Gogo Breeze

Gogo Breeze

Zambia's Radio Elder and the Voices of Free Speech

HARRI ENGLUND

The University of Chicago Press
Chicago and London

The University of Chicago Press, Chicago 60637
The University of Chicago Press, Ltd., London
© 2018 by The University of Chicago
Published 2018
Printed in the United States of America

27 26 25 24 23 22 21 20 19 18   1 2 3 4 5

ISBN-13: 978-0-226-49876-8 (cloth)
ISBN-13: 978-0-226-49893-5 (paper)
ISBN-13: 978-0-226-49909-3 (e-book)
DOI: 10.7208/chicago/9780226499093.001.0001

Library of Congress Cataloging-in-Publication Data

Names: Englund, Harri, author.
Title: Gogo Breeze : Zambia's radio elder and the voices of free speech /
    Harri Englund.
Description: Chicago ; London : The University of Chicago Press, 2018. |
    Includes bibliographical references and index.
Identifiers: LCCN 2017029781 | ISBN 9780226498768 (cloth : alk. paper) |
    ISBN 9780226498935 (pbk. : alk. paper) | ISBN 9780226499093 (e-book)
Subjects: LCSH: Gogo Breeze. | Radio broadcasting—Zambia. | Breeze FM
    (Radio station : Zambia) | Mass media—Social aspects—Zambia.
Classification: LCC HE8699.Z33 E54 2017 | DDC 384.54092 [B]—dc23
LC record available at https://lccn.loc.gov/2017029781

⊗ This paper meets the requirements of ANSI/NISO Z39.48-1992
(Permanence of Paper).

In memory of my parents

CONTENTS

ACKNOWLEDGMENTS

As a matter of protocol likely to be appreciated by the main subject of this book, I begin by acknowledging the unwavering support of Breeze FM's founder and director, M. Michael Daka. He opened the radio station for me in a way that made my anthropological study there not only possible but exhilarating. I never felt restrained or encountered red tape. The more I spent time at Breeze FM, the more Daka also became a formidable interlocutor, whose outlook on life will have a lasting impact on me as a person. While the following pages contain observations that he would hardly include in an authorized account of the station, I hope that they can convince him and his staff of the seriousness with which I have approached the task of writing about it.

Peter Grayson Nyozani Mwale, aka Gogo Breeze, was my first reason to go to Breeze FM and remained the linchpin of my research throughout. Having identified an exciting area of research in political and moral thought on vernacular radio in Malawi, I was intrigued to learn about this popular radio personality in Zambia's Eastern Province. Several visitors had interviewed him before my arrival, and I found a provincial celebrity so confident about his work that he seemed from the outset unperturbed by my shadowing him across the various spheres of his influence. As with Daka, our rapport grew into a collaboration with mutual, if distinct, benefits. Rarely had he met a foreigner whose passion for Chinyanja was virtually equal to his own. I salute him for the generosity of spirit he showed me as we learned more about one another's projects and for the countless hours spent discussing this or that aspect of Chinyanja and the other languages used on his programs.

Anyone reading this book will notice that it is not a biography, let alone a hagiography, of the man whose radio name it bears. My ethnographic approach was always going to accommodate a wide range of persons and programs at Breeze FM. Although Gogo Breeze was both the beginning and end of my research, it involved many more people at Breeze FM and in Eastern Province than are apparent in the book. Certain other radio personalities appear with their own names, while others, when the matter warrants it, are left anonymous. At any rate, I must register my debt of gratitude to the many employees at Breeze FM—from presenters and newsreaders to technicians and administrators—who made my work there so productive, including Juliana Banda, Peter Frank Banda, George Luanja, Glenda Matoto, Martin Mwape, Naomi Mwimba, Deliwe Ngoma, Samuel Njobvu, Mtwalo Nzima, Gift Phiri, and Pauline Phiri. It pleases me that my collaboration with this remarkable world of broadcasting will continue through a series of podcasts featuring Gogo Breeze's work.

I had the good fortune of making my first research trip to Eastern Province in the company of Giacomo Macola. An awe-inspiring historian and the truest of friends, he left an indelible mark of mirth on the place that made my subsequent solo sojourns there all the more enjoyable. Serving as Giacomo's interpreter when he interviewed Ngoni chiefs for his own research also provided an excellent way into the history and present circumstances of the province before I made the radio station my base. It also made Nkosi Nzamane IV our mutual friend; his kindness and good humor contributed to my favorable first impressions of the area. Giacomo also generously shared his extensive knowledge of Zambia when reading my draft chapters.

In Lusaka, I did a productive spell of research at the National Archives of Zambia, the Zambia National Broadcasting Corporation (ZNBC), and Muvi TV. I thank all those who shared their time and insights as I became acquainted with the broader media scene in Zambia. Ernst Wendland kindly allowed me to listen to his collection of tapes featuring Gogo Juli, the radio elder of the 1960s and 1970s, whose programs had sadly been lost at the ZNBC. I also remember with gratitude the kindness afforded by Marja Hinfelaar, Walima Kalusa, Bizeck Phiri, and Anthony Simpson.

I am grateful to all who listened to, and offered comments on, the many presentations I made on this research in seminars, workshops, and conferences. British Academy, Churchill College, and the University of Cambridge supported my research financially. At the University of Cambridge, scores of scholars and students provided an intellectually stimulating environment in which to think, discuss, and write. Serendipity made the Centre for Governance and Human Rights adopt radio broadcasts in Africa as its major focus as I was starting my fieldwork. Florence Brisset-Foucault,

Alastair Fraser, Iginio Gagliardone, and Sharath Srinivasan, some of whom carried out their own research at Breeze FM, allowed me to benefit from their findings and enabled me to see my own contribution more clearly.

The Division of Social Anthropology and the Centre of African Studies were other important hubs of intellectual life where colleagues and students responded to my work. Rupert Stasch put aside his own remarkable work to prepare a set of penetrating comments on draft chapters. I benefited from encouragement by, among many others, Matei Candea, Giovanni da Col, Andrea Grant, Paolo Heywood, George Karekwaivanane, James Laidlaw, Sian Lazar, and Joel Robbins, as I did from conversations with doctoral students whose writing-up I supervised alongside my own writing, including Clara Devlieger, Tom Neumark, Joe Philp, Jamie Wintrup, and Christina Woolner. Learning with Jessica Johnson has continued to be formative.

At the University of Chicago Press, I had the honor of working with T. David Brent before his retirement. He assigned impressive readers to my manuscript and ensured a smooth transition from review to production, after which the book was taken up by the eminently capable hands of Priya Nelson and Dylan Joseph Montanari.

While I was finalizing the manuscript in 2016, an *annus horribilis* in life as in so much of the world, my thoughts on more than one occasion turned to my parents, both of whom departed this life long before the present work was even conceived. It is in their memory that I offer the following observations on elderhood, still unsure of whether to mourn or to celebrate the passage of time.

Introduction

Soon after crossing the border from Malawi to Zambia on his bicycle, Maikolo Mbewe found himself talking to a radio journalist. Walking along the main road, the radio journalist stopped passersby to record his conversations with them. He wanted to know what had brought Mbewe to Zambia.

MAIKOLO MBEWE: I want to find piecework, casual labor.

RADIO JOURNALIST: Oh.

MAIKOLO MBEWE: Indeed, given the difficulties we face at home in Malawi.

RADIO JOURNALIST: What kind of difficulties? Please tell us.

MAIKOLO MBEWE: The lack of money.

RADIO JOURNALIST: How is it lacking?

MAIKOLO MBEWE: Well, the lack is not like here; in our place the lack is enormous.

RADIO JOURNALIST: Why?

MAIKOLO MBEWE: I don't know the reason why.

RADIO JOURNALIST: Have you had time to ask leaders/elders why money is lacking like that?

MAIKOLO MBEWE: Such opportunities don't exist.

RADIO JOURNALIST: Don't you have [elected] councillors?

MAIKOLO MBEWE: We have indeed, but councillors insult us; they even despise us. They don't give us the opportunity to speak with them.

RADIO JOURNALIST: Sure?

MAIKOLO MBEWE: Indeed, indeed.

RADIO JOURNALIST: So, after you have elected them, they just live on their own like that?

MAIKOLO MBEWE: That's it.[1]

Speaking the same language as Mbewe, though calling it Chinyanja rather than Chichewa as was common on the Malawian side of the border, the radio journalist was quick to establish enough rapport in this random encounter to trigger Mbewe's lament. The above exchange gives the perception that Zambia offered greater economic opportunities for Malawians like Mbewe, who moved back and forth across the border in search of casual employment on farms and in homes. Equally remarkable is that the exchange also concerned another opportunity to speak to leaders and elders about the lack of economic prospects. Whether Zambians were better endowed also in this regard was not explored in the conversation. The following chapters will describe numerous instances in which a similar lack of opportunities to be heard by leaders, whether elected or hereditary, was as pressing in Zambia as it appeared to be in Malawi. Yet in Eastern Province, where this exchange took place, Zambians did have at least one figure of authority to turn to when no one else seemed to listen to them. He was Gogo Breeze, the radio journalist who had stopped Maikolo Mbewe on the road.

Free speech found an unlikely champion in Gogo Breeze, whose radio name combined *gogo*, the Chinyanja term for grandparent, with Breeze FM, the name of the radio station he worked for. Gogo Breeze was his listeners' grandfather. Across a variety of programs, he dispensed sage advice on a range of matters of both intimate and public nature, admonished those whom he had found guilty of moral transgressions, and generally had the last word. His hierarchical demeanor was based on the wisdom that old age brought and that entailed obligations toward listeners, whom he addressed as his grandchildren. He was impelled not only to advise them over the airwaves but also to meet them and their adversaries in person in order to investigate grievances and other expressions of injustice. Some programs broadcast random encounters, such as the one with Maikolo Mbewe; on others he responded to listeners' letters and phone calls by leaving the studio to hear different sides in disputes. It is this effort to listen as well as to advise, and to broadcast multiple voices, that affords a perspective, however unlikely, on free speech. Free speech here had few of the connotations it has in the Euro-American debates on the topic. Equality and individual autonomy among speakers were overshadowed by the elder's prerogative to have the last word.

This book is an ethnographic exploration of the value of free speech in the specific conditions of its realization. At the same time, certain aspects of those conditions—such as the use of mass media and the predicament of socioeconomic inequality—are recognizable enough across the globe to suggest a perspective of comparative significance. What Zambia's radio elder compels us to consider in particular is moral authority in the pursuit of free speech. For it was in the morally charged maze of grievances, obligations, and hierarchy that different subjects could or could not speak. The authority to allocate opportunities to speak in public was a moral one and, as such, subject to constant revision and negotiation, not the automatic consequence of advanced age.

Although the focus is on one radio personality, the study inevitably requires attention to the station where he worked, his interactions with his listeners and with authorities of various kinds, and Zambia's place in the wider movement toward political and economic liberalization. Despite being introduced on several programs as "your grandfather on air, Grayson Peter Nyozani Mwale,"[2] it was the radio name Gogo Breeze by which he was commonly known—on air and off—and which will be used in the chapters to follow. He had joined the station when it was founded in 2003 in Chipata, his long-standing home and the capital of Zambia's Eastern Province, with some seventy thousand residents. His recruitment was consistent with the founder's vision of identifying local talent rather than importing presenters from the national capital, Lusaka. Mwale had not had any experience of media work when he engaged the founder in casual conversations as they were watching the construction of the station in central Chipata (see figure 1). He had recently retired as a schoolteacher, and it was his flair for storytelling, his passion for idiomatic Chinyanja, and the ease with which he seemed to relate to different people that convinced the founder of his promise as a broadcaster. Another crucial element in his evolving radio personality was the commitment he had previously shown, in a variety of institutional settings, to matters of justice. Gerontocratic as he might have sounded, Gogo Breeze brought to the airwaves a particular sensibility to speech as a medium through which those matters could be pursued.

Breeze FM owed its existence to the liberalization of Zambia's media landscape since the early 1990s. Following the country's return to multiparty democracy in the 1991 elections, when Frederick Chiluba and his Movement for Multiparty Democracy (MMD) swept to power, new constitutional provisions and various pieces of legislation came into force to open up broadcasting beyond the virtual monopoly enjoyed by the Zambia National Broadcasting Corporation (ZNBC). The founder of Breeze FM, Michael Daka, had intimate knowledge of broadcasting both before and after the liberalization. Initially a journalist at Zambia's official news agency and then the trainer of broadcasters, Daka had made his career in Lusaka and decided to spend his retirement in the province of his ancestry. He

came with lofty ideals and an acute sense of new business opportunities, both of which are themes that will keep appearing in this book. Sharply critical of the rush to establish radio stations in Lusaka and in towns along the Copperbelt, Daka took the media liberalization to mean, as he never tired of telling his staff and visitors, that radio stations could cater to local needs, in the languages that people used themselves. He offered biting sarcasm about the predominantly English-language commercial stations in Lusaka that played, in his view, identical pop music without much content otherwise. He, along with other staff members at Breeze FM, told me stories about stations seeking presenters who could speak English with an "American accent." With nine in ten persons living in rural areas, and being some 350 miles from Lusaka and even further away from the Copperbelt towns, Eastern Province had been poorly served by broadcasters despite the radio's importance as the main mass medium.[3] Broadcasts by the ZNBC had only limited local relevance, while the contents of community radio stations were very localized indeed. Eventually, Breeze FM's principal rivals in Eastern Province came to be Radio Maria, a Catholic station, and Feel Free FM, a commercial station whose content and geographical reach never really matched those of Breeze FM.

Daka's determination to serve "the people"—also expressed in the station's slogan, "Lifting the Spirit of the People"—harked back to the era of public broadcasting when he had become a journalist. Yet he also saw in this mission a means of generating revenue by providing news, music, and a whole variety of other program content that would attract local listeners; much of this programming would seek listeners' participation through phone-in programs as well as broadcasters' visits to rural and urban areas. Accordingly, with an ever-shifting constellation of partnerships with businesses, governmental departments, and nongovernmental organizations, Breeze FM grew to provide broadcasts every day of the week from 6:00 a.m. until midnight.[4] Chinyanja was the main language broadcast, the lingua franca of Eastern Province and the first language of over 80 percent of its population.[5] News and other programs in English were also broadcast, but the desire to allow local people to speak over the airwaves brought other languages on air, particularly Chinsenga and Chitumbuka. For several years, Breeze FM broadcast only in Chipata and the districts in its vicinity, including parts of neighboring Malawi and Mozambique. By the time it celebrated its tenth anniversary in 2013, the station had erected new transmitters that ensured coverage of virtually the entire Eastern Province.

"Serving the people" involved following Daka's own vision as much as popular preoccupations in the province. A predominantly Christian public tuned into Breeze FM, but Daka remained adamant that religion would play little role on his airwaves. His cosmopolitan agnosticism stood out among the many practicing Christians in his staff, and he never made a secret of his opinion that Africans spent excessive amounts of time reading the Bible rather than focusing on socioeconomic development. This opinion earned him a reputation for Satanism among some Pentecostals in Chipata, who had approached the station in the hope of beginning their own series of programs. Whether they were prepared to pay for the series or not, Daka had made it clear to them that such a program would not go on air under his regime. "They tried to intimidate me," he remarked to me afterward and asked rhetorically, "Intimidate how? It is not possible." Of Breeze FM's closest rivals in Chipata, Radio Maria as a Catholic station had the largest amount of religious content, but it could not accommodate evangelical or Pentecostal preaching for denominational reasons. Feel Free FM, on the other hand, allowed Pentecostal preachers to broadcast for a fee. In light of the expanding literature on religious (and particularly Pentecostal) public spheres in Africa (see, e.g., Meyer 2015; Pype 2012), Breeze FM's popularity in the absence of religious content deserves special mention.

What these preliminary observations about the station suggest are some of the actual conditions within which free speech as an abstract value had to be pursued. Only occasionally on air himself, Daka depended on local talent to make his station a success.[6] After spending a lifetime in Lusaka and traveling internationally on academic and professional assignments, Daka came to the province with cosmopolitan orientations that provided insufficient guidance on the specific ways in which the provincial public might be won over. As the chapters in part 3 will show in more detail, local talent came in various personal styles, of which Gogo Breeze's was only one. At the same time, by being the station's most recognizable voice, his radio personality indicated the popular appeal that elderhood could have despite all the exhortations, through Breeze FM and Zambia's other media, to participate in public speech as equals. Such personal characteristics gave the pursuit of free speech its locally salient forms, but they coexisted with a number of other practical challenges to its exercise. An obvious one was the station's dependence on generating revenue—its quest for sponsorship and advertisement was a constant feature of its operations. Just as local businesses had to be courted, so too could governmental and nongovernmental contacts be transformed into sponsorship arrangements if mutually beneficial projects could be devised. Although Zambia, renowned for its orderly changes of government through several general elections, had witnessed relatively little harassment of journalists, partisan reporting was anathema at Breeze FM.[7] Lofty ideals aside, all these potential "partners" in broadcasting—businesses, governmental and nongovernmental agencies, politicians, and pastors—presented risks as well as opportunities. The ways in which such challenges unfolded in practice are best tackled ethnographically, not by focusing on the stated principles alone.

In taking an ethnographic look into the conditions of free speech, I do not seek to expose the *value* of free speech as a mere chimera. The value, in all its historically contingent forms, should be kept separate from free speech as a supposedly self-evident state of affairs, whether or not spawned by appropriate legislation. In this book, free speech would need to be put within quotation marks throughout, as in "free speech," but such inelegance of exposition is unnecessary once this distinction is made. We may well agree with the title of Stanley Fish's book, *There's No Such Thing as Free Speech, and It's a Good Thing, Too* (1994), especially when he explains that free-speech advocates never protect speech per se. They would do so, he points out, only if speech would indeed trump everything else, in the sense that "no one gave a damn but just liked to hear talk" (Fish 1994:106). Protecting free speech is inevitably about protecting other values, not simply about fostering the ability to speak in public. The ethnographic task is to investigate what people do with the value of free speech, what effects its pursuit has, how it relates to their other values, and what it all can tell us about issues such as speech, mass media, voice, morality, obligation, freedom, and so on. In the best tradition of anthropology, this book arises from the hope that a close study of an unlikely instance—a radio station in provincial Zambia with a grandfather figure at the helm—can provoke thoughts that transcend itself.

From Free Speech to Multivocal Morality

In this book the provincial—in the sense of being located in a Zambian province—challenges the parochial in much of the Euro-American literature on free speech. For all its claims to elaborate on a universal value, that literature is remarkably consistent in tracing its intellectual resources to only two or three instances: the First Amendment to the US Constitution, the French Revolution, and the nature of democracy in ancient Athens. Such parochialism comes with the cost of failing to see, particularly in the debates around the First Amendment and the French Revolution, free speech in any other terms than autonomy and equality. Although a firm believer in the freedom of expression, Steven Heyman (2008) appears to endorse the point made above that it is not just any talk that free-speech advocates seek to protect. Talk typically addresses someone or something; it has a direction, an intent to have an impact: "Communicative impact is not an accidental but an essential feature of communication" (Heyman 2008:94). As a legal scholar, Heyman makes this point in response to what he calls the doctrine of content neutrality in the US Supreme Court—the notion that it has no power to restrict expression because of its subject matter or ideas. The oft-cited examples of hate speech and pornography furnish Heyman with evidence on the harmful effects of expression that has no constraints. He advocates, instead, a "rights-based" approach to the First Amendment freedom of speech. Its merits include, he writes, the protection of speech as "essential for individual self-realization, democratic self-government, and the pursuit of truth," along with legal provisions to "restrict speech that invades the rights of other people" (Heyman 2008:206–7). The ensuing refrain was often put forward by activists and politicians during democratization in Zambia and Malawi: "Where one's rights end is where another one's rights begin" (Englund 2006:67).

Heyman (2008:7–22) reminds his readers of the influence that Lockean thought on natural rights had on the eighteenth-century authors of the First Amendment. Although a rights-based approach in the twenty-first century can hardly claim such continuity with the natural rights tradition (see Moyn 2010), Heyman usefully situates the appeal to republican values in the notion of social contract. The traditions of thought regarding social contract have their well-known differences between the Anglo-American and French ideas of government, associated with Locke and Rousseau respectively, but common to both is the idea that governmental authority is something external to the citizen. Whether it is the Lockean notion of government as forever "ready to tyrannize and enslave the free people by whom it was created" (Saxonhouse 2006:23) or Rousseau's rather more trusting injunction to submit oneself to the law, the social contract has two parties: one the citizen, the other the more or less sinister government. Ancient Athens offers in this regard a different set of concerns to explore in relation to free speech. Here, particularly as can be gleaned from texts produced in the fourth century BCE, living in a city with no external government that could oppress citizens made free speech "an aspect of their own capacity to rule themselves in a regime of equal citizens without hierarchy" (Saxonhouse 2006:30). By exploring speech one can appreciate a political subjectivity in which the quest for social contract has no meaning. *Parrhêsia* was the concept for speaking or saying everything—free speech as frank speech (Saxonhouse 2006:86–87; see also Foucault 2001 and 2011). It was not a matter of having rights that, in this perspective, attach themselves to a representative democracy in which "speech is not one's own nor is it revelatory of one's own views" (Saxonhouse 2006:87). By contrast, *parrhêsia* was a key feature of a democratic regime where citizens (freemen) participated by speaking their own minds as equals separate from the slave and the female. A corollary was the absence of a distinction between public speech and private speech, or an arena to which *parrhêsia* properly belonged (Saxonhouse 2006:28). Speech was an attribute of free people who knew how to govern themselves.

The interest in *parrhêsia* is welcome as a reminder that not all forms of democracy have been cloaked in a liberal garment, through which run the threads of rights and social contract. Its appeal is also evident as an aspect of the trend, over which looms the figure of Michel Foucault (1986 and 1988), to explore morality and ethics as matters of self-cultivation.[8] The demands it places on ethnography must, however, give us pause. For *parrhêsia* to travel across historical and ethnographic instances, it would, at a minimum, have to take heed of two central aspects of its original form in ancient Athens, both resolutely at odds with how the pursuit of free speech will look in the chapters to follow. The first is what Arlene Saxonhouse describes as "a vivid expression of the rejection of respect or reverence for ancient hierarchies and patterns of social organization" (2006:30). By contrast, Gogo Breeze built his radio personality on the cultivation of morally justified hierarchy and deployed notions such as custom (*mwambo*) to describe his work of moral education and practical intervention. The whole interest of exploring his radio personality is, of course, to consider the actual revisions and negotiations that this approach to free speech and broadcasting entailed. Yet negotiating hierarchy is something very different from rejecting it, as appears to have been the case among the freemen of ancient Athens. The second aspect of *parrhêsia* to give us pause is another rejection it discharged. "The truly parrhesiastic speaker," Saxonhouse further remarks, "eschews the art of rhetoric" (2006:92). "Revealing speech" is another definition of *parrhêsia*, speech that "opens and uncovers" (Saxonhouse 2006:87). On this count alone, Gogo Breeze was not a "parrhesiast" (cf. Foucault 2001 and 2011). His passion for idiomatic Chinyanja, for proverbial expression and esoteric phrases, will be a major theme in this book, even when he addressed issues as urgent as exploitation in his listeners' efforts to make a living. At the same time, frank speech, sometimes culminating in direct and abrasive accusation, was certainly also a part of his rhetorical arsenal. The analytical task is to discern the contexts in which one register of speech was more appropriate than another, and how the different registers were integral to his efforts to generate moral authority. Critical here is the recognition that speakers were not generally assumed to be equal. Frank speech was the prerogative of specific speakers, such as the radio elder.

Anthropological and historical works on political communication in Africa are awash with examples of rhetoric (including poetry and praise singing) rather than frank speech as the appropriate register in which to speak to the powers that be (see, e.g., Barber 1991 and 2007; Furniss 1996; Finnegan 2007; Vail and White 1991). Where the genres involved display formalization, the initial challenge is to resist the early anthropological view that such speech allows for "hardly any choice of what can be said" and that, as a consequence, the creative potential of language becomes "impoverished" (Bloch 1975:17). Nothing could be further from the actual practice when it is studied in its ethnographic and linguistic richness (Werbner 1977). Writing about *akyeame* in Ghana, royal counselors gifted in public speaking, Kwesi Yankah shows that "it is within formal forums that creative wit in speaking finds its utmost fulfillment" (1995:58). Frank speech as audacity to speak truth to power is here dislodged by respect for authority, much as the incumbent may deserve criticism. "The challenge becomes that of creatively registering dissent, protest, or displeasure within the scope of the politeness frame" (Yankah 1995:58). The challenge that awaits the ethnography of mass-mediated speech in provincial Zambia is to understand direct speech—criticizing, for example, current gender relations or particular politicians—as coexisting with considerable popular fascination for the creative uses of language. Gogo Breeze stood at the intersection of these apparently contradictory language ideologies, a large part of his authority deriving from a judicious sense of when to deploy what sort of speech registers on and off air.[9]

The persuasive rhetorics of liberal democracy, as it has been pursued for nearly three decades now across the African continent, make it necessary to try and share some of Gogo Breeze's sensitivity to the multiple registers of speech. While local oral expression, typically through song and drama, has been harnessed by political parties and donor agencies alike to transmit messages about new freedoms both at independence and during subsequent transitions to multiparty democracy, not all vernacular expression has been as eagerly embraced, or even understood, by the self-appointed guardians of democracy.[10] Jennifer Jackson (2013:193–98), for example, shows how newspaper cartoons were a genre that found support among expatriate technocrats keen to build a civil society in Madagascar.[11] On the other hand, the genre of *kabary politika*, political oratory that made copious use of indirect language, metaphors, proverbs, and poetry, could be dismissed as so much obfuscation. While both genres were very popular, the cartoons were thought to teach people the values of transparency and truth telling, against which was the political oratory that was felt to hide the truth and even provide the linguistic equivalent of the expatriate technocrats' ultimate nightmare: corruption. Jackson reports a different concern with transparency among the audiences of *kabary politika*, a desire to follow the orator's reasoning through his use of metaphors and proverbs rather than focusing on the message as a finished product. Here as in Ghana and with Gogo Breeze, speaking truth to power is again an act that cannot be analyzed in isolation from the specific genres and the specific social relations that make it possible.

Although Gogo Breeze would often urge his interlocutors to say what is true (*choona*) and to "tell us for real" (*tauzeni nkoni*), the very phrase "speaking truth to power" may have to be suspended. He would prod his interlocutors in this way when they were the ordinary folk (*anthu wamba*) he encountered in the streets and villages. But other rhetorical means were at his disposal when he visited civil servants or company managers in their offices. Respectful as his address was on those occasions, matched by their consistent use of the term *gogo* in return, he did not enter the offices as though he was an outsider, a representative of citizens seeking social contract with external bodies. As will be seen throughout this book, the grandfather appellation was no gimmick. It summoned kinship in virtually every encounter he had, not least when he addressed the government as the parent of the grandchildren on whose behalf he spoke. The government, in other words, was not allowed to be a force apart, much as its operations often seemed to be so, and responsiveness to obligations rather than to rights was what the radio grandfather sought to instill in its functionaries.

The courage required in such address reveals aspects of personhood that are incompatible with Foucault's (2001 and 2011) emphasis on the government of *the self* in *parrhêsia*. For Foucault, *parrhêsia* involves a risk of offending the other person, even to the point of the relationship facing a violent end. The *parrhêsiast* takes "the risk of breaking or ending the relationship to the other person which was precisely what made his discourse possible" (2011:11). Foucault's description of the relationship as "friendship" introduces a measure of optionality that Gogo Breeze's radio kinship did not have. The grandfatherly courage was to insist on an enduring obligation even when the relationship was regarded as contractual by his interlocutors in government or commerce. The last word that the grandfather had on these and other occasions was, of course, a provisional one, only to be superseded by others as events unfolded. An exception was those people who so decisively cut themselves off from his mass-mediated kinship that the radio grandfather did not even attempt to address them. A prominent example was the recent Chinese arrivals in the province (see Englund 2015a and chapter 3 below).

The multiple registers and genres of speech, along with kinship and personhood, serve to nuance the actual ways in which the value of free speech might be pursued in any given instance. No one principle recovered from the Euro-American past—whether natural rights, social contract, or *parrhêsia*—can ensure such nuance in the ethnography of free speech, whether in Africa or in Euro-America itself, although they can certainly help to specify the challenge of the provincial to the parochial. Indeed, anthropologists have contributed to debates about free speech by considering what sort of injury or offense has been committed in specific historical circumstances, such as by those who have published cartoons about Prophet Muhammad (Asad 2009; Mahmood 2009; Keane 2009). For Webb Keane, the offense, so poorly understood by the mainstream media in Euro-America, revealed different views on what pictures and words were. As "representational acts" (Keane 2009:57), they were mere information for those who defended the publication of the cartoons, the purpose and validity of which were left to each recipient to ascertain. A basic mistake made by those who protested violently against the cartoons, the defenders seemed to think, was to take representations for reality. To the extent that the controversy evoked blasphemy, it only confirmed to the self-proclaimed liberal defenders of press freedom that blasphemy as an offense belonged to Europe's past, not to its present. At issue, Keane argues, were distinct semiotic ideologies, one subscribing to the view that words and pictures were "vehicles for the transmission of opinion or information among otherwise autonomous and unengaged parties" (2009:58), another to the view of words and pictures as modes of action within particular social relations, not as information detached from anyone's interest in them. As Keane emphasizes, semiotic ideologies do not divide the world into distinct civilizations—more than one semiotic ideology can be present in the same polity. And affinities can obtain between seemingly incompatible semiotic ideologies, not least when they share themes—for example, in the Abrahamic scriptural religions (Keane 2009:59).

Sensitivity to different semiotic ideologies is necessary not only to nuance what words might stand for in free speech, such as when metaphors and proverbs are preferred in political communication, but also to interrogate the notion that the freedom of expression ensures that a *voice* can be heard (see Keane 2009:63). If autonomy should characterize the subjects evaluating the information and the opinions they are presented with, then voice is what each of them ought to have the freedom to exercise in making their own opinions count. "The subject's body, affections, and speech are regarded as *personal property* because they constitute the person," Talal Asad (2009:30; emphasis original) has pointed out with regard to a central tenet in liberal thought. Yet identifying a central tenet is not the same as to have exhausted the scope and possibilities of liberal thought. Even Asad (2009:25), a trenchant critic of liberalism, assures his readers that liberalism is "a complex historical tradition," full of "contradictions and ambiguities" that animate constant debate. As such, the study of free speech as one of liberalism's constitutive controversies stands to benefit from other instances than the canonical ones mentioned above (First Amendment, French Revolution, ancient Athens). The interest in voice, in particular, may take critics beyond the threadbare theme of possessive individualism and open up fresh prospects for inserting unlikely characters, such as Gogo Breeze, into the debates about free speech. "Despite the importance of speech to liberalism," Marianne Constable has remarked, "critics tend to dwell on the liberal construction of autonomous rights-bearing subjects, rather than on liberalism's constitution of speaking subjects" (2005:57).

The recent anthropology of voice has highlighted the dual nature of voice in many of its contemporary evocations (Weidman 2014). On one hand is voice as a metaphor for empowerment, self-representation, and agency, as in "finding one's voice" or "giving voice to the voiceless." On the other is voice in its physical and sonic dimensions. Both of these aspects are highly pertinent to the study of the radio as a medium of free speech. Voice as a metaphor for empowerment was one of the underlying justifications for having local people speak their local languages on Breeze FM. At the same time, Gogo Breeze's role in gathering and mediating those voices underscores the importance of studying closely the actual manner in which voices—and the opinions they conveyed—came on air. The chapters in part 3 will describe programs on which voices were broadcast apparently with no intervention by the presenter. By contrast, Gogo Breeze rarely abrogated the grandfatherly prerogative to engage his interlocutors even when urging them to express their own views.

Gogo Breeze's approach to the pursuit of free speech had an element of the argumentative stance that informed John Stuart Mill's (1998) mid-nineteenth-century thoughts on the liberty of thought and discussion. No such parallel would be admissible if we were to follow those readings of Mill, common among liberalism's critics, that emphasize his thoughts as an invitation "to cultivate one's own unique sense of self, to cherish a realm of autonomy, and to engage in public discussion with others in order to challenge the truthfulness of their own individual opinions" (Roberts 2004:72). To suggest any degree of equivalence between Gogo Breeze and John Stuart Mill would indeed be a step too far.[12] But in Mill's idea of truth as a matter of "reconciling and combining of oppositions" (1998:54) lies an important opportunity to insert Gogo Breeze's radio work into the complex tradition of liberal thought. Chapter 2 will introduce more fully multivocality as a key feature of that work, but Mill's thoughts on the collision, and particularly *combining*, of views are not altogether inapposite here.[13] They allude, among other things, to the importance of hearing, and not just expressing, opinions (O'Rourke 2001). It will be a recurring theme in the following chapters that Gogo Breeze combined multiple voices in his own radio personality as much as he did so by broadcasting voices emanating from other bodies. His moral authority was, in other words, multivocal, not based on the monological speech from which communication between autonomous individuals might be thought to emanate.

Along with the multiple registers and genres of speech in which his voice could be heard, its sonic texture also varied according to the moment. A whole range of moods could be evoked by a voice that was variously soothing, stern, sober, and ludic. Although the emphasis in what follows is on what Gogo Breeze and his interlocutors said, and how they said it by deploying particular words and genres, mention will be made of their tone and other sonic elements. The sonic aspects of voice, in other words, must not be thought of as being subordinate to the message (Weidman 2006:289). The early history of commercial radio, in the United States for example, teaches us as much, confronted as it was by the challenge to overcome "the listener's sense of being stuck in a mass audience without mutual interaction or awareness, with one-way flow of communication and anonymous styles of talk" (Peters 1999:214). Breeze FM, as will be seen below, emerged against the background of well-established patterns of radio communication in Zambia and elsewhere that involved recognizable personalities. Their conversational styles and intimate address mitigated listeners' sense of belonging to a mass audience. Public intimacy may well be the particular forte of the radio everywhere, but its material qualities as technology are always subject to specific social and historical influences (Kunreuther 2014:151). In Zambia, for example, its public intimacy owes something to the way in which radio reception has often been a social and shared occasion, from the positioning of loudspeakers in public places by the colonial government to the frequent borrowing and mobility of radio receivers once they had become widely affordable (see Spitulnik 2000 and 2002).

The limitations imposed by physical absence are not necessarily overcome by the indiscriminate broadcast of as many voices as possible. An ideology of voice, no less than the language ideology mentioned above, informs who is allowed to speak and how (Weidman 2014:45). Silence, as such, can very much be a part of free speech as it is locally pursued, and the radio's special stake in apparently direct communication need not erase the practice of indirection. Speaking through an intermediary such as Gogo Breeze, what Yankah calls "surrogate oratory" (1995:8), becomes compelling on the airwaves when the speaker interacts with his listeners through various other media—from letters to mobile phones—and in person off as well as on air. Moreover, multivocality involves tacit awareness of "all the other—possibly mute—people who enable and structure even the most fleeting moment of dialogue" (Sterne 2005:344–45; see also Hill 1995; Keane 2010). Moral authority inheres in knowing how to manage silences as well as voices in the pursuit of free speech.

Mass Media and the Moral Market

Where the freedom of expression has constitutional guarantees and is jealously guarded by journalists, political interference may give way to other threats. Critical theory, addressing the so-called old democracies in the North, has long given form to anxieties about the adverse effects of the market on mass-mediated free speech.[14] One formative approach came from Jürgen Habermas, whose early work interrogated "systematically distorted communication" (1972) with a view to offering interpretations of public discourses that would disabuse the public of those distortions. His theory of the decline of the public sphere came to attach particular importance to the commercialization of mass communications (Habermas 1989). In an apparently more empirical perspective on this theme, Pierre Bourdieu (1998) investigated the effects of different fields—such as the mass media and the economy—on one another and came to the conclusion that the media and artistic fields were being colonized by the economic field. Journalists' work for media companies bent on making profit (through advertising and cheap stories) and artists' dependence on private patronage subverted, in this view, their critical and creative potential (see also Bourdieu and Haacke 1995). To the extent that such anxieties were voiced with regard to old media, including television (Bourdieu 1998; Herman and Chomsky 1988), the emancipatory prospects afforded by new media did not take long to be dimmed by critics' rediscovery of "communicative capitalism" (Dean 2009). The Internet, for example, not only made consumers coproducers of media content, it also produced "massive distortions and concentrations of wealth as communicative exchanges and their technological preconditions [became] commodified and capitalized" (Dean 2010:4). Apart from the promise of civic engagement and participation stood the user's "economic meaning as a producer, consumer and data provider" (van Dijck 2009:55).

The repetitive nature of media critics' arguments should not mask their substantive differences on matters of theoretical detail or their serious attention to the ways in which technological changes have precipitated fresh constellations of power.[15] However, less subtle is the ease with which the market and the corporation are often conflated in these critiques. It ought to make a difference whether the media outlet under investigation is a giant transnational corporation or a small provincial radio station.[16] Both may strive to make profit, but the settings they provide for journalistic practice are not the same. As one cautionary comment on dismissing the media's commercial basis notes, the market can actually enable a recognition of the public's internal diversity in media content (Curran 1991:48). The obstacles to exploring the interface between the market and the media go deeper than critical theory's anxieties about distorted communication. They include the old separation between money and morality, as though the two were irrevocably opposed.[17] They also mirror the laxity characteristic of much critique at the turn of the millennium when "neoliberalism" became the catchphrase for everything that was wrong with political and economic liberalization.[18] Too often the catchphrase evoked little else than market fundamentalism instead of inspiring close investigation of the ways in which the market may have intersected with moral thought and practice.[19] The challenge of studying a privately owned provincial radio station in Zambia is to confront these established and recent critical impulses with insights acquired through ethnographic fieldwork.

Breeze FM had two shareholders: Michael Daka as its founder-director and his British acquaintance from his time in Lusaka. The Briton had remained detached from the station's operations all along and appeared to have fallen out of favor with the founder-director by the time of my fieldwork. At any rate, with Daka holding 80 percent of the shares and the Briton 20 percent, the latter's input to Breeze FM as a business was bound to be modest.[20] Indeed, Daka never tired of reminding his staff and visitors of the extent to which he had invested personally in the station as a business. The land and the building that it occupied were investments from which his extended family may well have wanted to reap some benefit. Instead, the family effectively subsidized the business by charging rent below the market price. What Daka mentioned less often was his involvement in commercial agriculture just outside Chipata. His farm employed a farm manager and ten farm workers, who cultivated maize and an increasing variety of vegetables that he hoped to supply to Chipata's best hotels. Although not spoken about publicly at the station, the farm and the station were sometimes complementary businesses. When a presenter working on a program about sweet potatoes received a large amount of them for free, Daka took five bags to be used as seed potatoes on his farm. On the other hand, a part-time staff member, whose self-styled patriarchal radio personality is examined in part 3, was a successful farmer and had helped Daka to get started with his own farm. Possibly because of this connection, the patriarch's controversial views on air attracted less comment from Daka than might have been the case otherwise.

Daka's preferred method of making his staff aware that Breeze FM was a business was to draw a contrast to government departments and nongovernmental organizations (NGOs). A repeated theme in the speeches he delivered at the weekly staff meetings was to ask the broadcasters to consider themselves as running their own companies within the infrastructure provided by Breeze FM. The contrast to civil service was clear in that work for the station was expected to be profitable and based on the employee's own initiative. NGOs, on the other hand, appeared frequently in Daka's reflections. He saw them as ephemeral, dependent on donor support that itself was notoriously unreliable. He recalled Chipata in the early days of Breeze FM when the town, in his estimation, had many more NGOs than it had a decade later. This observation would often extend into a diatribe against development aid overall, drawing on the critique of dependency he had encountered during his university studies and culminating in the claim that countries like Zambia were kept underdeveloped by aid itself. He would also point at me during staff meetings and say that I could confirm that Europe was in an economic crisis and should not be relied on for funding. Another problem with NGOs, he would also often argue, was their urban bias, while he had established Breeze FM to reach out to "the people" in rural areas and urged his staff to use every opportunity to seek news and stories beyond the offices of the government and NGOs.

Daka's definition of Breeze FM as a business was compatible with apparently contradictory rhetorics and practice. He actively sought revenue from the government departments and NGOs that he criticized. He would publicly rebuke presenters who had not seized the opportunity to ask visiting civil servants about the possibility of starting a sponsored series on matters falling within their remit. He bemoaned that his station was supporting the government for free by carrying its messages through interviews and news items. In an apparent contradistinction to his ambition to hear the voices of the people on the radio, spoken in their own languages, he framed the government's anticipated contribution as an opportunity for civil servants and politicians to "explain" its policies to the public in exchange for a fee. The idiom of "explaining" seemed at variance with the democratic era, but a part of the package that he would offer to civil servants and politicians included interaction with the public through a live phone-in element. Politicians already paid a fee when they came to the studio to be interviewed, as did the members of the public who wanted to put announcements on air. NGOs rarely needed to be encouraged to use the radio and, when well funded themselves, could offer relatively lucrative, if prescriptive, contracts, as will be seen in part 3. The presence of competing stations in Chipata had, however, made their contribution somewhat erratic.

Despite Daka's wish to diversify its revenue base, Breeze FM, like other commercial stations in Zambia, received most of its income from NGOs and corporations, particularly mobile phone companies, that sponsored daily programs, such as popular morning shows (see Willems 2013:229–30). The revenue from local businesses in Eastern Province was around 20 to 30 percent in 2012–13, while Daka's ambition was to increase it to 40 percent. It was in this context that he would sometimes give disparaging comments on the staff's commitment to achieving his ambition. At a staff meeting, he expressed regret at the failure to properly "monetize" Gogo Breeze, whose rapport with local businesses should have been taken, in his view, to a higher level of revenue than this radio personality seemed capable of even imagining. As mentioned, a similar pressure to generate revenue was placed on all staff members and not only on the station's most popular presenter. Daka had introduced a scheme by which staff members would be paid a commission for the advertisements or sponsored programs they had been able to source (see figure 2). When the first quarter of 2012 showed loss on a scale unseen before, largely as the consequence of a major new investment in transmitters to cover virtually the entire province, Daka reprimanded his staff by saying that it was "sad" that no check for commissions had been written that year. He juxtaposed the attitude among his staff with the energy with which street vendors pursued their livelihoods. Instead of waiting for money to come to them, vendors were active in selling their merchandise and in cultivating relationships with customers. Daka described with some admiration one vendor of secondhand clothes (*salaula*) who would not be discouraged by his consistent refusal to buy from him. Daka had never bought secondhand clothes, not even as a graduate student in the United Kingdom, but the vendor would continue to come back to him regardless.

"When you wake up in the morning," he urged his staff in several meetings I attended, "think that you are going to make money, not to work for someone else." What informed this imperative to make money—and to regard everyone who was encountered during broadcasting assignments as a potential "client"—was not some neoliberal impulse but a curious mix of commerce, paternalism, and public-service ethos.[21] As Debra Spitulnik (2010) has discussed, a shift toward "making money" had occurred within ZNBC before the airwaves were liberalized. Daka had grown accustomed to seeing broadcasting and business as mutually compatible activities, but he entered the era of liberalization with a public-service ethos that wanted to make the market moral. When a presenter reported from a workshop he had attended in Lusaka that participation in agricultural production had been mentioned as one way of securing income for Breeze FM, Daka dismissed the idea as potentially exploitative of small-scale farmers. Money,

Definition

Commission is payment made to a full time or part time member of staff who has sought and secured business for the company in form of;

1. Programmes
2. Advertisements
3. Consultancy work

Mode of Payment

Commission will be paid only in cases where;

i). A full time member of staff secures;

13 series programmes – 10%
26 series and above – 15%
10 advertisements – 7.5 %
Long-term consultancy work – 20 %

ii) A part time member of staff secures;

13 series programmes - 15%
26 series and above – 20 %
10 advertisements – 10%
Long-term consultancy work – 20%

The full time or part time member of staff who has secured business will be paid ONLY after the payment from the client has been made in FULL. Payment by way of a bank certified cheque should be encouraged when negotiating for business with the client.

If the payment is by ordinary cheque, then the payment of the commission will be delayed until after the cheque is cleared in the bank. The closing date for submission of commission forms will be on the 19th day of every month.

Terms and Conditions

All claims for commission should be supported by a signed Customer Call Card.

If a full time or part time member of staff brings back a client for repeat business, he/she will receive 50% of the standard rates, thereafter 25% of the standard rates. This business will be supported by signed Customer Call Cards.

On the other hand, if the client's contract expires and the company or organization decides to come back on its own, no commission will be paid on the new contracts.

FIGURE 2

in other words, would not be made at any cost, whatever his own private involvement in commercial agriculture. The issue here was Breeze FM's reputation among the public it claimed to serve, and it would have been damaging to its mandate had it been discovered to engage in the same exploitative practices as those its listeners complained about.

Making money acquired moral content also in Daka's demand for each staff member to contribute to the station's revenue. It was moral concern over his employees' growth as persons, not simply a capitalist's interest to make his workers pay for their wages. In one-to-one meetings with young presenters in particular, he would compare their trajectory to his own and point out that when he was their age, he had been following a plan to make his career and domestic life a success. Staff members whom he had employed as unmarried youths had gotten married and had children without any obvious effort to further their professional lives. It was the apparent lack of planning that puzzled him the most in his staff members' attitude to making money. The scheme for commissions had been introduced, he said, for people to set targets for themselves so that they could realize their ambitions. It was disappointing, he remarked, that no one on his team had purchased a car during the station's first decade.

Breeze FM was, in other words, a site where profit and paternalism sat side by side. Daka's demeanor at the station had more than a hint of a master running a workshop, unquestioned in his authority but also keenly interested in his subjects' welfare. No doubt the failure among staff to purchase private cars reflected adversely on his own capacity to generate and distribute wealth in the province, with his Toyota Hilux cutting a rather imposing figure as the sole vehicle parked outside the station.

Gogo Breeze inserted his own combination of hierarchy and amity into this regime of work ruled by a highly personalized form of capital. He often mentioned to me that the relationship between him and Daka was one between cousins (*chisuweni*), a joking relationship based on their clan names. Yet I never witnessed him offering Daka anything else except deference, at times adopting the kneeling posture familiar from village settings when subjects greeted and addressed their superiors. As Breeze FM's most recognizable personality, Gogo Breeze was himself an asset on a par with the technology required to run a radio station. Daka's concern to monetize him aside, Gogo Breeze worked tirelessly as a part of the station's marketing team and did more than most to honor Daka's injunction to treat every new contact as a potentially revenue-generating client. This orientation was as steeped in moral considerations as was the founder-director's own. Not only was his advice on and off air generally rendered free of charge, save the services he provided for individuals looking for partners to marry (see chapter 5); he also sought to turn advertising contracts into long-term relationships on the basis of the hierarchical amity that his radio personality represented (see chapter 1). It was, in point of fact, in Gogo Breeze's work that the interface between the market and morality appeared in a particularly compelling form. The prospect of free speech was never without complications when subject to the need to make money. But precisely by making money, and by attending to the injustices of other people's efforts to make money, Gogo Breeze brought his moral authority to bear on market relations.

The Radio Grandfather

While liberalization introduced new challenges and opportunities to broadcasting in Zambia, it took place after the radio had established itself as the most popular mass medium. Across Africa, the medium's particular (and continuing) appeal came to be documented relatively recently (see Fardon and Furniss 2000; Gunner et al. 2011), and the volume of scholarly work on this medium is hardly on a par with its reach and influence. Affordability, broadcasting in African languages (in contexts where newspapers typically cater to publics able to read in languages introduced by European colonialism), and the intricate ways in which the medium taps into oral expression are all reasons for the radio's status as the continent's principal mass medium. Zambia's role as a pioneer in broadcasting to African audiences makes the historical background particularly pertinent. A small government broadcasting station had been established in Lusaka in 1940 to bring war news to African miners in the politically volatile Copperbelt (OSISA 2010:11; Smyth 1984). This effort to counter what colonial authorities regarded as rumor mongering evolved into a full menu of programs to inform, educate, and entertain Africans at the Central African Broadcasting Station (CABS), which from 1950 was broadcasting initially in four and then in seven languages (apart from English) from Lusaka to Zambia (then Northern Rhodesia) and Malawi (Nyasaland), with Zimbabwe (Southern Rhodesia) added in 1957 when the three territories were joined to form the Federation of Rhodesia and Nyasaland. Despite being the organ of the federation that became a target of nationalist agitation, the station was itself a remarkably cosmopolitan space in which "color-discrimination was completely unknown" (Fraenkel 1959:23–24; see also Heinze 2014:625). The tone of some of its programs was accordingly very different from the white supremacist content in the settler press and the separate broadcasting service provided from Southern Rhodesia to the small white population in the three territories. The Chibemba program *Imikalile Yesu* (*The Way We Live*), for example, enabled listeners to hear "views on the air that most emphatically did not sound like the Government handouts" (Fraenkel 1959:211).

From the outset, the CABS brought on air a feature that also underlies Gogo Breeze's popularity: a sense of intimacy fostered through radio personalities. Various "agony aunts" had begun to appear in colonial newspapers to dispense advice on relationships (Chaplin 1962), but the anonymity of their authors suggested that the role may have been adopted by white editors themselves. The absence of a physical voice did nothing to match the intimacy that radio personalities were able to achieve. Portuguese settlers in Mozambique, for example, noted with alarm the popularity of African presenters in neighboring territories, including the state-controlled Radio Bantu in South Africa (Power 2000:617). Censorship was indeed the corollary of permitting broadcasts to Africans in their own languages, but subversive messages could be hidden in idioms and proverbs that took vernacular proficiency to detect (Lekgoathi 2011:126; see also Lekgoathi 2009). Innocuous programs such as sports reporting could transport their listeners to places far afield in ways that were not available to them under the conditions of racial segregation and poverty, contributing to new possibilities to imagine home and even the nation (Gunner 2011:166). Above all, a cast of radio friends and regional celebrities emerged, their voices keenly followed across different programs (Coplan 2011:144). "Malome Atšona" (Senior Uncle) on Radio Bantu's Northern Sotho service (Lekgoathi 2011:122) was just one of the many nicknames these radio personalities assumed. In Zambia, the practice more than survived national independence, with the 1950s nicknames often combining allusions to sound and constant activity (Vidali-Spitulnik 2012:255–56), followed by others as the broadcaster changed its own name several times, most recently in 1988 when it became the Zambia National Broadcasting Corporation (ZNBC) to indicate its status as a statutory body responsible for generating some of its revenue (Spitulnik 2010). In Zimbabwe, where freedom of expression fared much worse than in Zambia, the popular radio personalities who started to emigrate to the United Kingdom proved instrumental in recreating a sense of the old public broadcaster on a clandestine radio aimed from London to Zimbabwe (Moyo 2011:54).

Gogo Breeze's most obvious predecessor among Zambian radio personalities was Gogo Juli, real name Julius Chongo. Gogo Juli was the most popular radio personality on Zambian Broadcasting Services between 1966 and 1976, the period when the man who would become Gogo Breeze was beginning his career as a schoolteacher.[22] Gogo Juli, by contrast, had been trained as a journalist and worked for several years as a subeditor at the Zambia News Agency (see Wendland 1979). *The National Mass Media Audi-*

ence Survey noted in 1971 "the enormous popularity of *Poceza M'madzulo*" (Mytton 1971:13), the program of Chinyanja storytelling that Chongo was renowned for.[23] It found out that "people of all language groups" mentioned it as one of their favorite programs and that it appealed to "young and old, educated and uneducated, male and female, and listeners of all tribes" (Mytton 1971:13). Gogo Breeze performed stories from Gogo Juli's published repertoire (Wendland 2004), with due acknowledgements, but he never eulogized about, or otherwise mentioned, his predecessor, whether on air or not. The two men never met, Chongo having died in 1995, and despite the common grandfather appellation, their radio personalities had important differences. Not only did Gogo Breeze sound and look the part by being a de facto grandfather when he achieved fame on the airwaves, but the range of programs associated with his radio name was much wider than the storytelling shows run by Gogo Juli. Although both of them commented on listener feedback on air, Gogo Breeze broadcast in an era of much more intense interaction between radio personalities and their publics. This development was partly caused by commercial imperatives and new technologies such as mobile phones, but it also coincided with Gogo Breeze's desire to take the grandfather from the studio to the streets and villages, something that Gogo Juli never attempted.[24]

The customary codes of conduct in the grandparent-grandchild relationship on which Gogo Breeze built his radio personality were described with remarkable consistency by midcentury anthropologists working in Zambia's predominantly matrilineal settings. Closest to Gogo Breeze's sphere of influence had been Max Marwick (1965), whose fieldwork in Eastern Province in the 1940s and 1950s confirmed that grandparents and grandchildren engaged in a joking relationship. This "friendly, sometimes hilarious, relationship" (1965:134) was a somewhat tempered version of the one that obtained between cross-cousins (*asuweni*), who could indulge in banter and behavior that bordered on the obscene. Grandchildren, on the other hand, were tied to their grandparents, particularly through the mother, by a coresidence that combined physical intimacy with the moral lessons of "bedtime stories" (1965:34). Elizabeth Colson, in turn, reported that a joking relationship between grandparents and grandchildren in Southern Zambia "play[ed] upon marriage and sex in a restrained fashion, without the boisterous quality which appears in the joking of cross-cousins" (1958:57). Victor Turner observed similar behavior in North-Western Zambia with greater attention to how the relationship was expected to evolve: "Although a young child is often allowed to take considerable liberties with his or her grandparents, when the child reaches adolescence he or she must behave with greater respect towards them" (1958:245). Nevertheless, the grandparents would often remain "the genial advisers and instructors of the grandchildren," able to discuss matters that were beyond the pale in the more formal display of respect between parents and children.

Gogo Breeze had not read these anthropological studies, but his demeanor on the airwaves approximated the customary conduct they depicted. He was affable and amusing when with those he called his grandchildren, but stern with wrongdoers and in his advice. The next chapter provides more ethnographic and linguistic detail on the ways in which he sought to achieve and maintain the status of a radio grandfather. But was his choice of idioms for the kind of elderhood he wanted to identify with, and his efforts to summon a public of grandchildren, out of step with the aspirations of Zambia's youthful population? Working in North-Western Zambia in the 1980s, James Pritchett noted the continuing friendship between grandparents and grandchildren but added a sobering thought: "The gulf of experience between them tempers the relevance and meaning of any advice given" (2001:117). Also working in 1980s Zambia, this time in the very district where Breeze FM came to be established two decades later, Mark Auslander (1993) observed the gulf between elders and youths culminating in an open rift when the itinerant witchfinder Doctor Moses visited the area. When witchcraft paraphernalia were found among elderly women and men, the former were resented, in Auslander's interpretation, because of their exclusive knowledge of matters to do with sexuality and reproduction, and the latter suspected to block young people's economic pursuits. For young men, Auslander contended, "the barrier to their economic betterment is not the Zambian State or the International Monetary Fund but the elders of the community, and the moral, political, and economic obligations on which they insist" (1993:181–82).

The disastrous macroeconomic policies of the 1980s and 1990s aside, the economic situation in Eastern Province had not improved in the 2000s to the extent of rendering these acute observations of a gulf irrelevant.[25] The much-debated crisis of reproduction in many African countries—often brought to a head by the combination of the HIV/AIDS pandemic and receding opportunities among young men to amass enough wealth for marriage—would seem to render obsolete Meyer Fortes's description of how "involvement in responsible social relations expands through marriage, fatherhood, economic independence, family headship and lineage eldership" (1959:19).[26] As a result, elderhood in contemporary Africa came to be discussed through the more narrow lens of aging (Bledsoe 2002; Cattell 1997; Makoni and Stroeken 2002; van der Geest 1997 and 2002) and the work of care performed by grand*mothers* (Geissler and Prince 2004; Notermans 2004). Along with the veritable boom in the anthropology of youth in Africa, these studies rarely considered how elderhood might still be an index of authority in societies with young populations and obvious generational tensions.[27] The well-taken corrective to an earlier anthropological emphasis on elderly men's public roles, for example, inadvertently harked back to another source of elderhood's diminishing visibility in scholarship. An early wave of feminism and Marxism in anthropology reduced male elders' authority to a patriarchy in which young men's fortunes were subject to elderly men's control of marriageable women.[28] "Stripped away," Richard Werbner notes, "were the virtues," and the trend in scholarship offered few insights into the "local perceptions of authority and maturation" (2004:134).

While the empirical and theoretical reasons for elderhood's virtual disappearance from the study of Africa may have coalesced, they raised the question of what constituted authority amid the moral, political, and economic turmoil that recent studies highlighted. New forms of authority, decoupled from age-related considerations, certainly emerged in this turmoil, whether of religious or (quasi-)criminal nature,[29] but the case of Gogo Breeze confronts them with an unblinking claim to authority based on age. This empirical finding must be theoretically consequential lest scholarship is transported back to the past. The midcentury anthropologists cited above worked in an intellectual milieu in which the relations between different generations were an issue of comparative interest. Looking for conditions of "equilibrium" in social relations, A. R. Radcliffe-Brown, for example, abstracted a "structural principle" in the "contrast between restraint in the presence of a father or his brother and the freedom of joking with a grandfather" (1950:30–31). The anthropologists working in Zambia and elsewhere in South-Central Africa shared this comparative interest, but many of them were at the forefront of delivering anthropology from the confines of structural-functionalism (see Gluckman 1961; van Velsen 1967). The very notion of equilibrium, where it appeared, was an analytical conceit to envisage change rather than stasis (Gluckman 1968; see also Kapferer 2006:127). The analytical import of "as-if" models could, therefore, be mistaken for unreflexive naïveté about the complexity of social life (see Gluckman 1964). When not detained by undue abstraction, anthropologists working in South-Central Africa anticipated, in fact, perspectives on kinship as contingent and performative rather than as strictly genealogical or biogenetic.[30] However, as much as this intellectual legacy would make possible a shift from the "as-if" models of bounded social units to "an open network of relations" (Werbner 2004:135), it could also lead analysts to neglect the codes of conduct that subjects themselves attributed to specific relationships. "The people's freedom to revise their kin relationships," Marshall Sahlins recently pointed out, "does not mean that the relationships as such are under revision" (2011:5). Kin relationships, in order to be recognized as such, carry determinate properties and codes of conduct.

By evoking elderhood in the idiom of kinship, Gogo Breeze made himself vulnerable to the customary codes of conduct he himself promoted over the airwaves. Unlike perhaps the elders of, for example, Auslander's (1993) study, Gogo Breeze could not control those he deemed his juniors. His was a voice on a privately owned radio station keen to secure revenue as well as listenership from its provincial publics. "Moral, political, and economic obligations" (Auslander 1993:181–82) were not simply an elder's ploy to be resented but a set of relational properties to be engaged. The mass-mediated nature of his elderhood is, therefore, key to understanding the purchase his apparently anachronistic idioms had. The radio was not used in this instance to connect spatially dispersed persons who considered themselves kin irrespective of the radio itself (see Fisher 2016; Mano 2011:115). All grandparenthood involves "the mediated quality of relating to the child of a child" (Whyte and Whyte 2004:83), but mediation here was on another scale, an invitation to a vast assemblage of mutual strangers to consider themselves related to the radio grandfather—and therefore to one another. Gogo Breeze's self-imposed imperative to fulfill the role of the grandfather was consistent with the long-established insight of much anthropology of Africa: life stages such as grandparenthood are to be achieved as moral positions and are not merely given by biological processes (see Johnson-Hanks 2002). What was new was the association of the grandfather's moral position with how he managed to meet his obligations to a potentially infinite public. In an echo of both Turner's (1957:245) observation of shifting qualities in the grandparent-grandchild relationship as the latter matured and Pritchett's (2001:117) skepticism about the continuing relevance of grandparents' advice, Sjaak van der Geest reported from Ghana that "the wisdom of the grandparents may no longer have relevance to the young generation" (2004:57). It was precisely in the extension of the grandfather's wisdom into the areas that really mattered to his public that Gogo Breeze had a chance of imbuing elderhood with moral authority.

Knowing Gogo Breeze

Although Gogo Breeze was still working at Breeze FM when this book went to press, I use the past tense to indicate that the reference is to 2012–13 when I carried out my fieldwork. Life at Breeze FM does not stand still, and a number of programs and personalities not mentioned here went on air before, during, and after my period of research. My conversations with Gogo Breeze, the founder-director, and a number of other present-ers, administrators, and technicians improved my understanding of the sta-tion's first decade before my fieldwork. My main method of inquiry was participant observation, punctuated more by ad hoc conversations than by formal interviews. Using the Breeze FM building as my base, I would spend whole days there to attend various meetings, observe the making of programs, linger in the administrative office that doubled as the station's marketing department, and be close by when visitors came to the station. When the occasion seemed to require it, I left the staff members to their chores and immersed myself in the letters that Gogo Breeze had received or in the digital archives of his and other presenters' programs. Those ar-chives had received little systematic attention and generally did not extend more than two or three years back in time. As such, most of the programs discussed here came on air during or around the period of my research in 2012–13.

Reception, in the sense in which I studied it for my book on the public radio in Malawi (Englund 2011), was not a distinct part of this project. Al-though I spent time in Chipata's markets and high-density residential areas unaccompanied by anyone from Breeze FM, I did not establish a base in those areas for a sustained study of radio reception in all its complexity. Yet important aspects of reception were available to observe in the process of production itself.[31] My primary interest was Gogo Breeze's radio personal-ity and its place in the province's public life, and my insights evolved or-ganically from the many letters and visitors he received, along with his and my own casual encounters during fieldwork. At the station and beyond, two important elements of fieldwork complemented participant observa-tion. Although formal interviewing was a marginal part of my methods, I did sit down with Gogo Breeze and a number of other presenters, particu-larly those described in part 3, to elicit their life histories and reflections on various issues. Another aspect of these repeated sessions was to present my draft transcriptions of program content for their comments. While invalu-able corrections and insights would emerge, it took some time to convince Gogo Breeze in particular that my aim was not to produce transcriptions from which all nonstandard linguistic elements would have been removed. Possibly because of his background as a schoolteacher specializing in Chinyanja, or his understanding of my own interest in the language, he would strike over and replace words or phrases that were either too colloquial to him or borrowed from other languages, especially Chinsenga. It was a learning experience for both us, with Gogo Breeze coming to appreciate that I was as interested in the spontaneous and improvised language characteristic of his everyday encounters as in the carefully articulated Chinyanja of his storytelling performed in the studio.

The other aspect of fieldwork that took me beyond participant observation at the station was to accompany Gogo Breeze and other staff members when they visited Chipata's stores, markets, offices, and townships (the high-density residential areas known as compounds in Zambian towns), or villages, clinics, chiefs' courts, and primary schools in rural areas. Some of these excursions were personal errands with little connection to their radio work, while others were sponsored trips to gather interviews and sounds for broadcast. Accompanying Gogo Breeze involved a particularly wide range of locations and activities, and it was not always clear where his radio work began and ended. He would normally carry a voice recorder with him and turn even the most casual of encounters into a verbal exchange to be recorded. Crucial to my understanding of how his on-air output drew on off-air events and negotiations was to observe when he did *not* turn the voice recorder on, such as when he was in the early stages of investigating grievances. It was equally interesting to note what of the recorded material did not end up on air.

Sometimes the participant aspect of my observer status became rather more prominent than I had wished for. Referring to me as "my grandfather friend from Finland" (*gogo anzanga wa ku Finland*) and sometimes using the clan name Phiri, which I had been given while living in Malawi, Gogo Breeze seemed determined to turn our rapport into a double act, both on air and off. When people we met in the streets and villages realized that they had heard the two of us on the radio, some mirth inevitably ensued, but it was a measure of Gogo Breeze's confidence in his own public personality that he would turn to me for comment and advice when he was considering issues raised in letters or in casual encounters. For it was Gogo Breeze, admittedly aided by my reluctance to have any of his limelight, who had the last word on these as on other occasions. I was merely drawn into his mass-mediated world of kinship like many others he interacted with. Apart from being invited to appear on certain programs run by other presenters at Breeze FM, *Makalata* (*Letters*) and *Landirani Alendo* (*Welcome*

FIGURE 3

Visitors) were the only Gogo Breeze programs on which I appeared. As I became more at ease with playing the rather absurd role of a "grandfather from Finland," I settled into a self-effacing routine of being the man of few words, as seemed to befit the role, while answering listeners' letters. Most episodes discussed in this book did not have me in the studio when they were recorded.

Makalata and *Landirani Alendo* were Gogo Breeze's long-standing signature programs. The letters program involved a "granddaughter"—a female member of staff—reading out listeners' letters before the grandfather answered them, at times complemented by recordings from his investigations (figure 3). The practice of having a granddaughter read out the letters summoned the presence of a village elder, illiterate and yet authoritative in his responses. *Landirani Alendo* could include interviews with visitors to the province, whether in the studio or beyond it, but it also commonly broadcast various kinds of random encounters that Gogo Breeze had, as was seen at the beginning of this introduction. Another long-time program he was particularly famous for was *Zotigwera* (*What Befalls Us*), which Gogo Breeze described as a program of "fireside stories," storytelling involving his own narratives as well as those from Gogo Juli. *Makalata* stood out among his programs as the one with a regular sponsor,[32] but my fieldwork coincided with another sponsored series to which Gogo Breeze contributed along with other presenters. It was *Chidwi Pa Anthu* (*Interest in People*), an initiative of a foreign media charity that gave Breeze FM the opportunity to visit rural areas in search of stories and issues that mattered to its publics. These trips were important occasions to accompany and observe Gogo Breeze and his colleagues as they engaged with villagers and various local authorities and professionals. A further dimension of Gogo Breeze's prolific presence on air was the programs he devoted to the riches of Chinyanja, such as *Chinyanja China* (*More Chinyanja*) and *Mawu Okuluwika* (*Idioms*, lit., "hidden words"). Most of his programs were prerecorded and broadcast at least once a week in the evenings, but he was also live on air three evenings every week, playing music, reading out announcements, and taking phone calls and SMS messages from listeners. The result of all this activity on air, including the use of his voice in many ads, was that his indeed was the most common voice on Breeze FM, to the extent that many listeners seemed to think that the station belonged to him, much to the founder-director's chagrin.

The pair of chapters that constitute part 1 examine in more detail what being Gogo Breeze entailed. Elderhood's mass-mediated parameters are explored in chapter 1 and contrasted with the paucity of scholarly attention to elders as producers of popular culture in Africa. In this chapter, the radio personality's life history before he became Gogo Breeze precedes a discussion of the idioms by which he distinguished himself from others on the provincial airwaves. The chapter also considers his interactions with a number of other authority figures in the province, from traditional and government officials to Chipata's business leaders, many of whom were of South Asian extraction. Chapter 2 presents a case study of his involvement in a particular controversy. Responding to a listener's letter about mill owners in Chipata overcharging their customers, Gogo Breeze embarked on a project that exceeded the purpose of investigative journalism. Here was an elder who wanted to hear all sides in the dispute so as to pronounce his own view with moral authority. The case study gives some of the issues raised in this introduction further conceptual and ethnographic content, such as multivocality and the uses of different media technologies in Gogo Breeze's work. The chapter draws a contrast to another project, not involving Gogo Breeze, that also sought to enhance listener participation at Breeze FM, this time by producing statistical results from listeners' SMS messages to the station. Its plurality of voices turned out to be rather monologic, while the grandfather's concluding speech in the mills controversy was itself multivocal.

The chapters in part 2 take a close look at the grievances and concerns that Gogo Breeze was presented with. Chapters 3 and 4 examine his engagement with them on air and off, respectively, and revolve around the ways in which grandfatherly compassion could be qualified by grandfatherly reprimand. Many listeners' self-identification as the poor victims of their circumstances could make him particularly irate, but he did not hesitate to attack instances of exploitation when he saw them. Chinese involvement in cotton cultivation as well as in retail trade, along with leadership issues in agricultural cooperatives, stand out in chapter 3 as some of the pressing concerns for which Gogo Breeze came to offer his idioms of exploitation drawn from the depths of Chinyanja. Chapter 4 makes a distinction between privacy and intimacy in the radio grandfather's work by exploring how some grievances were addressed without putting them on air. He regularly broadcast intimate matters, but this public intimacy contrasted with his private service. Multivocality remained essential to his work even off air, such as when he confronted a village headman with critical views on his practice or when he painstakingly discerned the many perspectives pertaining to a woman's efforts to access her deceased father's estate. Free speech, in other words, did not always require broadcasting the views he encountered. It could also depend on respecting the boundaries of disclosure with which his listeners confided in him.

Gender relations and children's prospects were matters of public concern in Eastern Province that threw pubic intimacy and multivocality into starker relief. They engaged, as the chapters in part 3 show, a number of presenters at Breeze FM whose distinct styles of voice revealed considerable differences among themselves as well as between them and Gogo Breeze. In chapter 5, gender appears as one of the most controversial issues in the province, matched by a spectrum of voices at Breeze FM from different kinds of feminism to a patriarchy that shared—despite the neo-traditionalist discourse of the particular radio presenter who advocated it—certain misogynist themes with contemporary Zambian popular music. Gogo Breeze enjoyed more approval among his female colleagues and listeners than this self-styled patriarch, largely as a consequence of his multivocal approach to the range of views that gendered controversies provoked. Chapter 5 ends with a description of one of his most popular services over the airwaves—the grandfather as a matchmaker between women and men whose HIV status and previous marital history he accepted without moralizing remarks. Children, on the other hand, rarely had their voices on his programs in any other capacity than as entertaining sideshows, the bulk of debate and conversation being conducted in adult voices. Gogo Breeze's approach stood here in an unacknowledged contrast to much governmental and nongovernmental rhetoric about giving children their voices in both domestic and policy affairs. Chapter 6 follows the preparation of two series of programs at Breeze FM sponsored by a major NGO and their partial resonance with the personal convictions of a senior female presenter. When the second series, focusing on child protection, was being launched, a riot erupted in one of the province's trading centers over the alleged occult killing of a schoolgirl. While the series launch ignored this turmoil, Gogo Breeze came to appreciate the anxieties on the ground. The radio elder's obligations toward his public again dictated the need to attend to vernacular expressions with the seriousness they deserved. It is the specificity of the radio as a medium in this quest for free speech, obligations, and the moral market with which the book concludes in chapter 7.

PART ONE

Being Gogo Breeze

ONE

Mass-Mediated Elderhood

Gogo Breeze's burden was to make judgments and advice appear as though they stemmed from his own wisdom. Much as his authoritative voice was based on assembling other people's voices, the raison d'être of his radio personality was to offer an infallible source of guidance. *Imvi* or gray hair was an idiom, among others to be discussed in this chapter, that Gogo Breeze used to explain his privileged condition. It was an idiom he evoked not only with the Chinyanja-speaking public but also with foreign visitors, such as when he answered a visiting academic's question about the sources of his advice with a chuckle: "Well, the gray hair here is doing something!"[1] On air, he would occasionally use it to underscore the gray hair as an index of his moral authority but also, importantly, to address the discrimination elderly people could face. For example, while explaining the proverb "the scared crow died of old age" (*khwangwala wa mantha anafa ndi ukalamba*), he referred to his gray hair as proof of having lived like the scared crow.[2] "What about you?" he asked his listeners. "Do you want to see gray hair on your head?"[3] His advice was to "be afraid of things that can destroy your life."[4] On another program, however, the question was different. "When a person has grown gray hair like your grandfather here, do you assume that he does sorcery?"[5] Gogo Breeze posed the question during his concluding comments on a short story, and he answered it with a defiant riposte. "Who knows? It is up to you what you think, but understand this: elders are required among us, because when we are in various kinds of trouble, elders are the ones who know how to solve them."[6]

The response alluded to a counterargument about elderhood as a condition that could conceal occult knowledge within the depths of its language and experience—a kind of knowledge as exclusive as the wisdom that elders so freely displayed otherwise. Gogo Breeze did not often engage the counterargument in his broadcasts, but its effects were apparent in comments such as the question about sorcery quoted above and in his reluctance to admit any knowledge of witchcraft when it featured in stories and listeners' letters. Mass-mediated elderhood was a tightrope suspended between suspicion and intimacy. Too much insolence could give rise to fear and cost him listeners. Too much amity risked making him sound like any other presenter on the radio, barely distinguishable for his moral authority as the grandfather. "I deserve respect" was what he said to the letter writer who had assumed undue parity with him in the way he had addressed the grandfather (see below). From time to time, the public had to be reminded that grandfatherly amity did not entail egalitarianism. Here also stood a contrast to the populism that his willingness to assist the disadvantaged might be seen to represent. Gogo Breeze did not hesitate to scold or reprimand the very populace whose experiences of injustice he otherwise sought to investigate and ameliorate.

When examining how an elder figure could command a vast following in a popular culture saturated with youthful styles and concerns, it is important to bear in mind the mass-mediated nature of Gogo Breeze's elderhood. It was a disposition he inhabited with a particular public in mind—the countless listeners he addressed as his grandchildren. While aware of the plight of some elders in Zambia as burdens to their families or as susceptible to accusations of witchcraft, Gogo Breeze asserted an engaged elderhood. Some of its attributes did have a nostalgic flavor, not least when he interspersed contemporary pop music during his late-night shifts with the midcentury classics of Congolese and Zambian music. Yet he mitigated the "stranger intimacy" (Warner 2002) of mass mediation by becoming personally involved in the lives of his public. One challenge of addressing the public as his grandchildren was, therefore, to adopt the lifestyle of a village elder living by modest material means rather than that of an urban professional. He summoned his mass-mediated grandchildren through idioms that supported this identification with the village and, equally importantly, lived the part by refusing to use motor vehicles to move from one place to another unless he was visiting rural areas. Instead, his off-air personality of an elderly man either walking or cycling to his destinations became a much-remarked aspect of his local popularity that soon gave rise to accompanying idioms on air.[7] His past as a schoolteacher was an important aspect of his elderhood, but Gogo Breeze was not an "urban elder" of the kind described for Kinshasa (capital of the Democratic Republic of Congo)—a figure embodying nostalgia for an urban past (Pype 2017). Despite Zambia's historically high rate of industrialization, retirement and retrenchment there had often resulted in attempts to find land to cultivate in rural areas (Ferguson 1999). Certainly in the predominantly rural Eastern Province, whether an elder was rural or urban was not an important distinction.

To build a radio personality on generational differences was not merely to expose oneself to the stereotypical ideas of elderhood, whether for better or for worse. It also brought differences in life courses to the fore (see Whyte and Whyte 2004). Across much of Africa, opportunities for mobility and employment enjoyed by persons who now belong to the grandparents' generation have shrunk as new generations have come of age. Gogo Breeze's life course did not involve as much travel as did those of his generation who took part in labor migration to the mines, but he had pursued spatial mobility and professional advancement on a scale that was beyond the reach of many of his contemporaries.[8] Indeed, several aspects of his life contradicted the image of a village elder. His wife was a highly qualified nurse, and by virtue of her employment, the couple had been able to purchase a spacious government-owned house when Chiluba's regime began its program of privatization. The house was on a large plot of land in central Chipata, away from the town's high-density slum areas. None of this was specifically hidden from the public—including his poultry farming on the plot, which he would sometimes mention on air—and so widely known was his residence that people would pay him impromptu visits at home. As is discussed in chapter 5, he also opened his home for listeners who needed privacy to meet their prospective spouses. Before considering Gogo Breeze's on-air idioms and behavior in detail, it is therefore worth examining his life story as he presented it to me over several interviews and encounters. Language that he deployed on his programs and his emphasis on delivering justice through moral authority had evolved over a long period and were not easily shed when the radio personality was ostensibly taking a break.

The Path to Elderhood

Born in 1946, the man who called himself Gogo Breeze told me, in private, that he considered himself a "young grandfather" (*gogo wachinyamata*). Gray hair and de facto grandfatherhood were not sufficient to make him look and sound like the true octogenarian he longed to become. Yet by the time he made the remark to me, he had already been Gogo Breeze for a decade. Elderhood had been from the start a way of distinguishing himself from other aspiring broadcasters when Breeze FM was established, and the specific properties of mass-mediated elderhood took shape as a process that he could not fully control. Key to his evolving sense of being Gogo Breeze was a narrative about his life before he had become a provincial celebrity. It is a life story that brings the historical forces of colonialism, Christianity, and postcolonial politics to bear on a particular life, its disparate moments conjoined by an abiding commitment to justice.

Introduced on several programs as "your grandfather on air, Grayson Peter Nyozani Mwale,"[9] Gogo Breeze carried in his proper names some of the different influences that had shaped his life course. Grayson, he told me, was the name he had given himself as an adolescent, while Nyozani was his father's first name and Mwale the clan name that derived from his father. Peter had been given to him as a mark of respect for Bwana Peter, a colonial officer (*mtsamunda*) for whom his father had worked.[10] Mwale was among the younger of nine siblings in a family that lived some twenty miles from the administrative center of Fort Jameson, now Chipata. His father's occupation as driver for Bwana Peter suggests a measure of material security for the family. His father's death in 1958, though, raised the question of which school Mwale should attend. His mother wanted him to go to a school run by the Catholic mission in accordance with her and the late father's denomination, but his maternal uncle intervened to place him in a school that was closer to their home village, a decision that Mwale himself endorsed.[11] Thus started his lifelong affiliation with the Seventh-day Adventist Church, first at this local school run by the church and then at a boarding school near the border with Malawi. He had made an impression on the Adventist missionaries, who had decided to transfer him to the boarding school. As his choice of a new name later in life would also attest, Mwale had no qualms about following his own path in life. He responded to my comment on his "courage" (*kulimba mtima*) in rejecting his father's denomination by saying that "the religion that the father had followed was not the same as what is said in the Bible."[12] "I chose that church on my own,"[13] he added, alluding to a degree of separation between him and the rest of his family. Seventh-day Adventists commonly see Roman Catholics as their major theological adversaries.

In practice, of course, Mwale's own path was paved with contacts and opportunities that others presented. In his early years, the church provided key contacts, not only through the teacher who agreed to waive Mwale's fees at the boarding school for his domestic work at the teacher's house, but also when the missionaries encouraged him to embark on training to become a pastor. This phase in life took him to Mzimba in Northern Malawi, where young men from the three territories that had recently comprised the federation—Malawi, Zambia, and Zimbabwe—studied together. While Mwale had gotten used to the idea that people from these territories belonged to "one country" (*dziko limodzi*), no such solidarity could be taken for granted in a region now partitioned by national boundaries.[14] Envious of the missionaries' decision to elevate Mwale to the status of a leader (*mtsogoleri*) among the African students, a Zimbabwean student had gone to the police to report that Mwale was not in possession of a passport. Mwale was thus deported from Malawi in 1967. He saw his ambition to become a pastor vanish but found work in the church as its auditor. He was initially stationed in Southern Province but soon became a national auditor, gaining knowledge of Zambia and its languages that would serve him well later in life. The role did not appeal to him, however, because of pastors who "wasted church money" (*anaononga ndalama za mpingo*). Attempts to solve disputes (*milandu*) led to acrimony. After receiving a death threat on the Copperbelt, he stepped down to pursue a career as a primary school teacher.

Schoolteacher (*mphunzitsi*) became his defining profession and would occasionally be mentioned in his broadcasts. By contrast, as subsequent chapters will discuss, although he remained an active Seventh-day Adventist, references to his past in the service of the church, and to religion overall, were more rare on air.[15] After taking a teacher training course in Livingstone in 1970, Mwale spent his teaching career in Eastern Province, working in a range of rural schools until the 1990s, when he joined a school in Chipata. His experiences in different schools also gave rise to stories about his witnessing or confronting misconduct and injustice. For example, in one school near the Malawian border, his success in keeping chickens caused envy that led to his transfer to another school, where he inadvertently became embroiled in examination malpractice. What he narrated as his superior's wrongdoing resulted in the "punishment" (*chilango*) of being transferred to a particularly remote school, where he stayed from 1981 to 1992. He attributed his eventual move to Chipata to the newly elected president Fredrick Chiluba's intervention. Mwale had served as the interpreter for him and his entourage when they visited the area. Impressed with his skills and demeanor, Chiluba had queried why he was kept so far from Chipata, where he could be of more use to the Movement for Multiparty Democracy (MMD), the new ruling party. He then taught in Chipata until his retirement in 2001, devoting most of his teaching to the relatively advanced Chinyanja in grades seven to nine.

The encounter with Chiluba was not Mwale's first taste of politics. In 1988, he had contested the preliminaries in the then-one-party state and had ended up in the second position. The transition to multipartyism made him join the MMD, but the affiliation proved to be short lived when, by his own account, the expectations of bribes (*ziphuphu*) within the party effectively marginalized members of modest means like himself. He contested the parliamentary elections once in the 1990s as an independent candidate, proudly describing how his minimal campaign had involved him distributing flyers with his bicycle. After the votes had been counted, he emerged as the third in these elections. He also contested the parliamentary elections once as an independent candidate after he had become Gogo Breeze, but the seat in parliament remained elusive. These efforts to enter politics were well known among his listeners and colleagues, some of whom would point out that his failure to advance within the MMD had less to do with his refusal to pay bribes than with party leaders' genuine preference for other kinds of candidates. The founder-director of Breeze FM was particularly scathing about his political ambitions. His criticism was not about improper conduct while on duty, because Mwale had taken a leave of absence when he campaigned during his employment at the radio station. Rather, the founder-director took exception to the very idea that Mwale would, on the basis of the renown he had achieved as Gogo Breeze, move to the distant Lusaka. This would have alienated him from the very base that had made him popular in the first place. While the founder-director had an obvious interest in keeping Gogo Breeze at his station, he also offered an interpretation of Gogo Breeze's success that emphasized patterns of behavior distinct from those of the political class.

By the time I got to know him in 2012, Gogo Breeze no longer appeared to harbor political ambitions and conveyed few preferences in the hotly contested landscape that Chipata and certain other areas in Eastern Province had become.[16] Rather than putting too much weight on his attempts to enter politics, it is more plausible to see them as aspects of the same life that had involved various efforts to play a public role. From his leadership among his fellow students to his role as the church auditor to his career as a schoolteacher, Mwale had grown accustomed to presenting himself as the champion of justice before he became Gogo Breeze. It is not necessary to take all aspects of his life story at face value to appreciate his striving for a life of exceptional service. Instead of exposing self-serving rhetoric that may well have been present in his life story, I believe it is more pertinent to recognize that this grandfather had come to his radio personality not as the village elder he often presented himself as on air but as a highly aspirational individual embracing the opportunities presented by the church, school, and politics.

Among other examples is his realization of the importance of language. While the family into which he was born, like other families living in and around Chipata, mixed Chinyanja with Chinsenga, he early on saw it as his calling to speak "proper Chinyanja" (*chinyanja cholongosoka*). He drew inspiration from the Chinyanja Bible and the clarity and depth that, in his view, Malawians brought to the language. This ambition to explore the riches of the language to harness it better for moral education by no means precluded his appreciation of a wide range of Zambian languages, which he had gained during his travels; some of these he was pleased to speak on the radio when the opportunity arose. Rather, in his choice of language he once again demonstrated his commitment both to building on what was locally available and to distinguishing himself as a custodian of those linguistic-cum-moral resources.

Idioms of Elderhood

When he became Gogo Breeze, Mwale found an outlet for his long-standing interest in studying and teaching Chinyanja on programs such as *Chinyanja China* (*More Chinyanja*) and *Mawu Okuluwika* (*Idioms*). Never slow to insert idioms and proverbs into his speech on other programs, he kept producing these language programs for several years, ostensibly to help schoolchildren to prepare themselves for their classes and examinations but also to establish a link between his knowledge of language and moral authority. Underlying this process was a language ideology that attributed to certain words an opacity only accessible to those who had lived long enough to appreciate the complexities of life.[17] One of his regular introductions to *Mawu Okuluwika* stated, "Idioms are words that hide Chinyanja from children so that when the words are said young children are not able to know what is said by elders unless the issue requires that they know it."[18] The association of elderhood with linguistic prowess was also explicit on *Chinyanja China*, for instance in the statement that "if an issue seemed difficult for someone to understand, elders used words that were said in a short form."[19] While most adults would be expected to know the meanings of such words and phrases, Gogo Breeze situated their usage particularly in deliberations on disputes that elders conducted: "These words are said during court cases if someone has fallen into trouble and lacks help. . . . People judging disputes use short words/phrases so that the words/phrases cover the whole dispute for those who appreciate the kind of Chinyanja that elders a long time ago spoke."[20] It was the brevity of expression that distinguished idiomatic Chinyanja: "Words/phrases said in a short form but planted with meanings" (*mawu okambidwa mwachidule koma ndi mawu obzala ndi matanthauzo*). By presenting himself as an elder who could both apply them when delivering judgments or advice and uncover their hidden meanings, Gogo Breeze traced the sources of moral authority to language itself.

A certain democratization of language use was implicit in this explication of esoteric idioms. However, neither was all revealed, as is discussed later in this chapter, nor was Gogo Breeze prepared to relinquish his role as the one with exceptional wisdom (*nzeru*). Mass-mediated elderhood summoned a public of grandchildren to listen to the grandfather's advice on a vast range of issues, some of which evoked dilemmas of justice on a scale well beyond the competence or interests of the prototypical village elder. Yet the idioms favored by Gogo Breeze often represented the encounter between him and his public as though it was taking place in a village setting far removed from the world of exploitative labor relations, greedy entrepreneurs, and other problems associated with the contemporary forms of poverty. At the same time, the instances discussed throughout this book indicate that his registers of speech during broadcasts were not confined to such idioms of village elderhood. The effect of those idioms was to generate, at least in specific program formats, a particular ambience within which the grandfather could attribute moral authority to his views.

"Take care! Your grandfather is helping you to correct your behavior."[21] Such direct appeals to listeners were common on Gogo Breeze's programs, some of which devoted considerable time to creating the sense of a grandfather addressing his juniors. *Zotigwera* (*What Befalls Us*), a program of short stories whose title Gogo Breeze himself translated as "Fireside Stories," often included allusions to a village gathering. For example, "This moment, my grandchildren, is very good, because different kinds of food are available as they should be this time. When you come to chat with your grandfather, do not forget, you children, to take up small pieces of firewood so that if you come, we shall make a big fire to fry the food we came with. . . . You did well to come with your friends who want to hear stories that your grandfather tells. . . . You do well to do like that, and I would be happy if you called more of your friends who are just sitting in their houses. If they continue to sit like that in their houses without listening to these stories, they remain ignorant/misbehaving children."[22] It is notable that Gogo Breeze spoke these words on a program that had no audience in the studio and whose content and late broadcast time resulted in a predominantly adult listenership. On a program about proverbs, he conjured an intimate gathering by remarking on the ways in which people might be seated: "If you have already sat down on chairs, you have done well. If some of you don't have chairs but stools, there is a small chair too. Others among you may not even have a little stool, but if you have a goat hide, you are able to sit comfortably to listen carefully to today's program."[23] This sense of conviviality did not preclude comments on how a bygone era could be revisited over the airwaves: "The aim is for you to be people who know how our ancestors used to live, because it is very difficult to find people together carving hoe handles, making hoes or axes; very few make these things. . . . Today we are fortunate to have your house on air, Breeze FM, here in the district of Chipata."[24]

Sharing food and listening to the grandfather's storytelling while pursuing various crafts were some of the most common rhetorical devices that Gogo Breeze used to summon his public. On many other programs, however, he interacted with his colleagues or his guests to produce similar encounters between the grandfather and his grandchildren. Once when one of the granddaughters who read letters for him on *Makalata* had brought to the studio a young woman he did not know, Gogo Breeze expressed delight that the newcomer had arrived to help others with work.[25] He noted that he now had no fewer than three granddaughters helping him, commenting that it showed "the grandfather's prosperity" (*kulemera kwa gogo*) by indicating that "the grandfather ha[d] grandchildren" (*agogo ali ndi adzukulu*). While many letter writers would ask him to act on their behalf as their grandfather, the idiom was also actively used by the female colleagues reading letters. A typical way for them to appeal to the grandfather can be seen in this conclusion improvised by one of the granddaughters in the studio: "They say that they are asking because they have not received salaries for three months now. Grandfather, you should go to the company boss so that he explains. Workers are saying that they don't understand why they are not paid. Perhaps you, the grandfather, can assist them, your grandchildren."[26] As these examples suggest, it was a short step from Gogo Breeze's own efforts to summon a public of grandchildren to demands that he serve them as their grandfather.

"I Deserve Respect"

When members of Gogo Breeze's public took his mass-mediated intimacy for granted, they risked becoming subject to sharp rebuke by the grandfather. Particularly hapless was the young man who had written his entire letter in English, possibly to show off his academic credentials, and addressed Gogo Breeze as "Dear Grayson Mwale."[27] The granddaughter got no further than reading the letter's first line—"Dear Grayson Mwale, first and foremost I would like to pass my greetings to you and your colleagues"—before Gogo Breeze stopped her: "Did he write like that, 'Dear Grayson Mwale'?"[28] To the granddaughter's confirmation that this was indeed the case, he uttered, "Aa" in apparent frustration. The granddaughter laughed and said, "Meaning you, grandfather" (*kutanthauza inuyo, agogo*), but Gogo Breeze did not sound amused. On the contrary, he broke the conventions of the program and found out from the granddaughter the name and village of the letter writer. Mixing Chinyanja and English, he brought the issue to a close with these words:

> Without respect. You wrote there in the village of Kalunga; your name you gave as Izeki Jere. Can you please go back to your school where you did your grade twelve? Ask your English teacher to show you how to address people. Letters like that, you are writing as if you were writing to your friend; we don't write like that. I deserve respect. My granddaughter here deserves respect. And if you write like that it means you don't even qualify to be picked in [admitted to] the college you are writing about. We don't do like that; let us give each other enough respect. When writing an application letter, we write well; don't write like you have written here. Had you written, "Dear Editor," or had you written, "The Director," it would have been a letter to the head of work here. But you just wrote "Dear Grayson Mwale"; that is an insult to me. Can we please learn how to address people? Thank you very much for your letter, but I am not giving you any advice on it or your problem.[29]

Granddaughters normally made a point of omitting personal names from the letters they read out, with only the chiefdom or urban area where the letter had come from mentioned, but it was a measure of Gogo Breeze's agitation that he went on to repeat the letter writer's name and village in his closing comments. At one point he even addressed the letter writer in the second-person-singular *iwe*, a pronoun that is usually considered impolite among adults.[30] Humiliation was also reinforced by his injunction that the letter writer return to his secondary school to consult his former English teacher. Competence in the English language is one of the main indices of academic achievement in Zambia, but by alluding to the letter writer's application for college education after this rebuke, Gogo Breeze came close to crushing his aspirations. Here was the grandfather at his most unforgiving, refusing to assist only because of what he saw as a lack of respect in the manner he had been addressed.

Moral education as delivered by Gogo Breeze did not, therefore, take the form of advice alone. It could also involve teaching people modes of conduct that would transform them from disrespectful or negligent subjects into properly behaving moral persons. Such attempts at moral education were not confined to his moments on air; they took place whenever the occasion seemed to warrant them. Regardless of whether he was recognized as Gogo Breeze, he would interfere with conduct that violated his sense of propriety. For example, once when we were standing by the street in Chipata, he suddenly shouted at a man passing us by that the child he was with should walk on the side of the pavement, not on the side where the cars were. It was not uncommon for such interventions to become episodes on his programs, particularly *Landirani Alendo*, on which he broadcast his encounters in townships and villages. After noticing a young child with his private parts exposed because he did not wear a pair of shorts, he engaged the mother in an exchange:

GOGO BREEZE: Where are the shorts so that we can see if it is true that you forgot the shorts?
MOTHER: They are at home.
GOGO BREEZE: At home?
MOTHER: Yes.
GOGO BREEZE: Is the home here?
MOTHER: No, I left to buy charcoal=
GOGO BREEZE: =No, children, children, you have to dress them up. When the child wakes up, you dress him in the shorts, because if a child is naked, he shows the father naked, the mother naked. That sort of thing should not be seen in the open. Do we understand each other?
MOTHER: Mm.
GOGO BREEZE: Yes, dress the child in shorts.[31]

Not all of Gogo Breeze's interventions came in the form of solemn rebuke. He could deploy humor by smiling or laughing while delivering his stern views, but he was consistently unfazed by strangers whose behavior he felt able to correct. His off-air outings were invariably punctuated by such interventions, often good humored, such as when he walked past a man pushing a bicycle uphill and remarked, "You are lazy" (*ndinu waulesi*). His frequent quips to smokers that "you are spoiling the air" (*mukuononga mphepo*) provoked laughter from onlookers, especially if he merely continued his journey without stopping to hear the smoker's response. On one occasion broadcast on *Landirani Alendo* when he again condemned smoking in public, the response in a crowded beer garden was almost more than he could handle:

GOGO BREEZE: Now when you smoke you take a small disease, but those who don't smoke and are far from you take a big disease because of the smoke you let out from your mouth. Are you doing the right thing?

SMOKER: No, we are not doing the right thing=

GOGO BREEZE: =If it is true that you live in Katete, change [yourselves]. You the people from Katete should not smoke, because we have banned smoking here in Chipata.

DRUNKARD: Listen, I have something true to say=

GOGO BREEZE: =Who is telling me that I should listen to you? Who are you?

DRUNKARD: I am a human being.

GOGO BREEZE: Is that how you answer?

DRUNKARD: Yes.

GOGO BREEZE: Now, what do you mean? You should not answer like a cockroach, because the cockroach=

DRUNKARD: =What about human being?=

GOGO BREEZE: =fell into somebody else's sweet beer.

DRUNKARD: Who created the human being?

GOGO BREEZE: No, carry on smoking. Am I preaching here?[32]

When faced with a challenge, sometimes fueled by alcohol, Gogo Breeze would withdraw by making a comment such as the one above that he did not preach. What is remarkable about these exchanges, however, is how his mass-mediated elderhood was not an instance of populism in any straightforward sense. A populist would hardly call a man on the street, however drunk, a cockroach. If populism assumes "the moral purity of the oppressed" (Wolfe 1989:234), then Gogo Breeze was not a populist, as his responses to, for example, the frequent references to poverty and hardship will also attest in the next chapter.[33] While amity and compassion certainly characterized the interactions with his public, his grandfatherly demeanor displayed no qualms about taking poor people as well as their better-off tormentors to task. "You are now contradicting yourself," he said in English to an interviewee who had first complained about his lack of a stall inside the Petauke market and then claimed that he made better money by selling his goods outside the market.[34] It was precisely because he presented himself as a grandfather rather than as a politician or a pastor that his occasional diatribes or quips against the common people were only to be expected and added to the credibility of his radio personality. The discovery of self-serving rhetorics among those complaining about their difficulties was no less intriguing than engagement with administrative and business leaders.

Addressing Authorities

Gogo Breeze generally spent more time away from the Breeze FM building than in it, recording the voices of those he met as he walked the streets of Chipata on his way to sell slots for advertisements among shopkeepers and to pursue various complaints with authorities. His approach to government departments had developed into a routine by which he would walk, usually unannounced, into the office of the department's most senior civil servant rather than attempting to seek a response from low-ranking officers. The reason for this routine was not simply Gogo Breeze's own sense of self-worth but also, inextricably, his understanding that as an elder, he should address only those who were elders (*akuluakulu*) in their offices. Afraid of being seen as subversive, anyone more junior than the provincial officer in any particular department would refer him to their superior. Bureaucratic and commercial interests, as is discussed in the next section, circumscribed the scope of what Gogo Breeze could hope to achieve during these forays, but his ways of addressing these authorities were consistent with his radio personality. In return, he would also often be addressed as grandfather, whether on or off air, evoking a hierarchy within which even the highest-ranking civil servants would cast their responses in a deferential language.

Such exchanges had their humorous moments, but the realization that civil servants' responses could become mass-mediated pronouncements was never far from the interlocutors' minds. In contrast to the mill owners described in the next chapter, Gogo Breeze rarely raised his voice or used disrespectful language during these exchanges. However, he was usually forthright about the hierarchy he wished to see in such encounters. During one of our visits to the provincial local courts officer to investigate yet another complaint about bribery in a particular court, the officer began to read the Local Courts Handbook to us and remarked, "You should send them here: 'Go and see that child; he will explain/translate for you.'"[35] To Gogo Breeze's question, "Where?" (*kuti?*), the officer answered, "Myself" (*ine*). The officer's attempt to appropriate the role he occupied in the grandfather's scheme involved a subtle shift in the identity in which authoritative statements were vested. Quick to restore his prerogative to make such statements, Gogo Breeze asserted the proper order with these words: "The child should explain/translate, but the gray hair should also know, because we cannot speak as though we were speaking on behalf of government. We speak in accordance with the radio program, but the child responds in accordance with custom. We shall only confirm whether what the child says is true."[36]

Referring to himself in the first person plural as "we" (*ife*), Gogo Breeze seized on the officer's self-description as "child" (*mwana*) but cut short the officer's attempt to enlist the grandfather as a mere messenger between claimants and the officer. The radio stood in contrast to the government, a contrast conducive to free speech, albeit mediated by hierarchies other than those between the bureaucrat and the common people. The officer was obliged to submit to custom (*mwambo*) and allow the grandfather to have the last word on whether the response was acceptable. Such off-air exchanges often involved subtle negotiations about procedure and outcome between persons who were both public figures but had strikingly different mandates to consider claims and complaints from their respective publics. The provincial social welfare officer, for example, was familiar to Gogo Breeze not only because many of the letters he received concerned this department but also because the two attended the same Seventh-day Adventist Church on Saturdays. Though not close in social terms, they would exchange pieces of information on these occasions and would maintain amicable relations when Gogo Breeze visited his office. Amity did not preclude disagreement over procedure, such as when Gogo Breeze brought two letters from orphans (*ana a masiye*) to the officer. The complaint was a familiar one from the *Makalata* program: eligible children were excluded from financial assistance because members on the local committees selecting the deserving children had preferred to support their own relatives.

Gogo Breeze told the officer that such letters "burdened" (*kulema*) him, but the officer's first reaction was to explain that local committees were expected to fill out forms about the eligible children in their areas and to submit those forms to the department's district offices. A further bureaucratic rule was that only three children could be selected from each area for support. In an apparent gesture of compassion to qualify his opening remarks on the bureaucratic procedures, the officer then told Gogo Breeze that he could consider if the two letters he had brought would warrant exceptions to the rules. Gogo Breeze opposed the idea by saying that "I have many letters" (*ndili ndi makalata ambiri*) and that he had brought these two only as examples. Against the officer's offer of discretion, he asserted that the scale of the problem was too large to be ameliorated by such individual remedies. Two aspects of this moment in their conversation were especially notable. One was the officer's alignment with bureaucratic power in which he articulated both the rule and its exception.[37] The other was the way in which Gogo Breeze's preference for structural rather than individual considerations was likely to indicate his particular obligations to his listening public. Although no allusion was made to bribes in the officer's tolerance of exceptions, Gogo Breeze was only too aware of how his association with such bureaucratic discretion might be viewed as corruption. Much as his obligations were expressed in the intimate register of grandfatherhood, they were not supposed to expose him to charges of favoritism.

The officer made a swift return to bureaucratic rules when Gogo Breeze suggested that he bring him all the letters. "That is not the procedure," he said in English with a somewhat irritated tone, adding that it would have "implications." Requests for assistance should not come through the radio, he explained, but by observing the procedures he had already outlined. As if to anticipate the deadlock to which their conversation was heading, the officer then pointed out that his department had only secondary-school students' welfare issues in its remit while the Ministry of Education looked after those issues among basic-school students. Both men seemed to sense an opportunity for compromise here, and Gogo Breeze offered to group his letters into two categories according to which type of school they referred to. The officer welcomed the idea that Gogo Breeze would come back to him with a small number of letters pertaining to his department, and the two men parted in good humor. Before they did so, the officer mentioned something he had taken up with Gogo Breeze when they had met before: the possibility that his department would buy regular slots on Breeze FM's broadcasts to, as he said by deploying the English term, "sensitize" people about the work of his department. Gogo Breeze was enthusiastic about the possibility both with the officer and afterward as he reflected on the amount of revenue a series of thirteen slots would bring to the station. What was striking to me was the officer's desire to use the radio only insofar as his department could have an outlet for its own messages, not as a tool to gather grievances from the public. Gogo Breeze's obligations to his public, however, ensured a different order of free speech, one in which the officer was likely to remain subject to such grievances.

An important element in encounters such as this one was Gogo Breeze's assurance that he would not record anything at that point but was simply visiting the office to obtain information. When he did take out his voice recorder in offices, senior civil servants were invariably deferential in their address, often making great effort not to mix Chinyanja with English phrases as they did in their off-air talk. "Thank you, grandfather" (*zikomo gogo*), the provincial education officer began his recorded response to Gogo Breeze when faced with the question of whose duty it was to clean pit latrines in schools. Gogo Breeze had received a letter complaining about the practice at one particular school, where parents' monetary contribution to the school's upkeep had not prevented teachers from ordering pupils to clean pit latrines. Gogo Breeze had developed a view on the matter already before arriving in this office, and the two men were in agreement that money contributed by the parents was unlikely to be enough to employ a full-time cleaner and that the pupils had to take responsibility for cleaning pit latrines. More remarkable than the agreement was the officer's obliging attitude to a question that might have been well below the provincial education officer's status, ensconced as he was in a spacious, air-conditioned office furnished with armchairs, sofas, a flat-screen television, and trophies from his sporting activities (see figure 4). Rather than attributing this attitude entirely to this particular officer's magnanimity, we might plausibly find in his deferential address an indication of how much he recognized the authority entailed by the radio grandfather's mass-mediated obligations.

The encounters with top provincial civil servants indicated a degree of familiarity, even of mutual dependence, that was less apparent in Gogo

FIGURE 4

Breeze's approach to other kinds of authorities. While no leader—whether from religious, business, political, or traditional spheres—would be subjected to vitriol, he could be more direct about his disapproval of them than of the civil servants with whom he had established working relationships. The practice on the letters program of not mentioning personal names applied to these leaders and their churches or businesses too, but some listeners could apply their local knowledge to identify the leaders. Yet this was by no means the most significant consequence of broadcasting critical perspectives on leadership.[38] Even when unnamed, leaders came under fire in a way that could only too readily be extended to any other leader. For example, a bricklayer wrote a letter to complain that after he had worked for five months at a daily rate of ZMK 25,000, the owner of the company had reduced the rate to ZMK 20,000, announcing that "anyone who does not want to work should leave."[39] Gogo Breeze gave a rebuke as his response: "When you have money, you can employ your friends to work for you. It is not proper to treat them badly, because the work would not be done if the people were not there. That is fraud that we are talking about, or theft."[40] Careful not to reveal the businessman's name to listeners, the granddaughter reading the letter had a suggestion to make to the grandfather: "The company they mentioned here, it belongs to a very well-known person here in Chipata District. Please go and talk to him."[41] She then showed the name to the grandfather, who exclaimed, "Oh, it is that one!" (*Oh, ndi awa!*), to which the granddaughter replied, laughing, "Do you know him?" (*muwadziwa?*). The grandfather expressed more disapproval by saying, "Ah, is that how we do things? No, you are bringing discord/conflict" (*aa, nanga timatero? A-a, mukuputa ndewu kumeneku*).

By addressing the flawed businessman directly as "you," Gogo Breeze asserted familiarity with him even when he remained nameless, but also made all employers vulnerable to similar charges of exploitation. Such categorical appeals to authorities were not uncommon on his programs. At the end of a short story, broadcast in three parts, he summed up its narrative about the fatal consequences of a self-appointed chief's unpopular rule and addressed the chiefs who were listening to the broadcast. "You, the chiefs, they gave you the responsibility [lit., "the chair"], but is it yours? If the responsibility that you received is indeed yours, work in the way that your chieftainship requires you to work."[42] Chiefs and village headmen were the authorities to whom Gogo Breeze would often refer aggrieved listeners in rural areas, such as when he received a letter complaining that the chairman of a local farmers' cooperative had helped himself to more bags of fertilizer than he had been entitled to. Gogo Breeze's comments and

exchange with the granddaughter in the studio assumed that his public included traditional authorities from this particular area:

GOGO BREEZE: I ask you, my brother, that if he really did that to you, go to the
 headman; the headman should take you to the chief with the scepter.[43] I
 don't believe that Paramount Chief[44] Mpezeni would accept wrongdoing by
 the chair of the cooperative, because Paramount Chief wants his people to
 have food in their houses. Now, you gave that one responsibility, but he gives
 money back to you instead of giving you one small bag. He took two, three,
 four bags, just because he is a leader in the cooperative. No. Mpezeni has his
 elders with whom he will sit down to examine=

GRANDDAUGHTER: =But does he not hear us talking?

GOGO BREEZE: If the program has reached there to the Paramount Chief, this
 person should go there tomorrow to explain the issue is like this, this, this,
 so that they will put him [the chair of the cooperative] under the kachere
 tree. Do you know kachere tree, how things are?

GRANDDAUGHTER: You are able to say.

GOGO BREEZE: Ants.[45]

The image of the chair tormented by ants while sitting under the kachere tree made both Gogo Breeze and the granddaughter laugh, but the
exchange subtly highlighted how subjects could use traditional authority
to control its incumbents. Not only were the headman and the paramount
chief expected to provide justice when a local cooperative had fallen under
poor leadership; these authorities were themselves given a standard to measure up to by the radio grandfather's comment that the paramount chief
wanted his people to have enough food. Reminiscent of praise singing in
Southern Africa (see Vail and White 1991), the comment obliged the chief
to commit himself to his subjects' welfare by asserting such commitment
as a fact. By the same token, the comment also invited the grandfather's
mass-mediated public to witness what the paramount chief, himself assumed to be listening to the program, would do in response to it. For many
listeners in Chipata and in Mpezeni's territory, Gogo Breeze's mention of
this particular paramount chief was also charged with special significance.
The incumbent's reputation had been tarnished by his disagreements with
other Ngoni chiefs, some of whom were more educated than him, and by
allegations of sexual misconduct. Although he was never directly accused
of such failings by Gogo Breeze over the airwaves, this was not the only occasion when Mpezeni was the recipient of advice and reminders from the

radio grandfather, whatever the respectful and laudatory register in which they were delivered.[46]

Elected representatives, such as local councillors and members of parliament, were no less subject to Gogo Breeze's grandfatherly advice, but letter writers had to be seen to bring up genuine grievances rather than partisan claims. "Their question is very good" (*funso lawo ndi labwino kwambiri*), he remarked to endorse a letter in which listeners reported that "we voted for the MMD [Movement for Multiparty Democracy] for both councillor and the MP, but what is surprising is that the development that came here is salt, soap, blankets, and games of football as well as handball."[47] The granddaughter read out what the politicians had promised before their election: "They told us that if you vote for us, first roads, bridges, we shall repair. Of the two I mentioned here, not one thing has happened; it has failed. The question, grandfather, is whether salt, football, blankets are development."[48] Gogo Breeze's response began by asking if the letter writers had sat down (*kukhala pansi*) to discuss their grievances with the elected representatives, but he quickly proceeded to reprimand the politicians and suggested that he would call them on the telephone to make them explain the situation to him. Anticipating their difficulties of meeting popular demands, he ended his comments with words directed to the politicians:

> It's therefore necessary for us who are on the front [ahead] that if we told people that when you vote for us, we will assist you in various ways, please make the effort [to fulfill promises]. I know that it is difficult to find assistance because you don't have money. Money can be found during the campaign, but now when you look into your pocket, it is empty because you took so much. To replenish it, it is difficult, but please try to meet other people who might assist you so that what you promised to people you will fulfill.[49]

Here the radio elder, himself an austere figure, reconfigured the elected politicians as needy, themselves requiring assistance in order to meet their campaign promises. He suggested that their status as the prototypical distributors of patronage depended on cultivating contacts with people other than those who had voted for them. At the same time, Gogo Breeze may have given the politicians the benefit of the doubt, because rather than suspecting them of wasting their resources, he gave their plight the sympathetic interpretation that they simply lacked money when the campaign was over. The effect of his advice over the airwaves was, however, to make

the politicians all the more answerable to their constituents in a way that
was analogous to the burden of responsibility he placed in the guise of
praise on the paramount chief. The elected politicians found themselves
subject to demands for proper development not because they were regarded
to have failed in moral terms, but because their assumed uprightness was
compromised by their lack of means to bring development. It is important
to note that this charitable attitude had nothing to do with Gogo Breeze's
own political preferences. He could be sharply critical of MMD politicians
who indeed were found to have neglected their constituents, as will be seen
in chapter 4, just as he would dismiss inappropriate attacks on the Patriotic
Front (PF), Zambia's ruling party after the 2011 elections. For example, he
cut short the reading of a letter that began with the words, "I ask the government of PF, the governor, cabinet minister here in Chipata, on behalf of
the whole Zambia."[50] The large number of demands in the letter, though
not read out, caused considerable amusement in the studio, but Gogo
Breeze dismissed it with the words, "Thank you very much. I have heard
your complaints, but you must begin by considering, 'Are these issues appropriate to write the grandfather about?'"[51] Unlike the letter about the
MMD politicians, this letter did not emanate from a recognizable constituency of grandchildren. By answering it, Gogo Breeze could have entered
partisan politics in which the government and the ruling party in general
would have stood on trial. Obligations, despite their mass-mediated scale,
had to be traced to specific relationships for the grandfather to intervene.

The Value of Gogo Breeze

Among its listeners, Breeze FM was so much associated with Gogo Breeze
that many would assume, to the founder-director's chagrin, that he was
the station's owner. His popularity was a major asset to the station that
was, despite its ethos of public service, run on commercial principles. That
Gogo Breeze was frequently absent from the studio was by no means only
because of his investigations into misconduct and injustice. A typical day
would see him visiting several businesses in town between the morning
and early afternoon in order to pursue what he described as "marketing."
These outings were often interspersed with visits to authorities on behalf
of his listeners, but he would retire to his house in the afternoon to rest
and to write scripts for the advertisements that he had sold. Late-evening
shifts at the station would then provide the peace and quiet to record and
edit the ads as well as programs. The same combination of commercial
and public-service principles that characterized Breeze FM as a whole was

epitomized by Gogo Breeze. Rather than leading us to conclude that Breeze FM was implicated in making local listening communities vulnerable to market expansion, the figure of Gogo Breeze affords harder questions to be asked about the relationship between private capital and public service in the twenty-first century.[52]

The founder-director's frustration, as mentioned in the introduction, over his efforts to "monetize" Gogo Breeze masked the many benefits, tangible and intangible, that this radio personality brought to the station. Beyond the rapport he had established with his public, Gogo Breeze also acted as an elder in the station's daily life. He offered advice to other members of staff on a variety of personal and professional matters and was consulted whenever issues arose in the station's relationship to traditional authorities. For example, when another broadcaster had produced a program about Ngoni history that alluded to their victory over the Chewa, it was Gogo Breeze whom colleagues at Breeze FM asked to mediate when the Chewa paramount chief Undi made his displeasure at the program known. Gogo Breeze was instrumental in arranging his colleagues' visits to rural areas and frequently provided not only local contacts but also advice on appropriate protocol. No one was more reliant on such advice than the founder-director himself, whose long career in Lusaka had done little to prepare him for the linguistic and cultural conditions of broadcasting in Eastern Province. He rarely ventured into the field, but when he did so, usually to accompany donor representatives and other visitors, Gogo Breeze's presence was often crucial.

An illustration is the one-day visit in 2013 by two representatives, a man and a woman, from an organization supporting Breeze FM's work in rural areas. Zimbabweans by nationality, they represented a Dutch organization. After collecting the visitors from Chipata's premier hotel, Michael Daka, the founder-director, returned to the station, where several staff members were preparing for the field trip. He asked me to sit in his Toyota Hilux with the visitors while the staff members, Gogo Breeze included, crammed into another vehicle. During the drive, Daka told the visitors about the need for his staff to leave Chipata in order to "serve the people" in rural areas, which he used, as he had done in conversations with me, to distinguish the station from NGOs. When we reached our destination, we followed the other car to the chief's house, also known as his "palace." Daka snorted and said, "Oh no, this is some serious traditional stuff now," when he saw Gogo Breeze leaving the other car to talk to Daka. A brief discussion between the men ensued when Daka questioned Gogo Breeze's request to bring the visitors to meet the chief. Gogo Breeze pointed out that they had now entered the chief's territory (*dziko*; also translated as "country") and were obliged to pay a courtesy call to him. When Gogo Breeze went into the house to ask for permission to introduce the visitors to the chief, Daka and the donor representatives exchanged views on the insignificance of traditional authorities who, they agreed, existed mainly to be manipulated by politicians. We were then led by Gogo Breeze into the chief's house, where the visitors remained silent while Gogo Breeze and Daka explained to the chief the purpose of their visit. In another indication of his lack of consideration for customary codes, Daka regretted that he had not brought a windup radio to give to the chief as a token of their gratitude. He resolved to send Gogo Breeze to deliver the gift on another occasion.

Gogo Breeze was no less indispensable in approaching the chief's subjects than he was in soliciting the chief's permission to be in the area. While the other broadcasters played little role in the villages other than interviewing selected people for their programs, Gogo Breeze was again the one who facilitated the delegation's encounters with various local dignitaries, such as the heads of primary schools, and with the crowds that thronged to see them. Although he invited Daka to speak when the delegation was seated before a vast audience of schoolchildren, teachers, and parents, Gogo Breeze kept the crowd entertained and interested with his witticisms and interactive methods of communication. Using the female donor representative as a role model for girls, he urged that girls had to resist boys' advances even if their breasts had started to grow. He pointed to her and asked rhetorically if she had no breasts (*mawere*), and when the audience affirmed with a roar, he remarked that she had been able to get far by focusing on her studies instead of playing (*kusewera*) with boys. Daka and other Breeze FM members laughed along with the crowd rather nervously, but the subject of Gogo Breeze's remarks appeared to have escaped the donor representatives, who spoke no Zambian language. As we were walking in one of the villages, his role as the intermediary between the visitors and the locals was commented on by a man who, possibly encouraged by a taste of alcohol, observed in English that "Gogo Breeze is an international man" (see figure 5).

Daka left the area soon so that the donor representatives could catch a flight back to Lusaka, but I stayed behind and returned to Chipata at the end of the day with the rest of the Breeze FM crew. Two incidents during our journey further indicated Gogo Breeze's unique standing among his colleagues. A traffic policeman stopped our vehicle on the road, and when he was inspecting the driver's license, Gogo Breeze tried to engage him in a conversation. "May I know you?" (*ndikudziweni*), the policeman asked,

FIGURE 5

to which came the reply, "Gogo Breeze."[53] "Oh," said the policeman and waved the driver to continue driving, with the conversation in the vehicle revolving around the traffic police's habit of "becoming rich" (*kulemera*) by stopping vehicles in order to extract bribes from their drivers. The team was convinced that the policeman would have asked for a bribe had he not recognized Gogo Breeze. As we reached Chipata, a female presenter, whose makeup and jeans had stood out in the village setting, sighed in English, "Back to civilization." A sometime "granddaughter" on the letters program, this presenter possessed rather more local linguistic and cultural competence than Daka and his visitors, but her sigh of relief betrayed a measure of distance toward rural areas that could not be associated with Gogo Breeze. He did not comment on the female colleague's words, but the excursion could have taken a rather different form had it not been for his skills in navigating local hierarchies and in ensuring popular participation in Breeze FM's projects. In fact, the visit was hardly a "field trip" for him as it had been for Daka and some members of the team. The interactions with the chief, the schoolteachers, their pupils, and other villagers were no different from his daily routines in Chipata.

His unique standing among Breeze FM's staff could, of course, be a source of envy, but an important aspect of his modest, if hierarchical, demeanor was his effort to defuse such a possibility. He rarely spoke more than others at staff meetings and never missed a chance to announce how much praise colleagues' programs had received during his interactions outside the station. His elderhood could not secure uncontested authority, but it was more the suspected material and monetary gains of his popularity than his elderhood as such that sometimes caused friction at the station. On one particularly tense occasion during and after a staff meeting in 2012, Gogo Breeze withdrew into silence when his younger colleagues expressed their concerns over the use of an ad he had prepared for Breeze FM. Several colleagues had heard the advertisement on the two rival stations, Radio Maria and Feel Free FM, but as one of them pointed out, Gogo Breeze's voice was "unmistakable" and therefore likely to confuse listeners who might think that they had tuned into Breeze FM. At first he had tried to calm his colleagues down by warning against alienating the client who had commissioned the ad and who had given Breeze FM business for five years. A young news reporter said that he had been present when Gogo Breeze had agreed on the price of the ad, but no mention had been made of the client's right to take it to other stations. Gogo Breeze remained silent when the group resolved to order him to ensure that the ad was removed from the other stations.

Breeze FM had two or three staff members assigned to its marketing department, but as mentioned, Daka saw it as every presenter's duty to generate revenue for the station. Few were able to do so, much as they might have wanted to report to the weekly staff meeting that they had found new advertisement or sponsorship. It was Gogo Breeze's relentless socializing with people beyond the station that made him particularly well placed to expand both listenership and sponsorship. Just as he engaged strangers in conversations, so too did he often endear himself to entrepreneurs through his skills in communication. While he always seemed alert to opportunities to sell advertisement slots whenever he visited businesses, such as during "field trips," he also had long-established acquaintances among the local business elite, particularly in Chipata town. Some of those acquaintances had become regular advertisers on Breeze FM; others were especially inclined to extend gestures of generosity to Gogo Breeze himself. Here was another source of tension between his radio personality and the world in which the personality was embedded. On one hand, the source of advertising revenue in the personality's popularity could provoke envy among other broadcasters. On the other, by accepting gifts from sponsors, he became vulnerable to the same accusations of bribery that filled some of his programs.

Gogo Breeze's popularity on the airwaves was, however, only one aspect of his rapport with Chipata's business elite. Particularly when dealing with entrepreneurs of Indian origin, he brought not so much his radio personality as his pre–Gogo Breeze life history to bear on his relationships with them.[54] Although avid advertisers and, as third- or fourth-generation Chipata residents, fluent in Chinyanja, few of the Indian entrepreneurs appeared to follow the contents of Breeze FM, unlike many of the African entrepreneurs Gogo Breeze also interacted with. It was in his past as a schoolteacher that Gogo Breeze found an interface between his experiences and those of the Indian entrepreneurs. Although he had not taught them, schooled as they had been in institutions catering primarily for Indian settlers, his postings as a teacher in various parts of Eastern Province had brought him into contact with their fathers and other relatives who had visited the areas for their businesses. Remarkably, and in line with the rest of his off-air interactions in public, Gogo Breeze's evocations of the past called forth hierarchy as well as amity. To the apparent amazement of their African workers loitering within hearing distance, these Indians—almost invariably bearded, dressed in white robes, and habitually stern looking—were subject to good-humored reminders of having been mere "boys" (anyamata) when Gogo Breeze had already been a teacher. Unlikely associations came to the fore when he recalled, for example, a shopkeeper's visit as a member of a soccer team to the rural primary school where he had been teaching. This familiarity, when kept within the bounds of acceptable humor, tended to ensure advertising revenue that was not unduly restrained by the entrepreneurs' notoriously mean ways. Some of them had, in fact, developed the expectation that it would be Gogo Breeze who came to collect the payment and the message for the next advertisement. I often observed them complaining to him that "girls" (atsikana) from Breeze FM's marketing department had visited them but had not been able to convince them to agree on another ad.

At the end of a day spent visiting businesses in Chipata, Gogo Breeze would sometimes remind me that he had achieved success in marketing without any formal training in it. While Daka told me that he wanted to enhance this department with someone who had professional training in marketing, Gogo Breeze's contribution to the advertising revenue also indicated how linguistic and cultural competence may have been more important than training disembedded from the relationships in which so-called marketing had to take place. Making money was, for Gogo Breeze, more than a contribution to the station's finances. It involved cultivating relationships and using language in creative ways. Once when an African shopkeeper started to write down the phrases he wished to hear in his advertisement, Gogo Breeze interrupted him by saying, "Don't worry; we have the language" (*musavutike,* language *tili nayo*). He put virtually as much effort into writing and performing the ads as he did into programs devoted to the riches of Chinyanja, often deploying idioms or esoteric words (*mawu okuluwika*) in both. The language in the ads had to be entertaining as well as esoteric, such as when he used the English word "trailer" to describe the women serving food in a restaurant that was being advertised. The image was of a plump woman with a protruding rear end. Although he was intrigued to hear sponsors' comments on ads after they had been broadcast, he rarely consulted them about the actual phrases he would use and seemed to safeguard his authorship of them with some resolve.[55]

The hierarchical amity of commercial relationships trod the thin line between gifts (*mphatso*) and bribes (*ziphuphu*), and Gogo Breeze had to be constantly vigilant to ensure it did not compromise his moral authority to pronounce on businesses' abuses. Anonymity among companies and protagonists on the letters program allowed for investigations without necessarily severing a commercially important relationship. Unlike the other authorities on whose cooperation Gogo Breeze's investigations also depended, however, business elites were particularly disposed to giving him gifts. He accepted some gifts when it was made public that he was not alone in receiving them. For example, Breeze FM's tenth anniversary in 2013 saw gifts and donations flowing to various presenters, including a suit for Gogo Breeze from one of Chipata's upmarket retailers. The gift of a motorbike in 2013 emanated, in the words of the prominent African entrepreneur who donated it, from "compassion" (*chisoni*) for the aging radio personality who chose to walk and cycle. Yet even the motorbike came to be absorbed in Gogo Breeze's carefully cultivated modesty, because he made it known that he could ride it only after negotiating allowances for fuel with the founder-director. How much such modesty distanced him from the specter of bribes—and what took place in private when I was not present—are questions that I cannot answer with any precision. At any rate, his mass-mediated elderhood had made his lifelong commitment to public service subject to new kinds of challenges. The exposure of bribes, fraud, and exploitation in other people's lives could not exonerate the radio elder from such practices in his own life.

TWO

The Grandfather's Voices

How many voices must be heard when addressing matters of public concern? The World Bank answered this question with some precision in 2002 when it brought to a conclusion its project titled *Voices of the Poor*. This three-volume initiative presented the views and aspirations of sixty thousand poor men and women in sixty countries (Narayan and Petesch 2002). It employed life histories, group discussions, and individual interviews to capture their voices. While translations of what had been said enlivened the texts, the researchers were required to aggregate their findings upon producing them, resulting in data subsets and frequency counts on particular topics (Narayan and Petesch 2002:5). The World Bank's established habits of knowledge production necessitated a study "on a sufficiently large scale to reduce the probability that it would be dismissed as producing merely interesting anecdotes" (Narayan and Petesch 2002:3). Yet this emphasis on statistical knowledge cannot be explained solely by the fact that economics enjoys a dominant status in organizations such as the World Bank. As histories of statistical thinking have demonstrated, statistics evolved into a technology of government by which society became knowable (Porter 1986). Reducing a population to a small number of variables was by no means the inevitable consequence of this technology. The increasing sophistication of statistical methods entailed individualizing rather than totalizing. Aggregation was, and is, a method of differentiation.

Once the plurality of voices becomes an object of interest, neither quantitative nor qualitative approaches to identifying and representing them have any intrinsic advantage over one another. In 2002, the same year as the World Bank study was published, a historian used the phrase *voices of the poor* to offer an altogether different perspective (see Isichei 2002). Here "truth from below" indeed came as so many anecdotes. Isichei (2002:4) likens her interpretations of them to literary criticism. In contrast to the tales of material hardship and deprivation collected in the World Bank project, the themes of vampirism, witchcraft, and magic dominated the voices of the African poor in the historian's account. Despite this contrast, both studies took as their task to recover those voices from the policy and academic orthodoxy in which they had been drowned. In neither instance was the possibility of constituting, rather than recovering, these voices contemplated. Whether analyzed through aggregation or in terms of symbolism, the resulting voices were by no means as authentic—or as plural—as the authors of these studies seemed to suggest. Using statistics produced patterns and frequencies that no participant in the World Bank project was likely to be aware of. Interpreting symbolism framed and explained anecdotes about vampirism, witchcraft, and magic in ways that made them intelligible to far-flung audiences. As such, both studies constituted voices by managing plurality—as a matter of statistical interest in one case and as an interpretative challenge in the other.

If free speech, by definition, requires multiple speakers, then the question of how to describe the plurality of voices must lie at the heart of any effort to account for it ethnographically. Studying a radio elder in contemporary Zambia helps us to confront this question with particular acuity. His status as an elder, avowedly omniscient and assured, is all too easily associated with the singularity of voice rather than its plurality. But in provincial Zambia as elsewhere, the radio also exists at the intersection of media technologies that seem poised to increase the number and range of voices heard on air. According to one observer of the radio in Africa, it appears to be transforming from a "mono-modal" medium to a "multi-modal" one, combining the voice with written words (such as blogs), pictures, and even video (Moyo 2013:211). The prospect of individual empowerment promised by mobile phones in Africa is especially bright when they are understood to "put the power of *instant content and reaction* into the hands of the listener" (Smith 2011:267; emphasis original). More globally, new media technologies are said to enable not just more voices to be heard in public but to engage "a vastly increased range of people" (Couldry 2010:140).

Studies documenting the social and cultural consequences of the rapid, large-scale rollout of mobile phones in the Global South have demonstrated just how integral they have become to various aspects of life, from intimate relationships and secrecy (Archambault 2017; Pype 2016), to linguistic innovation (MacIntosh 2010), to money transfers (Kusimba et al. 2016), and much else (Jeffrey and Doron 2013). Their interface with the radio is a corollary of their ubiquity. While interactive shows facilitated by mobile phones have become de rigueur across Africa, there is no denying empirical research into their actual procedures and contents. A recurrent finding in studies on political and current affairs programs, for example, is the influence wielded by so-called serial callers, small cohorts of recurrent characters who call radio stations several times a week (Brisset-Foucault 2016; Gagliardone 2016; Tettey 2011). Mostly young or middle-aged men, they can be affiliated with particular political parties or business interests but are also in some cases spurred by personal ambition to showcase their academic knowledge in the absence of other opportunities to do so. It appears unlikely that such participation amounts to the emancipatory, citizen-led deliberation predicted in the more triumphalist accounts of interactive radio. In Zambia, where the mobile phone subscription rate was 71.5 percent in 2013,[1] partisanship has been no less blatant on phone-in shows than in some areas of the country's print media. Particularly in the politically contentious Western and Copperbelt Provinces, "name calling, libel and rumour" (Fraser 2016a:9) have been reported to be the staple of phone-in shows.

Chapter 6 describes how popular anger could also take over phone-in shows in Eastern Province when rumors about an occult attack began to circulate there. At the same time, it is important not to overstate the power of mobile telephony in public deliberation, partly for reasons indicated above and partly because of the deeper questions to be asked about technology and voice. Breeze FM, along with other radio stations all over the world, is a site on which various media technologies meet. Its media ecology extends beyond broadcasts through the letters, phone calls, photos, SMS messages, and emails it receives, some of which refer to further technologies of mediation, such as bureaucratic forms (compare Kunreuther 2014:202). It also has an online presence through a website and Facebook. Its publics are invited to contribute to its programs through these media on several occasions every day. The uses of these varied technologies, and the meanings attributed to them, differ not only between radio stations in different parts of the world, but also within Breeze FM itself. I witnessed the founder-director admonishing his newsroom staff for mentioning the email and Facebook addresses before the telephone number and postal address when urging listeners to contact the station. Email and Facebook, he pointed out, reached the station's "secondary audience," while the other methods of contact were more accessible to the "target audience" and should be mentioned first when soliciting comments and contributions. In this regard, Gogo Breeze practiced what the founder-director preached. His elderhood was no impediment to making use of mobile phones on his programs, such as when he fielded phone calls and SMS messages live on air during his late-evening shifts at the station. Yet letters, typically handwritten, were the principal media by which his public became known to him, along with people who visited him at the station or at home and his own frequent excursions to urban and rural areas in the province. Although he had become accustomed to the editing software and edited all his programs by himself, Gogo Breeze's limited knowledge of computing, including the Internet, was mocked by some of his younger colleagues when he was not present.

What is particularly interesting in the work of Gogo Breeze is that these limitations in using new-media technologies by no means rendered his programs less attuned to the plurality of voices than the ostensibly interactive and participatory programs that used those technologies more extensively. A part of the challenge recognized in the recent anthropology of voice is precisely to understand the variable technological and institutional conditions of producing and staging voice beyond its evocation as "expressive agency" (Fisher 2016:113; see also Kunreuther 2014:16). Media technologies that enable the broadcast of multiple voices are not intrinsically more multivocal than a radio elder speaking alone in the studio. Much hinges on whether the technologies are harnessed to render voices as dialogical rather than monological. At issue is not only dialogue as conversation between speakers but the extent to which dialogue makes explicit the need to listen as well as to speak. Broadcasting voices for their own sake misses a crucial element of Gogo Breeze's multivocality: the summoning of subjects, including the radio elder himself, who listen and not only speak.

Multivocality, which is thus not the same as free speech, came in different modalities on Breeze FM. Moreover, Gogo Breeze's habit of having the last word on many of his programs could easily be mistaken for monovocality. Underlying this mistake is the view that, on one hand, voice properly belongs to each speaker, which makes it desirable to broadcast as many voices as possible in order to ensure pluralism and free speech. On the other hand, the mistake also fails to identify a potentially monologic order in which multivocality is thought to exist, as Mikhail Bakhtin (1984) argued with respect to earlier interpretations of polyphony in Dostoevsky's work. At issue was what sort of unity might emerge from, or perhaps even order, the many voices and perspectives that carried Dostoevsky's novels. Against the previous celebrations of multivocality, Bakhtin insisted that no such unity was intended by the author, because the unity would monologize polyphony by reducing it to some singular authorial or philosophical worldview. Instead, words such as simultaneity, juxtaposition, and counterposing enabled Bakhtin to conceptualize Dostoevsky's "stubborn urge to see everything as coexisting, to perceive and show all things side by side and simultaneous" (1984:28). This approach to multivocality has sometimes been seen as a precursor to poststructuralist notions of distributed agency and fragmented subjectivity, or even as a challenge to the very idea of the author (see Barthes 1977). Ethnographers may balk at following these notions to the letter, especially when they seem to bypass "the person's embeddedness in concrete social relations" (Barber 2007:106). No less problematic to contemporary sensibilities is Bakhtin's acceptance of the view that, prior to the destruction of isolated social worlds by capitalism, those worlds "which collide in Dostoevsky's work were each self-sufficient, organically sealed, and stable" (1984:19). Such sources of discord with ethnography should not diminish the value of Bakhtin's original insights into the issue that matters here: multivocality.

This is not the first time that Bakhtin's discussion of Dostoevsky's poetics appears congenial to studying oral expression in Africa. In her work on Yoruba praise poetry, Karin Barber notes that "Bakhtin uses language that seems made for *oríkì*" (1991:37). Indeed, both *oríkì* and Gogo Breeze, whether in his encounters with others or in his solo performances of storytelling, worked "to concentrate and enhance the dialogic capacity of all discourse to bring the other into relationship with the self, and in so doing, to constitute social being" (Barber 1991:37). Here the parallel might end, because inevitably, it seems, Gogo Breeze's was "a fixed authorial point of view" (Barber 1991:37). His public was left in no doubt that it was listening to their grandfather on air, nor did he hold back advice when confronted with grievances. Yet the apparent finality of his judgments should not mask the multivocality of their production and, by the same token, their ultimate status as another point of view. The radio grandfather typically assembled so many points of view before pronouncing on issues that the ensuing advice or judgment could only come into being with his public's full awareness that it was one point of view among others, however ardently advocated by the radio grandfather. His propensity to dispense didactic messages distinguished his work from what might otherwise seem mere good practice in investigative journalism. Even more importantly, this propensity made his programs participatory in a different way from those programs, discussed toward the end of this chapter, that were based on a monologic sense of multivocality. Reminiscent of the way the viewer, in Bakhtin's (1984:18) notion of the polyphonic novel, also became a participant by being drawn into its dialogic unfolding, Gogo Breeze's public was engaged as participants rather than as spectators to consider whose point of view they might align themselves with. It was participation without the participatory injunction to identify oneself with a particular frame (see Cooke and Kothari 2001). Crucial to understanding the different modes of multivocality, even within Breeze FM itself, is the distinction between *combining* voices, as on Gogo Breeze's programs, and *merging* them, as on certain other programs more explicitly devoted to the cause of participatory development.

Just as Barber's study of *oríkì* had to begin from within the *oríkì* tradition itself rather than by applying Bakhtin's thought, so too must these preliminary remarks on intellectual resources give way to a consideration of multivocality in Gogo Breeze's practice of broadcasting. As a way into the subsequent chapters, where a host of on-air and off-air aspects of his practice are examined, the following pages are devoted to a detailed account of a single incident. The focus is on a controversy over grinding mills that had started to charge extra if their customers wanted to take with them maize husks and not only maize flour. Gogo Breeze's involvement in this controversy extended across different programs and was based on listeners' participation through various media. He announced his commitment to hearing all sides. The voices he eventually assembled for his judgment remained irreducibly plural. The chapter ends by comparing this mode of multivocality with the mode that was adopted on Breeze FM by those programs that sought listener participation through SMS messages with a view to producing opinion polls and other statistical genres.

Gogo on Gaga

The founder-director of Breeze FM shook his head in mock despair in 2012 when I told him that maize husks had become a hot topic on his airwaves. "It shows you what kind of place this is," the well-traveled cosmopolitan remarked on the apparent backwardness of Eastern Province. Yet the controversy over grinding mills and maize husks convened its public to debate widespread exploitation in one of the essential domains of everyday life. It is hard to find a rural or urban household in Zambia's Eastern Province and beyond that does not need to use the services of grinding mills (*zigayo*)[2] in order to obtain *ufa*, the maize flour that is used in cooking *nsima*, the staple food without which no meal is considered complete. Few households can afford to buy *ufa*, so most cultivate or buy maize, which is then pounded into a form that can be brought to a mill. The husks (*gaga*) that appear in the process are waste products in one sense, but as the complaint that initiated the controversy indicated, they can be used to make profit as animal feed. Although not made explicit in the controversy, maize husks and grinding mills also carry specific meanings in the wider moral imagination. *Gaga,* also known as *madeya,* is used for human consumption during periods of hunger, particularly in neighboring Malawi, where food shortages tend to become more severe than in Zambia; it therefore represents a measure of food security for the poor and not a commodity for profiteering.[3] Grinding mills, on the other hand, often attract suspicion and rumor as businesses in which sinister, even occult, schemes take place. While their owners are often seen to make considerable profit, the relatively high capital costs of mills put them beyond the investment opportunities of most entrepreneurs.

Figures 6 and 7 show the letters that marked, as far as Gogo Breeze was concerned, the beginning and end of the controversy. Under the heading

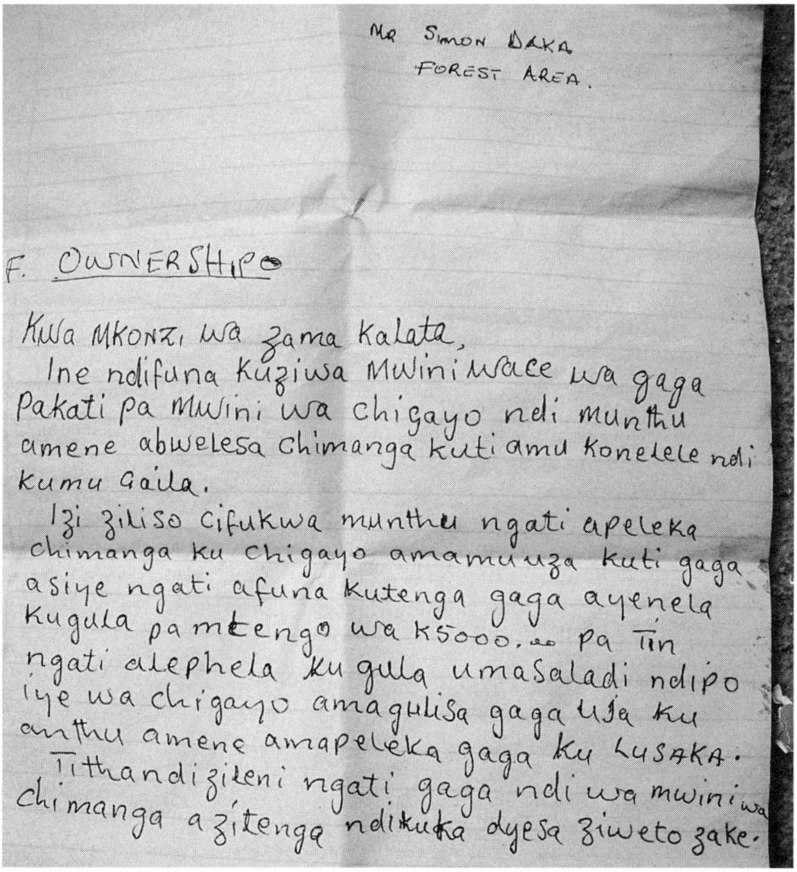

MR SIMON DAKA
FOREST AREA.

F. OWNERSHIP

Kwa Mkonzi wa zama Kalata,
Ine ndifuna kuziwa Mwinimwace wa gaga Pakati pa Mwini wa chigayo ndi munthu amene abwelesa chimanga kuti amu konelele ndi kumu gaila.
Izi ziliso cifukwa munthu ngati apeleka chimanga ku chigayo amamuuza kuti gaga asiye ngati afuna kutenga gaga ayenela kugula pamtengo wa K5000.00 pa Tin ngati alephela kugula umasaladi ndipo iye wa chigayo amagulisa gaga uja ku anthu amene amapeleka gaga ku LUSAKA.
Tithandizileni ngati gaga ndi wa mwini wa chimanga azitenga ndikuka dyesa ziweto zake.

FIGURE 6

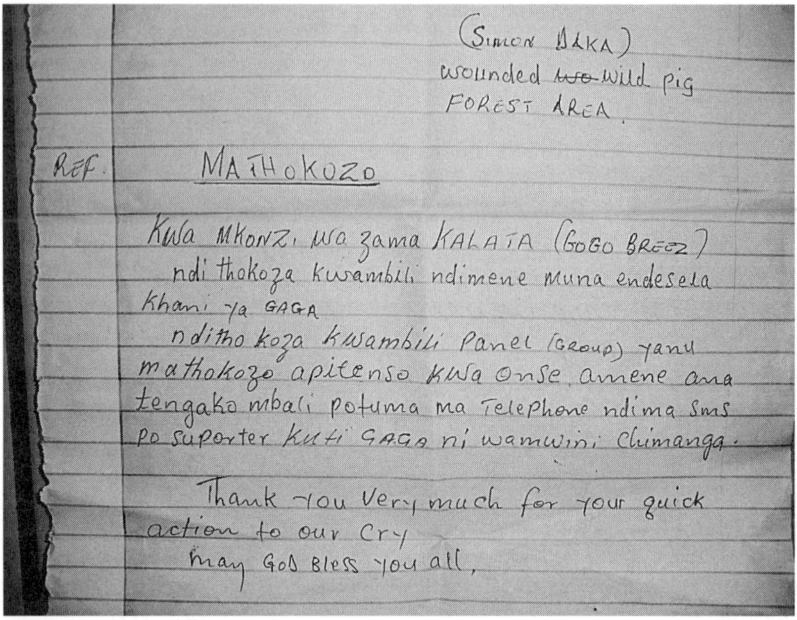
(SIMON DAKA)
wounded ~~wo~~ wild pig
FOREST AREA.

REF. MATHOKOZO

KWA MKONZI WA ZAMA KALATA (GOGO BREEZ)
ndi thokoza kwambili ndimene muna endesela
khani ya GAGA
ndithokoza kwambili Panel (GROUP) yanu
mathokozo apitenso kwa onse amene ana
tengako mbali potuma ma Telephone ndima SMS
po suporter kuti GAGA ni wamwini Chimanga.

Thank you very much for your quick
action to our Cry
may God Bless you all,

FIGURE 7

"Ownership," the letter writer asked whether the owner of maize husks was the owner of the grinding mill or the one who brought the maize to be milled. The query arose from some mill owners' practice of charging ZMK 5,000[4] and, if the customer was unable to pay that amount, of keeping the husks to themselves. The letter reported that the husks thus obtained would be sold to businessmen who took them to Lusaka to be sold further. His question was whether the actual owner was the one with maize who would then use the husks to feed his or her own domestic animals. The author appeared satisfied with both the procedure and the conclusion when he wrote a month later to Gogo Breeze under the heading "Thanks" (*Mathokozo*). "I thank you very much for the way in which you conducted the story of maize husks,"[5] he began, ending with the English words, "Thank you very much for your quick action to our cry. May God bless you all." That his first letter had actually been a complaint rather than a query was evident in his praise for Gogo Breeze's "panel" that had concluded the dispute in the maize owner's favor. It is not clear if the author identified the panel with those broadcasters who had initially discussed the topic or with all those members of the public, also thanked in the letter, who subsequently participated through phone calls and SMS messages.

The issue first came on air on *Makalata*, the letters program that included a female presenter, addressed as "grandchild" (*mdzukulu*)[6] by Gogo Breeze, who read each letter before he began his response. On this occasion, there were two granddaughters in the studio along with Gogo Breeze and the anthropologist. As the introductory greetings were exchanged at the very beginning of the program, Pauline Phiri, one of the women whose form of feminism will be the subject of more discussion in chapter 5, commented on the presence of two women and two men: "Here is gender" (*jenda kaya muno*). Once the other granddaughter had finished reading the letter about *gaga* after these introductions, Gogo Breeze began by commenting on the subject of gender:

> Now this issue concerns women, the ones who go to the grinding mill. It is
> not possible for you to say gender. It is not many men who go to the grind-
> ing mill. You are the ones who encounter these things. Give [the query] to
> your friend so that she may enlighten us who the owner of maize husks is.
> Then come to us.[7]

Gender equality as a matter of carefully managed balance, popularized in Zambia through, among others, the phrase "fifty-fifty," had become one of the most contentious issues associated with the country's democratization, as chapter 5 will show in more detail. At the same time, Zambians found many activities unthinkable as devoid of gendered responsibilities and privileges, among them the processing and preparation of food. By commenting on *jenda*, Gogo Breeze not only drew attention to women as the typical customers at grinding mills; he also reminded the granddaughters and listeners of constitutive difference and hierarchy in social life, which influential campaigns for gender equality seemed to bypass. It was an early indication of what the exercise of free speech might involve in this case. A multivocal affirmation of difference and hierarchy was integral to the very possibility of free speech, because the query had come to the radio grandfather as the one who had moral authority to pronounce on the case. In practice, however, the grandfather became a medium through which public speech could occur, from the contributions by the granddaughters in the studio to a much wider range of listeners on a subsequent program. Gogo Breeze, in effect, suspended his right to speak in public in order to let others express their views, but it was his moral authority that attracted those multiple voices in the first place. A difference-blind democracy had no place in these deliberations.[8]

The granddaughters in the studio seized on their chance to express opinions with some bravado. "Is this a moot point, grandfather?" (*Nanga nkhaniyi ndi yovuta iyi, agogo?*), one of them exclaimed, to which Gogo Breeze replied with *kaya* (I don't know), a position of apparent neutrality on his part. The granddaughter then engaged her colleague in a dialogue:

PAULINE PHIRI: I carry maize, so where do the husks come from, my friend?
JULIANA BANDA: From my maize.
PAULINE PHIRI: From whose maize?
JULIANA BANDA: Mine.
PAULINE PHIRI: Making my husks, whose husks are they?[9]

The granddaughter who initiated this exchange was the more vocal one and offered these further reflections: "Because husks as goods actually find a market out there, people take husks with them back to the village while mill owners say that 'husks are mine.' You, the owners of mills, you do not have the power to say that husks are yours. They [customers] gave you money to grind what they had brought. We have domestic animals, and we want to give husks to animals such as small pigs, small goats, so the husks do not belong to the mill owners."[10] "They should not make us talk beside the point" (*asatilankhulitse pakhundu*), the granddaughter concluded, drawing laughter from everyone in the studio.

Despite his apparently neutral demeanor, Gogo Breeze allowed his own voice to sound passionate in the excerpts from his interviews with mill owners in Chipata District, carried out after he had seen the letter but before this *Makalata* program had been recorded. He introduced the excerpts by explaining how he saw his own role in the dispute: "Now for the grandfather to speak; his job is to investigate so that we can see what is true about what is happening."[11] He added, "I took my bicycle to go around to investigate how the issue of husks is. Is it true that mill owners take husks? What is the reason for taking husks? I asked the mill owners to speak, then we shall see what the end of this issue will be."[12] Neutrality as detachment was far from Gogo Breeze's agenda in these interviews, as the following example of interrupted speech demonstrates:

MILL OWNER: They must ask.
GOGO BREEZE: They must ask for their maize husks?
MILL OWNER: Yes, they must ask.
GOGO BREEZE: They must ask from you?
MILL OWNER: Yes.

GOGO BREEZE: Are the husks yours?

MILL OWNER: Yes, they are ours because=

GOGO BREEZE: =How are they yours when you have no maize?

MILL OWNER: Those coming to grind=

GOGO BREEZE: =Stealing is not acceptable.

MILL OWNER: Eh?

GOGO BREEZE: Do you hear?

MILL OWNER: Yes, I can hear.

GOGO BREEZE: Do not steal from people!

MILL OWNER: Okay, okay.[13]

Gogo Breeze's and the mill owner's speech, raising in anger, overlapped on occasions (indicated with equals signs, =). This exchange was preceded by the mill owner's response to three female customers, all of whom had criticized the charge on maize husks. When Gogo Breeze asked what the women wanted the mill owners to do with regard to charging for maize husks, one of them had in no uncertain terms shouted, "They must stop!" (*aleke*). The mill owner defended the practice by saying that "electricity needs money, workers need money, the owner of the mill needs money, so I saw that money to give is scarce, but it is better to find money in maize husks because we might find a little something."[14] Before launching into the above exchange, Gogo Breeze confronted the mill owner by asking, "Are you able to steal maize husks from people?"[15] To the owner's denial he fired another question, "If you cannot, why do you continue to steal from the common person?"[16] Gogo Breeze's inquisitive style and his angry tone allowed for little ambiguity about his sympathies. By referring to the customer as *munthu wamba*, the common person, rather than as *wosauka*, the poor, he framed the subjects of exploitation as ordinary, honest people and demanded justice more than charity from the mill owner.

Gogo Breeze's neutrality was an engaged one, committed to hearing all sides as a good journalist and a good elder might be expected to do, yet at the same time prepared to attack injustice where he found it.[17] The broadcast excerpt continued with the voices of other mill owners, five of whom tried to assure Gogo Breeze that they did not follow the practice under investigation. Humor is rarely far from his affective arsenal, even in moments of controversy and anger. When the owner of the mill that had prompted the letter denied the practice in a telephone interview, Gogo Breeze exclaimed, "You have been caught!" (*wagwidwa*), to the laughter of those who were present during the recording. As will also be discussed in subsequent chapters, it was this presence of an audience in his investigations that often constituted a public event quite apart from what he later broadcast on the radio. As a celebrity figure, Gogo Breeze tended to attract a crowd of on-lookers wherever he stopped to interview people, and the interrogations at grinding mills were carried out in full view of customers and passers-by. At one point while taking his leave, I observed him saying to the owner, "The issue will trouble you in the future; I am off" (*nkhani idzakuvutani patsogolo; ndapita*). These words were left out from the broadcast excerpt, because, Gogo Breeze later explained to me, they could have sounded too ominous. The verbal threat of something bad happening to one's interlocutor in the future is the most common form of curse among Chinyanja/Chewa speakers. Although excised from the broadcast, Gogo Breeze's parting words had a local audience that witnessed more vitriol than the public convened by his radio programs.

Voice of the People

After the excerpts from his interviews and before continuing with other letters, Gogo Breeze concluded the topic with a promise to return to it on another program while inviting his granddaughters to make a final statement.

GOGO BREEZE: We shall hear people's thoughts on another day in the future, but we here, as Naphiri [Pauline Phiri] said: maize husks belong to whom?[18]
JULIANA BANDA: To the owner of maize.
GOGO BREEZE: To the owner of what?
JULIANA BANDA: Of maize.
GOGO BREEZE: Oh, thank you very much.
PAULINE PHIRI: Maize is mine, and I came from my house with it to the mill; somebody tells me to leave the husks. I don't want that; is not the maize mine?
GOGO BREEZE: Were they sued? [*laughs*]
PAULINE PHIRI: Ah!
GOGO BREEZE: Enough, that's it.
PAULINE PHIRI: Next letter.[19]

When the time came nine days later to open the telephone lines for listener participation on the issue of maize husks, it was during one of the grandfather's late-evening shifts at the station.[20] Three days a week he was in charge of the station from 7:00 p.m. until its closure at midnight, presenting the programs, reading out announcements, taking phone calls and

SMS messages, playing music, and chatting away, always referring to himself as his listeners' grandfather. During the maize husks controversy, his appearances on air at different times entailed different registers of voice, from his respectful, if humorous, exchanges with the granddaughters on the letters program, to his confrontational interviews at the grinding mills, to the late-evening moment with his audience when his voice became soothing and intimate. This range of sonic expression is important to keep in mind while exploring multivocality on Gogo Breeze's programs. It serves as an example of how studying the capacities of voice must extend from its metaphorical uses to its affective and physical properties. Uttered by the same radio personality, the sonic richness of voice indicates, for its part, multivocality within one person.

Gogo Breeze introduced the topic he wanted to talk about with his audience by first summarizing the letter and explaining how he had made investigations at several grinding mills. He then invited listeners to tell him who the owner of maize husks was and added, "We are waiting for you to tell us, because no, the grandfather is unable to understand fully how this issue will be."[21] The emphasis was again on the grandfather's need to consult and on the need to include multiple perspectives in the discussion. Overall he fielded twenty-three telephone calls that evening and read out fourteen SMS messages, all of which supported the notion that the owner of maize was also the owner of maize husks. Those who called were assertive in their tone, often angry, and repeatedly concerned with the money that they thought the mill owners were making from maize husks by selling them to people with domestic animals. One of the first callers gave Dzuwalatsoka[22] as his name and offered a testimony of having confronted a mill owner over the issue. He described the owner as "one who loves money" (*wokonda ndalama*) and how he and the owner had "quarreled" (*tinakangana*) over maize husks. Echoing the claim in the original letter, Dzuwalatsoka emphasized that "they make a lot of money in Lusaka when they pick up husks from here" (*amapanganso ndalama zambiri ku Lusaka akanyamula gaga kuno*), raising his voice in anger when he pronounced the word *zambiri* for "a lot." Then, lowering his voice almost to a whisper, he continued, "What they do is theft in the open" (*chimene amachita ndi ukamatule wapoyera*), pausing slightly between "theft" and "in the open." To Dzuwalatsoka's use of the word *ukamatule* for "theft," Gogo Breeze responded, chuckling, with the word *unjivi*, another somewhat uncommon word for stealing. *Ukamatule* was familiar to Gogo Breeze's listeners as one of his favored words for stealing, which is normally talked about as *kuba* or *ukavalala*. One caller's flawed rendition of the word as *ukalamatule* was perhaps an indication that the word was not in frequent use beyond Gogo Breeze's programs.

Rather than remarking on the caller's mistake, Gogo Breeze commented that "the word *ukamatule* is coming out" (*liwu la ukamatule likutuluka*), pointing out the callers' consensus that charging for maize husks was theft. Consensus about the issue was, in fact, only one aspect of this opportunity to hear the vox populi. Equally important was the sense of a community that Gogo Breeze's ways of addressing his public helped to generate. Most of the callers were unfamiliar to him,[23] but through their participation in word play and speaking in different affective registers, they coconstructed with Gogo Breeze a public that was as intimate as it was physically dispersed. Some, as seen above, subscribed to his choice of relatively esoteric words, while others tried to match his preference for idioms and proverbs, such as the caller who urged mill owners "not to deceive people" with the idiom whose literal translation is "do not grab people by the eyes" (*osagwira anthu m'maso*). Gogo Breeze, in turn, participated in this coconstruction with his catchphrases, humor, and voice, which conveyed his loyalties even when his words did not make them explicit. He would take new calls with the greeting, "You have reached the house on air, Breeze FM; who are you?" (*mwafika nyumba ya mphepo; ndinu yani?*) and addressed youthful male callers as *mkulu wanga* (my brother/friend).[24] His voice became particularly soothing when he received calls from female listeners, who constituted only four of the twenty-three callers that evening despite their preponderance among the customers of grinding mills, as recognized on the letters program.[25] The following appreciation Gogo Breeze gave to a female caller summed up this aspect of the program: "All right, mama; sleep tight, mama. Thank you very much. I myself will be around; no sleep now. I will be around for several hours until I go home to sleep. You sleep, Mtoliro's mom; thank you very much for your words."[26]

Here the grandfather used his voice in its most intimate register to thank the female caller, whom he addressed with one of his catchphrases as *make Mtoliro* (Mtoliro's mom). Gogo Breeze was not assuming that the caller actually had a child by the name of Mtoliro; rather, he was deploying his favorite appellation for all women, which he had discovered in a short story. In the above extract, he did not use *mayi*, the most common term for mother, but *make* and *mama*, terms that are more affectionate and intimate than *mayi*. He also assured his listener that he would be on air for hours to come, to see this issue to its conclusion, while he wished good night to her.

Through the use of voice and the choice of terms, it was clear whose side he was on in the dispute between male mill owners and their predominantly female clients. Another female caller gave him the opportunity to remind the listeners of the gendered nature of the dispute: "Mama, I thank you very much; sleep well; thank you very much. Praise God that you, mother, also took part, because as on the letters program, I told my women that it concerns you; what do you say? They explained for their part."[27]

Gogo Breeze began to read out SMS messages before taking the last of the phone calls. A message from Navutika, one of Chipata town's high-density residential areas, popularly known as compounds (*makomboni*),[28] made him reflect on his use of voice:

> Where I went to follow up on the letters program, my granddaughter Mrs. Phiri [Pauline Phiri in the above extracts] told me when she came today that "ah, grandfather, you had shouted in Navutika." No, because I was not pleased with the answers the boys were giving me, I raised voice. Because of raising my voice a little, someone says that I shouted, but I did not shout; I wanted to find the truth.[29]

Although the message made no mention of Gogo Breeze's investigations in Navutika, noting merely that "without maize there cannot be husks" (*popanda chimanga gaga sungapezeke*), the colleague's comment was another indication of a local audience that witnessed more than what went on air. As was seen above, parts of his aggressive interrogation did get broadcast, but through his denial that he had shouted, Gogo Breeze sought to defend his moral authority against the accusation of improper conduct. Coming from the very colleague who had been the first to condemn the practice of charging for maize husks, and embedded in phone calls and SMS messages that conveyed unanimity, the accusation was less about a lack of neutrality than a failure to observe the radio grandfather's expected demeanor. For Chinyanja speakers, shouting often signifies either a loss of self-control, typically under the influence of alcohol, or a person of mean or malicious disposition (*wankhanza*), such as those employers whose loud reprimands are a mere step away from physical punishment. For Gogo Breeze to embody moral authority, his use of voice had to conform with his commitment to justice. His alleged shouting attracted comment, in fact, because voice was not simply an index of such commitment; it actually was an act with affective and ethical consequences. In this regard, his soothing voice in the exchanges with female callers contributed more to his moral authority as grandfather than did the apparent loss of temper with mill owners. The soothing voice added a sense of "soft masculinity" to grandfatherly authority (compare Gunner 2014).

Because it was not neutrality as detachment that was required of Gogo Breeze, the absence of any phone calls or SMS messages from mill owners attracted little comment during this late-evening program. It was after he had received twelve of the twenty-three calls that he began to address them. Despite allowing the tone of his voice to betray his sympathies, he had all along refrained from making his own statement on the issue and had merely encouraged and facilitated callers to speak. Mill owners emerged as outsiders in the community that his intimate speech had helped to construct, merely listening to the various points raised by the community of callers rather than participating in its deliberations. The first time he addressed mill owners was when he said, "I believe that mill owners are listening to what people are saying. It sounds as though husks belong to their owners."[30] Later, after reading out some of the SMS messages, he again alluded to his own role in the dispute: "I believe that you, the mill owners, you hear what people are saying; it is not the grandfather who is saying."[31] In effect, the radio grandfather accentuated the presence of multiple points of view even when some of them were not voiced through phone calls or SMS messages. In this instance, silence did not mark the boundaries of multivocality.

Polyphony in a Monologue

This positioning of the grandfather as a mere conduit for other people's voices resulted in the apparent paradox that while those who contributed to the program through their phone calls and SMS messages spoke in one voice, Gogo Breeze's ostensibly monologic summary at the end was the most multivocal part of the program. A transcription and translation of the summary can be found in appendix A, but only a few themes can be selected for discussion here from the thicket of its language.[32] One obvious source of such complexity is the linguistic diversity itself, with Chinyanja providing a foundation upon which English and Chinsenga expressions added a layer of code switching, as they often do among Chinyanja speakers in Eastern Province.[33] More relevant to this chapter, however, is the way in which the clarity of the grandfather's judgment did not undermine the capacity of his voice to encompass various subject positions, spatial locations, and intertextual references. Moral authority, in this regard, was by no means a prerogative to pronounce from a distance. It was based on a carefully cultivated skill to bring all relevant considerations and subject positions to bear on the final judgment, which, as such, did not resolve the dispute by merging the diverse interests into one harmonious totality. The voices embodying those interests were combined rather than merged in the grandfather's judgment, their irreducible polyphony related to the operations of the market.

Gogo Breeze started his summary by bringing in one more voice that had not been heard during the deliberations. Petauke, a district adjacent to Chipata, was home to a practice that he wanted to highlight as the solution to the controversy. Gogo Breeze had come to learn about it from a person whom he had met during his investigations in Chipata but who worked in the Nyampinga area of Petauke. "I would have been pleased if people in Petauke had phoned me to explain how things are," he said as he began the summary. Because no such call had been received, he explained that people in Petauke had agreed to take husks with them while mill owners charged only one price. The notion of "agreeing" (*kugwirizana*) was crucial here as in other attempts to solve disputes, and Gogo Breeze continued by describing the consequences of Chipata's mill owners charging two prices according to whether the customer wanted to take or leave the husks. Heart beating fast, or rising blood pressure, was conveyed by his use of the phrase *chimtima pyukupyuku* to indicate the irritation that the practice in Chipata caused among customers, an image complemented a little later by people "rolling up sleeves" (*kupinda mashati*) to fight with fists (*nkhonya*). "I congratulate people in Petauke," he said in English when he returned to this example to urge others in Chipata and elsewhere to also agree. The grandfather's solution to the problem was not, in other words, delivered as a scheme contrived by himself but as an exemplary practice already adopted elsewhere. He spoke in what he thought might have been the voice of people in Petauke to present their practice in the best possible light. Agreement contrasted with irritation and fighting.

A sense of diverse and conflicting interests was palpable in Gogo Breeze's summary, but while the voices of mill owners were muted, they were by no means eliminated altogether from his judgment. His words addressed them in the registers of pleading and threat and ended up including their voices even when no mill owner had contacted his phone-in program. According to Gogo Breeze, mill owners had found a "ladder" to develop, the word for ladder, *manera*, ingeniously combined with the verb for developing, *kutukuka*, that connotes lifting up. Bribes (*ziphuphu*) were key to this climbing at others' expense. As will be seen in subsequent chapters, bribery appears in a wide variety of contexts to provoke comment and intervention from the grandfather. Here the seemingly legitimate practice of entrepreneurs deciding on how to set prices assumed connotations of fraud. By describing his own experience, Gogo Breeze consolidated his identification with *anthu wamba* (the common people) as the victims of mill owners' theft, as he had claimed in the extract above from his interviews at grinding mills. For the first time in these deliberations, he drew on his own experience as a customer rather than as the grandfather investigating matters. He told his listeners that he had once gone to a mill to buy husks for his chickens. The phrase he used for the chickens—*nkhuku zachiboyi*, "local" or "African" chickens[34]—alluded to a pattern of business that was modest and homely. His comment that he was not certain whether the money he gave for the husks went to the boss was a way of connecting his experience to the bribery that seemed to inform the current practice in Chipata. It gave another opportunity to present Petauke as the place of exemplary practice, because the agreement on one price was thought to preempt bribes. Agreement here contrasted with every customer attempting "on their own" (*payekhapayekha*) to deal with mill owners' demands.

Unity, such as there was, referred therefore to the market in which conflicting interests collided but which the radio grandfather sought to make moral in its multivocality. Gogo Breeze, as mentioned, was not looking for mill owners' charity. *Anthu wamba* were not evoked as objects of pity but as knowledgeable customers who had their own business interests to protect. "Nobody wants to throw away something that might give them money," he pointed out, and he asserted that it was easy to find a market for husks among the many people who kept chickens. The one incentive beyond pleading and threat that he offered to mill owners was customers' capacity to pay for milling as long as they could take the husks with them for their own business. The more time he spent on the issue, the more its ramifications also became apparent. As he was finishing reading the SMS messages and preparing to begin his summary, one more phone call arrived. The caller extended the issue to concern sunflower (*mpenyadzuwa*) that was also brought to grinding mills. While turning sunflower seeds into oil, these mills also produced flour known as cakes (*vikoko*) that could be used for both human and animal consumption. Gogo Breeze replied to the last caller that "the issue is the same, my brother. Time does not permit me to bring it to the group [of people listening]."[35] Just as maize husks belonged to the owner of maize, so too did the byproducts of other items taken to mills. Although it came late on the program, the call indicated listeners' willingness to extend the discussion to other instances of fraud and exploitation.

This extension was also implicit in the language Gogo Breeze used in his summary. Avid listeners could identify intertextual references in the idioms that had become his stock-in-trade. For example, while pleading with mill owners, he warned that the issue of maize husks "will bring you trouble." The idiom *idzakuutsirani kaligone* is richly allusive and often deployed by Gogo Breeze to describe the dangers of provoking authorities with illegitimate aims. The underlying image, he explained to me, is that of a stranger and a sleeping dog. If the stranger moves with a stick (*kamtengo*, lit., "a little piece of wood"), the dog may bite him or her if it wakes up and sees the stick, while it would not bite if the stranger did not carry any weapon.[36] Malpractice can, therefore, become the provocation to attract authorities' retaliation. One example of its use elsewhere on Gogo Breeze's program was when he deployed the idiom after criticizing Chinese investors in Eastern Province. "We finish here for the time being lest I bring misfortune" (*talekera pamenepo poyamba, ndingautsi kaligone*), he said in an allusion to the government's sensitivity to such criticisms (see Englund 2015a).[37] Another idiom, used toward the end of the summary, was not a warning about consequences but an accusation of exploitation. Referring to the "boy" (*mnyamata*) he had spoken with at a mill, Gogo Breeze rejected his argument for profit by describing the practice as "stealing wild fruit from people's heads" (*kuombera mapiru pamutu*). The image here was of a person carrying fruits in a basket on her or his head and being the victim of theft without noticing it.

The idiom *kuombera mapiru pamutu* became one of Gogo Breeze's favorite phrases in a variety of contexts during the maize husks controversy. He had first introduced it, only four days before this late-evening broadcast, on *Chinyanja China* (*More Chinyanja*), the program devoted to Chinyanja idioms.[38] Most idioms he explained were from John Gwengwe's (1964) collection of the same title as his program. He read out verbatim Gwengwe's exegesis of this particular idiom before adding further reflections and examples of his own. Gwengwe (1964:61) had already related the idiom to labor relations by beginning with an instance in which a person worked on someone else's farm but, receiving "very small wages" (*malipiro ochepa koposa*), "at the end of the work did not look rich or any different from when he/she entered the work."[39] Gwengwe then extended the idiom to all those situations in which "one person benefits because of other people's strength."[40] On the *Chinyanja China* program, Gogo Breeze began his own comments by pointing out that "these words are very deep/meaningful, and it is important to use them a lot."[41] He immediately provided more examples of where the idiom could be put to use: when people are employed to work in someone's house, to dig a pit latrine, to build a house, or "any other work you give someone without paying adequate wages, such that when the person leaves your house, your work, he or she is poorer than when he or she started."[42] Four days later, Gogo Breeze extended the idiom to cover the kind of profiteering—if not theft, as he had suggested in his interviews—that the owners of grinding mills were seen to be culpable of. Conversely, this example of exploitation referred back to other instances of exploitation that listeners could also be mindful of. The last caller's question about milling sunflower was only a first step in that direction.

By connecting different programs with their different examples, Gogo Breeze produced continuity between his different appearances on air and a consistent moral position on exploitation in the social world he inhabited with his public. Yet another ramification of the polyphony was that the social world was not a spatially confined unit. Not only did he discover a solution in another district, he also made explicit the reach of his words: "This story has now gone far, because the radio Breeze FM reaches far. In Mozambique, in Malawi, yes, when we reach Malawi, we reach Mzimba there in Bangweni and in Mzuzu we are there."[43] The grandfather's voices traversed geopolitical locations as much as they did hierarchical social relations and different program formats. By appealing to his listeners' assistance in judging the case, he defused any idea of being alone capable of pronouncing on the case. Rather, in his pronouncements multiple voices were combined in a self-conscious act of coconstruction, as his very last words in the summary, before the voice of the late South African reggae star Lucky Dube went on air, made clear: "Thank you very much for taking part in this program. You helped the grandfather to answer the letter someone wrote to us. Let's do like that every time to assist each other for the country to be good."[44]

Modes of Multivocality

Grinding mills in Chipata District discontinued the practice of charging two prices in the aftermath of this controversy. While the decision seemed to hold when I visited them a year later, the interesting question presented by this case is not whether Gogo Breeze's judgments achieved a permanent change in exploitative practices. Without backing in law and its enforcement, they were unlikely to do so. Rather, the interesting issue is the mode of multivocality in his efforts to pursue this particular exploitative practice as a matter of public concern and, by the same token, the ways in which his efforts contrasted with other exhortations to respect the plurality of voices at Breeze FM and beyond. The controversy over grinding mills and maize husks is an example of the reach and multiple registers of Gogo Breeze's voice. By taking place on different programs—and by alluding to further programs through his choice of idiomatic language—the controversy shows how listeners were able to follow his voice beyond the format of particular programs and therefore acquired several viewpoints on the same issue. While another way in which they were exposed to different viewpoints was the more conventional journalistic practice of letting different voices in the dispute have their say, important to the achievement of multivocality was not simply the gradual increase in the number of voices. Gogo Breeze's achievement lay in argument rather than in aggregation, in combining multiple voices rather than in pretending that they could all be merged to form a coherent whole.

When appealing to different parties in a dispute, Gogo Breeze could certainly evoke ideas whose moral scope was expected to encompass the conflicting parties, such as "country" (*chalo*) in his conclusion above or, more commonly, "custom" (*mwambo*). These appeals were not attempts to impose a monological unity on the plurality of voices. Crucial to combination as a model for multivocality is, as Bakhtin understood it, that "the voices remain independent" (1984:21). Gogo Breeze cultivated "a plurality of independent and unmerged voices and consciousnesses, a genuine polyphony of fully valid voices" to use Bakhtin's description of Dostoyevsky's poetics (Bakhtin 1984:6). Because he made no secret of his disagreement with some of those voices, his was also a viewpoint among others, though put forward as being based on the moral authority of elderhood. The plurality in the case discussed here was understood by the radio grandfather to be a feature of the market in which the controversy unfolded. It was not the market that he criticized in his judgment but the exploitative condition of profiteering, if not stealing, that a market divested of moral considerations was prone to generate. While the theme of the market will loom large in much of this book, not least because Breeze FM as a commercial entity was itself embedded in market relations, the specific instances of plurality in Gogo Breeze's work will also emerge from linguistic, gendered, and generational considerations. Such considerations were not, of course, solely his prerogative among the programs that Breeze FM put on air. The mode of multivocality associated with his programs—indeed with his radio personality—appears more clearly when it is compared to other instances of plurality over the airwaves.

So entrenched was the plurality of voices on Breeze FM and many other Zambian radio stations that few programs got broadcast without explicit requests for listeners to contribute their views and comments. Interactive radio took several forms, but the three rival stations in Chipata—Breeze FM, Radio Maria, and Feel Free FM—all gave airtime to its most common practices by inviting questions for a guest in the studio, on one hand, and by carrying out, on the other hand, phone-in shows on set topics, facilitated by a presenter.[45] A degree of competition was evident in the extent to which they could secure high-profile guests. Breeze FM's founder-director shared with me stories about amateurish standards at Feel Free FM, including the incident when their representative had been waiting outside the Breeze FM building to meet a visiting party president in order to persuade him to follow his vehicle to Feel Free FM's studio. The founder-director was also inclined to point out that his station tended to receive more calls representing a larger geographical area than Feel Free FM, whose transmissions were confined to Chipata District.[46] For their part, politicians also appeared to compete over the airwaves. Not only would the visit by an opposition politician trigger a visit by a government one (and vice versa), but during my research I also witnessed a deputy minister's phone-in show being followed after a few days by another one with a minister who, staff at Breeze FM told me, feared being overshadowed by his junior partner. Such ministerial visits had a monetary aspect not mentioned on air, because politicians were liable to pay fees to the stations for both the time they were on air and the slots used to advertise their appearances.[47] Nothing in the conduct of these shows suggested that money entailed influence over their contents. Regardless of who was in the studio, the stations would field critical questions and comments which, if nothing else, tested politicians' patience.

Although the relatively fearless expression of opinions during these programs indicated the health of Zambia's political pluralism, the voices heard on air were not as plural as the remit of these shows might have suggested. Callers were almost exclusively male, English dominated even when the politician was supposedly answering in Chinyanja, and the phenomenon of serial callers, some of whom had partisan interests, was not unfamiliar at Breeze FM (compare Brisset-Foucault 2016; Gagliardone 2016; Tettey 2011). Despite the veneer of tolerance that democratic politicians were expected to maintain when they were under pressure, some of them found more or less subtle ways to caution, even intimidate, their callers. "I think I know Mr. Chuzu, even though he doesn't know me," one government minister remarked before addressing Mr. Chuzu's criticisms. A distance between the guest in the studio and people making calls could be particularly obvious when the guest was a technocrat rather than an elected representative. Such encounters could take the form of an expert lecturing to the listeners about the subject of his or her knowledge. Chapters in part 3 contain examples of this distance being asserted by both some Breeze FM presenters and their guests on phone-in programs. Yet the question of distance is only one way to qualify the plurality of voices. More pertinent to the discussion here is the manner in which multivocality could actually be monologic.

The convergence of callers' opinions on Gogo Breeze's phone-in program described above is one example of several persons speaking and yet only a limited range of voices being heard. Monologism as this kind of convergence could also occur on programs that adopted a statistical interest in the plurality of voices. My fieldwork in 2012–13 coincided with a pilot project in which Breeze FM was included along with a number of other radio stations in Ghana, Kenya, Malawi, Mozambique, Uganda, and Sierra Leone. *Africa's Voices* was the initiative of a research team at the University of Cambridge in the United Kingdom that sought to utilize open-source software FrontlineSMS and FreedomFone to generate data from the SMS messages that listeners sent to these stations.[48] A part of the interest was, therefore, to explore the emerging interface between radio broadcasting and new communication technologies, particularly mobile phones, so as "to promote engaged citizen participation in governance" (Abreu Lopes and Srinivasan 2014:5). Public opinion was the domain within which this exploration took place during the pilot project. Apart from helping the stations to use the open-source software to collect and manage SMS messages on a large scale, *Africa's Voices* supplied them with questions on which the public's opinions were sought. Sensitivity to technological, ethical, and topical experimentation was built into the project design, with six "rounds" of questions carried out and some modifications made each time (Abreu Lopes and Srinivasan 2014:9–10). Among other changes, the first two questions were asked in English and the subsequent ones in the main languages in which the stations broadcast. The questions also became binary options after an unsuccessful attempt to offer four alternative answers to a question. The plurality of voices appeared to be advanced by the finding that the initial attempt to encourage anonymity was discarded by some stations, including Breeze FM, when it was realized that listeners wanted their names to be identified with their messages.

Along with the admission of personal identification came an attempt to create space in listeners' responses for justifications of their answers (Abreu Lopes and Srinivasan 2014:13). A striking degree of conformism resulted from this additional concession to the plurality of voices. Rather than producing multiple, competing justifications for the same opinions, let alone argument between them, the SMS messages in round 4, for example, converged on a small number of phrases.[49] The questions were, "Which one of these diseases do you fear more: AIDS or malaria? Why?" The justifications for each of the two answers converged on phrases such as "it has no cure" for AIDS and "it kills fast" and "it kills innocent people" for malaria. While the repetitive use of the word "fear" at the beginning of the answers was required to filter the messages related to *Africa's Voices*, no such conformity was expected from the justifications. On the contrary, their inclusion in the pilot project was thought to be "useful to contextualize crude percentages" (Abreu Lopes and Srinivasan 2014:13). Yet the resulting conformism casts some doubt over the extent to which the voices thus collected were "independent" in the Bakhtinian sense. They did the same as the phone calls and SMS messages on Gogo Breeze's program described above: despite being identified with named individuals in particular locations, they actually merged the voices into one totality (or two binary totalities in the question about AIDS and malaria). Far from individuating each participant, the use of individual names appeared to swear the participants' allegiance to one or the other of the available alternatives. In the absence of research among the participants in the *Africa's Voices* pilot project, it seems inadvisable to speculate why and how this convergence of not only justifications but also the phrases used took place. The contrast, nonetheless, is clear to the ways in which Gogo Breeze, who was not involved in *Africa's Voices*, pursued "a genuine polyphony of fully valid voices" (Bakhtin 1984:6) by refusing to compromise multivocality with a creeping monologism.

It is easy to imagine an *Africa's Voices* question about the controversy discussed in this chapter. After considering the various stages of the controversy over Breeze FM's airwaves, it should be equally possible to imagine what would be lost if the ownership of maize husks was reduced to a binary opposition with limited space for justifications. Among other things, the gendered nature of the controversy, conveyed by actual human voices, along with comparisons between locations and the idioms used to envisage exploitation beyond the case itself, would all become inaudible. At the same time, to recall the point made at the start of this chapter, the statistical interest in knowledge production has no monopoly over monologism. Conversely, as projects such as *Africa's Voices* develop, they will have every opportunity to harness the radio–mobile phone interface in the service of adequately situated public-opinion surveys. The critical question is how alternative notions of voice can be wrested from influential policy and political agendas that celebrate the plurality of voices by monologizing them. To the well-established argument that, because of his or her position in a discourse determined by others, the subaltern cannot speak (Spivak 1988), the case of Gogo Breeze adds the possibility that speaking may occur without a voice, as it were. At issue is more than the entirely plausible observation that for anyone to claim and exercise free speech, there has to be someone to communicate with (Brysk 2013:167). The challenge mounted by public speech in contexts ravaged by socioeconomic inequalities is to understand how communication *through*, rather than merely with, someone gives free speech its locally salient form.

PART TWO

Obligations On and Off Air

THREE

On Air: Beyond Charity

Despite the poverty and hardship of its public, Breeze FM refused to become a medium for appeals to charity and donations to the poor. Time and again, journalists who visited members of the public had to explain their reluctance to countenance such appeals. Confronted with tales of misery and deprivation on a visit to a rural area, a despairing journalist reported to the group he had gathered there the question he invariably received on his excursions: "Do you not take our complaints?" (*simutenga madandaulo athu?*). He used the question to drive home to the group that Breeze FM was not in the business of simply collecting its listeners' grievances. If it was to broadcast only complaints, no one would want to listen to the radio. Crucial to successful broadcasting was *chidwi*, an *interest* that stories and reports might evoke in listeners. It was clear from the journalist's explanation that *chidwi* could unite the radio and its public in a complementary quest for recognition. Just as the radio needed people to generate interest for it to attract listeners and advertisers, so too could the interest it broadcast result in new investments in a particular area.

The journalist, whose specialty was agricultural and environmental programs, used as an example his earlier visit to a cotton-growing area. He had accompanied white people (*azungu*), who had provided inputs, but discovered during the visit that farmers had not been weeding their fields. The journalist described the disappointment and embarrassment that the farmers' lack of *chidwi* had caused. He told the story when we were visiting an area with a sizable pond in its vicinity. It was when the journalist asked how local people made use of this resource that the litany of complaints ensued. Schoolchildren's project of fish farming, for example, had come to nothing when thieves had stolen their fish. A recurrent idiom in the locals' complaints was *waya*, a word used for the string or "wire" to tie together wooden elements in house construction but here evoked as the assistance that resource-poor people would need. Before the journalist had made his exasperation explicit, the group had on several occasions used the idiom to complain about the lack of development in the area. "Government should give us wire" (*boma litipatse waya*), participants repeated in dull conformity. When the journalist spoke after he had turned off his voice recorder, he pointed out that the locals had not used the water to establish *madimba* gardens to cultivate maize and vegetables outside the rainy season. Their appeal to *waya* stood in contrast to the *chidwi* they ought to have shown for anyone to take interest in their predicament.

I use this off-air cri de coeur as an insight into the forms that Breeze FM's on-air encounters with poverty and deprivation were supposed to take. Gogo Breeze gave those encounters his own distinct flavor, as this chapter will describe, but common to the programs that were not commissioned by the government or NGOs was the refusal to accord the impoverished public the subject position of victimhood. Such a subject position came naturally, however, to those who found themselves interviewed by the radio. Decades of state monopoly over the airwaves had inculcated in the listening public the idea that development and poverty alleviation were the government's responsibility. The end of that monopoly, along with an enhanced sense of political opposition in the country, made it possible to talk back to the government about its failure to deliver development. Yet such talking back was likely to build on what state broadcasting had established as the listening public's subject position—that of aid recipients. Grievances were voiced from the viewpoint of those who had not received enough assistance. As victims, they needed *waya* before they could show *chidwi*. As a private entity with a public-service ethos, Breeze FM summoned its public in a different way. *Chidwi* and *waya* were not temporally separate but interdependent. The injunction to exhibit interest and initiative had superficial similarity with another developmentalist trope, the one that recruited the poor to participate in their own development in the name of self-help. An acute sense of hierarchy, however, tempered such recruitment through Breeze FM. Particularly on the programs featuring Gogo Breeze, the public was understood to be enmeshed in relations of hierarchy through which its various grievances and aspirations had to be pursued. The ethos of public service here involved the effort to make those with capital and influence aware of their obligations.

At the same time, the recognition of hierarchy was not driven by the populism of serving the people. As was seen in the previous chapter, Gogo

Breeze used his own radio personality to convey what productive hierarchy and dependence should entail. This chapter follows him across a wider range of moments on air when he had no hesitation to scold the self-styled poor for their deception and greed. The virtually instinctive association with victimhood unraveled in ways that were both harsh and entertaining. It was another way of keeping listeners tuned into Breeze FM, not only by broadcasting examples of how impoverished people showed initiative but also by exposing the fraud they indulged in when poverty became their excuse. Common to both approaches was obligation as a matter of the market rather than charity. Rather than being recipients of charity, the public Gogo Breeze summoned was expected to be fully equipped to advance its aspirations in the market whose morality the radio elder policed with vigilance. Where evidence of exploitation convinced him, such as in the Chinese involvement in cotton cultivation and retail trade, his commitment to the cause of the exploited took over the airwaves. It did so, as this chapter also shows, not only through his own style of investigative journalism but also by devoting other programs to teaching the public idioms in which exploitation could be recognized and debated. By learning idioms other than those asserting their victimhood, the public of grandchildren could discover opportunities for free speech in the radio grandfather's combination of moral authority and language.

Self-Pity and Greed

Alcohol consumption was one of the vices that Gogo Breeze attacked with merciless wit. Although a teetotaler in accordance with his Seventh-day Adventist faith, he never condemned alcohol as such on air. Instead, he would confront, particularly on the program *Landirani Alendo* (*Welcome Visitors*), drunkards when he met them, undeterred by their raucous responses to his criticisms. While some would explain their behavior as "having fun" (*kusangalala*), a more common response, and one that Gogo Breeze attacked with particular vigor, was to make excuses with reference to the poverty in which the drunkards found themselves. Their intent appeared to be both to evoke pity (*chisoni*; also translated as "grief" and "sadness") and to normalize their indulgence by appealing to what they wanted to regard as a widely shared predicament. Gogo Breeze's condemnation of their behavior refused compassion and typically involved evoking the obligations that the drunkards were neglecting.

Once when visiting a beer party in a rural area, he got into a heated argument with a group of young men.[1] After listening to their complaints about "thoughts" (*maganizo*) that plagued them when sober, he became decidedly confrontational.

GOGO BREEZE: You little boys, [your] beard has just now started to grow, but now you are pouring spirits into the head. What kind of benefit is there in drinking that beer?

YOUNG MAN: Ah, that beer. I am killing thoughts that are happening in the head.

GOGO BREEZE: What kind of thoughts?

YOUNG MAN: Like thoughts that I quarreled with someone=

GOGO BREEZE: =And you want to go and kill that person? When you drink beer thoughts don't stop=

YOUNG MAN: =Ah, Grandfather, that beer, or when I promised a woman.

GOGO BREEZE: That?

YOUNG MAN: That we should meet in a certain place.

GOGO BREEZE: To meet for what kind of work?

YOUNG MAN: To get rid of thoughts, because that little part, that part is good.

GOGO BREEZE: So you went to a woman? Are you not married?

YOUNG MAN: Ah, I am talking about the part=

GOGO BREEZE: =I am saying that you talked about a woman; are you married?

YOUNG MAN: Ah, I am married=

GOGO BREEZE: =How come you left the wife?

YOUNG MAN: Ah, I am saying that=

GOGO BREEZE: =Explain to me this thing: how come you left the wife?[2]

It was by reference to other relationships than those between the drinking partners and their girlfriends that Gogo Breeze sought to make apparent the young men's selfishness. Although *maganizo* is a common idiom for worries and even depression, selfishness could be detected in these youth's withdrawal from the obligations that they should have honored. One set of relationships revolved around the village where they lived. Appealing to their sense of citizenship in the village, Gogo Breeze rebuked them by saying, "Boys, boys, you are destroying Thondweni village if you continue to drink beer and smoke tobacco. Stop! The village has to be well organized with strong youths."[3] Women, whether as wives or mothers, represented another set of relationships that provided a contrast to the drunkards' indulgence. After hearing that their wives were planting crops for the new season while the men were at the beer party, Gogo Breeze remarked: "The time to cultivate has arrived; I know it is women who will cultivate much.

You will say, 'I should go and ask for tobacco from Jomba,' then you are gone."[4] The image he conjured was of a man with his wife in the field, using the excuse of borrowing tobacco from his friend Jomba as a way of escaping from the obligation to cultivate with her.

On this occasion, obligations to mothers also became vividly apparent when Gogo Breeze realized that one of the drunkards had his mother nearby. He started by examining the extent to which the mother had carried out her own parental duties.

GOGO BREEZE: Did you give birth to your child?

MOTHER: Indeed.

GOGO BREEZE: Did you instruct him one day about the good and bad aspects of beer?

MOTHER: Yes, indeed.

GOGO BREEZE: What did you tell him?

MOTHER: I said that there is no benefit [profit] in beer. The benefit of beer is fighting, quarrel with wife at home. If schooling eludes you, you can find yours in the garden.

GOGO BREEZE: Did he understand those words?

MOTHER: He looks like he has forgotten them.[5]

Here the mother affirmed her work of moral education as a parent, including her advice to the son to toil in the garden if he found school too difficult. Gogo Breeze seized on the opportunity to bring the mother and son into direct conversation with one another and urged her, "Ask him, 'Why did you forget my words?'" (*mufunseni "Chifukwa chiyani mwaiwala mawu anga?"*). The mother laughed but agreed to summon her son, Gilini (Green), to answer the question. The son's response was to evoke poverty.

GILINI: Those words are problematic, because my parents, you did not educate me; now I stopped school at Grade 11. It hurt me a lot to lack money, no parents—that's why I am drinking beer. To say that I would reenter school, it is not possible for me.

GOGO BREEZE: So what she is saying is true. You are drinking beer because you don't have money. Why did you give up growing cabbage [to find money] to continue schooling?

GILINI: I am a young child; that's why I have failed to find everything that is needed.

GOGO BREEZE: You as well, you are feeding me with smoke. I don't want to eat smoke. Extinguish your cigarette; what's wrong with you? See your mother here; maybe you could have bought her a cloth to wear on her head. But you escaped from the window in Grade 11; is that proper?[6]

Listeners were able to envision a morally charged situation by hearing not only the words but also the voices of the drunk young man, the radio grandfather, and the elderly, soft-spoken mother. The young man's dubious excuses for drinking beer were further undermined by the obvious disrespect he showed by exhaling smoke into the radio grandfather's face. The son's failure to provide the mother with a simple headcloth gave further evidence of his withdrawal from obligations. The self-pity that he expressed by claiming that his poverty amounted to having no parents at all contrasted with Gogo Breeze's view that he could have helped himself and his mother by cultivating cabbage. To end this encounter, Gogo Breeze turned to the mother and asked, "Now, what kind of advice do you have to give to children who do not understand?" (*tsono inuyo muli ndi malangizo otani kwa aja ana amene sakumva?*). The mother replied in a sad voice, "Mm, when giving birth, we, the parents, suffer. The child will suffer when he grows up" (*mm, pobereka ana ife makolo tavutika. Mwana avutikira akakula*). Gogo Breeze's parting words were directed to the son: "Do you hear, Gilini? Mother is complaining here." (*Wamva Gilini? Akudandaula mayi apa*).

Alongside self-pity stood greed as another of poverty's corollaries. Here the targets of Gogo Breeze's rebuke were entrepreneurs who cut corners to maximize profit. Transport was a particularly controversial business, because the drivers of taxis and minibuses routinely loaded their vehicles with more people and cargo than they were supposed to carry. The importance of trade to local economies, and the scarcity of car ownership among the populace, kept the demand high for transport services in spite of the adverse consequences for road safety. *Landirani Alendo* was again the program on which Gogo Breeze would most often confront such breaches of responsibility for passengers' welfare. One episode began with the voice of a female passenger exclaiming, "He loves money" (*amakonda ndalama*).[7] To Gogo Breeze's question, "He loves what?" (*amakonda chiyani?*), accompanied by laughter from onlookers, the woman repeated, "Money" (*ndalama*). It immediately became clear that the reference was to the driver of an overcrowded taxi, and Gogo Breeze began his interrogation of this man by asking where he lived, with the woman still shouting "money lover" (*wokonda ndalama*) in the background. The man, who gave Ng'ombe as his name, claimed to live in Chipata, to which Gogo Breeze responded by asking him to specify his area and house number. Ng'ombe obliged, but Gogo

Breeze sounded highly skeptical. He had established that the passengers were from Katete, another small town in the province. Before turning to speak to one of the passengers, he rebuked Ng'ombe: "People you have picked up are from Katete; the car is going to Katete; you claim you live in Chipata. Mr. Ng'ombe, lying is not acceptable; do you hear? This sort of transport is not acceptable. Only five people can be in a taxi. Oh, Ng'ombe, oh, well, carry on. Yes, my teacher colleague."[8]

Gogo Breeze had earlier realized that among the passengers was a primary-school teacher, and he engaged him in a conversation about the driver's conduct.

GOGO BREEZE: You should not allow=
TEACHER: =We don't allow it, but still I feel compassion for these young men/
  boys who squeeze in people. The cars are theirs; they want to find a little
  something.
GOGO BREEZE: Now to find a little something, they can't find it, because when
  the car overturns, everything=
TEACHER: =Everything gets destroyed; that's right.[9]

The teacher's voice, and not only his profession, suggested seniority that gave him and Gogo Breeze a shared vantage point. The teacher's reference to the drivers as boys (*anyamata*) reinforced this commonality between the two elders, but Gogo Breeze refused to be moved by the compassion (*chifundo*; also translated as "mercy") that the teacher admitted to feeling. Notable was also the teacher's idiom of *kangachepe* for the "little something" that the drivers would acquire through their dubious practice. It often appears as a way of appealing to charity in both asking for and giving money or favors.[10] The teacher was prepared to grant the "boys" some charity but was also swift in aligning his position with Gogo Breeze's when the latter insisted on the destructive side of their practice. He lent similar support to Gogo Breeze's subsequent remark that they would not be able to afford another car if they destroyed the one they had. The teacher also agreed with his assertion that "it is not good to squeeze in like pumpkins" (*tsono sibwino akungopanikiza ngati maungu wotere ayi*). With this image of passenger inconvenience in mind, Gogo Breeze took leave of the driver by exclaiming, "Mr. Ng'ombe, you ought to stop this issue. We understand each other, right? Thank you very much; I am off" (*A Ng'ombe muleke nkhani imeneyi. Tamvana eti? Zikomo kwambiri; ndapita*).

This brief encounter contained divergent perspectives—from the female passenger's accusation of greed in her remark on "money lover" to the

teacher's initial admission of charity—as well as the radio grandfather's unwavering condemnation of an unjust and destructive practice. While allowing, and even asking for, other views to be expressed, he reserved to himself the right to judge. Yet the voices he assembled remained independent
instead of becoming subsumed under the radio grandfather's authoritative
pronouncements. Even more argument could be heard in longer exchanges
with entrepreneurs and other interlocutors who resisted his interpretation
of the situation. A driver of a minibus who had loaded his vehicle with
cargo rather than people exclaimed, "We are poor" when Gogo Breeze had
accused him of wanting to get rich quickly.[11] The accusation followed a
series of questions the radio grandfather had fired at the driver, including
whether his license permitted the transportation of cargo. To the driver's
confirmation that the license encompassed "especially people" Gogo
Breeze gave the caustic remark, "Today sugar has transformed into people."
He quickly dismissed the driver's suggestion that the cargo of sugar and
bread was being used to prepare tea in the bus. Listeners could hear Gogo
Breeze touching several bags and counting the few spaces that might be
available for passengers. His unfavorable opinion was strengthened by
what he considered to be an unhygienic way of treating bread. The main
issue, however, was likely to be familiar to most listeners as the practice by
which minibuses, overloaded and accident prone, were used along with
other types of vehicles to transport goods for sale in villages and trading
centers. While the driver maintained until the end that the cargo belonged
to several passengers who would all return to the bus in due course, Gogo
Breeze's judgment evoked a business that the driver, possibly with accom-
plices,[12] had in transporting and selling the cargo. The driver would not
concede much in this argument, but Gogo Breeze's questions made him
contradict himself on several occasions. For example, in another allusion
to poverty, the driver claimed that "here in the village, we transport cargo,
but it is different in town. In town people only go to work." After clarify-
ing that Chipata was a village rather than a town, Gogo Breeze confronted
the driver again to see whether it followed that he was allowed to transport
cargo on the minibus.

Poverty could be evoked, in sum, as an excuse for self-pity that justified
withdrawal from obligations as much as it could be an excuse for greed that
endangered the lives of those whom it preyed upon. While self-pity turned
into laziness and lack of effort in Gogo Breeze's judgment, the abundance
of effort involved in transporting overloaded vehicles was no more acceptable to him. As other examples will show, the value of work and effort
was measured by the extent to which it contributed to fulfilling obligations

toward others. Important in the exchanges described above was also Gogo Breeze's uninhibited use of moral authority to advance his own views. Various voices were heard and juxtaposed, but in the encounters cited here, they never unsettled the radio elder's prerogative to have the last word, just as his last word could not erase the multivocality it presupposed.

Cotton Cultivation and Chinese Exploitation

The register in which Gogo Breeze delivered his judgments on air was by no means confined to the confrontational, ill-tempered disposition described in the above examples. As I have already suggested, his popularity owed much to his judicious use of humor and wit. In fact, many of the exchanges he recorded during his excursions went on air because of the entertaining interactions they involved, not because he had necessarily set out to expose injustices and abuse. At the same time, it would be wrong to create the impression that the remit of his moral authority was restricted to small-scale, face-to-face encounters. On one hand, even the face-to-face interactions, when broadcast over the airwaves, assumed a scale that surpassed what might have been a fleeting, virtually private moment.[13] The controversy over maize husks discussed in the previous chapter, on the other hand, indicated how Gogo Breeze was also the recipient of grievances about injustices that went beyond individual perpetrators. Exploitation committed by companies and foreign investors was no less his concern than the small acts of fraud he discovered in the streets of Chipata.

The turn of the millennium had seen an increase in Chinese investment in Zambia, and the radio elder had begun to receive complaints about their activities in Eastern Province. Much coverage in national media and academic research has highlighted problems with Chinese investment in Zambia's mining sector, such as its inability to create employment and its lack of consideration for the provision of social welfare that characterized mining compounds during the boom years of the midcentury.[14] The rural outlook of Eastern Province gave the issues a somewhat different tenor, although the question of job creation was pressing there too. I have elsewhere presented the case of a labor dispute that Gogo Breeze helped to mediate in the context of abundant labor and Chinese investment in agricultural processing in Chipata (see Englund 2015a).[15] Here I follow Gogo Breeze on his visits to rural areas where he encountered irate smallholders supplying produce for the Chinese investors. These visits took place under the auspices of the program *Chidwi Pa Anthu* (*Interest in People*) in 2012–13, sponsored by a foreign media NGO.[16] The bulk of the series consisted of conversations Gogo Breeze had with groups of men and women, in which he actively sought contributions from a cross section of participants and referred to the gathering as *bwalo*, the public arena often associated with the village headman's court and a term he also commonly used on air to refer to his listeners.[17]

Following the favorable price villagers' cotton had reached in the 2010–11 season, many smallholders had increased the area devoted to the crop.[18] To their shock, however, smallholders discovered that the price of ZMK 3,600 per kilogram had more than halved to become a mere ZMK 1,600 in the new season. Reports on smallholder discontent taking various forms appeared in local and national news—for instance, truckloads of cotton being burned before they had been delivered to ginning companies in Chipata.[19] Some farmers felt that harvesting the crop would signal their acceptance of the price offered by the companies and decided to leave it in the field. Others disagreed and pointed out that leaving the crop unharvested for too long would damage its quality. This local discontent culminated not only in attacks on trucks but also on the harvests of fellow villagers who were accused of betraying the rest by agreeing to the low price. The predicament had the hallmarks of what some might regard as a local-global interface: villagers' livelihoods and interpersonal relationships had come under pressure because of a poor price offered by companies that were under Chinese management and that claimed to use the world market as their guide in setting the price.

Smallholders' prospects for making profit were further dimmed by the inputs such as seeds and pesticides they had already obtained on credit from the companies to which they were obliged to sell their crop. It was unlikely that they could have made any profit when the price was so low, but another source of injustice for many farmers—and for the broadcasters at Breeze FM with whom I reflected on the issue—was the arrangement by which they became suppliers for companies at the beginning of the agricultural season when the price was not yet known. This capture by a particular company, along with the tedium of tending a highly vulnerable crop, evoked long-standing idioms for exploitation, such as slavery (*ukapolo*). Gogo Breeze came to nourish and mediate those idioms with his own definition of the parent whose responsibility it was to look after the welfare of smallholder farmers.

Njala, hunger, was the common complaint Gogo Breeze recorded when he started the series of programs in late 2012.[20] "Look at the price of cotton," one man in Mambwe District said. "We are crying. There is hunger."[21] It was not an acute shortage of food that Gogo Breeze discovered in rural areas but rather widespread concern over the strategy many villagers had chosen for the season. "On the issue of cotton, we are crying," a woman in the same gathering added. "This year we don't cultivate much maize. We cultivate a lot of cotton so that we find money, maybe to buy maize, but everything is overwhelming, only problems here: pesticides on credit, seeds on credit."[22] Confronted with a consistent narrative about hard work and crushed expectations, Gogo Breeze did not frame the grievances in terms of self-pity or greed. He listened to (and broadcast) expressions of smallholder pride in their livelihoods, such as when in a subsequent installment a man pointed out, "We make an effort since we don't have cattle to help us."[23] His reference was to ploughing, a rare possibility among Eastern Province's smallholders, but the man made a virtue out of lack. "We don't count on having cattle because the one with cattle does not have strength. We who don't cultivate with cattle have more strength than the one with cattle. When the cattle run away from him/her, he/she will not be able to cultivate."[24] It was Gogo Breeze who introduced the topic of hunger in this case.

GOGO BREEZE: What about hunger?
MALE SMALLHOLDER: There is hunger as much of this year's cultivation went straight to cotton. There is the expectation that cotton would bring a lot of wealth, but the trouble we complain about concerns those of our friends who went straight to cotton. Companies that buy cotton destroyed agriculture. There is hunger because many didn't cultivate maize; they cultivated cotton so that we would find a little money to buy food. Now money is missing in cotton. What will they eat?[25]

This smallholder's judgment that "companies that buy cotton destroyed agriculture" contained a clear message about exploitative practice, a criticism echoed by many others whom Gogo Breeze talked to during these encounters. The management of Chipata's cotton companies by Chinese nationals was not mentioned in this series, although as will be seen below, it did mention the adverse impact of the Chinese on local trade, and the Chinese involvement in the labor dispute at a cotton company became news when the series was being broadcast (see Englund 2015a). Yet Gogo Breeze's questions and comments alluded to what most listeners knew: the cotton companies were managed by foreigners. Unlike in the cases of exploitation involving Zambian bosses, he did not suggest that he would pay a visit to the management. Instead, he allocated responsibility to those elected officers whom he expected to care for villagers' welfare. "Do you have leaders, councillors, an MP? What is it that they have done about the complaints?" he asked the man in Mambwe District who was cited above.[26] The response was dismal. "Well, to say honestly, there are none this year; councillors, an MP—there are none this year. They hear people's complaints at headmen's meetings. When they have meetings, they invite chiefs, but there is nothing that happens."[27] The man described here the pattern by which elected representatives in local government and parliament used village headmen and chiefs to gather crowds for their meetings but turned a deaf ear to what the chiefs might have told them about local grievances. On several occasions throughout the series, Gogo Breeze concluded by appealing to leaders' sense of the people they served as their children. The idioms he deployed were variations on the theme of a crying child, such as when upon listening to similar complaints in Petauke, he observed, "When a child cries for sweets, give them to him/her to eat. Don't tell him/her lies that you will bring sweets when you bring a stone which the child cannot eat."[28]

Such idioms were his stock-in-trade, grandfatherly prompts for other authorities to show their care within hierarchical relationships. When broadcast over the airwaves, as I argue throughout this book, they became public interventions on behalf of exploited and injured subjects, bringing shame to authorities by amplifying popular grievances. Yet I also argue that Gogo Breeze's idioms for care and exploitation did not simply hark back to an idealized kinship society in which everyone met their obligations toward each other. As his life history indicated, the man who inhabited this radio personality had come of age during late-colonial developments and nationalist agitation. Familial idioms were compatible with memories of colonial violence. When carrying out deliberations near Mfuwe, a location renowned for its proximity to the South Luangwa National Park that drew tourists to Eastern Province, he met people whose chief complaint was about destructive wildlife. One man contrasted foreign visitors' care for wild animals with the plight of local villagers: "They don't care about the welfare of people. They care about the welfare of wild animals. . . . They forget that when they came here, to live here, they were taken care of by people; they were not taken care of by wild animals. So, that is why our agriculture is also going wrong."[29] Rather than helping villagers to protect themselves against wildlife, mainly elephants, that destroyed their crops, the foreigners who were seen to visit and run the National Park appeared to have forgotten who their actual hosts were. Gogo Breeze's comment, accompanied by the interjections of "yes!" (*ee!*) from his audience, drew a striking historical parallel:

What grabbed my heart was slavery, the way slavery was in the past. In the past, they were taking black people to countries in Europe so that they would work in their sugar cane fields. But today the white person has left his home to come here to Zambia, to come here to Africa, to make a slave of the person whose soil it is. Here I don't know how government representatives will be thinking about this slavery.[30]

The appeal was again to authorities in government as the ones whose responsibility it was to care for people in the villages, as parents would care for their children, but Gogo Breeze's comment arose from historical consciousness that had sharpened imaginative weapons against the kind of dependency that slavery epitomized. Nor was his—and his interlocutors'—evocation of kinship obligations averse to the market as the principal institution through which villagers might hope to achieve prosperity. Immediately after the comment cited above, Gogo Breeze inserted a song he played on virtually every program in this series.[31] It began by asking, "How do I stop complaining when we farmers here are exploited?"[32] The contrast between farmers' efforts and the state of the market became clear in the next lines: "To cultivate, we try to spend the day in the sun, at the time of the market you abuse us / I say I try to grow cotton; its price is depressing."[33] Before the last line—"But at the time of the market, you steal from us again"[34]—the singer made a familiar appeal to the government: "Please, government, care for us. We, the farmers, are just being exploited."[35] The appeal was not to the government as the opposite of the market, still less to overthrowing the market economy, but to a hierarchical relationship in which those in authority ensured the fair and just functioning of the market. Not unlike the free speech that the radio elder mediated through his moral authority, free trade required similar alignment with morally legitimate authority to ensure that justice prevailed.

In this regard, Chinese investors were outside of the relationships in which such appeals and claims could be made.[36] Their presence was, however, made explicit in another context that programs in the *Chidwi Pa Anthu* series highlighted. The Chinese had also begun to make inroads into local trade in secondhand clothes and other minor commodities. Upon hearing about problems with business at Petauke's trading center, Gogo Breeze asked for more specificity: "How come business has problems?"[37] A female trader called a spade a spade:

FEMALE TRADER: The Chinese are difficult. We are not selling here at the stands because of the Chinese.

GOGO BREEZE: What have the Chinese done?

FEMALE TRADER: The Chinese left Lusaka to sell here. Now the way they sell, they sell in the method of Lusaka. Now for us to sell here, they [customers] say that the Chinese make things cheaper here, so they run to the Chinese; they say that the Chinese sell well.[38]

Without indicating his own opinion on the matter, Gogo Breeze turned to other traders for alternative opinions but found only unanimity about the adverse impact of the Chinese on local trading. Another woman remarked, in a phrase that carried its own historical reference to how trading by South Asians had been restricted, "The Chinese should be in town, not here" (Chinese *afunika kutawuni* not *muno*). One man began to describe the changing pattern of trade in secondhand clothing and emphasized local traders' commitment to developing Zambia. It was only when Gogo Breeze asked him specifically about the Chinese that he mentioned them.

MALE TRADER: We are selling well. Yes, secondhand clothing used to come from Malawi; now it comes from Lusaka. In Malawi it was difficult. Transport, customs, they used to detain people. We saw, well, let's now start buying in our country of Zambia. Let's develop our country. Let's start ordering [stock] here at home nowadays. That is the stock you see there at the stands.

GOGO BREEZE: Aha.

MALE TRADER: Yes.

GOGO BREEZE: The Chinese don't bother you?

MALE TRADER: The Chinese, ah, they lower the prices. They don't bother us by beating us but by lowering the prices.[39]

This trader's assertion of patriotism appeared in the context of his vociferous colleagues explaining to Gogo Breeze the damage that the Chinese were doing to local trade. "Developing Zambia" was another phrase with thick historical resonances in a country where successive governments had set development as their primary objective. It was a way of claiming membership in that project and the care that the government as its custodian was expected to provide. Gogo Breeze's question of what elected leaders were doing received a familiar response: "Councillors don't hear the complaints of the people" (*akansala sakumva madandaulo a anthu*), a woman said. She described the local traders' repeated efforts to petition the local government to "repair" (*kukonza*) the prices. Gogo Breeze's conclusion on this occasion found the crying child demanding his/her mother's breast: "When the child cries it means he/she wants his/her mother's breast. And if the mother does not care for the child's crying, the child will fall down and start hurting him- or herself. Let's see how everything we do for our people would make them happy all the time."[40]

Idioms of Exploitation

A female smallholder complaining about dysfunctional markets deployed an idiom familiar from several of Gogo Breeze's programs. She referred to the companies and entrepreneurs buying agricultural produce as those who steal wild fruits from the top of other people's heads:

> They are cheating people [lit., "They are grabbing people's eyes"], to tell the truth. We, the farmers, are not pleased because we suffer in order to find things we need to help ourselves, but they deceive us; they steal wild fruits from the top of the head. They benefit; we don't benefit. So, we very much ask them to open proper markets for us to sell the crops we cultivate so that we can be assisted especially on the issue of schoolchildren['s fees].[41]

As was seen in the previous chapter, *kubera* (to steal) or *kudyera* (to eat) *masuku/mapira pamutu* was an idiom that Gogo Breeze had introduced and explained, drawing on Gwengwe (1964:61), on the *Chinyanja China* program in April 2012. His explanation drew on examples from exploitative labor relations, but the previous chapter also showed him using the idiom for the deceit that mill owners were accused of. The appearance of the same idiom in his listeners' talk attested to its resonance with their experiences and to the radio elder's provision of imaginative resources for talking about exploitation and injustice.[42] His repeated use of this idiom had begun already before he had explained it on *Chinyanja China*. It appeared, for example, as a way of telling a chief on the letters program about misconduct among the leaders of an agricultural cooperative in his area. The claim was that the leaders were not distributing fertilizer according to the rules of the cooperative. The letter Gogo Breeze had received described a familiar situation in which people's complaints were falling on deaf ears.

NAOMI MWIMBA: They are saying that when they ask the leaders of the cooperative, they insult them, saying, "Get off; what are you claiming?"
GOGO BREEZE: "You are making noise."
NAOMI MWIMBA: "You are making noise." Maybe the leaders of the cooperative were given fertilizer, but they want to use it on their own. They don't want

others to benefit. That is what they see, and "can we be helped now?" They have included the names of the small organization's leaders.[43]

In response, Gogo Breeze pointed out that the letter had come from Chief Kapatamoyo's area. In a vein similar to the statement he made over the airwaves that Chief Mpezeni would care for his subjects (see chapter 1), Gogo Breeze made it difficult for the chief and his aides to ignore their obligation to intervene on their subjects' behalf. The idiom of wild fruits being eaten from the top of the subjects' heads alluded to exploitation in the chief's area:

> On Monday morning if Chief Kapatamoyo has come back from the Ngoni ceremony Ncwala,[44] go to the palace, go and explain to the chief that the leaders of the cooperative have not taken good care of us. They have eaten wild fruits from the top of the head so that Chief Kapatamoyo can deal with these people. What I am saying here, if Chief Kapatamoyo is not at home, the wife is at home, and the elders who sit by the kachere tree are at home— some of them did not go to the ceremony—they are listening. They will expect you on Monday. Go and give this issue so that they can see precisely who took the fertilizer. Tell them that when you ask, they yell at you.[45]

The idiom would speak where the leaders of their cooperative left the villagers muted. It would help the chief to recognize the uncaring leaders as exploiters. Gogo Breeze demonstrated by his own repeated use of the idiom just how versatile it was: its application extended to a variety of situations in which unjust advantage or benefit was damaging other people's prospects. The trouble with the distribution of fertilizer mentioned above resembled other local projects that unscrupulous leaders exploited for their own benefit. In response to a letter complaining about some villagers soliciting charitable aid without passing it on to the needy, Gogo Breeze urged, "We who register orphans or elderly people for others to assist them, let's be trustworthy. Do not eat wild fruits from the top of the head; that is what the grandfather says."[46] The same idiom could be applied to any hierarchical relationship that violated a sense of obligation, including marriage. One letter gave insight into the domestic affairs of a man who had been employed by a cotton company in Chipata.[47] His wife wrote the letter to complain that after only one year in marriage, the husband was not sharing his money at home but demanded that the wife use the money she earned through trading on food and other necessities. Moreover, when the wife inherited a substantial amount of money from her late father, the husband insisted on using it at once while the wife hoped to keep it in a bank for their children's future benefit. Naomi Mwimba, who was also on this occasion the granddaughter reading the letter, voiced the wife's concern and question: "She says the man is like that, grandfather. 'How will you help me, please? I am impoverished; what should I do with him?'"[48] Gogo Breeze exclaimed before he used the idiom to preface his response:

GOGO BREEZE: Goodness! That man my friend. Harassment!

NAOMI MWIMBA: Mm.

GOGO BREEZE: Now what is evil here is that they got married last year.

NAOMI MWIMBA: Last year!

GOGO BREEZE: Now last year was the year when he was supposed to demonstrate the good side of his masculinity.

NAOMI MWIMBA: Mm.

GOGO BREEZE: And he just wants to eat wild fruits from the top of the wife's head—is that how it is done?[49]

He then launched into a lengthy discourse repeating the details about the couple's separate sources of income and the husband's habit of using his wife's money for the household. Gogo Breeze spoke as though he assumed that married couples' joint planning of household budget (*bajeti*) was the norm and rebuked the husband by saying, "Sometimes we have to feel shame" (*tizimva manyazi nthawi zina*). As long as the husband also had an income, exploitative as it was likely to be for a cotton worker, Gogo Breeze expected him to bring it home. By using and explaining another idiom, he advised the wife of what she should be mindful of:

Do you know that he might throw his money into the water? Now when the grandfather says that he throws into the water, don't worry [about understanding the meaning]; let me explain to you. Water is women who just move around in a disorderly way. They are looking for money at night; that is where your husband's money is going. I haven't seen him, but I am telling how it is if he does not have money. "I don't have money, give money." Now where did his money go because he has an income? Mother, take care of the money you took from the state, the money that your father left behind. Take care of it because you will not live long with that man. I know that he will leave you soon. If he is difficult, let the marriage guardians deal with him. You sit down and explain the problems your husband has.[50] Then you will examine the way in which you can look after the children.[51]

Exploitation at work was not, in other words, acceptable as an excuse for exploitation at home. By using the same idiom for different injustices, Gogo Breeze made them all appear as instances of exploitation. A range of words in more common use were also at his disposal, such as *mazunzo* (harassment) in his exclamation above, and its corresponding verb *kuzunza* for "harassing" or "oppressing," along with *kuvutika* for "having problems" or "suffering," a word that was particularly ubiquitous among the populace. Precisely because idiomatic language distinguished Gogo Breeze as an elder, he provided imaginative resources for talking about exploitation, injustice, and inequality beyond the litanies of complaints that many of his listeners were likely to offer. Moreover, because moral authority was not based on an egalitarian vision of social relations, the perpetrators of exploitation and injustice were not a self-evident category of people. Just as exploitation could occur at home and not only at work, so too was it possible that the evocations of self-pity and victimhood masked a disposition far more ungenerous than any associated with those who had power and wealth. Such a dilemma became particularly apparent through the proverb *pasambira mfulu, kapolo asambira pomwepo*, "Where the free person washes, there the slave washes," broadcast on the *Chinyanja China* program.[52]

Gogo Breeze told the illustrative story by reading again Gwengwe's text (1964:44–45) virtually verbatim. The story described how people fleeing hunger had found a chief (*mfumu*) eating his meal openly in the verandah of his house. Despite fear in their hearts (*anachita mantha mumtima mwawo*), the passersby decided to approach the chief in the hope of sharing his meal. Gogo Breeze explained, with Gwengwe, the risk they were taking: "In those days, there was an important custom that the person who was not a chief or wealthy was not allowed to eat with famous people, and if it happened, the person had a big case to answer for."[53] The "ordinary people" (*anthu wamba*) nevertheless proceeded to tell the chief the lie that they "had established your chieftaincy before you had been born"[54] and that they were now chasing their slaves (*akapolo*) who had run away. The chief invited these "famous chiefs" (*mafumu omveka*) to eat with him but wondered why they were wearing "torn clothing" (*zobvala zakutha*). He accepted their explanation that bandits (*anthu achifwamba*) had attacked them on the road. A play of words ensued when the chief overheard them saying to one another, "Let us do the washing of the free person" (*tidzachite pasambira mfulu*). To the chief's question of what they were talking about, they responded by using the word *fulu* (tortoise) to divert the attention from *mfulu* (free person) and claimed that they had mentioned tortoises because they liked to eat them in their own village.

As always, Gogo Breeze had not chosen to elucidate this proverb in order to highlight an obsolete custom. Before offering his own reflections, he read out, without mentioning that the words came from Gwengwe, the conclusion to the story: "This just means that the free person's good fortune/opportunity often likes to reach to ordinary people, but people who are not free persons are selfish and do not want their good fortune/opportunity to suffice for others."[55] Short-term gain, based on deception, revealed the ordinary people in this example as selfish, the actual word for the disposition—*odzikonda*—evoking the specter of self-love. Gogo Breeze added his own example after this conclusion by alluding to the time when he was summoned to serve as the state president's interpreter during a visit to Eastern Province:[56] "I remember one day when the country's leader came they called me to be among them to carry out some work. So we went together to St. Monica to eat. When you eat with leaders/elders, when they are full, you are also full, no matter how sweet it is—that's the challenge. So because of being a grandfather, he started to pick up scones to put into a bag in order to eat them in the car."[57] The example was interspersed with Gogo Breeze's laughter, and the reference to the grandfather in the third person contributed to a sense of self-mockery. Eating in the car was an instance of the kind of self-love that the conclusion had admonished. While having the good fortune of both eating well and being ferried in a car that belonged to the head of state's convoy, the grandfather had little regard for other ordinary people and continued to eat in the privacy of the car. As a discursive resource to think about injustice, the proverb could, in other words, be used to reflect on greed among the unfree, the ordinary people whose complaints and grievances filled Gogo Breeze's time on and off air.

Among the examples considered in this chapter, the case of Chinese exploitation involved apparent irony. Gogo Breeze came to broadcast grievances about foreign investors in a series sponsored by a foreign NGO. As chapter 6 will show, NGOs' hold on Breeze FM could be stifling, despite its founder-director's inclination to distance the station from the NGO economy. Yet here the irony was only apparent, because the NGO sponsoring this series gave Gogo Breeze the leeway to collect stories as he wished. It was, of course, not the status of the Chinese as foreigners that was the issue, although when exploiters could be identified as foreigners, the idiom of slavery was readily available to connect them to the deplorable past. Nor was the issue some inherent antagonism between the bosses and the masses. Hierarchy was assumed in Gogo Breeze's vision of moral market, and the more those with the wherewithal to provide employment and development treated their subjects as their children, the more moral was the market in which everyone was expected to operate. The moral market according to Gogo Breeze was a regulated one, such as when he allowed small-scale traders to demand intervention from the government against Chinese incursion into their trade. The desired regulation would usually take this form of governmental oversight, but its more profound element was the sense of obligation that ought to prevail in the moral market's hierarchies. Charity based on the model of the gift was an anathema to this sense of obligation. Not only were obligations animated by claim making for which Gogo Breeze offered specific idioms, but subjects' propensity to situate themselves as recipients of assistance was no more acceptable than exploitation by those with capital and influence. It was in his accusations of self-pity and deception that Gogo Breeze dissociated himself from populism in which the people would always be put on a pedestal.

FOUR

Off Air: Private Service

During one of our many conversations about Breeze FM as a kind of public-service broadcaster, Michael Daka, the founder-director, again voiced his frustration that the station was subsidizing the state. When he asserted that the state should support Breeze FM's contribution to public-service broadcasting, I raised the prospect of the support coming with strings attached. Daka replied by denying that he had direct monetary assistance in mind. Rather, the state should enter into a contract with the station to sponsor a series of phone-in programs on which senior state officials would field questions from the public. Soon afterward, as will be seen in chapter 6, Daka did initiate a meeting with the province's minister to discuss the idea of inviting senior civil servants to "explain" matters relevant to their departments. This sense of public service reflected Daka's own past in Zambia's national news agency. Having cut his journalist's teeth at the high point of postcolonial state building, he owed more than a little to the notion that the public as "the people" stood to be educated, informed, and entertained by public-service broadcasting. Although of the same generation as Daka, Gogo Breeze had established his radio personality on a rather different sense of public service. Here it was the grandfather who had the prerogative to explain, but as has been seen in the previous chapters, precisely because he was his listeners' grandfather, the distance between him and his public was not the same as that between a senior civil servant and citizens. Distance there was nevertheless, maintained through hierarchy in which the grandfather had the last word. Yet it was an intimate hierarchy, a congenial inequality that, in actual fact, depended on intimacy as much as it did on distance.

In order to gauge Gogo Breeze's style of public service more fully, it is therefore important to consider intimacy as well as hierarchy in his work.

An influential definition of "publics" emphasizes their nature as "stranger-sociability" (Warner 2002:56). They are, in this perspective, different from nations, religion, or race, which issue "tests of membership" on the basis of territory, belief, or identity. The only test of belonging to a public is participation by reading newspapers, watching or listening to broadcasts, logging into websites, and so on. While this perspective elaborates on the peculiar form of intimacy in stranger-sociability, it seems inaccurate as a description of what took place at Breeze FM. Gogo Breeze and many other presenters were known to their publics as persons who could be visited at the station just as they themselves paid frequent visits to the province's rural and urban areas. Gogo Breeze also mitigated stranger-sociability by defining his listeners as his grandchildren. This definition of a public came with its off-air consequences of obligations toward particular persons. Although he had no way of meeting everyone who tuned into his programs, so tireless was he in attending to specific listeners that the number of people he had engaged with in person—whether by listening to them and investigating their grievances or by helping them to find spouses—ran into thousands after his first decade as a radio personality. Indeed, some programs may have been launched without plans to send the radio elder out of the studio, but it was his sense of obligation to his grandchildren that made, for example, the letters program acquire an off-air life of its own. In this regard, Laura Kunreuther, while writing about Nepal, captured something of comparative significance in her statement that "contrary to much research on publics, anonymity was not an essential or key component of FM radio publics" (2014:141).

Recent studies of intimacy and the public sphere across the world have emphasized a historical shift by which intimate affairs have become the staple of print and electronic media, not merely as scandals but also as opportunities to explore the self in public (e.g., Berlant 1997; Illouz 2003; Kunreuther 2014; Lofton 2011; Matza 2009). Gogo Breeze addressed intimate issues, as indeed did other presenters on Breeze FM.[1] It may be as true of Breeze FM as of the FM radio in Nepal to say that their programs reveal "an overlapping dynamic between a subjectivity centered on interior desire, affect, and individuality and a subjectivity that emphasizes the centrality of familial roles, duties, and moral obligations" (Kunreuther 2014:167). This sense of an *overlap* is essential to keep in mind, because moral obligations must not be regarded as mere constraints. The question of intimacy on and off the airwaves can also be posed in other terms than as an "affective public" (Kunreuther 2014:167) that serves to counter the rationality associated with Habermas's (1989) theory of the public sphere. If the objective is to understand the place of the intimate in a particular approach to public-service broadcasting in twenty-first-century Zambia, it is even less advisable to build an analysis around notions such as "the neoliberal public" characterized by "the collapse of private and public, the flooding of the public with a proliferation of private emotion" (Muehlebach 2012:133). Instead, this chapter follows Gogo Breeze off air as he negotiated the intimate and the private with members of his public. Rather than allowing private emotion to flood his programs, he made a distinction between what should go on air and what should be kept off air. Yet by excluding some encounters from the airwaves, he did not necessarily disengage from them. On the contrary, public service could extend into private service in which the radio grandfather owed it to his public not to put everything on air.

It is obvious that Gogo Breeze's decisions about what to put on air were often editorial ones, based on what he considered appropriate to each of the genres and formats in which he broadcast. Editorial decisions are not merely technical ones, because they can reveal major political and aesthetic tensions between broadcasters and their public, not least in radio genres that deploy apparently unmediated notions of the people or the self (see Englund 2011:127–45; Kunreuther 2014:165). Although such genres often provide the clearest challenge to analytical models that separate the production of media forms from their reception, Gogo Breeze's radio personality was distinct in its aversion to populism. As was seen in the previous chapter, listeners could actually hear him excluding or rejecting viewpoints put forward by his public, whether when he met its members in person or considered their letters in the studio. It was the grandfatherly prerogative for high-handedness that made it somewhat redundant to conceal editorial discretion. By the same token, the grandfatherly prerogative, building on what grandparents were thought to be in the idealized village, was also to seek intimacy with his public. In order to properly investigate their grievances, or to dispense advice, he needed to meet some of them in private, the voice recorder switched off or, if on, with the assurance that the conversation would not be broadcast. Even when face to face, Gogo Breeze and members of his public did not entertain the notion that such encounters were somehow less mediated than those that went on air. Here, "Historical formations of power and knowledge," as Brian Axel has suggested, hardly "compelled face-to-face subjects to identify themselves with images of distinct, separable, total, and isolable bodies" (2006:374). Being face to face with one's radio grandfather was a moment of mutuality and hierarchy, interdependence that made communication possible.[2]

When following Gogo Breeze in his off-air engagements, it is important to avoid conflating the private with the intimate. His "public intimacy" (Kunreuther 2014) was distinct from his private service. Public intimacy, as critical scholars would know by now, can be a way of authorizing a particular type of life rather than allowing a whole range of possible lives to flourish.[3] The merits of this critical perspective on intimacy are best evaluated in the next two chapters that examine the ways in which women and children appeared on Breeze FM. Here the interest is in privacy as a matter of *not* putting on air everything Gogo Breeze saw and heard. Intimacy informed his private service as the above-mentioned rapport between a grandfather and his grandchildren, but the off-air encounters are important to investigate precisely because they show how his public service—indeed his radio personality—required privacy as much as publicness. In this regard, the catchphrase he often used for the studio—*kapinda komata* (a plastered/coated small room)—played on privacy in a different register. It alluded to a common idiom for the hut used in initiations to supply novices with esoteric knowledge.[4] *Nyumba yomata* is a house or hut that is so well plastered that no voices uttered inside it can be heard outside by those not privy to such knowledge. To refer to a broadcasting studio in a similar idiom is of course to transform private intimacy into a public one. This was the paradox, noted in chapter 1, by which the radio grandfather explained on the program *Chinyanja China* esoteric idioms that were not supposed to be available to children (*ana*). Private service, on the other hand, involved observing the boundaries separating one community of knowledge from another.

For Gogo Breeze's private service to be appreciated as an integral element of his public service, rather than as a pursuit of personal gain, I present in this chapter detailed accounts of two instances in which what went on air was only an aspect of the work he performed for his listeners. The instances are different enough to indicate the range of his private service. The first one arose from a public meeting he held in a village. Although recorded, the exchanges that took place among villagers and their headman were broadcast only to the extent that they conveyed dissatisfaction with the government and the area's member of Parliament. Allegations about the headman's own complicity in villagers' difficulties in accessing fertilizer and medicine did not appear on air, but the questions and provocations fired at him by Gogo Breeze rendered a service that stayed private for the concerned community of interlocutors. The second instance of private service took place under altogether more circumscribed conditions. Here a woman responded to Gogo Breeze's on-air invitation to come and explain the circumstances described in her letter to him. In this instance, the studio indeed became a well-plastered room when the three of us held a long unbroadcast meeting to discuss the woman's tribulations in her attempts to access her deceased father's estate. After a careful consideration of the social and spatial aspects of the woman's grievances, Gogo Breeze came to appreciate the dangers of intimate relationships within which she was pursuing justice. Our closed meeting, itself an intimate encounter, concluded that the woman's best hope lay in following the procedures of anonymous bureaucracy. Taken together, the two examples reveal an important facet of the moral market that Gogo Breeze summoned on his programs. Conversations carried out off air could be just as crucial to honoring obligations as were the advice and interviews he broadcast. For some grievances, the prospect of obligations being honored in unequal relationships was the brightest when the radio grandfather engaged in private service.

A Headman's Interrogation

The flow of letters and phone calls, along with the interest aroused by his appearances in the streets and villages, would make it seem that Gogo Breeze's radio personality was greeted with uniform enthusiasm. Yet not only the authorities he confronted with his listeners' grievances but also the people he met more casually could have reason to ask him to stop recording their encounters—or to avoid him outright. During one of our visits to Chipata's major marketplace, for example, female traders refused to talk to him because, they said, "You are going to record us" (*mutijambula*). Their challenge was voiced as banter with the radio grandfather they knew well, but he could also be rejected with a wall of silence. This was the case when he decided to stop by a rural clinic while collecting stories in the area. I observed him at first attempting to joke with the women who had accompanied patients to the clinic. His good-humored remarks on the food he found them cooking for the patients did little to loosen their tongues, aware as they were of his status as a radio personality. When he took out his voice recorder and asked them about the availability of medicine at the clinic, the women fell completely silent and stared at the cooking pots they were tending. Overseeing the encounter was the clinic's nurse, an imposing figure in a dazzling white uniform. When she heard Gogo Breeze's question, she shouted, "Yes, there is medicine!" (*ee, mankhwala alipo!*). His question had been motivated by the reports he had heard during this visit, and indeed in other rural areas, that nurses and other staff members were selling medicine that was supposed to be given free. Frustrated at the women's unwillingness to speak, Gogo Breeze left the scene

by saying, "That is your own problem; I am off" (*zili ndi imwe; ine ndapita*).
I lingered near the women and could hear one of them remarking to the
others in a despairing voice, "Now leaders [elders] will think that we have
enough medicine" (*panopa akuluakulu adzaganiza kuti tili ndi mankhwala ok-
wanira*). I told Gogo Breeze what I had heard, and he replied with the English words, "They have started talking."

It was this sense of opening out new opportunities for talking that informed Gogo Breeze's private service. His radio personality sometimes
summoned communities of deliberation even when he failed to capture
the proceedings on his voice recorder. A clear instance was another visit
to a rural area in 2013, where the familiar problems with the provision
of medicine and fertilizer led him to interrogate a village headman in the
presence of some one hundred villagers (see figure 8). The interrogation
did not become a part of the broadcast in the series *Chidwi Pa Anthu* that
had brought Gogo Breeze to this village.[5] While the broadcast was explicit
about the accusations of neglect that the crowd leveled against their member of Parliament, Gogo Breeze kept the tension between the headman and
his subjects off air. As other examples in previous chapters have indicated,
he had no qualms about mentioning traditional authorities by name on
air if he thought they should be subjected to special pleading or repri-

FIGURE 8

mand. On this occasion, as he explained to me afterward, his questions to the headman were so sharp, and the meeting so public, that broadcasting the whole episode would have seemed like a concentrated attack on one local person. As in the previous example, that people had "started talking" locally was the consequence of the service he had rendered to a particular community of deliberation.

After gathering a series of complaints from the crowd regarding the misallocation of fertilizer that local cooperatives were expected to receive from the Ministry of Agriculture and Cooperatives, Gogo Breeze raised the prospect of making these grievances public through letters to his program. "Elders, do you write letters? You must not hide stories/issues, because in the letters you write you can elaborate on the bad behavior of those who are executives."[6] With these words in mind, he turned to the headman: "Headman, explain well: maybe you received lots of fertilizer as a headman. They gave you many more bags than other people. Explain well."[7] In response, the headman promised to explain the situation "in detail" (*mwatsatanetsatane*) and asserted that the government (*boma*)[8] had changed its mind about the number of bags the members of cooperatives were entitled to. Betraying his own close link to the local member of Parliament, now on the opposition benches, the headman associated the change of policy with the change of the governing party. Rather than giving eight bags to every registered household, the new government had cut the entitlement in half. "Where does hatred reside?" (*udani ukhala kuti?*), the headman asked rhetorically. "Here, here in the village" (*kuno, kuno kumudzi*), he said, answering his own question as a way of alluding to villagers' misdirected anger. He sounded pragmatic in his suggestion for the way forward. "What can we do to share? No, but it is possible that fertilizer arrived only in small quantities. What can we do? Let us share little by little."[9] Unpersuaded, Gogo Breeze addressed the headman with his own advice. "Headman, you should not be the one who hides the child who made a mistake."[10] It evoked collusion between the headman and the leaders of the cooperative in ensuring that they received more fertilizer than others. The headman's response was to assert shared misery. "We are suffering together. There is no fertilizer."[11]

A man sitting next to me in the crowd, some distance away from Gogo Breeze and the headman, drove home to me the high stakes of this interrogation. "When they divide the fertilizer, he takes lots of it" (*Akagawana feteleza amatenga ambiri*). It was apparent from the crowd's interjections and body language that the headman was unpopular, not least because of his failure to participate in condemning Vincent Mwale, the area's member of Parliament, who was seen to spend most of his time in Lusaka. When visiting his constituency, people in the crowd asserted, he only spoke to trusted local contacts such as the headman himself. A further challenge was his status as an opposition politician, because he had won his parliamentary seat as a member of the Movement for Multiparty Democracy in the same 2011 elections that brought the Patriotic Front to power. Combined with his absence from the constituency, the area's apparent belonging to the opposition was feared by many in the crowd to result in its double marginalization. After interrogating the headman, Gogo Breeze asked the crowd for comments (*ndemanga*). An elderly man raised his arm to take the floor and pointed out, in a sad voice, "Justice is a problem" (*chilungamo chimakhala chovuta*). "Agriculture has gone down," he observed, "because of leaders and the government. The government should think hard about us living here in the village. Poverty has arrived because of the problem with fertilizer."[12]

Gogo Breeze rode a wave of popular sentiment when he engaged the crowd in questions and answers:

GOGO BREEZE: So, let us find evidence here. Because if someone, yeah, entered somebody else's house or grabbed a young girl, evidence exists because the young girl has what, a pregnant stomach. Is that not so, elders?

CROWD: Yes.

GOGO BREEZE: Now the issue that has come up here, let us compare the fields between you and me as the chairman or committee member. Does the maize, after it grew and matured, look the same when we go and look at your field and that of the chairman?

MAN IN THE CROWD: The maize is different.

GOGO BREEZE: How is it different?

MAN IN THE CROWD: It is different because elders and leaders have a different way [of doing things]. Justice is a problem among leaders, justice is a problem.

GOGO BREEZE: So, here we have evidence because the chairman's maize is good while my maize has done what?

CROWD: Withered.[13]

The deliberation on fertilizer had been preceded by a discussion about the availability of medicine in the local clinic. The headman had set the tone for Gogo Breeze's interrogation by assuring him that what he had reported from other areas about nurses diverting free medicine did not apply here. The headman received a less overt challenge from the crowd on this occasion than he would when the distribution of fertilizer was discussed later on, but another man sitting near me remarked to me and others around him that "it is not true" (*si zoona*) when the headman talked about the availability of medicine. The man told us about Mrs. Tembo, a nurse who had acquired considerable respect locally for her evenhanded provision of medicine. Yet she had been transferred to work in Chipata, and the nurse who replaced her had begun to take bribes (*ziphuphu*) for medicine. As was seen above, such direct expressions of discontent with named authorities, including the headman himself, remained murmurs among the crowd. Gogo Breeze, on the other hand, was altogether more direct in his interrogation of the headman and again became the vehicle for multiple voices of discontent. "Justice is a problem among leaders," as the elderly man quoted above put it, was an intervention that certainly implicated the headman, but no one in the crowd seemed prepared to confront him directly. The absent member of Parliament was subject to more vitriol and became the focus of the broadcast deliberation. Although the headman's interrogation kept discontent against him as a private matter between him and his subjects, Gogo Breeze's very presence, and his capacity to give voice to such discontent, rendered public service within duly observed limits.

The Moral Market of the Cooperative

Although the need for chemical fertilizers in large parts of Eastern Province may have been less acute than what the villagers were inclined to think, the degree to which they had vested moral considerations in its distribution indicated more than narrowly agrarian concerns. Access to fertilizer carried the promise of prosperity and all the potential for morally appropriate conduct that food security and the capacity to participate in exchanges entailed.[14] Because the government had instituted cooperatives as its mechanisms of distribution, the local focus inevitably was on how well they responded to villagers' moral expectations. Gogo Breeze's question about evidence visualized the morally barren state of local leaders' lush maize fields. Situated, in this image, next to the withering maize of ordinary cooperative members, the leaders' maize showed no promise of sustaining obligations beyond those immediately associated with it. Acquired through fraud and selfishness, their maize looked as healthy as it was incapable of making its owners morally upright.[15] Gogo Breeze conjured an image of inequality, but it was not any inequality that he attacked. Taking his cue from the sentiments expressed by the crowd, his voice gave an image of leadership that was not worthy of its status.

The moral market that Gogo Breeze helped to articulate was distinct from the ways in which Zambia's different governments had envisaged cooperatives. The cooperative movement enjoyed something of a renaissance as a method of distributing farming inputs after a period of official indifference in the 1990s when the government was more preoccupied with a program of privatization than with smallholder agriculture. This lack of interest came after considerable official attention to maize as a cash crop that smallholders would cultivate as members of cooperatives. The period from the late 1970s until the late 1980s, and its resonances with the agricultural policies of the late colonial period, have been critically assessed elsewhere.[16] Beyond its association with particular policies on agricultural subsidies and marketing, the cooperative movement in Zambia also reflects changes and continuities in official views on its benefits for local democracy. In Zambia's broadly socialist outlook of the 1970s and 1980s, defined as "Humanism" by President Kaunda, cooperatives signified solidarity and self-help in rural communities. The roots of African socialism were thought to rest on the soil of African tradition. "I am a firm believer," Kaunda stated, "in a co-operative way of life as it was practiced in simple village-like fashion. . . . The general rule was everyone helping their relatives and friends" (1966:32). Less prominent in such a view was the capacity of some smallholders to use their farming experience and their business and political connections to their own advantage. The principle of shareholding, by which each member bought shares in the cooperative, was thought to be compatible with democracy when everyone had only one vote regardless of the number of their shares. In the era of a greater emphasis on entrepreneurship, by contrast, shareholding could acquire meanings that were more congenial to the market economy.

These meanings became apparent to me when I interviewed a civil servant at the Chipata branch of the Ministry of Agriculture and Cooperatives. He affirmed that cooperatives were more than instruments by the government to provide fertilizer among smallholders. They were also, he stated, a means by which these farmers could be encouraged to think of their livelihoods as businesses. To this end, the members of cooperatives had to be made to understand the principle of shareholding as a future-oriented investment. If they managed their farms well, they would make a profit on their shares when they left the cooperative. Democratic decision making, based on having a single vote however many shares a member might possess, did not feature in the officer's reflections. Instead, he continued by stressing the benefits of cooperative membership to poor villagers in particular. They would learn the values and skills of entrepreneurship by participating in a profit-making economic activity together with other villagers, some of whom had those values and skills in greater abundance than others. The officer expected this exposure to business practices to result in improved standards of living, not only through farming for the market but also through other enterprises that members might be inspired to try out. Note that the officer's reflections can be interpreted as expressions of neoliberal rhetoric only if his insights into cooperation, imitation, and mentorship are ignored. Rather than casting the cooperative movement into the mold of market fundamentalism and unbridled individualism, he understood entrepreneurship to depend on a set of values and skills that could best be acquired by working with others. A certain egalitarian vision of individual thriving nevertheless informed the desired future outcome—that everyone, and not least the poor, would put their new values and skills to independent use.

If solidarity had given way to entrepreneurship and profit making in this vision of the cooperative movement, it is worth pointing out that the standard opposite of the individual had not disappeared from the government's efforts to entice villagers into cooperatives. An emphasis on group or communal cooperation lived on in *Buku La Alimi* (*The Book of Farmers*), the Chinyanja newsletter published for smallholders by the Ministry of Agriculture and Cooperatives. An article titled "Profit in the Cooperative" (*Phindu lokhala m'chigwirizano*) described what a cooperative in Nyimba District had achieved.[17] It had more than doubled its membership from the initial thirty-five members when it was founded in 2003 to seventy-five; it had sold fifty bags of maize cultivated in its garden to the Food Reserve Agency and bought inputs for the following season with the money it had earned; it kept twelve goats; it gave credit to its members "to develop on their own" (*atukuke wayekha wayekha*), including the building of "good houses" (*manyumba abwino*); it had a fund to assist its members to cultivate their gardens when they fell sick and to buy coffins when they had funerals; and it was building a house where classes for adult education and radio listening clubs could be held. Although the emphasis on self-improvement that the officer had put forward in his interview with me was not absent from this narrative, its contrasting emphasis was on collective effort in many more areas of life than in the procurement of fertilizer.

What both emphases papered over was what Gogo Breeze took as his point of departure when engaging with the practice of cooperatives in a particular setting. Leadership, with its concomitant questions of authority and inequality, was as invisible in the officer's appeal for individual entrepreneurship as it was in the newsletter's depiction of common causes.

Gogo Breeze's off-air intervention, by contrast, took seriously villagers' desire for better leadership and made no effort to educate them on the virtues of either individual entrepreneurship or collective work. Underlying both aspects of the official rhetoric was a certain egalitarianism, also apparent in the change of policy, correctly identified above by the headman whom Gogo Breeze interrogated, by which the amount of fertilizer per farming family had been halved. While the officer explained the new policy to me as an attempt to make the same amount of fertilizer reach double the previous number of smallholders, such seemingly even distribution of scarcity only fueled discontent with leadership. The various viewpoints—including those of the Ministry, the headman, the villagers, and Gogo Breeze himself—were united in one respect. They all took the desire to thrive in the market for granted. What divided them was more consequential than what united them, because any attempt to either ignore or whitewash leadership undermined the moral conditions of villagers' participation in the market.

Off-Air Intimacy

Gogo Breeze's off-air service to his listeners took on an even more private form when he rendered it in secluded spaces such as the station's *kapinda komata*, the soundproof studio mentioned above. Unbroadcast even when recorded for the radio grandfather's own use, the conversations were held in the ambience of trust and intimacy. Such ambience arose from Gogo Breeze's assurances of confidentiality and his efforts to make the visitors feel at ease. For their part, the visitors often came to see him predisposed to share intimate aspects of their lives with the radio grandfather. The prospects for intimacy were the greatest when the visits were not impromptu but were preceded by Gogo Breeze's on-air responses to the visitors' letters. He would comment on their lack of detail that made it impossible for him to answer them without meeting the letter writers, and he would state the specific date when he expected them to find him at the station. One example of such encounters is Miriam Nkhoma's case in 2012, an instance of suspected embezzlement of her deceased father's estate by the person who had taken on the role of administering it. It is a case that not only highlights the often complex relationships that Gogo Breeze found himself exploring when he moved beyond letters and phone calls as the means by which he interacted with his public. It also indicates the different registers of intimacy that such complexity could entail. Nkhoma's intimacy with her kin—with both the dead and the self-appointed administrator of the estate—evoked fear in her, while her intimacy with the radio grandfather was built on trust. The predicament illustrates, in Peter Geschiere's words, a "complex intertwinement of security and fear in people's experience of intimacy" (2013:28).

In her short letter, Nkhoma had stated that her father had died in Lusaka while working in the Office of the President, a government department responsible for various bureaucratic matters (see figure 9).[18] The family member acting as the administrator dealing with the estate was the focus of her grievance, because she thought that the person had concealed money and information from her. She mentioned that she had gone to Lusaka to sign papers, and the administrator had promised to call her when the estate's money was available, but no further communication had reached her. In his response on air, Gogo Breeze complained that "sometimes when you write, you write a little and don't explain everything about how things might be."[19] He posed a number of questions to Nkhoma, including "When choosing the administrator, how many of you were there?" and "What sort of kinship does the administrator have with you?" He invited Nkhoma to see him by saying, "I ask you to come next week on Monday to see the grandfather so that when you come we sit down for you to explain well to me how everything is." Yet even if the letter was brief, he understood the predicament behind it. "What is known is that the people who are chosen to be administrators sometimes have a hidden agenda to eat the money that belongs to the bereaved." He used the idiom *kampeni kumphasa* for what he translated for me as "hidden agenda." In a literal sense, the idiom alludes to a small knife (*kampeni*) hidden in a mat (*mphasa*) in order to be used to attack another person. When urging listeners to respect the dead, Gogo Breeze also alluded to the dangers of intimacy. "Now remember that it is not good to eat the property of the bereaved by force, because when you just eat the property of the bereaved, eating anyhow, you will pick up misfortune." The allusion here was to the intimacy between the dead and their living relatives. Although people in Eastern Province do not generally seek to stay in contact with their departed relatives, the dead are thought to be capable of harming the living if funerals and subsequent memorial services in churches are not conducted in a proper way. Discord among the bereaved over the estate can also expose people to the misfortune (*tsoka*) that Gogo Breeze alluded to. While the Christian God is the most acceptable source of protection, along with, in a more mundane sense, relatives who have the wherewithal to assist others, the relationship between the living and the dead entails largely nega-

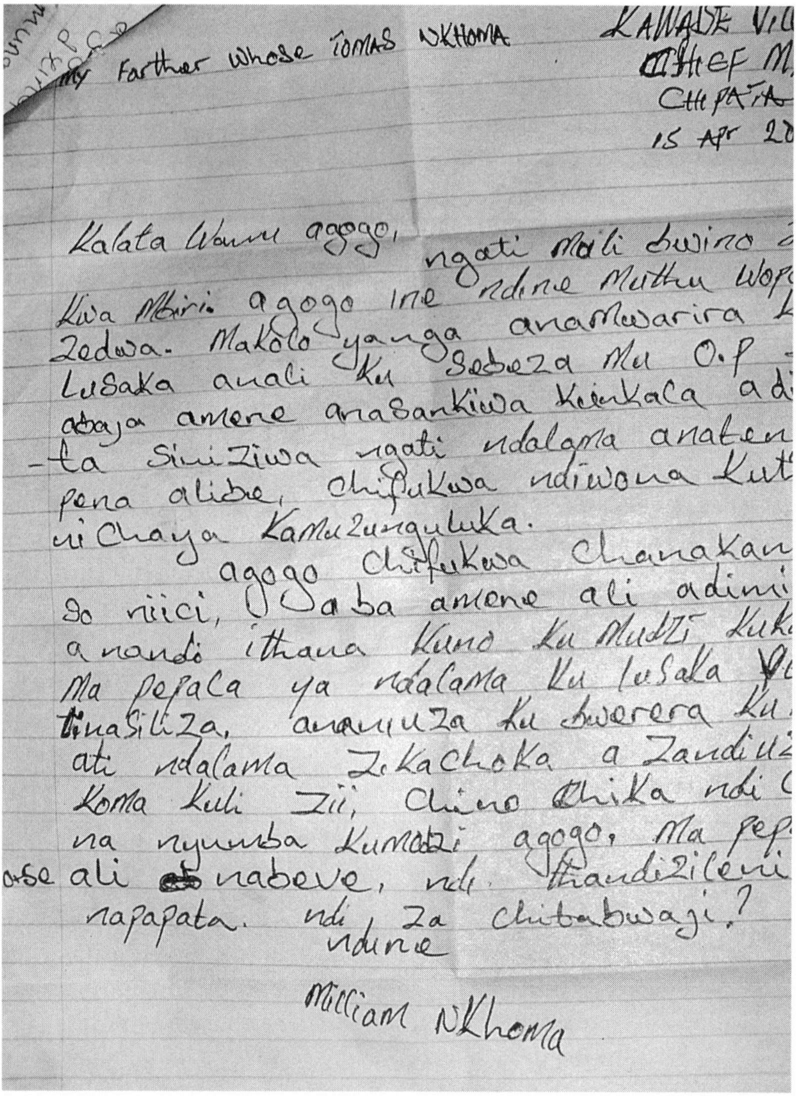

My Farther whose TOMAS NKHOMA

KAWADE VIL
CHIEF M
CHIPATA
15 Apr 20

Kalata Wanu agogo, ngati muli bwino
Kwa Mbiri agogo ine ndine Muthu Wop
Zedwa. Makolo yanga anamwarira
Lusaka anali ku Sebeza mu O.P
abaja amene anasankiwa kuinkala adi
-ta Siniziwa ngati ndalama anaten
pena alibe, chifukwa ndiwona kut
ni Chaya Kamuzungulika.
agogo chifukwa chanakan
So niici, Saba amene ali adini
anando ithana kuno ku Mudzi kuk
Ma pepala ya ndalama ku Lusaka
tinasiliza, ananuza ku bwerera ku
ati ndalama Zikachoka a Zandiu
Koma kuli Zii, Chino chika ndi
na nyumba kumudzi agogo, Ma pep
ose ali nabeve, ndi thandizileni
napapata. ndi, Za chitabwaji?
ndine

William NKhoma

FIGURE 9

tive intimacy, afflictions such as possession by spirits (*mizimu*), madness (*misala*), and even death if the dead have cause to be dissatisfied with the way they have been treated.

When Nkhoma duly appeared at the station on the prescribed date, Gogo Breeze was quick to establish grandfatherly intimacy with her. A woman in her early thirties, she came carrying an infant on her back. While adjusting the child to rest on her lap after she had been ushered into the *kapinda komata*, Gogo Breeze encouraged her to be relaxed about the noises the baby was making: "Let that one cry; no problem; don't worry." His opening remarks also affirmed his advice as a form of service: "We did not answer you in full to satisfy you on what you described. That is why I said, 'You should come to tell us the whole story, how it happened that you wrote the letter to ask for assistance from this house on air, Breeze FM.'" Nkhoma readily described her quest for assistance as an attempt to talk to her grandfather, speaking of Gogo Breeze in the third person: "Now my thoughts [were that] I should go and ask if the grandfather might help me on how things are. . . . I should complain to the grandfather; perhaps he can help me." Gogo Breeze also cultivated intimacy by sharing his personal experiences later on during the conversation, such as when he mentioned that he had a relative who had, three months after retiring from the Office of the President, received his retirement payment. Even more intimate was his recollection that after his son had died, the widow became the administrator of his estate, assisted by her brother-in-law, who "was only in the background." Personal experience combined with the grandfather's wisdom about matters to do with both family and bureaucracy. Indeed, a major issue to be negotiated between him and his visitor was whether the matter could be resolved within the family or if it needed to be taken to a court of law. Gogo Breeze had anticipated the latter course of action in his initial response to the letter on air, but when off air with Nkhoma, he used a good deal of time to establish the nature of her conflict with the administrator of her late father's estate. As is described below, Gogo Breeze's understanding of her particular circumstances took its time to emerge. Nkhoma's gradual and somewhat erratic presentation of facts—compounded by Chinyanja's gender-neutral pronouns and expansive kin terms—did little to afford clarity to the complexity of those circumstances. In the end, Gogo Breeze felt obliged to provide the same advice he had mentioned on air, but the way in which his emerging understanding of Nkhoma's intimate relationships eventually compelled him to recommend a bureaucratic and judicial solution is interesting. Bureaucracy and intimacy were not mutually exclusive but were entangled with each other in the search for justice.

Obligations to Whom?

Only the three of us—and the infant—were present in the *kapinda komata* when Gogo Breeze explored with Nkhoma the details of her grievance. He would turn to me, as he did when I participated in the letters program, to seek my comments as his "fellow grandfather" (*gogo mnzanga*). I had little to offer, but as can be seen below, my comments came to affirm his view on the different attitudes toward bureaucracy among Zambians and white people (*azungu*). This view was an aspect of the radio elder's usual confidence in mediating multiple perspectives, whether based on a comparison between racially indexed cultures or on cultural competence about his client's personal circumstances. Yet because the subject of Nkhoma's grievance was not with us in the room, her narrative was all that Gogo Breeze had to work with in order to imagine the motivations that had given rise to the grievance. Cultural competence was required to ask the right kinds of questions that would begin to identify salient details in Nkhoma's understandably one-sided narrative. Distance and proximity, in both social and spatial senses, turned out to be major themes in these efforts to get to the heart of the matter.

The administrator's precise genealogical link to Nkhoma took some time to emerge. At issue was the degree of intimacy—and the extent of legitimacy—in the administrator's claim to be representing the family's interests. Early on in the conversation, Gogo Breeze confirmed that the administrator, or *muimiliri*, "the one who stands for others," had been selected in Nkhoma's absence and without her knowledge. To his question about the kind of responsibility or duty (*udindo*) that the person had in the family, Nkhoma replied by saying that the person was the deceased's elder sibling. The phrase *akulu wawo* is gender neutral,[20] as are the personal pronouns in Chinyanja. Gogo Breeze had assumed that the elder sibling was the deceased's brother and had proceeded to ask about Nkhoma's mother and other senior relatives before the actual state of affairs started to dawn on him. After affirming that her mother had also died and that she was the oldest child, Nkhoma had answered Gogo Breeze's questions about her communications with the administrator before it became apparent that the person was a woman. This detail only emerged when Nkhoma was describing how the administrator's elder sibling, again an *mkulu*, had come to her to explain that she should not worry and that "your mother will tell you" when the inherited money is available. Having recently affirmed that her mother was dead, Nkhoma put an end to the confusion Gogo Breeze experienced by stating that "the old man's elder sibling, I used to live with her, so by habit I call her 'mother.'" A little later she noted that the administrator could also be called an aunt (*anti*) and that Nkhoma had lived with her after her own mother had died. Not only was the administrator revealed to be a woman, another layer of intimacy was added to the narrative when Gogo Breeze realized that the administrator could actually be seen as a mother by Nkhoma. Further complexity awaited him when he came to understand how this proximity could also be undone by social and spatial distance.

The administrator's siblingship with the deceased derived from the sisterhood between their mothers. Using the idiom for what anthropologists working in the region have called a matrilineal segment (Mitchell 1956:134; Richards 1950:230–36), Nkhoma explained that the administrator was from the "small breast" (*bele laling'ono*) while the father's mother was the older of the two sisters. In other words, he was of the more senior segment than the administrator, and a classic theme in the above-mentioned anthropology was to locate the roots of lineage fission in cleavages between such matrilineally related segments. It is not necessary to share these anthropologists' vocabulary of lineages and their segments to recognize in Nkhoma's grievance a sense of simultaneous proximity and distance. The administrator had, in her view, made a statement about who mattered to her the most by giving the clothes of Nkhoma's father to her own mother, the younger of the two sisters. This woman had allegedly used the clothes as payments for having her land farmed. Nkhoma also noted with some bitterness that the administrator was using the estate to educate her own children. As such, her grievance began to cohere around the claim that the estate was being appropriated for the benefit of the administrator's closest relatives rather than the deceased's own children. Nkhoma's past as a member of the administrator's household appeared to do little to put her on a par with these other beneficiaries of the administrator's largesse. Relationships also took specific spatial forms when the administrator's mother, for example, had an obligation to pay those who cultivated for her in Malawi and when the administrator appeared to make plans to generate wealth from the estate in Lusaka. She had explained to Nkhoma that the deceased's house in Lusaka's Chipata Compound[21] had to be sold so that another house closer to where she lived in Lusaka could be purchased and used to generate rent income that she would share with Nkhoma. Unaware whether this plan had been realized or not, and what had happened to the money that the deceased's estate should have obtained from his workplace, Nkhoma had tried to contact the administrator by phone. The tension between her and the administrator had reached a new level when it became apparent that the administrator would switch off the phone when the call was from Nkhoma.

Gogo Breeze's initial advice sought to find ways in which the distance between Nkhoma and the administrator could be bridged. If phone calls would not serve as the bridge, it was better that Nkhoma went to Lusaka herself. In order to avoid outright confrontation, Nkhoma was to tread carefully, "step by step" or "*khwerero* (ladder step) after *khwerero*," taking up sensitive issues in the afternoon or evening because "chatting (story) goes well" (*nkhani imakoma*) then. Two further pieces of advice are noteworthy. First, Gogo Breeze pressed it on Nkhoma not to consider herself as a child to the administrator, as her subordinate, but to assert, "I have grown up now" (*nakula tsopano*). Second, he urged her to pursue the matter of clothes, because it could furnish evidence (*umboni*) of embezzlement, if the administrator admitted that she had given the clothes away without consulting Nkhoma. Nkhoma's response to this advice was lukewarm, only endorsing Gogo Breeze's warning that death might await her if she did not make the journey with money in her own pocket to "avoid the food she will give you" (*kupewa zakudya zokupatsani iwo*). His remark that "here is both life and death" (*apa tsopano pali moyo na imfa*) was emphatically accepted by Nkhoma's "that is very true" (*ndi zoona ngako*). Still pursuing the option of traveling to Lusaka, Gogo Breeze was not discouraged when Nkhoma announced that she had no other relatives to stay with in Lusaka. He described the capacity of a particular Chipata-based bus company to diminish the effects of distance by making it possible to travel to and from the capital in one day. It was Nkhoma's appeal to poverty as a further obstacle to traveling—"Here is the village, grandfather; where would you find money to go from here to there?"—that crystallized Gogo Breeze's advice. The best route, after all, was the bureaucratic one by which Nkhoma would issue a summons to get the administrator to come to court. The evidence was the deceased's clothes—they must have come to the village in Eastern Province to be used as payments for farming in Malawi. Questioning the administrator in court about the clothes would open out the opportunity for the court to decide on the case more broadly. The clothes contrasted, in this regard, with Nkhoma's diffuse suspicions as something concrete that could be used to bring witnesses to court and to unravel the administrator's dishonesty.

An appropriate distribution of obligations was articulated by Gogo Breeze's assertion that Nkhoma had grown to take up the burdens of managing her father's estate. Once the relevant details had dawned on him, the radio elder understood how the time Nkhoma had spent with her surrogate mother was no guarantee of justice. Their belonging to different "breasts," along with contingent factors such as Nkhoma's status as her father's eldest child and the presence of the surrogate mother's own mother, created a situation in which competing obligations tore asunder whatever compassion might have made her assume the role of Nkhoma's mother. It was not greed that Nkhoma accused her of. Rather, she and the radio elder shared an understanding that the surrogate mother was driven by obligations to others rather than to the deceased's own children. Not entirely unlike the gluttonous witch, however, the surrogate mother came to embody the dark side of kinship intimacy in the fear that she might try to kill Nkhoma if she was to succumb to apparent acts of conviviality at the surrogate mother's house. Nkhoma's growth as an adult person entailed obligations of her own, not only to the infant she had brought with her but, as I established with her after she had taken leave of Gogo Breeze, to the three other children she had with two different men, neither of whom had stayed with her, alongside two more children left behind by her deceased younger sister. The bureaucratic route on which she and the radio elder settled arose, rather than stood apart from his mismatch of obligations.

The Intimacy of Bureaucracy

Before he had realized that the administrator was the surrogate mother Nkhoma had already mentioned, rather than the deceased's elder brother as he had assumed, Gogo Breeze turned to me to inquire about the management of estates in England: "Would you be able to take and use your younger sibling's property while the children in his/her family are left behind? Would that be possible?" My response asserted the power of law in "our place" (*kwathu*), the practice of having "well-documented" estates that made it difficult for anyone to run away with money that did not belong to them. What I brought to the discussion, on Gogo Breeze's initiative, was another perspective on bureaucracy that he deployed later on as a foil to consider Nkhoma's options. The faith "our friends," a reference to white people in general, put in *pepa* (paper) stood in contrast to the ways in which "we fear writing" and "we only keep it in our head what belongs to whom." The foil my presence provided was similar to the on-air occasions when Gogo Breeze would turn to me to seek my comments on issues raised in listeners' letters, whether teenage pregnancies or labor relations. He would express such requests by addressing me as "my grandfather friend/colleague" (*gogo mnzanga*) or by my first name or the clan name Phiri, which I had brought with me from my earlier projects in Malawi. It was intimacy based on alterity, different and yet complementary perspectives on shared concerns.

The dichotomy that Gogo Breeze had drawn between white people's bureaucratic practices and Africans' aversion to documents did not survive the complexity of Nkhoma's case. The mention of white people led him to recall a program one of his colleagues had recently put on air about the importance of preparing wills. No sooner had he made the comment than it transpired that Nkhoma's father had indeed written a will. Nkhoma's nonchalant remark that her father had done so left Gogo Breeze momentarily dumbfounded, exclaiming to me that "it's a big case!" This was the point at which he began to build the case for taking the question of the deceased's clothes as the first step toward an evidence-based prosecution against the administrator. Rather than seeking to validate the will in the first instance, his advice was to present a case about the missing clothes to the court, with the prospect of the administrator finding herself sleeping in a prison cell.[22] What had begun as a family dispute with complex intimacies between the living and the dead, and between the carer and the cared-for, took a bureaucratic turn when it had been established that neither a phone call nor a journey to Lusaka was going to provide a solution. Nkhoma would only need to meet the cost of postage to avail herself of a different solution. To convince her of the solution, Gogo Breeze evoked a pair of bureaucratic figures. A court messenger allayed Nkhoma's concerns about financial loss and poison or occult attacks if she was to deliver the court summons herself. A presiding officer in Lusaka was there to ensure the transformation of the case into a bureaucratic matter. Upon receiving the instructions from a court in Chipata, he would give the messenger the house number where to deliver the summons. In this bureaucratic move, the house that had been Nkhoma's home following her mother's death became a number in the administration of justice. Yet the detachment afforded by bureaucracy was motivated by intimacy. It was the negation of care, evident in the possibility of intimacy turning into occult attacks, that made bureaucracy the best option.

Nkhoma did not rush into endorsing the radio elder's recommended course of action. Before they drew their conversation to a close, she introduced her father's workplace as one further sphere for seeking justice. Upon establishing that the father had died while still employed by the Office of the President in Lusaka, Gogo Breeze had another set of documents in mind. A pay slip or the death certificate would be required for the employer to answer any questions about money it might owe to the bereaved. Because Nkhoma had no such documents, she was back to square one in her dependency on the administrator to pursue this path. At the same time, Gogo Breeze sensed Nkhoma's unvoiced wish for mediation. It would have been a role familiar to him and his public as the grandfather investigating listeners' grievances in offices which they were too intimidated to visit on their own accord. "If you had the documents, I would have told you to write, to make photocopies, and to enclose them with the letter so that I could have asked them here [the Chipata branch of the Office of the President]." Intimacy was again entwined with bureaucracy, now as a requirement to furnish the radio elder with the photocopies of the right kinds of documents. To Nkhoma's evocation of "fear" (*mantha*) as the impediment to pursue the case on her own, Gogo Breeze responded with an idiom that made us all laugh: "When sharing maize flour, do not be embarrassed or fearful. For you to share maize flour, you also want to have a full stomach." Gogo Breeze prepared Nkhoma to face the challenge by insisting that if the surrogate mother had taken her share, it was now time for Nkhoma to take hers. His final words, before thanking Nkhoma for visiting him, reasserted Breeze FM as a particular kind of public-service provider: "The house on air is yours. If you have difficulties, come, ask; we will try to answer."

Gogo Breeze's dichotomy reversed the stereotype, familiar from a variety of historical situations, by which the poor are subject to bureaucratic domination.[23] The reversal was itself too much like a stereotype to offer much practical guidance in his deliberation on Nkhoma's case, but his remark that "we fear writing" alluded to a sophisticated understanding of what documents can signify in social relations. Rather than ensuring a fair procedure, documents can exude danger, a capacity to undermine whatever room for negotiation and selective memory keeping things "in our head" might allow for. At the same time, Nkhoma's case unsettles any understanding that takes documents and bureaucratic categories for granted. The intimacy of bureaucracy was implicit in Gogo Breeze's comment that the deceased's employers would need to see his pay slip or death certificate in order to process Nkhoma's claim. The comment appreciated the specificities of documents (see Hull 2008:503), the different people, objects, and affects their circulation requires. Pay slips and death certificates were some of the most intimate documents a person could possess, affectively charged when they carried information not everyone was supposed to be privy to (see Navaro-Yashin 2007:81).[24] Here the bureaucratic category of "administrator" also revealed its moral and affective ambiguities. Gogo Breeze wasted no time imagining an administrator who was known to the claimant only through a bureaucratic category. Both when answering Nkhoma's letter on air and when meeting her face to face, one of his first questions was about kinship. It was about legitimacy in representing the bereaved, based on the convention that estates are usually administered by spouses or close kin. The administrator's possession of the deceased's intimate documents, along with her role as Nkhoma's surrogate mother, was not enough to confer legitimacy on her self-appointed status. The management and division of the estate was a bureaucratic task, but its moral execution was something that the radio elder could readily evaluate. Grandfatherly intimacy compelled trust in bureaucracy precisely because in its procedures there was, as expressed in Hannah Arendt's critical remark, "nobody left with whom one could argue" and "to whom one could present one's griev-ances" (1970:81). Grievances that evoked the perils of intimacy had the best prospect of facing their demise in the anonymity of bureaucracy.

Radio Intimacies

The two instances of Gogo Breeze's off-air service discussed in this chap-ter provide a standpoint from which to ask further comparative questions about the role of radio in producing intimacies between broadcasters and their publics, and among publics themselves. As was noted from the out-set, intimacy and privacy are not the same. Much of Gogo Breeze's on-air personality was built on grandfatherly intimacy, evident in his capacity to engage in both banter and biting criticism with his listeners. Intimacy was often a matter of voice as much as words, as seen in chapter 2 when the stern, roaring voice he used with the owners of grinding mills changed into a soothing one when he took late-evening calls from people affected by the owners' profiteering. It was certainly the case that the topics he brought on air involved detail about intimate matters such as marital and sexual life or, as in Nkhoma's case, death and inheritance. While the letters program omitted personal names, many of the encounters he broadcast did begin with his inquiries into the interlocutor's name and origins. Yet grandfa-therly intimacy involved discretion about the extent to which some issues should become public. Gogo Breeze's private service arose from common Zambian expectations that moral authority to consider, and to give ad-vice on, sensitive matters often depended on meeting supplicants behind closed doors—and on switching off the voice recorder.

Beyond the contrast between intimacy and privacy, the ethnography presented here permits comparative perspectives into the kind of economy in which the radio had come to mediate grandfatherly intimacy. Com-menting on the rise of radio talk shows in post-Soviet Russia, Tomas Matza has noted their involvement in a "new psychotherapy market" in which "therapeutic idioms like self-esteem, self-realization, self-knowledge, self-management, independence, personal potential, and responsibility have articulated with consumer desire, capitalist self-fashioning, and careerism"

(2009:492). The idioms identified in Matza's study are of course reminiscent of the idiom of voice as the property individuals need to discover and use.[25] In this regard, the moral authority that radio psychotherapists and radio grandfathers exude may be based on very different notions of voice and the self. Both can take intimate affairs as the focus of the expertise their moral authority allows them to assert, but where voice is not necessarily individual property but comes to have an effect in and through the moral authority of others, the emphasis on techniques of the self is much less salient as an analytical concern in ethnography.[26]

A variety of self-help manuals have also appeared on the shelves of Zambia's bookstores, along with ubiquitous Pentecostal exhortations to prosper through individual, divinely inspired effort. Psychotherapeutic counseling has gained a foothold in Zambia as in many other African countries in recent decades, not least in response to the HIV/AIDS pandemic. One of its effects may be a heightened awareness that previously persons seeking help "would be 'talked to' and 'advised' by people usually older than themselves but would rarely be listened to in an open-ended way" (Vaughan 2016:511). Against the dichotomy between advice and listening stands their interdependence in Gogo Breeze's practice. The challenge it poses to analysts is to devise a perspective that is more attuned to the idioms deployed by the radio elder and his listeners than to those peddled in the psychotherapy market.

In the moral market that Gogo Breeze's programs mediated, the judicious evocation of obligation rather than the techniques of the self was at the center of radio intimacy. The grandfather was needed to know when and how claims were to be made in the quest for justice within unequal relationships. In the first instance discussed in this chapter, discrediting a local leader over the airwaves could have dealt too big a blow to efforts to make him honor his obligations toward villagers. A broadcast that transcended the local community was better suited to criticizing the member of Parliament, a leader operating in national politics and whose commitment to the locality had become uncertain. Leadership (*utsogoleri*) was also at the heart of Nkhoma's grievance about the administration of her father's estate. Here the radio elder was required to advise on how to negotiate the multiple obstacles presented by kinship divisions, occult threats, and bureaucratic procedures. Gogo Breeze's response to Nkhoma's letter on air made public his disapproval of administrators who mismanaged estates and may have, as such, supported many others than Nkhoma herself in generating claims for justice in similar circumstances. Yet the specificities of her situation could emerge only in private and be addressed once the grandfather had developed a complete picture of the options available to her. Critical to this process was to withhold some information from the public lest it could have hampered Nkhoma's quest for justice.

It was an integral part of grandfatherly intimacy that Gogo Breeze allowed himself to be influenced by those who sought his advice. The headman's interrogation was indeed a service rendered rather than a verdict delivered from on high. The twists and turns in Nkhoma's case, on the other hand, tested the radio elder's capacity to recommend a specific course of action, and her own sense of what was feasible played a significant role in steering their conversation.[27] Gogo Breeze was himself embedded in the moral market he helped to summon. Grandfatherly intimacy entailed grandfatherly obligation, the burden to listen to other voices in order to mediate them. Private service was not the moment when Grayson Peter Nyozani Mwale would shed Gogo Breeze's radio personality. On the contrary, it was precisely an occasion when the man and the radio personality were most convincingly proved to be one, bound by the obligations toward his listeners even when off air. By introducing Breeze FM's other personalities who also addressed intimate questions with regard to gender and generational tensions, the next two chapters throw Gogo Breeze's particular ethos into sharper relief.

PART THREE

Women and Children

FIVE

Between Feminisms and Paternalisms

Virgin *nkhote alibe maliketi,* "The old virgin has no market." The key line in a hit song by the Zambian artist B1 caused controversy in 2012. In Lusaka and Chipata alike, the airwaves were filled with the song, titled "Perfecto," mixing Chinyanja and English to convey what some considered a timely message against NGO-led campaigns to assert women's independence from men, while others were scandalized by its apparent misogynist attempt to thwart female ambition, also evident in the refrain, *kulibe perfecto,* "There is nothing that is perfect" (or, more idiomatically, "Nobody's perfect"). Both sides appeared to understand the song as an invitation for women to reject the NGO advice to postpone sexual affairs until they were properly educated and ready to assume economic independence. Better to have a man, however imperfect, than to face the diminishing marital market as an old virgin. Appearing in an interview with Muvi TV—a commercial channel available in Zambia's urban areas—B1 sought to play down the song's misogynistic tone and urged everyone, without elaborating, "to listen to the whole song." Meanwhile, newspapers reported that the public broadcaster ZNBC had launched an investigation into the controversy after receiving several complaints about the song's "degrading" portrayal of women.[1]

Breeze FM played its part in giving the song air time. Although it did not accord with the station's formal commitment to progressive gender relations, I never heard its message being debated over Breeze FM's airwaves. It got absorbed in the daily flow of popular music, along with B1's other risqué tunes,[2] without comment or reflection, even when the presenters were the feminists described later in this chapter. When it did become the subject of reflection, "Perfecto" revealed some of the station's gendered fault lines. One young male presenter expressed his admiration for the song with particularly striking enthusiasm. Responsible for many of the station's key talk shows, including those sponsored by NGOs, he never made his admiration apparent on air. Instead, he had the song as his mobile phone's ring tone and followed with great interest the evolving controversy elsewhere in Zambia's media. Sensing my own interest in the matter, he would seek me out to tell me the latest developments and to offer his views on them. He was adamant that "Perfecto" was indeed about warning women against unrealistic expectations in life. He described how the campaign slogan "Virgin Power, Virgin Pride," also mentioned in the song, had earlier saturated the public sphere, against which B1's intervention stood as a welcome corrective.[3] He dismissed the newspaper reports on complaints about the song and claimed to know that "only one man" had gone to the ZNBC to protest. This one complaint, he asserted, was now used in attempts to remove the song from the radio.

This young male presenter's investment in the controversy provides one point of entry into Breeze FM's multifaceted role in fostering debate about gender relations. He inhabited dispositions that appeared to be mutually contradictory while giving rise to a sharply articulated position on the proper balance between the male and female domains. He was, among other things, closely involved in producing and presenting the NGO-sponsored program series on the girl child that will be discussed in the next chapter. He was much in the founder-director's favor for ensuring that the talk shows he hosted were sponsored and had as their guests representatives from the government, NGOs, and businesses. His status as one of Breeze FM's up-and-coming radio personalities had been boosted by his selection to participate in a short course in Europe. His personal plans also supported the founder-director's desire to see the young members of his staff advancing in their careers so as to acquire the outwardly appearance of a successful life, such as marriage and material possessions. At the same time as "Perfecto" was all over the airwaves, this presenter was preparing to marry his longtime fiancée. Both upwardly mobile in their careers, the couple seemed set to consolidate their position among Zambia's middle class.

In order to understand how this presenter—and perhaps many who found B1's message compelling—could live with the apparently contradictory dispositions, it may be advisable to dispense with the notion of misogyny. While violence against women was a public concern in Zambia,[4] its associated sentiments were never condoned by those among the Breeze FM staff who were critical of certain governmental and NGO-led campaigns for gender equality. A clue to this young presenter's frustration with such campaigns lies in his assertion that it was a man who had sparked the ZNBC's investigation into "Perfecto." Rather than blaming women, he attributed the complaint to male zeal. For this presenter as presumably for B1, it was in women's own best interests to ignore the NGO call for virginity and to insert themselves into relationships with men. One form of paternalism was here pitted against another—both the presenter's appreciation of "Perfecto" and the alleged lone complainant's action on women's behalf were guided by a male sense of what was best for women. Yet as an insight into debates about gender within Breeze FM, the actual interest in the young presenter's paternalism is the way in which it drew on contemporary electronic popular music, infused with hip-hop influences, and appeared alongside middle-class aspirations for professional advancement and marital bliss. Another form of paternalism found its place on Breeze FM's airwaves through a self-styled patriarch, who built his radio personality on altogether more traditional referents. In contrast to these paternalisms stood a variety of feminisms that owed their specific features to particular female presenters' personal experiences. By comparing these paternalisms and feminisms at Breeze FM—on air and off—it is possible to arrive at a more nuanced sense of the value of free speech in the gender debate as it actually unfolded amid the highly polarized concepts of women and men.

Such a comparison is essential to understand Gogo Breeze's particular position in the debate. He too spent a considerable proportion of his time exploring and advocating certain ideas of what the relationships between women and men should look like. The previous chapters have included several instances in which his authority appeared to be based not only on generational but also on gendered differences. He had grand*daughters* in the studio to read out letters for him, while some of his humor described earlier had a flavor that may strike some as sexist. For example, in chapter 1, to joke about a visiting donor representative's breasts and to use the word "trailer" for a woman's backside in an ad was to perpetrate a popular culture that objectified women. Yet the interest in exploring Gogo Breeze's position in Breeze FM's gender debate is not simply to demonstrate the limited extent to which he had adopted governmental and nongovernmental policies on gender equality. It is to investigate the actual ways in which gender relations featured in his moral authority to mediate his public's grievances and aspirations. Toward the end of this chapter, a closer look at how he could be challenged by the granddaughters, and a comparison with the station's self-styled patriarch, reveal multivocality similar to the work that the radio elder performed in less obviously gendered contexts.

The themes that appear in this comparison of paternalisms and feminisms at Breeze FM are familiar from the literature on colonial and postcolonial Africa. As in late-colonial newspapers and fictional works in Zambia and elsewhere, women's behavior provided a prism into the contested meanings that different protagonists attributed to socioeconomic change (see Barber 2012; Englund 2015c; Newell 2000). On one hand, the more things changed, the more they remained the same. The twenty-first century and the late-colonial period alike gave rise to concerns about polygamy, women's health, and childcare duties, along with an emphasis on Christian marriage and morals. On the other, the mass-mediated gender debate had to contend with issues that were barely imaginable half a century before. They included HIV/AIDS and the proliferation of organizations and campaigns committed to women's rights. While diverse viewpoints could be discerned even in colonial debates if the analyst looked hard enough (see Englund 2015c:242–43), diversity itself had become far more of a public concern at the dawn of the new millennium. Yet by comparing the positions different radio personalities took, it is possible to do more than simply demonstrate how polarized the gender debate had become. The above observations on the male presenter's apparently contradictory dispositions indicate what lies ahead in this chapter. Feminists and patriarchs at Breeze FM could be antagonistic, but when each of them is considered in turn, surprising nuance begins to emerge, with interesting consequences for the ways in which the freedom of speech could be deployed to pursue justice in gender relations.

Paternal Feminism

Governmental and nongovernmental authorities tasked with promoting gender equality rarely came to Gogo Breeze's notice on his excursions in villages and townships. A division of broadcasting labor was implicit in his mandate to record the voices of the sundry ordinary folks featured on programs such as *Landirani Alendo* (*Welcome Visitors*), *Makalata* (*Letters*), and *Chidwi Pa Anthu* (*Interest in People*). Whether or not they were sponsored by NGOs or the government, programs on agriculture and on gender were the domains in which officers' perspectives on gender were broadcast. An exception in Gogo Breeze's remit was the episode of *Landirani Alendo* where he broadcast some of his encounters at a training meeting in Lusaka.[5] Called to attend the meeting along with other Zambian broadcasters in order to learn about the topic of gender, Gogo Breeze introduced one of the governmental organizers by saying, "Mother, here in Lusaka, at Mika Hotel, I am wondering that you spent a long time at school to prepare the studies for which we have come here. I heard 'gender,' 'responsibility,' whatever our friends speak in English. People especially want to know your name to start with."[6]

Although respectfully convivial with the organizer and with the lecturers he also encountered during the program, Gogo Breeze established through this introduction a certain distance between his interlocutor and listeners. The radio elder had been transported to an unfamiliar place to be exposed to foreign terms in the presence of highly educated women. Trying to pronounce the English words "gender" and "responsibility," he gave the listeners a flavor of the language that fitted the exotic ambiance of a hotel in the capital city. After saying her name, the organizer explained the purpose of the meeting to be to train Zambian journalists on involving both women and men on their programs about development. Gogo Breeze sought clarification: "At first in the past, were there no stories about women when reporters wrote their stories as well as their programs?"[7] The organizer replied by mixing English and Chinyanja: "There were not so many stories about women especially in Zambia, so we want that man and woman are on the same, same level. Equal, equal."[8] It was as though the desired new state of being would be so novel that Chinyanja could not capture what the English words "same" and "equal" conveyed. Gogo Breeze encouraged her and others he encountered at the meeting to speak their own languages if they were unaccustomed to Chinyanja. "Your Chinyanja is extraordinary, had it been Chibemba," he started to say but was interrupted by the organizer's use of the English-language slogan for national unity, "One Zambia, one nation."[9]

Gogo Breeze's characteristic vigilance with linguistic expressions made apparent what has, along with gender relations, been a long-standing subject of controversy in Zambia: the would-be elite's penchant for English that both asserted national unity and set them apart from the masses who spoke vernaculars. In a subtle way, the distance he created between his listeners and the gender trainers also alluded to a hierarchy that was distinct from the one that the radio elder himself promoted. While it was possible in the grandfatherly hierarchy to seek his advice and intervention in the spirit of intimacy and trust, the paternalistic hierarchy of gender trainers left little room for two-way communication. Yet it was not only in the capital city's hotels where paternalistic feminism could be detected. It also characterized the programs prepared by one of Breeze FM's own presenters, whose short-lived association with the station indicates why this form of feminism had few prospects of meeting popular demand.

The feminists and patriarchs at Breeze FM had been recruited on the basis of their local talent just as the station's other presenters had been.

It was their fluency in Chinyanja and other languages spoken in Eastern Province that formed an important part of their capacity to communicate. Yet Deliwe Ngoma's linguistic skills—in her case Chinyanja and Chitumbuka as well as English—were not enough to establish the kind of rapport with her listeners and her colleagues that had contributed to the success of Gogo Breeze's radio personality. A large middle-aged woman with a resounding voice and infectious laughter, Ngoma shared with Gogo Breeze a late arrival in the world of broadcasting. She had spent twenty-seven years working as a nurse. What made her different from anyone else at the station, including its founder, were the many years she had been abroad. While working in Lusaka Province in the 1980s, the Provincial Nursing Officer placed her among those privileged few who stood the chance of entering government-sponsored schemes for further education. The opportunity availed itself in the form of training in pediatrics nursing in Edinburgh. Ngoma chose to stay on in Scotland after her course, followed by more nursing work elsewhere in the United Kingdom. She interspersed these periods of work with visits to Zambia, where she would also work as a nurse before moving abroad again. In her conversations with me, she explained her frequent stints abroad as necessary to her ambition to educate, as a single mother, her three children to a level that was out of reach for nurses in Zambia. When I interviewed her in 2012, she was of the view that the period she spent working in the United Arab Emirates in 2007 would be her last foreign stint. After a short stay there, she explained, "The heart said that I want to return home, not to return to Lusaka but to Chipata."[10]

Eastern Province, particularly the district of Lundazi, was Ngoma's *mudzi*, a word that translates as both "home" and "village." In actual fact, her schoolteacher father had taken the family to his various postings elsewhere in the province before settling on a farm far from Lundazi. There was no village to which Ngoma could have returned, and it proved to be more difficult than she had anticipated to create a sense of *mudzi* in Chipata. "It is very hard to establish yourself when you come from abroad," she sighed.[11] She described the suspicion that a returnee "would take our work."[12] "You work with all your heart [diligently], [but] they say, 'You are showing off.'"[13] After encountering such suspicions and resistance in the health profession, she took a short course to start her own business as a florist in one of Chipata's supermarkets. In order to advertise her business at Christmas, she decided to buy airtime on Breeze FM but lacked money to have her ad on air more than once. She therefore requested, through a female presenter who appears later in this chapter, an audience with Michael Daka, the founder-director, to discuss the possibility of getting more airtime on credit. When he heard about Ngoma's extensive professional experience, Daka instead suggested that she help the other female presenter prepare programs on cooking (*maphikidwe*). In Ngoma's own estimation, Daka was "impressed" with her performance and offered her the chance to start producing her own program series. She gave her series the title *Your Healthy Living* and dedicated it, largely in Chinyanja but also in English and Chitumbuka, to issues concerning maternal and infant health.

Apart from applying some of her knowledge as a nurse, Ngoma started to read the information she could obtain from aid organizations in Chipata and on the Internet. For example, she told me enthusiastically about the "holistic health" concept she had found in the information about the World Health Organization. It involved, she listed to me, "psychological, socioeconomic, physical, emotional, as well as spiritual health." At the same time, such enthusiasm for studying health-related matters did little to improve Ngoma's capacity to communicate with her provincial listeners or with her colleagues. Only a month into her employment at Breeze FM, I could observe tension arising between her and other presenters. She had started to receive feedback at the weekly staff meetings about her style of presentation which, to begin with, consisted of monologues that gave her programs the air of lecturing rather than interaction. She was instructed at the meetings by her more experienced peers to frame the programs as dialogues so as to make them sound more interesting. Although it was Ngoma's intent to invite speakers from aid and governmental organizations, she was unsuccessful in bringing them to the studio and assumed herself the role of an expert. As such, the programs sounded more like interviews than dialogues, not least because the interviewers worked with scripts she had prepared for them and showed little personal interest in the topics. They were young men working at the station, but Ngoma complained that the "boys" (*anyamata*) often claimed to be busy when she wanted to go into the studio to record her program. The following excerpts, from a program about breastfeeding,[14] give some sense of the stilted performances on *Your Healthy Living*. It is worth noting that in this case, the young man's lackluster reading of Ngoma's questions took place only a few days before he was suspended by Daka for impregnating a schoolgirl. While his offence was not known at the station when the recording took place, the irony of his involvement in a program on the welfare of mothers and their infants was not lost on staff members when they found out the reason for his suspension.

A notable feature of the scripts Ngoma prepared for her programs was not only their basis in her readings but also the status she accorded to herself as an expert. She announced Aunt Deliwe as her radio name, but the health professional's tone of voice was not eliminated. On this occasion, the young man introduced the topic and Ngoma by saying, "So, today we look into the problem of nutrition among children who are less than two years old. Aunt Deliwe, you know a lot about this issue; please explain to us."[15] Knowledge quickly became the key distinguishing factor in Ngoma's views on malnutrition among young children. She explained, "When we talk about malnutrition, we mean that the body is not receiving the food it needs to receive. Especially when there are children, if she has several children, she struggles a lot because the mother does not know how to prepare food and does not know how to find that food."[16] By referring to "malnutrition" in English while otherwise speaking Chinyanja, Ngoma already created the impression of a technical issue requiring a particular kind of expertise. This impression was reinforced by the young man's subsequent question and Ngoma's answer to it:

YOUNG MAN: Now, Aunt Deliwe, what is it that prevents the child from eating enough?

NGOMA: What prevents the child from eating enough are mothers who don't know how to feed the child well. That is why we want to inform the mother so that she knows.[17]

Here Ngoma adopted a point of view that was little different from the many governmental and NGO campaigns, from colonial to postcolonial times, to define motherhood as a site of intervention by nonkin experts.[18] The specter of malnutrition arose from mothers' lack of knowledge, never mind the intergenerational care that attended childbirth even among residents in Chipata town.[19] That some mothers may not have access to enough food was not mentioned, in spite of Ngoma's enthusiasm for the "holistic health" concept mentioned above that included socioeconomic dimensions. Yet Ngoma did not typecast her public of young mothers merely as ignorant village women, because she also had in mind the predicament of motherhood in urban areas. While expounding on the benefits of breastfeeding, she had the young man read out a question about that predicament:

YOUNG MAN: But Aunt Deliwe, there are mothers who work, who cannot breastfeed the child twenty-four seven. They buy milk from shops. What kind of problem is that?

NGOMA: There indeed is a problem. Mothers who work, there are many jobs where they give leave for them to be with the child, so that they may breast-feed him or her well. And, secondly, to add to that, the person who wants to have a child, what's important is that we don't want her to just give birth over and again. At school a girl child is already giving birth. That is why we want the person to make a plan so that when she has a child, she is in a well-established marriage. Don't just give birth anyhow.[20]

Ngoma managed at a stroke to combine advice to working women with admonishing schoolgirls against pregnancies. Just as her emphasis on mothers' ignorance left little space to reflect on the possibility that some of them found it difficult to secure enough food, so too did her statement about working conditions leave out the possibility that a great many of the jobs that were available to women did not make any such provisions for maternity leave. Those who were fortunate enough to get employment as professionals in government departments and NGOs were sometimes able to negotiate short periods of leave. By contrast, the vast majority of working women in Eastern Province were domestic servants or employed on short-term contracts (or without contracts at all) by commercial farms and agricultural industries. They belonged to the surplus people whose leave entitlements were subject to the employer's discretion, all too often undermined by the vast pool of unemployed or underemployed women competing for the same jobs.[21] Ngoma's warning to schoolgirls sounded an exhortation familiar from other programs on Breeze FM, including those run by Gogo Breeze, but her suggestion of rampant sexuality resulting in multiple unplanned pregnancies amplified the expert's tone with striking colonial and postcolonial resonances. Female sexuality risked running out of control unless there were experts like Aunt Deliwe to advise girls of the proper order of doing things.

If Ngoma's radio personality came across as rather overbearing on air, her demeanor at the station was no less immodest and contributed to her swift departure. Before the first month of her employment at Breeze FM was over, she announced that she had already submitted eleven proposals for sponsored programs to different organizations in Chipata. Each proposal seemed to identify a specific disease or health issue to be discussed by Ngoma and selected professionals in the studio. Although her proactive approach to her new career seemed to embrace Daka's plea for his staff members to bring in revenue, Ngoma quickly antagonized both her boss and her colleagues. At staff meetings, where deferential behavior was expected especially when Daka was present, she would dwell on the companies and organizations where she had sent proposals, declaring that she had in her sights a sponsor that would be bigger than the mobile-phone provider Airtel, then Breeze FM's key partner through advertisement and funding for a morning show. She was particularly enthusiastic about establishing a contact with an expatriate staff member at USAID, the international development agency of the United States government, who had introduced her to a project promoting the cultivation and use of sweet potatoes. "Vitamin A–rich yellow sweet potato" became something of a mantra for her, a phrase she could be heard repeating in her final days of employment as one solution to the province's problems with nutrition. "Sweet potatoes are sweet only when they start bringing us money," Daka remarked wryly at one staff meeting, without mentioning that his own farm had already benefited from Ngoma's contact through five complimentary bags of sweet potatoes. No program sponsorship was forthcoming, though, and Daka's patience was also tried by Ngoma's interventions in the presence of other staff members. When he announced his travel plans at a meeting, Ngoma pointed out that he had other commitments on those days. Daka replied curtly that he would perform his work before his travels. On another occasion, as he was leaving the meeting midway, Ngoma stopped him to ask publicly when he would be traveling in the coming week. Not only was such behavior exceptionally casual, it also undermined Daka's authority by asking him to divulge information that he liked to share with his staff at his discretion. Ngoma was eventually dismissed when the relationship between her and one young woman in the marketing department deteriorated to the point of verbal insult and aggression.

It would be wrong to assume that Ngoma faced her demise at Breeze FM solely on the basis of her failure to adapt to the station's particular organizational ethos. Although the failure did trigger her dismissal, it is also worth reflecting on the extent to which she advanced a similar paternal feminism as Gogo Breeze's interviewee earlier in this chapter. Whatever the sentiment that brought her back to Eastern Province, Ngoma's approach to her new career as a radio personality was based on the conviction that her medical expertise and her linguistic skills could surmount any communication problems after her long absence from the province. When describing her work to me, she often used the verb for announcing, *kumemeza*, for the type of activity she performed over the airwaves. Her feminism was paternal because it involved handing knowledge down in a manner that presumed to know what the public's deficiencies were. It was feminism none the less in its insistence on women's health and on their advancement through schooling, but its paternalism was revealed in the distance that Ngoma generated between her listeners and herself. Both she and

Gogo Breeze's interlocutor in a Lusaka hotel used the distance to announce rather than to engage. As such, the hierarchy they established was distinct from the grandfatherly hierarchy in which intimacy rather than distance constituted the foundation for communication. Announcing left no space for multivocal morality.

Provincial Feminism

Although she was the contact who facilitated Ngoma's first meeting with Daka, Glenda Matoto could not have been more different from Ngoma in her on-air and off-air demeanor. A mature woman herself, Matoto had begun to work at Breeze FM in 2009 upon her graduation from secondary school. She had returned to school as an adult with her husband's encouragement, after the birth of their children. She told me that she had wondered, "Where do I go now?" (*ndilowera kuti?*) before she heard about vacancies for part-time staff at Breeze FM. With no background in journalism and little experience of using her voice in public except as a member of her church choir, she found herself succeeding in the tests that the station had set to her and other applicants.[22] She described finding her "calling" (*maitanidwe*) when she started to prepare news and reports and was reading out news live on air from her second year onward. She was quickly promoted to a full-time position based in the programs department, but she continued to read news while assuming responsibility for a number of programs. Her remit was to produce and present programs about family life and various topics associated with women, such as on the programs *Maphikidwe* (*Cooking*), *Azimayi Angakwanitse* (*Women Are Able*), and *Zam'mabanja* (*About Families/Marriages*). These programs were either without sponsors or generated sporadic advertisement revenue, but as will be seen in the next chapter, she was also involved in NGO- and government-sponsored series on women's and children's affairs. The feminism she brought to bear on her radio work was less obviously tied to a particular profession than Ngoma's was. The pragmatic concessions she made especially when in debate with the station's self-styled patriarch also had much to do with her lifelong immersion in Eastern Province's social world. In sharp contrast to Ngoma, she had never traveled abroad and had lived all her life in Chipata District.

Matoto's personal trajectory from a poorly educated mother to a mature pupil in a secondary school made her particularly passionate about the program *Azimayi Angakwanitse*. She regarded it as her "big program" (*pologamu yaikulu*) and described to me the program's purpose to be to show how "although they are women, they are doing different kinds of development which can teach other women who are passive and thinking that they are not able to do anything in their lives. When they hear what their peers are doing, perhaps they can follow the example."[23] Her vision of connecting mutual strangers through broadcasting was clear, as was her appreciation of the lack of self-confidence among many women in the province. The format of the program involved chatting with women about their experiences within the broad theme of development (*chitukuko*). Although the lack of sponsorship prevented her from moving far beyond the confines of Chipata District, Matoto often carried out the recordings on site, whether in marketplaces, shops, or gardens, with their respective background noises contributing to the aural definition of a location. Among the issues highlighted on the program, always in terms of women's life histories, were gardening that had made it possible to acquire cattle and to educate children,[24] a return to school by a forty-year-old hospital cleaner who eventually took the examination at the same time as her child,[25] assiduous piecework (*ganyu*) in a township,[26] and the importance of educating girls.[27] By selecting the participants from the everyday contexts of township and village life, Matoto made expertise less prominent a feature on *Azimayi Angakwanitse* than it was on Ngoma's *Your Healthy Living*. The didactic tone came in various female voices, dialects, and languages rather than in the monotony of an expert's lecture. Female pride and potential were asserted by Matoto's interlocutors even when they urged, as they often did, girls and women to take formal education seriously. "Women, women, we are the nation of Zambia," one woman pleaded. "Women must be strong and not stay behind. Women are the ones who look after the house, women are the ones who look after children as well as men."[28]

It was this combination of pride in women's conventional roles in housekeeping and childcare with uplifting tales of female advancement through education and business that gave feminism a flavor compatible with women's experiences in Eastern Province. Yet this provincial feminism was subject to challenge, even vitriol, as Matoto realized on the program about family life, *Zam'mabanja*. Its format had witnessed changes over the years, but by 2012 it had substituted responses to listeners' letters with a dialogue between Matoto and the station's self-styled patriarch, Mtwalo Nzima. The dialogic principle was regularly undermined by Nzima's commanding presence in the studio. Although Matoto often tried to talk back to him, sometimes to the point of acrimony, her role as the program's presenter made Nzima seem from the outset as the elder whose advice was being sought on various topics. Buttressing Nzima's elderhood was his identification as Ngoni, the ethnic identity associated with often violent migrations from Southern Africa in the nineteenth century (Barnes 1954; Langworthy 1975).

The format of *Zam'mabanja* involved Matoto welcoming listeners and Nzima to the program, followed by her explanation of the topic. The topics (*mitu*) could arise from the letters that the program received even though they were no longer read on the program but more often had been selected by Matoto herself from the topical issues she had encountered in everyday life and in the media. Just as Gogo Breeze's letters program was rarely based on its presenters reading and discussing the letters before going to the studio, so too was *Zam'mabanja*'s dialogue unrehearsed and based on the long-term collaboration between Matoto and Nzima rather than on any careful planning of what they should say in the studio. In her reflections on the program with me, though, Matoto made clear her dissatisfaction with it. She felt that Nzima's firm views required a "panel" that would represent "different sides" (*mbali zosiyanasiyana*) and "disagree" (*kutsutsa*) with him. Her efforts to counterbalance his views were indeed readily seized by Nzima as examples of metropolitan feminism. Its assertion of gender equality in the slogan "fifty-fifty," exhorting an equal share between men and women in all aspects of life and work, was an anathema to healthy marriages as Nzima saw them. The English word "gender" had become *jenda* and stood for the radical change that people like Nzima saw taking place in the relations between men and women.

Nzima's off-air personality had its paradoxes, as will be seen below, but his on-air personality as an Ngoni patriarch left no ambiguity about his views on gender relations. Expressed in his deep voice and in a mixture of Chinsenga and Chinyanja, his contributions sounded like they emanated from a venerable elder immersed in village life. The topics courted controversy and often entailed fervent moral discourse. They addressed, among others, weddings in rural and urban areas,[29] disciplined and undisciplined children,[30] the upbringing of unmarried parents' orphans,[31] and beer drinking.[32] Whether men should report incidents of domestic violence to the police was a topic that brought out particularly vividly the extent to which the notion of gender equality had incensed Nzima, with Matoto attempting in vain to substitute the polarized discourse with a more conciliatory tone.[33] The topic arose from high-profile campaigns against so-called gender-based violence in which women always appeared to be the victims and men the perpetrators. Should a man, Matoto asked in her introductory remarks, also report an incident to the police when he was attacked by his wife? As soon as Nzima began to talk, he asserted himself not as the advocate of a partisan perspective but as the one who was able to pronounce on the institution of marriage. He stated the proper order by remarking, "Before I answer this question, I should say that in every marriage/family, when it is a marriage, the most important thing in a marriage is respect. The husband should respect his wife, the wife should also respect her husband. What is it that brings quarrelling or fighting into the house?"[34] The measured tone in this initial remark was carried in Chinyanja, but the more heated the argument subsequently became, the more Nzima used Chinsenga, a language of his everyday communication and therefore more intimate to him than Chinyanja. As always, a part of his appeal on *Zam'mabanja*, the only program he contributed to, was his charismatic presence that both conveyed the patriarch's stern views and entertained the listeners with anecdotes and comical performances of fictional protagonists' voices, in this case a wife beating up her husband with a cooking pot. His charisma found no match in Matoto's more subdued personality and left her doubly disadvantaged in her attempts to counter his views.

In Nzima's interventions, it was a short step from the mutuality of respect to a fierce attack on the fifty-fifty agenda of current gender campaigns in Zambia. He endorsed men's prerogative to report domestic violence more as a revenge on this agenda than as a way of upholding the principle of gender equality. Fifty-fifty evoked tit for tat.

NZIMA: You started it yourself. Gender, gender is fifty-fifty. The husband must give a report when he has been beaten.
MATOTO: [*laughs*] Who will look after the house?
NZIMA: I will with the children.
MATOTO: Who will cook for you?
NZIMA: I will on my own.[35]

Rather than explaining the fifty-fifty agenda, Matoto challenged Nzima's reasoning with the notion of complementarity between the genders in which cooking and housekeeping were women's tasks. It was an instance of the provincial feminism that she broadcast on her other programs—female advancement through schooling compatible with pride in female domains of work—but when confronted by an unreformed patriarch, it risked becoming submerged in a polarized debate. Matoto did her best to avoid such antagonism by accepting the gendered division of labor. She was in agreement with Nzima even on the question of who the head of household was.

NZIMA: The important point is that the husband is the owner of the household=

MATOTO: =All right.

NZIMA: It is not the man who is courted; the woman is courted by the man.

MATOTO: Mm.

NZIMA: Now the gender you have is confusing women for nothing. Wanting to be the same as men.

MATOTO: Could we not talk about responsibilities, the rules of work which anyone can perform? Could we not talk about sharing power/abilities?

NZIMA: No, you want to say that you and I are the same. Now, we are not the same at all, because your work is to sweep, to cook, and to bathe. Sweeping in the house while I am at work.[36]

Nzima mentioned the grammatical feature, common to languages in the region, by which the verbs for courting and marrying are used in the passive tense for women and in the active tense for men. In his conversation with me, Nzima elaborated on this point by asserting that courting (*kukonshera* in Chinsenga; *kufunsira* in Chinyanja) is men's prerogative. During the program, in one of his verbal enactments of an illustrative case, Nzima went on to describe how the man of the house is a driver transporting heavy loads between Zambia and South Africa. Upon his return home and faced with demands for consumer goods, the husband says to the wife, "You are just eating" (*mukudya chabe*) and "You don't feel pain" (*simukumva kuwawa*), because all she ever does is to stay at home. Matoto, on the other hand, tried to establish a distinction between rule and responsibility in the household, but it took some time to make Nzima listen to her point of view. "Nzima, when we talk about work such as washing plates, cooking food, work in the kitchen, on the side of the kitchen women are the ones who rule. But when we talk about the rules of running the household, the husband is indeed the head of the household."[37] Nzima interrupted her by asserting, "In everything, the man is the owner; the woman comes behind" (*vonse mwanalume ndi mwini; mwanakazi awera pavuli*). The argument was becoming heated, and Matoto reprimanded Nzima for interrupting her.

MATOTO: Nzima, I want to finish; you interrupted me [lit., "you grabbed me by the mouth"].

NZIMA: Finish it, all right, I stop=

MATOTO: =When we are on the subject of rule, the head of the household is the husband=

NZIMA: =Mm=

MATOTO: =The one who rules everything. But when we come to responsibilities—for example you, Nzima, you have gone away from home. You will find that the wife is acting like an assistant manager, because the manager is away. I am the wife who says, ah, this we do like that, but when you come back one day, you will come back to be my husband. Can we say that I took over ruling there?

NZIMA: You see, let us talk about things so that they may be understood, mother. The main thing we should be talking about here is rules as they relate to marriage. We have the rules of marriage, but these days, gender has killed them, because the woman only wants to have more power than the man.[38]

"Gender has killed" (*jenda yapaya*) was the climax of Nzima's attack on the gender campaign, an accusation he fired out with a yell. It did little to reciprocate Matoto's conciliatory tone or even to accept her as an equal partner in their conversation. Nzima protected his position in the conversation as the one who was consulted for views and whose prerogative it was to explain issues, put forward by expressions such as "you see" and by defining the parameters of the conversation. The fifty-fifty agenda was, in this perspective, revealed to harbor not simply unrealistic expectations of sameness but actually a plot to transfer more power to women than to men. By contrast, Matoto, resorting to English, claimed no more than that the wife was an "assistant manager" when her husband was absent. To be sure, her apparent submissiveness and his violently assertive tone drew on widely circulating views and practices, not only with regard to the polarized gender debate but also as they were experienced and negotiated in the province. Wedding ceremonies often involved speeches or written materials that quite explicitly defined the bride as the bridegroom's helper in all matters to do with the family, health, and prosperity. At the same time, all this talk about women assisting men seemed curiously out of tune with the measure of economic and social leverage women could exert in the historically matrilineal Eastern Province. Access to land through the female line, and children's primary identification with their maternal rather than paternal kin, made the loud proclamation of patriarchy a rather shallow one. Nzima's off-air personality as a successful farmer, as is discussed below, was hardly as consistently patriarchal as his on-air personality might have suggested. He freely described to me how his wife was in charge of their farm's financial accounting. In her conversations with me, Matoto vented some of her frustration about Nzima by pointing out that she saw little trace of Ngoni heroism in him. Having married an Nsenga woman, she said, Nzima had become more Nsenga than Ngoni, evident in his limited linguistic skills that included only the odd archaic Chingoni words that all who were aware of the province's Ngoni revivalism could utter.

Despite Matoto's complaint that *Zam'mabanja* was "not going well" (*si-kuyenda bwino*), its format had not changed by the time I carried out my second period of fieldwork in Chipata in 2013. She found it difficult to recruit anyone with suitable gravitas to provide an alternative to Nzima's convictions.[39] Yet it is possible to gain from her very frustration a perspective on the complex circumstances under which speech about gender relations was supposed to flow freely. Nzima's patriarchy was never so misogynistic as to deny girls the opportunity to pursue their aspirations through schooling. Nor was Matoto's provincial feminism so well articulated as to present an ideologically coherent alternative to metropolitan feminism. Instead, both Nzima and Matoto were feeling their way in the midst of diverse influences and aspirations. Patriarchy polarized the gender debate in response to well-resourced campaigns for gender equality and, put forward by Nzima's forceful personality, made Matoto's willingness to negotiate sound like a series of regrettable concessions to the cause of male supremacy. What the fury of patriarchy on the radio risked rendering inaudible was the basis of provincial feminism in difference. The gender trainer interviewed above by Gogo Breeze emphasized the English words "same, same" and "equal, equal" by repeating them, but no amount of emphasis could eliminate the differences between men and women that were experienced to be as real as they were desirable. Matoto's provincial feminism took difference as the foundation upon which pragmatic changes in gender relations could be negotiated. Because the radio personality Nzima had developed could not accept negotiation, Matoto found the most rewarding outlet for her aspirations in the conversations with fellow women on *Azimayi Angakwanitse*. Defined as a women's program, it had few prospects of attracting male listeners to consider its perspectives on gender relations.

Power and Authority

As Matoto's private doubts about Nzima's credentials as an Ngoni elder suggested, there was more to his personality than met the eye (or the ear) through the airwaves. In his conversations with me, Nzima shared aspects of his own history that made the role he had adopted on the radio rather surprising. He had been a civil servant in the census department of the Ministry of Finance and had traveled the length and breadth of Zambia to collect statistical data. During these visits, he came across information about farming that served him well when he settled to farm in Eastern Province after his retirement. The visits also made him acutely aware of the country's linguistic and cultural diversity. While still living in Lusaka before retirement in the early 2000s, Nzima had been approached by an academic there to conduct interviews among ten Ngoni chiefs in Eastern Province. Nzima and his team became interested in achieving unity (*umodzi*) among the chiefs and came to revive the first-fruit ceremony *Ncwala*, since then taking place annually in February and presided over by the paramount chief Mpezeni in the company of various other Ngoni chiefs and notables. In light of his role in Ngoni revivalism, Matoto's comments on his Nsenga identity, acquired through his wife, were rather subversive.[40] Yet such comments did not exhaust the paradoxes in Nzima's life. One of the first things he said to me was that he was "pro-British." It alluded to his keen interest in all things British, ignited before national independence by, among other things, the radio broadcasts he had listened to with other Zambians outside a social club frequented by whites. It was to these broadcasts in the 1950s that he traced the origins of his lifelong support for the Manchester United Football Club. A devout Anglican, he had been married, he proudly explained to me, "in the bishop's house" as the first African to be so honored.[41] Add to all this his taste for Scottish whiskey and the impossibility of describing him only as an Ngoni revivalist is clear.

Nzima was well aware of the provocative nature of his contributions to *Zam'mabanja* and chose to speak in metaphors when the point he was making seemed to require them. During the above broadcast, he digressed to express what Matoto took as a defense of polygamy (*mitala*), a practice associated with Ngoni elders but increasingly rare in Eastern Province and not, as seen above, observed by Nzima himself. He declared, "The one who is strong can manage to cultivate two gardens, cultivating a vegetable garden there, cultivating a rain-fed field" (*wolimba n'wokwanitsa kulima minda iwiri, kulima dimba uko, kulima munda*). Matoto understood the provocation and asked about justice (*chilungamo*) in the arrangement but could not get Nzima to defend polygamy as such. He later explained to me that "what she wanted was for me to say that 'yes, people should have polygamy,' but I feared that they would start saying, 'Oh, Breeze FM endorses polygamy.'"[42] Such acts of self-censorship, based on Nzima's understanding that Breeze FM promoted progressive gender relations and did not want to alienate its various constituencies, could still achieve his aim of provocation by deploying metaphorical speech. Yet it would be wrong to suggest that Nzima, in certain respects a sophisticated provincial cosmopolitan, used his radio personality to provoke merely as a form of entertainment. Although on re-flection, especially with interlocutors like myself, he would laugh at some of his exchanges with Matoto, he never sought to belittle the convictions he expressed on air. Instead, and in contrast to his radio personality, who rarely made explicit references to the Bible, he would reinforce his justifi-cations based on tradition (*mwambo*) with biblical references: "When we read the Bible, it says 'husband'—do you understand me here?—'love your wife and you the wife, obey your husband,' but Paul did not say, 'Husband and wife, your powers are the same; please love each other,' or he said in English, 'A man must love his wife and the wife must submit to her hus-band.'"[43] It is a biblical passage Zambians often use to justify inequality in gender relations and one of the influences that connected Nzima's radio personality to the person he was outside the broadcasts.

It is important to draw a contrast between Nzima and Gogo Breeze in order to understand their different positions toward the various feminisms that Breeze FM mediated. The two men were amicable when they met and had collaborated on Nzima's very first assignments at Breeze FM to pro-duce programs about Ngoni culture. Elderhood was central to both of their radio personalities, but Gogo Breeze's lifestyle outside broadcasts was not as sharply different from what he projected on the radio as were Nzima's Anglicanism, pro-British attitude, and consumption of whiskey. In fact, Nz-ima shared more similarities with Ngoma, the ill-fated paternal feminist, despite their obvious differences. Both had been absent from the province for a long time. Both returned to the province with a desire to pursue par-ticular agendas, Ngoma as a health professional and Nzima as a farmer and Ngoni revivalist. Dialogue on air did not come naturally to either of them, determined as they were to let the province know of their respective preoccupations.[44] As such, one contrast between Nzima and Gogo Breeze as male elders on air lay in their divergent approaches to speech. Gogo Breeze did not promote dialogue as an encounter between equals, but dia-logue nevertheless made him thrive and helped him to achieve a sense of intimacy between unequal subjects. The contrast between the two elders was, in effect, between Nzima's power that could quite literally shout down any challenges and Gogo Breeze's authority that required acknowledge-ment and accommodation of different viewpoints.

When talking to me, the female members of staff at Breeze FM often compared the two elders in ways that were favorable to Gogo Breeze. "He can change his thoughts" (*amatha kusintha maganizo awo*) was one descrip-tion of his capacity to accommodate other people's views. Yet from Gogo

Breeze's point of view, the grandfatherly prerogative to have the last word had to remain intact even when he adjusted his position on various issues. The previous chapters have indicated the resources he had at his disposal to protect his status when facing challenge, from his quick-witted deployment of idioms and proverbs to his good-natured humor. Another advantage he had was to edit out before broadcast those interjections and exchanges that undermined his authority. In his studio work, the so-called granddaughters who read listeners' letters for him varied greatly in the extent to which they sought to insert their own views into the matters raised by the letters. Gogo Breeze also addressed the granddaughters in different ways according to their own personalities on air. When Matoto read letters for him, he did not address her as granddaughter (*mdzukulu*) but as mother (*mayi*) and would engage her on issues appropriate to her mature character, such as marriage and female initiation ceremonies. Young women featured on the program were sometimes referred to as girls (*atsikana*) by the grandfather, but not all of them were content to merely defer to grandfatherly authority. Pauline Phiri, whose vocal opinions on mill owners appeared in chapter 2, was the most articulate and self-confident of these young women, clearly in the habit of regarding her role on the letters program as virtually equal to Gogo Breeze's in seeking answers to listeners' queries and complaints. Although their exchanges never became as acrimonious as those between Matoto and Nzima, Gogo Breeze would often say with a sigh, "This one!" (*uyu!*) and point to Phiri when they emerged from the studio after an intense recording session. Talking back to the grandfather seemed to come naturally to her, not least when the topic was gender relations.

Younger than Ngoma and Matoto, Phiri brought yet another style of feminism to the airwaves. In many respects compatible with Matoto's provincial feminism, hers was also committed to the institution of marriage as well as to female advancement through education. Apart from reading news and serving as an announcer, Phiri also contributed to programs designed for female listeners, including her own program titled *Kupirira M'banja* (*Persevering in Marriage*). There she interviewed women about their experiences of marriage, usually with a view to providing uplifting examples of women surmounting difficulties in their marital lives. Although her voice was obviously younger than the other two feminists', she did not present herself as someone who was too young to be married. As such, she carried some authority to talk about marriage, but the register in which she did so was different from Matoto's. Phiri came across as her younger version through her more direct speech patterns that often sought not so much to reconcile different viewpoints as to champion a female perspective. She also exuded a greater degree of ambition, having joined Breeze FM as a part-time sales representative in 2005 and having left it as a popular radio voice with full-time employment in 2009. She cited to me career prospects as her reason to take up a post as Information Officer at the Chipata branch of the Farm Association, but she was eventually able to combine this post with more part-time broadcasting on Breeze FM. By 2013, she had resigned from both responsibilities to accept an offer from the ZNBC to join its Chinyanja team in Lusaka. From then on, she could be heard reading news on the national radio.

It was particularly her interventions on the letters program that Gogo Breeze was inclined to excise in order to safeguard his grandfatherly authority. At the same time, as I was able to observe when I was with them in the studio, her comments and questions did shape the responses that went on air in Gogo Breeze's voice. An example comes from the same broadcast as was discussed in chapter 1 with regard to the controversy over maize husks.[45] Although Juliana Banda also contributed to debating a letter about a mature man leaving behind his wife and children for his girlfriend's sake, Phiri read out the letter and played a more active role in getting the grandfather to respond to it in a particular way. She gave an account of the letter's contents without commenting on its rather poor structure and expression (see figure 10). When the subject of the letter was described as having maize flour (*ufa*) in his hair, Gogo Breeze interjected, "Like me!" (*monga ine!*), in a familiar allusion to gray hair (*imvi*) as one of his favorite idioms for his age. The interjection survived his subsequent editing, establishing a degree of similarity that later became a basis for Gogo Breeze's direct appeal to the man. Phiri went on to say that the letter was about the letter writer's friend, whom he accused of prostitution (*uhule*). The man had stolen a car from his workplace, leaving his wife and children to struggle on their own, and had built a restaurant for his girlfriend to run. The initial debate in the studio, not broadcast on the program, revolved around the opposing views that Phiri and Gogo Breeze expressed on the matter. While Phiri had no doubt that the story was true and that the man had to be condemned, Gogo Breeze maintained that it could be based on hearsay (*khambamkamwa*). Both granddaughters sensed the specter of polygamy in this case and wanted to reject it in the strongest terms. "I don't want to be the second or the third" (*sindifuna kukhala wa* two *kapena wa* three), Banda declared. As always, Gogo Breeze gave no indication that he might endorse polygamy, but the women in the studio would not let him begin his response as long as he appeared to be taking the issue too lightly. Phiri kept interrupting him with her own views on the matter until she said sharply, "Grandfather, don't take just one side on this matter" (*agogo, musangotenge mbali imodzi pankhani imeneyi*). The following response then ensued, but between its first sentence and the rest was nearly three minutes of argument that did not end up on the program:

> I like to avoid hearsay. Perhaps what we can do is to help this fellow. If it is true that he caused his children and wife problems when he saw a young woman, he made a mistake. The young woman will leave him; the property he gave to this new woman will not stay his own. We are often talking about these things, and when stories like this reach here, they cause embarrassment. The one who wrote us the letter, yes, he did well, but let us all help one another, women, men. Let us watch carefully together. We must not drink water from many different wells, because by drinking water from many wells, we bring problems to our body and then we will go to the grave before the time is ripe. You, mister, who built a restaurant for the girlfriend, you made a mistake. What about the children you gave birth to with the woman who accompanied you when you came out of the bachelor's hut? What did you leave for her? C'mon, let's be careful, these are strange stories. I am pleading, ehe. Ah, you people, you, ah.[46]

The speech shared many common features, both in the message it conveyed and in the idioms through which it did so, with Gogo Breeze's other responses to cases of adultery and infidelity. He juxtaposed a long-standing relationship with the whimsical affair in which the young woman would eventually leave the man with the property he had used to help her. The word *kamoye* for the young woman summoned a girl in her puberty, possibly a virgin, rather like the word for a female initiate, *namwali*. By contrast, Gogo Breeze used the word *gowelo* to underline how far back the man's relationship with his wife went—all the way to the bachelor's abode from where his marriage to this woman had released him. He had, in other words, achieved his adulthood with the woman he had now left to struggle alone with their children. Gogo Breeze's moral perspective on the case had this betrayal of a long-term relationship in focus, but he also tended to add to such cases a warning against promiscuity as a source of disease. "Drinking from many different wells" alluded to promiscuity, but in another common turn of phrase, he also emphasized that both men and women should do their part to avoid destructive behavior. Although he ended by addressing the man directly, and accused him quite sharply of making a mistake,

Gogo Breeze often sought to convey a sense of balance in his judgments by calling on both women and men to consider their behavior.

The women in the studio chuckled to express their delight at the angry tone with which Gogo Breeze ended his response. By attributing responsibility to the old man, he also rejected the misogynistic impulse to blame the young woman for the affair. Such reasoning appeared to be in line with

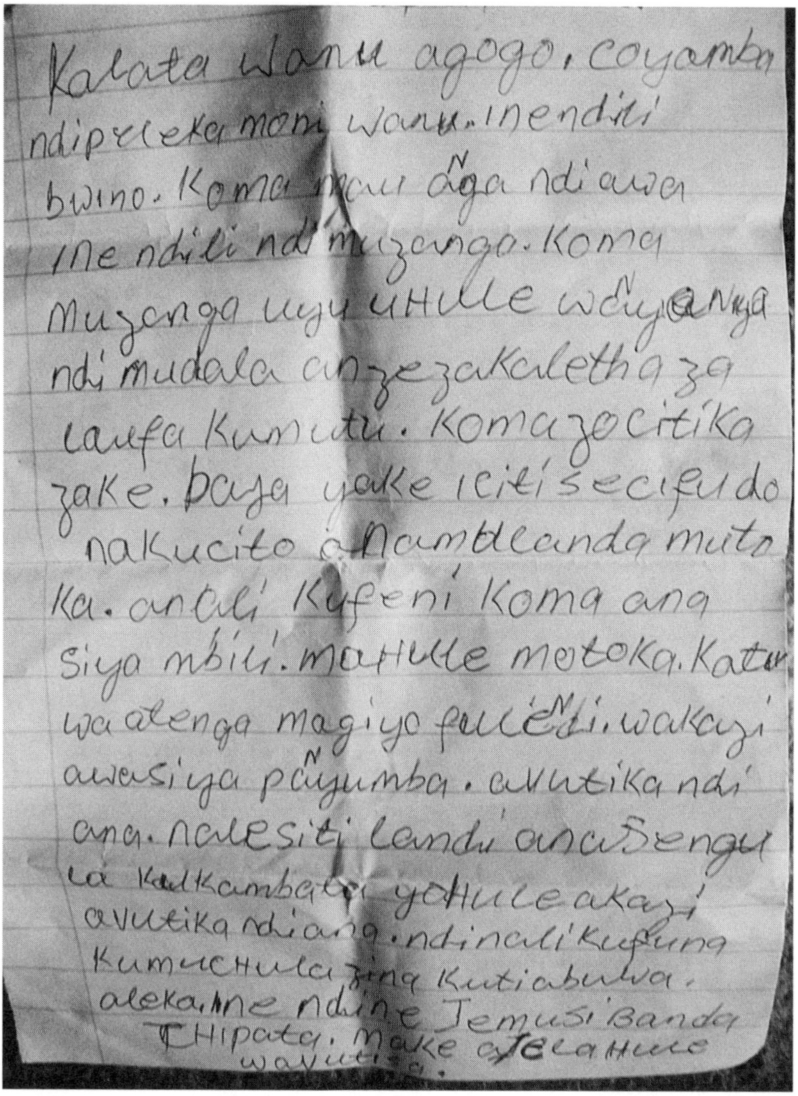
Kalata wanu agogo. coyamba
ndipeleka moni wanu. inendili
bwino. Koma nanu ŋga ndiawa
ine ndili ndi muzanga. Koma
muzanga uyu uHulle wdiyanga
ndi mudala anzezakaletha za
laufa Kumutu. Komazocitika
zake. baja yake iciti secifudo
nakucito anambleanda muto
ka. anali Kufeni Koma ana
siya nbili. maHulle motoka. Katu
waalenga magiyo fulendi. wakazi
awasiya pnyumba. avutika ndi
ana. nalesiti landi anaSengu
la Kalkambala yoHule akazi
avutika ndiana. ndinaliKufuna
KumucHula zina Kutiabulwa.
aleka. Ine ndine Jemusi Banda
CHipata. make ofelaHule
wayutsa.

FIGURE 10

the letter writer's intent to call the man a prostitute. In the subsequent exchange that was also broadcast, Phiri expounded on the self-destructive behavior the man was seen to indulge in:

PAULINE PHIRI: That is true, grandfather. In a person's life, everything has its time=
GOGO BREEZE: =You see now=
PAULINE PHIRI: =This old man can see that at the moment he is doing well, but when the day comes, everything will be revealed.[47]

In his final remarks, Gogo Breeze started to appeal to the wife's forgiveness, but Phiri made one more intervention to assert a female perspective, also broadcast as a conclusion to discussing this letter:

GOGO BREEZE: I would like to ask the wife to forgive that old man. Perhaps after the way we have talked, he can go to sleep at home.
PAULINE PHIRI: She has forgiven already, because this wife is strong when she is still in the house, while it is the old man who has to change.
GOGO BREEZE: Tell him.
PAULINE PHIRI: I told already. Should I carry on here?
GOGO BREEZE: Old man, you are causing us embarrassment. You see, grandfather is failing to speak because of your shameful story, ah![48]

Gogo Breeze was "failing to speak" not simply because he was scandalized by the case, but because he identified himself as the old man's peer, both of whom had gray hair. His doubts about the story's veracity had initially made him reluctant to speak, but what he eventually said was influenced by the two granddaughters who were with him. Such influence, coming as it did through a rather sharply worded argument, could not be put on air lest it would have undermined grandfatherly authority. What the example illustrates are some of the reasons for Gogo Breeze's popularity among his female colleagues and listeners. Just as when he provided a respectful and soothing partner for women to express their views on mill owners in chapter 2, so too did the broadcast response to this letter enable abandoned women to find sympathy on the airwaves, emanating from an exemplary elder who would identify wrongs irrespective of whether the perpetrator was a man or a woman. In a provincial public culture saturated with a polarized gender discourse, such wisdom had a distinct role to play. It sounded different from the roars of power with which Nzima drowned challenges to his male perspective. Yet the sound of authority was not as exclusively an elder's achievement as the edited broadcasts may have suggested. By allowing himself to be swayed by argument, Gogo Breeze based his judgments on negotiated authority. The morality he advocated was multivocal rather than patriarchal.

The Marital Market

A recent study on Zambia's Copperbelt finds that "gender-status inequalities have weakened with prolonged exposure to information that contradicts gender stereotypes, and with collective reflection upon these shared experiences" (Evans 2014:996). The finding highlights the economic imperative of relaxing the expectation that in these urban areas women should live up to the ideal of a housewife. By observing women engaging in tasks and occupations that used to be male preserves, people on the Copperbelt appear to have revised their views on what women can do. Eastern Province, despite its more rural outlook, has not been spared the increasing pressure on both men and women to generate income. It may be one reason for why Breeze FM's diverse commentators on gender relations converged on the need for girls to attend school. Yet the diversity—and, at times, the polarization—of their viewpoints also indicates how "exposure to information" is mediated by various competing registers of speech by which publics are summoned, from the campaigns for gender equality to alternative feminisms and paternalisms on the vernacular airwaves. Within this diversity, gender stereotypes may not so much be weakening as becoming recast, especially by those women who remain proud of their association with care and domestic work while pursuing new opportunities outside the home.

As has been seen, being married was, along with schooling, another taken-for-granted aspiration among the opposing views on gender relations that Breeze FM mediated.[49] In contrast to the view expressed in B1's song with which this chapter began—that "old virgins" faced a diminishing marital market—and to Nzima's equally rigid ideas of what marriages should look like, Gogo Breeze engaged with the widespread desire among women and men alike to be married.[50] Although in some parts of Eastern Province marital payments from the bridegroom to the bride's family, known as *lobola*, continued to be observed, many marriages, especially those that were not first marriages, arose from a range of far less formalized arrangements, sometimes involving few others than the couple themselves. Divorce and death were common and, as in the past in this region, made remarrying a somewhat unremarkable feature of the social world.

At the same time, B1's imagination of marriages as taking place within a market found a rather concrete instance in Gogo Breeze's efforts to facilitate romantic ties. Virtually every broadcast of the weekly letters program (*Makalata*) contained one or more requests for him to find a partner for the letter writer. This service became one of Gogo Breeze's signature activities, along with his investigations of listeners' grievances and his broadcasts of Chinyanja idioms, proverbs, and short stories. By 2012, on the founder-director's request, he had begun to charge a fee of ZMK 15,000 (just under US$3) for reading out such requests. It was the only fee associated with his programs, but Gogo Breeze went well beyond merely announcing the requests for partners. The marital market was a moral market in which the radio grandfather was not content to merely collect fees from his listeners but often added his own advice and reflections to what was being announced. Moreover, as is seen below, he even provided privacy for the men and women to meet after they had contacted him about the requests on the letters program. As such, Gogo Breeze considered himself responsible for a great many marriages in the province.

Two aspects of this service are particularly noteworthy. First, the marital market as mediated by Gogo Breeze was far more multifaceted than what B1's dichotomy of young and old virgins seemed to suggest. Second, while it was a moral market, it was not a moralizing market. Far from virginity being an issue in the letters that Gogo Breeze received, the real-life situations of HIV infection and children from previous liaisons loomed large in the letters. Since 2004, antiretroviral HIV treatment had become widely available in Zambia (Simpson and Bond 2014:1069–71), and the phrase "to drink medicine" (*kumwa mankhwala*) was in frequent use on the letters program to indicate the letter writers' HIV status. It was commonly understood that the medicine it referred to was the antiretroviral drugs and not any other medicine. The way in which the phrase appeared in letters requesting marriage partners made this association obvious, but it also alluded to the diminishing stigma associated with HIV infection and even to a degree of hope replacing fatalism (see Colson 2010:145; Johnson 2012). The radio elder's comments on letters using this phrase carried no trace of a moralizing discourse on sexuality. On the contrary, he could use the letter writer's admission of taking medicine to address his or her life prospects more generally. A typical instance was when he deemed the person requesting a partner to be too young to marry. After encouraging female listeners to come forward to see whether a twenty-five-year-old letter writer had any appeal to them, he proceeded to make a comment that cast some doubt over the wisdom of marrying at that age.[51] Using one of his favorite idioms for the wherewithal that a man starting a family ought to have, he wondered whether the letter writer had a blanket (*gombeza*) to cover himself and his bride. He seized on the letter writer's antiretroviral treatment as an opportunity to rethink his priorities:

> What is clear is what we are saying here: twenty-five years are too few. He should continue his studies to finish them. When he has finished in the college, he can go elsewhere to marry, because to be drinking medicine does not mean that his life has ended. People who are drinking medicine live many more years than those who are not drinking medicine.[52]

Rather than being content with merely announcing requests for partners, Gogo Breeze pursued the grandfatherly prerogative to pronounce on the issues that were drawn to his attention. It may have been rather more service than a listener looking for a partner was asking for—the abovementioned man had made no mention of how much education he had—but it also imbued the marital market with moral considerations without moralizing on people's past sexual encounters. In fact, the broadcast that contained the above letter also had two others that illustrate the range of circumstances and responses that shaped the marital market on Breeze FM. The next letter was from a twenty-eight-year-old mother of two looking for a husband. The granddaughter reading out the letter remarked, "She is saying that her status is that she is drinking medicine, so she is writing that any man who is on medicine as well as has employment, she says she could make a family with him. She has enclosed her picture and phone number and is a good-looking girl."[53] The practice of sending pictures along with letters was common, especially when the objective was to find a partner, and it contributed to the way in which Breeze FM accommodated multiple media in its interactions with its listeners, such as letters, pictures, and mobile phones (compare Kunreuther 2014:202). In this instance, Gogo Breeze referred back to the previous letter and regretted that the age difference was unfavorable to matching the two letter writers. Building on the unmentioned expectation that the man should always be of the same or higher age than the woman, he responded by concluding, "But let us just say that if there are men who have more years than this woman, they can come to see this picture and maybe they can agree to make a family."[54]

The high frequency with which drinking medicine was mentioned in letters seeking marriage partners made it a commonplace for those without HIV to also state their status. Yet the complications of everyday lives affected their marital prospects too. In the above broadcast, the third letter for the marital market came from a widower who had lost his wife in a road accident. The granddaughter introduced the letter by saying, "The man writing this letter says he is thirty-seven years old and that he wants a trustworthy and beautiful wife."[55] The granddaughter also affirmed, "He does not have the virus" (*alibe kalombo*)[56] and read out the letter's statement that its writer did not have the "disease of HIV" (*matenda a* HIV). The man described himself as being employed in an office in Chipata town and, alone with two children, welcomed marital candidates who had children of their own: "Please, grandfather, if it is possible to find a woman I can make a family with, and she has two children or one child, we can look after each other in my family."[57] Uninterested in having a housewife despite being employed in an office himself, the letter writer also specified that he was looking for a wife who traded in any of Chipata's markets. His final line was to praise Gogo Breeze for his services: "Grandfather, may God bless you because you make very many families."[58] Gogo Breeze responded by making public his offer of privacy to couples considering their marital options:

> If you like him, come over. A little shy mouse died in the hole. For if you just say, "Ah, he is here in Chipata; I cannot go," you make a mistake. If you come to see him, my girl, and when you have seen him, he will tell me, I will give you a place, a very private place, eh, in the middle of my household, behind the maize. After you have taken your time to discuss, when you have finished everything, you have agreed, I will tell you what you should do next. Women, there are many of you engaged in markets in compounds; you have no husband; the husband has been found. He is at work; he wants a woman who works at a market so that he can make a family with her.[59]

Gogo Breeze used a well-known proverb to warn against undue shyness. Just as the mouse died because it did not dare to leave its hole in good time before the hunter came, so too could a woman hesitating to see a man in the same town miss out on an opportunity to marry. The interplay between distance and intimacy came in several forms in this short speech. The prospect of courtship in the same town carried the risk of being revealed before the couple was ready to make it public. In response, the radio grandfather offered both intimacy and privacy. By addressing the female listener as "my girl," he sought to establish trust, further enhanced by opening the door to his household for the couple to meet, as he put it in English, in "a very private place." The reference to a place "behind the maize" was to the side of the granary that typically faced the household's edge, used for private conversations away from the spaces of socializing within the household. The radio grandfather also alluded to being available beyond this initial encounter by advising them, if all was well, what to do next. It would, Gogo Breeze explained to me later, involve encouraging the couple to approach witnesses to their prospective marriage, although he rarely had the time to monitor the next steps beyond this advice. At any rate, the service he offered again went well beyond mere announcing against a fee. It was another instance of mass-mediated intimacy in which a vast public was addressed in the intimate register of "my girl" and assured of privacy when reacting to the call over the airwaves. Privacy also set the limits of grandfatherly advice, because it was never Gogo Breeze's inclination to foretell which encounter would result in marriage. Within the parameters of compatible age, previous marital history, HIV status, and other such considerations, the ultimate arbiter was always the romantic pull between the couple, who were left to establish its extent on their own. As such, Gogo Breeze ended his response to this letter by declining to help with the letter writer's request for a beautiful woman: "But on beauty, he will have to see it for himself. If a woman comes, we will invite him to see if she is beautiful. It is he who can see if she is beautiful, because what I see as beautiful and what he sees will be different."[60]

Gogo Breeze's efforts at facilitating marriages put forward rather more complexity than what either B1 or Nzima allowed for in their different registers. The letters he received showed the illusory nature of B1's expectation that women married only once. They also revealed the range of issues to be negotiated between women and men in search of marriageable partners, in contrast to Nzima's assertions that it was the man who was the head of household and the active one in courtship. Many of the men writing to Gogo Breeze appeared to be looking for not only a romantic tie—a "beautiful woman," as in the letter above—but also a partner with her own contribution to household economics. At the same time, while the tenacity of marriage as an institution was by no means a result of Gogo Breeze's preferences alone, his efforts in the service of this institution may be interpreted as setting certain limits to the acceptable form of sexual relationships. The above letter's request to find a partner among women engaged in market trade was readily seized upon by the radio elder, who remarked on the abundance of market women without husbands. The implicit reference was to a long-standing male anxiety over economically independent women being particularly loose in their sexual morals, against which the institution of marriage carried the promise of establishing a proper order in relationships.[61] Yet Gogo Breeze's contribution in this instance was no more than to ride the mainstream wave of support for marriage. By allowing people with diverse personal circumstances to seek their fortunes on the marital market, he mediated free expression about relationships between men and women in a way that some of the more narrowly cast views described in this chapter did not.

SIX

Children's Voices

During one of his excursions, Gogo Breeze asked questions about children who beg for money and food. "There are certain things that happen in other places. I don't know if they happen here at your place in Lundazi, especially among those of you who are in the market. You are selling; you find that a young child walking down the street starts to beg, 'Father died, mother died, [or] they went to Malawi,' but it is the mother of the child who sent him/her to beg. Do such things happen here at your place in Lundazi?"[1] The market vendors he was chatting with at a rural trading center all corroborated Gogo Breeze's findings from other areas. One man added to his description of children's claims the assertion that the parents were in prison. Another man initiated a discussion about the causes of such wild claims. "It is true what my friend is saying. Children pose as street kids, but the parents indeed exist. That's the problem, but the problem is about their parents. They are the ones who cause this problem. The mother has nothing; the father is at a beer party. Yes, the problem exists; that's true."[2] A woman added, "It is true: children called street kids exist here at Lundazi Market Square. They are children whose parents are sometimes at a beer party at dawn. For the children to stay alone at home with hunger, it is a problem. That is why they come here to the market and start begging."[3]

At issue was more than an effort to expose cynical manipulation in the guise of destitution. Rather than being cold-hearted spectators of children's begging, Gogo Breeze's interlocutors were concerned to allocate responsibility for the predicament. Behind every child begging, they suggested, was an adult causing their unacceptable behavior, whether by sending them out to beg or by neglecting their parental duties to the extent that children were pushed to the streets to seek assistance. For his part, Gogo Breeze did not solicit the views of children who begged. He did sometimes broadcast encounters with young children, such as when he engaged them on the *Landirani Alendo* (*Welcome Visitors*) program in playful banter about what they might have learned at a nursery or school. The exchanges entertained by putting on air childish voices making childish points, but when he addressed youths, as was seen in chapter 3, he could substitute grandfatherly playfulness for grandfatherly reprimand. Responsibility grew with age, as did the expectation that a young person could speak for him- or herself. Multivocality assumed maturity—at its apotheosis the radio elder himself, who could, as in the maize-mill controversy in chapter 2, give expression to multiple voices in his own person. Gogo Breeze's approach to young children—attentive and affectionate whether on air or off and yet confined to childish concerns—was consistent with how he pursued the issue of begging. A serious social problem required a serious look at the adults whose obligation it was to care for the children found begging in the streets.

Even the plight of orphans (*ana a masiye*, lit., "children of the place where death has occurred"), a matter of public concern in the wake of the HIV/AIDS pandemic, could not distract from the need to identify responsible adults.[4] Here, as the above comments by market vendors indicated, children's voices were subject to similar views by the radio elder and the people he encountered during his excursion. No child was imagined to act entirely on his or her own accord, just as his or her requests to be assisted by strangers were bound to conceal their origin in an adult's machinations. The contrast is clear on the weight placed on giving children a voice in the promotion of their rights. Such promotion gained fresh momentum in 1989 when the UN Convention on the Rights of the Child declared in its Article 13 that "the child shall have the right to freedom of expression." Advocacy and research proliferated to establish children as "competent social actors" (James 2007:261) and so did the problems associated with such attempts.[5] The singular category of the child did nothing to identify historical, social, and biographical diversity among people defined as children by activists, officials, and academics. When children's voices were collected and put forward to advance particular policies or analytical commitments, basic questions to be asked about any such representations were not necessarily addressed, including whose voices were being represented, by whom, and why. Depending on the policy or moral position that the authors wished to take, children's voices could be inserted into a long history of Western imaginations of childhood as humanity bared of intrigue and conflict (see Malkki 2015:77–104).

This chapter is not the place to evaluate the extent to which the well-being of young people has been served by such moves toward representing children's voices. Rather, the aim is to take further the reflections on voice as a democratic capacity by investigating ethnographically how Breeze FM came to be situated in the mutually paradoxical currents of grandfatherly authority and high-minded advocacy with regard to children and youth. Children's rights, along with the controversies over gender relations discussed in the previous chapter, had become a matter of public concern in Eastern Province by the time Breeze FM went on air. In the above extract, the use of the English term "street kids" by Gogo Breeze's interlocutors indicated their exposure to new categories deployed in governmental and NGO campaigns. At the same time, Breeze FM was itself a key medium to stage these campaigns in Eastern Province. Despite its founder-director's strictures on NGOs organizing closed workshops in hotels rather than enabling his staff to go out in the field, the station did put on air a number of NGO-sponsored programs about children's rights. This chapter examines particularly the relationship between Breeze FM and one of its largest partners in this area. Plan Zambia, a part of Plan International which styles itself as "an international child-centered development organization," enlisted Breeze FM in the early 2010s to prepare two series of programs, the first with a focus on the girl child and the second with the aim of promoting child protection and participation. Off-air negotiations between the organization and Breeze FM's presenters indicated the close interest that the organization's officers took in every aspect of production and delivery. Although the scope for experimentation and spontaneity on Breeze FM's part was thus curtailed, the purpose here is not simply to give just another instance of NGO agendas overriding other concerns. Just as the debate on gender could speak to deeply felt convictions among the station's diverse presenters, so too did the radio campaigns on children's rights touch personally some of them.

Multivocality remained a feature of Breeze FM's airwaves despite this resonance of Plan Zambia's agenda with the experiences among some of its presenters. Gogo Breeze's approach to related issues is again important to investigate for the way in which he rejected, deliberately or not, many of the practices that characterized NGO-sponsored programs. Where Plan Zambia expected carefully staged encounters in which participants expressed views that had been agreed on prior to the recordings, Gogo Breeze broadcast more of the arguments that accompanied the encounters he facilitated. Where the voices on the NGO programs became rather monotonous in their convergence on a small number of key points, the radio elder actively solicited contrasting views by recognizing different interests among the people he spoke with. Underlying his achievement of multivocality was the firmness of his own views and the grandfatherly confidence with which he threw himself into argument with his diverse interlocutors. Rather than expecting a singular expression of an acceptable point of view, he used his own standpoint as a foil for other views. Toward the end of the chapter, the possible disconnect between Plan Zambia's mode of multivocality and the actual anxieties over children in Eastern Zambia becomes strikingly apparent during a riot in the trading center of Katete. The riot, sparked by the killing of a schoolgirl who was suspected to have fallen victim to a businessman engaged in occult practices, took place as the new series on child protection was being launched. The abstract discussion about children's rights in the studio contrasted with the urgency that many listeners felt about the incident as they called the province's radio stations. In the middle of this oversight and turmoil, Gogo Breeze's approach to the incident gave further insight into the relationship between free speech and moral authority.

Exemplary Girls

Because I Am a Girl / Chifukwa Ndine Mtsikana was the title of the campaign that Plan Zambia carried out in 2012 in Chadiza, the district where it concentrated its operations in Eastern Province. By sponsoring a series of radio programs in English and Chinyanja, it made the message of the campaign reach much further than one district. At the heart of the campaign was a focus on girls' schooling, not simply their access to it but their chances to continue with it if it had been interrupted by pregnancy. The policy by which schoolgirls had earlier been expelled when they became pregnant was modified by the government to encourage reentry after giving birth. A new policy thus in place, Plan Zambia's main objective was to spread awareness of it while at the same time warning girls against what the organization called early marriages. The agenda had little to say about broader policy questions, including the quality of primary education in provincial Zambia and the range of reasons behind high dropout rates among girls and boys alike.[6] The reentry policy enabled an emphasis on girls' own behavior and on so-called harmful cultural practices that included early marriages. Both emphases were present in the campaign over Breeze FM's airwaves, as they were in some of the encounters Gogo Breeze broadcast. Yet while the campaign's accusing finger appeared to be firmly pointed toward girls and their parents, it did not preclude identification with the cause among some of the presenters and listeners. The male presenter who appeared in the previous chapter as an admirer of B1's allegedly misogynistic song was involved in this series but never seemed particularly engaged with its message. By contrast, Glenda Matoto, the provincial feminist also introduced in the previous chapter, became its passionate advocate at Breeze FM.

Zam'mabanja, Matoto's signature program about family life, went on air without sponsorship during my fieldwork, but she rejected my suggestion that her work for NGOs such as Plan Zambia was somehow less meaningful to her than the production of her own programs. She asserted that she identified with the Plan Zambia programs "from the bottom of my heart" (*pansi pamtima wanga*) and felt "touched" (*kukhudzidwa*) by their topics. Alluding to her own modest educational background and to the didactic objectives of these programs, she said that she too learned many lessons through them (*ndimatenga maphunziro angapo*). By the same token, she was confident about her own value to organizations such as Plan Zambia because of her background both as a village woman and as someone who had gone back to school at a mature age. She admitted that the NGO had given detailed instructions on how to prepare the programs, but she thought it was natural for it to pay such close attention to the execution of what it sponsored, including the provision that Plan Zambia representatives had the prerogative of listening to the programs before they were put on air. At the same time, Matoto was not oblivious to the discrepancy between her conditions of work and those of her counterparts in the NGO. The only time when she could give these programs her full attention was when she was in the field recording their content. The editorial work in the studio, along with attending to NGO personnel who could pay impromptu visits to the broadcasting house, had to be accommodated within the busy daily schedules of other editorial work and newsreading. While she was trying to finish a piece of work before seeing the NGO worker who was waiting for her, I overheard her muttering to a colleague about NGO workers' access to allowances when they were out of the office. Yet she was hardly unique among Zambia's professional classes to move effortlessly from these critical observations to a thinly veiled desire to be employed by international organizations. Her current distance-learning course on journalism and public relations, she pointed out to me, could make her proven enthusiasm for advocacy all the more attractive to such organizations.

It was indeed this forward-looking attitude, buoyed by faith in formal education, that gave Matoto's work on these programs a personal flavor. When the *Because I Am a Girl* / *Chifukwa Ndine Mtsikana* campaign was launched on Breeze FM, Matoto was in the studio not as the presenter but as one of the mature women who served as "examples" (*zitsanzo*) of what girls could look forward to achieving if they focused on schooling.[7] Matoto was the first of the three women to tell her story. Delivered with some passion, it sounded like a testimony with unmistakably Christian themes of fall, repentance, and resurrection.[8] Matoto's schooling had gotten off to a good start. She had been selected to become subprefect in grade eight of primary school, followed by the promotion to become head girl in grade nine. Around that time, she earned the nickname Iron Lady for her resolve that left little time for boys. "Boys could not try to speak to me," she recalled. It was in grade ten that it all began to unravel. She attributed her downfall to her envious peers, who had seen how well she was doing at school and had begun to introduce her to the popular literature on romantic liaisons. A series titled *Love Principles* encouraged readers to write down their own thoughts on these matters, and Matoto was soon doing the same "nonsense" (*zachabechabe*) as her peers. Born in 1970, she first became pregnant in 1986. Far from acknowledging the prospect of a new life, she described the experience in morbid terms: "It was like I was digging a grave to bury myself." She was promptly expelled from school at a time when the reentry policy was not even imaginable. Moreover, the two pregnancies she had in rapid succession both resulted in premature births, evidence, she concluded, of her failure to follow the course that was best for her.

Matoto described her downfall not simply as an individual tragedy undoing whatever academic success she had been able to achieve. The downfall was situated in social relationships, from its origins in the machinations of her envious peers to the consequences it had for her standing both in her family and among her friends. She had started her testimony by noting her good Christian family background, but her early pregnancies had been received by her parents as though she had made a "very big mistake," while her married brothers refused to see her in their houses. When during her visits to town she saw former friends from school, now in good employment, she sought to hide from their view. In the home village where she had returned to marry after the end of her schooling, no one seemed inclined to contemplate any further studies. Under these circumstances, the radio became her friend, and it was through Breeze FM that she first heard about the new reentry policy for girls whose schooling had been interrupted by pregnancy. She reminisced about radio personalities who had since left Breeze FM, but it was the encouragement from her husband that made it possible for her in 2005, after giving birth to five children, to go back to school and to start again the grade ten that had been interrupted. She described how her child was taking the examination in grade nine as she was taking it in grade ten. If the expulsion from school had been like her burial, the reentry was the moment when she rose from the dead.

She continued with schooling until grade twelve in high school and wrote her final examinations in 2007. Still living in the village as a small-holder farmer and the mother of young children, she wondered what to do next. When Breeze FM announced in 2008 that it was looking for part-time members of staff, Matoto, a keen listener, decided to apply. Her description of how she applied and how she received the good news of acceptance underlined the rural character of the world from which she pursued her ambitions. She explained that she had written her personal statement with a ballpoint pen, and after the station's initial message of acceptance, Gogo Breeze himself called her to congratulate. She was working in her garden then and told her listeners how she had thrown the hoe away in joy after talking to him. Perhaps the act had metaphorical significance by marking a decisive break from the tedium of smallholder agriculture. At any rate, the redemptive nature of schooling was made plain in Matoto's testimony. It was only fitting that after describing her death and resurrection, her concluding image for finding employment was ascension to heaven. She also likened schooling to a key that opens windows, after having described earlier how the return to school had opened her eyes. The triumph, no less than the fall, was embedded in social relationships, now in the realization that those former friends who had shunned her were again pleased to know her. The culmination of the testimony was Matoto's next academic pursuit, the diploma in journalism and public relations.

After helping to launch the series with this testimony, Matoto produced a number of programs based on her interviews in Chadiza District. The two main categories of her interviewees were schoolgirls and mature women who as advisers (*alangizi*) were tasked with sexual and reproductive education in villages. It was women in this role, also known as *anamkungwi* when in charge of girls' initiation ceremonies, who had become the foci of governmental and NGO concerns over early marriages and so-called harmful cultural practices. Although the actual advice that these women dispensed was not widely known, and at any rate would have been secret when transmitted in the context of initiations, organizations such as Plan Zambia seemed to regard the women as culprits in promoting early marriages by transmitting knowledge about sex that, the organizations seemed to assume, girls would be eager to put into practice. Comfortable with various aspects of village life and idioms, Matoto nonetheless embraced these assumptions on her programs for the series. Rather than adopting the confrontational style that sometimes characterized Gogo Breeze's broadcasts on the same subject, she carefully selected girls and women who would speak in ways that supported Plan Zambia's agenda and put forward a single clear message. Plan Zambia expected as much from these programs, but as mentioned, Matoto felt no resentment against the expectation that she should follow their instructions. Such was her faith in schooling as the key to a better life that an argument between different viewpoints seemed unnecessary to her. The voices she broadcast represented exemplary conduct rather than a diversity of perspectives and circumstances.

Dialogue and argument were far from the discursive registers of statements and question-and-answer interviews that Matoto broadcast. The following three statements, for example, came on air one after another on one of the programs:

> My name is Susan Phiri, and I am a girl. Let me comment on what the teacher said. Parents may try their best so that we won't become pregnant, to advise us, but we the children do not hear what the parents say. Thank you.[9]

> My name is Ester Banda in Jolani Village. Let me comment that the advisers teach us so that it enters our ears, but let me comment that what the advisers tell us, it reaches our ears, but we don't do anything with it. We, the children, don't have ears. The advisers try to advise us, but for us the children to do anything, we just lack respect. We don't have respect so that we would obey parents. Thank you.[10]

> My name is Justina Mbewe, and I am a girl. Let me comment on what the advisers said about marriages, about pregnancies. We the children don't have ears, but parents/elders advise us, they really advise us by insisting that children must not get pregnant or be married quickly before the age is enough. When you get married before you are old enough, you find lots of problems; you won't be able to take care. Thank you.[11]

The formulaic nature of these statements betrayed their rehearsed rather than dialogic origins. Much in line with the emphasis placed on reciting and memorizing in Zambian schools (compare Serpell 1993:93; Simpson 2003:87–88), the girls had a previously agreed comment to make, their stilted performances befitting the classrooms where Matoto recorded them. Notable was also their self-identification as "girls" on a program devoted to the girl child and their attribution of blame to themselves. In the same spirit, the mature women whom Matoto interviewed were absolved of blame when they themselves asserted the value of schooling. One response to Matoto's question of "How do you know the project *Because I Am a Girl* brought by Plan Zambia?" went thus:

> Thank you, presenter. I know the project by Plan Zambia called *Because I Am a Girl* as follows. When it arrived, we received it with both hands. Ah, they did well to bring us the project to teach our children, because there are young children, fourteen years old, who are pregnant, and we try hard to advise these children that "you should not be doing that." Let us help together my adviser colleagues to enlighten children that "don't follow those things; through studying you will lead a good life in future. Don't rush to problems, because we as your parents have lots of problems: marriages, being beaten, being very oppressed if you haven't studied. If you don't study, you will find problems. Every little thing you will ask from men. You, the children, please study so that tomorrow your future will be good. You will also help us to be like me, an adviser." Thank you.[12]

A closer look at what the women and girls said to Matoto may qualify the impression created by the above quotes that all they did was to parrot the lines given to them by Plan Zambia. Despite the absence of the multivocal engagement that Gogo Breeze cultivated on his programs, some of the women and girls on Matoto's programs alluded to contentious claims that had the potential of reconfiguring gender relations. The woman quoted above mentioned the specter of unschooled girls having to ask from men every little thing they might need in life. Another woman on the same program made explicit the advantage that male pupils had when it was only girls who got punished for pregnancies. "Girls suffer in this country of Zambia. We explain to them that 'you girls, you have to listen to what we tell you. See, when there is a pregnancy among children, the male one who gave the pregnancy continues his studies, but the female one stops; that girl is left behind. The boy who gave the pregnancy is taking his future forward.'"[13] Even more radical in its implications was the point raised by a young woman who had returned to school after giving birth: "Even if you became pregnant like I did, you should not think of getting married. Let us return to school. Thank you, presenter."[14] Although not commented on by Matoto over the airwaves, such remarks on male children's relative advantage and on the possibility of not marrying when pregnant indicated more far-reaching reflections than Plan Zambia's focus on preventing early marriages and "harmful cultural practices" allowed for. In my conversations with her, I sensed that these reflections were almost too daring to Matoto as well, whose provincial feminism, as seen in the previous chapter, advocated opportunities for women within the conventions of marital life. While denying that she endorsed the idea of having children without marriage, she did think it was acceptable for young mothers to put their schooling before the expectation of being married.

Education and Its Discontents

A regular feature of the *Because I Am a Girl / Chifukwa Ndine Mtsikana* programs was the jingle in which a group of village women sang in praise of schooling. The choice it put forward was clear cut: "To stop schooling is bad, yeah / Law denies what is bad, yeah / To go to school is good, yeah / Law accepts what is good, yeah."[15] Along with the rest of the contents where statements and testimonies attested to the supreme value of schooling, the jingle did little to invite reflections on what might be wrong with schooling in Zambia, let alone what other forms of education constituted the life worlds of the girls and young women whom the program series tried to reach. School ethnographies from Africa have shown the complex ways in which youthful aspirations for advancement intersect with a host of material, religious, and historical factors influencing the experience of schooling (see Simpson 2003; Stambach 2000). In some countries, such as Sierra Leone, young people's failed "incorporation into a meritocratic order of education," pitted "against guidance and control of elders" (Bolten 2012:505), appears to have played its part in starting a war. The figure of Gogo Breeze adds to this literature on youth and education a perspective that qualifies the contrast between schooling and the moral authority of elderhood. Not only was his past career as a schoolteacher widely known, he also expanded the range of issues to be discussed around the theme of schoolgirl pregnancies.

Gogo Breeze did not challenge the perception that schoolgirl pregnancies and early marriages undermined prospects for a better future, but his focus was on the responsible adults who might be implicated in this predicament. As such, the perspective afforded by his work supports an insight emerging in childhood studies, namely the need to insert a notion of dependence into discussions about children's voices (see Meloni et al. 2015). While not making any reference to the UN Convention on the Rights of the Child, he restored what had been removed from its Article 28 concerning children's right to education: the interest in parental and other adult obligations (see Quennerstedt 2009). In line with his own prerogative to dispense moral education, he explored the kind of preparation that parents and mature women were expected to provide for girls. These perspectives on possibilities and constraints in girls' lives came on air through a program series around the same time as *Because I Am a Girl / Chifukwa Ndine Mtsikana*, also sponsored by an NGO. *Chidwi Pa Anthu* (*Interest in People*), as mentioned in chapter 3, involved Gogo Breeze visiting rural areas with a view to recording multiple voices addressing locally salient issues, but its contents had not been prescribed by the sponsoring foreign media NGO.

The state of local schools was a regular theme on these programs, along with Gogo Breeze's questions about issues such as agriculture and health facilities. On one program, for example, a discussion about the material constraints of schooling preceded his interrogation of the causes behind schoolgirl pregnancies.[16] Villagers' description of the poor roads and long distances that pupils had to endure on their way to school, and of the lack of housing for teachers, set the scene for girls' desolate fate in the hands of the very people who were supposed to teach them. Gogo Breeze introduced the topic with his usual allusion to what he had heard in other localities.

GOGO BREEZE: There is a problem I heard about while traveling. I heard the story that teachers, [when they see] children with a raised chest, oh yes, they are their wives. What about here in your place in Kagoro—is there an issue like that? If there is, what have you done about it?

MAN: It is true that this issue troubles us very much. Some of these teachers, when they see a woman, ah. Now we as the parents, we have discussed, that is not good behavior; children don't learn. They must stop; children should study. We have discussed.[17]

Gogo Breeze's idiom of a child with a "raised chest" (*chifuwa chokwera*) alluded to the breasts that schoolgirls of a certain age developed. Another elderly man confirmed the teachers' degradation by calling them "lustful teachers" (*aziphunzitsi ankhuli*). As with so many grievances that villagers had on this and other programs that Breeze FM broadcast, the man appealed to the government (*boma*). "Let us ask the government to bring ideas, to bring a law on the teachers who have damaged a child" (*timpemphe boma kuti liike nzeru, liike lamulo pa mphunzitsi akapezeka waononga mwana*). The mention of a higher authority beyond the teachers prompted this man to recall that "a long, long time ago when a teacher impregnated a child [pupil], he was no longer a teacher" (*kale, kale mphunzitsi akangopatsa mwana mimba sanakhalenso mphunzitsi ayi*). The search in these remarks was for moral authority when the custodians of the promise of schooling were themselves damaging pupils' prospects. The government as the ultimate parent was failing in its duties by allowing the transgressors to continue in the teaching profession. At issue were the parents' and elders', and not just the pupils', aspirations for a better life. "They must stop. We want the children of Kagolo to study. They should also become teachers. They should also become accountants; a bank recently came here. We want these children to study, not that the children give up [schooling]."[18]

Although Gogo Breeze did not draw on his past as a schoolteacher during these broadcasts, his listeners were generally aware of his past profession and likely to associate him with the era when teachers supposedly still focused on teaching. His postretirement career as a radio elder gave him leeway to consider other forms of education once the dismal infrastructural and moral state of schools had been established. Turning his attention to the women on whose shoulders rested girls' moral education, he made no effort to solicit the kinds of statements that filled the airwaves when the *Because I Am a Girl / Chifukwa Ndine Mtsikana* series was broadcast. Rather than expecting the women to repeat the value of schooling, he confronted them with the charge that their moral education actually caused girls to experiment with sex. "You women," he asked in the same episode, "I heard that you are the ones that when a [girl] child matures, is it true that you take her into a house to reveal everything to her, whatever it is, tell us for sure how it is?"[19] The radio elder, along with other men, was unaware of the actual contents of the women's teachings in the secluded space of a house.[20] Yet his cultural knowledge was enough to make the conjecture that the girls were being taught how to enjoy sex with men.

His preoccupation was to determine at what point the women "adjourned" (*kulekeza*) their teachings, but he faced considerable difficulties to elicit a straight answer. One elderly woman offered her own lament over the changing times: "To confirm that we take [girls] into the house, indeed we take. Even if we take her into the house, there is no benefit to us; children have no ears. In the past, we cried when a man seduced us, grabbing breasts. We simply married through the parents who would go to that person's place so that they pay. Today's child does not cry."[21] Another, somewhat younger woman shifted the blame from the girl to her parents and pointed out the limited time that the women had at their disposal to impart moral education: "Well, I want to tell the truth. When those children come from their parents, they have no ears. If I am with them for only a few days, I cannot prevent what is in the child's heart. Even I, as an adviser, I cannot prevent her. But it has been established by our custom that we take the child, we instruct her. After we have instructed her, we give her back to her parents, but we don't finish the whole custom."[22] It was this claim that the women knew where to stop, along with their pride in the custom (*mwambo*) as a whole, that provoked the radio grandfather, but the women would respond to his direct questions about where they stopped with laughter and decidedly innocuous observations. This woman's response was, "When we come to the house, what we begin with the child—we have taken the child, placed her in the house—the very first thing is that we want to teach her respect. That is the first thing. And dressing, we teach the child how to dress. She has to kneel down, but if the child is disobedient, she has come from her parents as a disobedient child."[23] To Gogo Breeze's question about the songs they teach the girls, she and her colleagues performed the one whose refrain was, "My husband, you don't have a secret / My husband, you don't have a secret / Things to do with the household we discuss as the two of us / Things to do with the household we discuss as the two of us."[24]

Instead of discovering rampant female sexuality fueled by immoral education, *Chidwi Pa Anthu*'s public was thus summoned to witness an argument in which multiple voices participated. While the advisers appearing on *Because I Am a Girl / Chifukwa Ndine Mtsikana* duly swore their allegiance to formal schooling and had little opportunity to highlight the positive aspects of their calling as customary advisers, their counterparts on Gogo Breeze's programs were able to insist that their custom taught respect in comportment and dress, a project undermined by the parents and teachers who no longer seemed concerned with discipline. Far from being obscene, the song cited above also seemed to assert intimacy as well as equality between marriage partners.[25] Gogo Breeze closed the focus on the women with a skeptical remark—"I say that maybe they don't adjourn" (*ine ndikunena kuti mwina salekeza*)—and brought fathers into focus instead. Here he felt able to suggest a degree of collusion between fathers and male teachers. He began his interrogation of fathers by saying, "Now when she is found with a man, you, the male parents, you say, 'Ah, I want him to give us a small cow—leave it; the child is mine.' Is it true that you make young children [girls] marry? Does it happen in Kagolo? If it happens, why does it happen?"[26] The first to respond was a woman who remarked that the practice was followed by "others, not here at our place" (*wena, osati kwa ife iyayi*). Gogo Breeze then turned to an elderly man and repeated the charge to him.

GOGO BREEZE: My age mate.
ELDERLY MAN: Yes, indeed.

GOGO BREEZE: I heard what you want: "They should give us cattle; [the girl] is theirs." You destroy the child.

ELDERLY MAN: On the issue being discussed here, it is not like that. We as the parents try to tell the children, "Ah, those thing no, those things no." The child is young; eighteen- or twenty-year should not marry. At first he/she must study. But there are other parents, as the woman here said, other parents take the child and make her marry, while other parents understand that no, a young child should not have a family [of her own].[27]

Gogo Breeze's identification as his interlocutor's age mate did not deter him from making the rather startling accusation that the age mate might be destroying children. The response implicating others than oneself was not what he received when he turned to yet another potential culprit in the predicament of schoolgirl pregnancies. In another episode of *Chidwi Pa Anthu*, he encountered a young man who admitted with some relish that his peers indeed visited schoolgirls for sex.[28] The interrogation followed a remark a woman had made to the effect that young men shared information about girls who were receptive to such visits.

GOGO BREEZE: Boys, you are the ones who bother girls. I heard that you tell each other, "Go to that one; I tasted already." How is it—is it true that you do so?

YOUNG MAN: What I can explain is that girls are undisciplined. After their parents have bought them a uniform, they go to school and want the boys to notice them, and when we lust for them, it is in our heart until we go and see them.

GOGO BREEZE: Is that what you do?

YOUNG MAN: Mm.

GOGO BREEZE: Do you do the right thing?

YOUNG MAN: Sure.[29]

The crowd witnessing the exchange erupted into laughter at this point, but the radio elder's tone became increasingly fierce when he confronted the young man by shouting, "You take somebody's child, you don't even own a blanket, you don't even own a mat, you damage her by taking her to the bush. Do you do the right thing?"[30] The blanket, *gombeza*, was one of his favorite idioms for the bare minimum a young man should have if he entertained a desire for a conjugal relationship. This young man's criticism of the way schoolgirls dressed regarded even the school uniform as a medium for seduction when worn in suggestive ways. The criticism elicited the radio elder's caustic remark on how young men themselves dressed.

GOGO BREEZE: You talked about the way girls dress. What about the way you boys dress? You keep your belt on your buttocks instead of on your hip. What is it that brings these things, because if you tie your belt on your buttocks, girls will also lust for your buttocks. Who is the bad one here?

YOUNG MAN: But we all are bad ones. As you are asking, grandfather, the difficulty is like that. They say, "That one looks good; he has money." Girls want that he shows what he has in the pocket.[31]

The young man's remarks had the same air of tit-for-tat as the responses to exhortations for gender equality described in the previous chapter. Gogo Breeze also assumed some parity between the sexual desires of boys and girls, but remarkable in his interventions was this effort to go beyond the current gender rhetorics by assembling multiple voices that all had something to say about schoolgirl pregnancies. It was, in this regard, only natural that he also sought official views on the matter. The above encounters that took place in Kagoro also resulted in air time for a local counselor who had come to hear Gogo Breeze's exchanges with villagers. Gogo Breeze turned to him toward the end of his session: "Counselor, you visit different areas, people you lead here; marriages among young children, don't they happen? If they happen, what is it that you as a counselor do? If they don't happen, anyway, tell us."[32] The counselor was pleased to report a decrease in the practice because of the cooperation between different organizations (*mabungwe*). "Yes, as you explained here, a child, in the past, it happened. When a child got pregnant, the parents forced her to marry with the aim of receiving cattle. But various organizations together with us, the counselors, are helping each other to educate children about the value of schooling. So now it is changing. I can say that some want their children to marry, but because of an agreement between church leaders and ourselves as counselors, now it is apparent that many children in Kagoro go to school."[33]

The politician's attribution of positive development to his and other leaders' efforts received no comment from Gogo Breeze. Instead, he paused the broadcast of his encounters in the village to play a song immediately after the counselor had spoken. The song was by Joseph Nkasa, one of Malawi's most popular singers, who had adopted the *phungu* appellation to style himself as the people's representative. The song demanded politicians to return the vote to the citizen because of betrayal. Gogo Breeze's invitation for his public to reflect on politicians' complacency was voiced through this song, but the counselor's voice did add yet another idea of education to the argument about schoolgirl pregnancies. Here education was something that enlightened leaders provided to children and adults alike. Although the counselor did not mention the phrase "harmful cultural practices," his perspective on the past habit of "forcing" children to marry with a view to receiving cattle accorded with much NGO and governmental civic education in the province. The resources it had at its disposal—including radio programs such as *Because I Am a Girl / Chifukwa Ndine Mtsikana*—far outweighed those among the advisers in villages who saw girls in the seclusion of their houses and stood accused of promoting so-called harmful cultural practices. What was remarkable about the programs Gogo Breeze put on air was a certain leveling effect they had among the different ideas of education. Those ideas were presented side by side, as aspects of the same life world where schoolgirl pregnancies were known to occur. Yet far from committing himself to some imagined neutrality of investigative journalism, he pursued the leveling effect by interrogating each stakeholder from his own point of view as the radio elder. It involved making explicit his faith in schooling and delayed marriages, but it also carried the grandfatherly prerogative of taking everyone to task, including teachers who could be the ones breaking the promise of schooling. Critical to that prerogative was hierarchically ordered multivocality, the broadcast of multiple voices framed and shaped by the grandfather's interventions.

Gogo Breeze deployed different modes of communication to make the grandfatherly interventions, from broadcasting a contentious song after a politician had spoken to charging advisers, fathers, and young men with complicity in schoolgirl pregnancies. These broadcasts are interesting in that they also show how different forms of education were expected to involve different kinds of speech and listening. The schoolgirls' stifled statements on Matoto's programs gave a sense of speech befitting provincial classrooms, but it is also worth noting that the diverse participants in the argument mediated by Gogo Breeze emphasized "ears" as a key idiom for the kind of maturation that a proper life cycle would entail. More than a voice, ears were what children and adults alike expected children and young persons to develop. The expectation resembles the ethical listening that anthropologists have explored in other settings (see Hirschkind 2006:34; Schulz 2012:117; Kunreuther 2014:173). They have qualified a focus on the speaker, the one with a voice, with an appreciation of the hearer's obligation to confirm in her or his comportment that she or he is capable of listening. Indeed, the Chinyanja word for "listening," *kum-*

vera, is also the most common word for "obeying."[34] Hence the emphasis one of the advisers participating in Gogo Breeze's program placed on respect as the key aim of the teachings in the secluded house. Their ethics of listening were contradicted by Gogo Breeze's direct questions about the contents of their teachings. As he pointed out to me in private, he was fully aware that he would not be able to elicit women's secrets, just as he judiciously avoided revealing everything on his own programs devoted to esoteric idioms and proverbs. It was precisely in the confrontation between the inquisitive radio personality and the secretive guardians of gendered knowledge that Gogo Breeze's public could get a glimpse of what the ethics of listening among girls might entail. In contrast to classroom recitations and the supposedly transparent messages spread by the government and NGOs, girls' learning to listen, their acquisition of ears, constituted them as specific kinds of persons—women. No one else but girls had the ears to listen to the secrets that would make them women.

Inside and Outside the NGO Economy

Ears came before the voice not only in girls' initiation but also in some exhortations to take schooling seriously. A representative of FAWEZA, another NGO devoted to the cause of women and girls' rights, had on one of its programs on Breeze FM asserted that "women who did not attend school, who did not study, don't have the freedom to speak on their own behalf."[35] The statement was descriptive as well as normative in that it drew attention to the difficulties unschooled women faced if they wanted to be heard. While the emphasis on the freedom (*ufulu*) to speak on one's own behalf (*paokha*, lit., "alone") foreclosed multivocality as mediated by Gogo Breeze, schooling was imagined here to be constitutive of voice in a manner that paralleled initiation. By contrast, the program series that Plan Zambia brought on air in 2013, after *Because I Am a Girl / Chifukwa Ndine Mtsikana* had ended, promoted children as subjects with voice, even if it was just one voice. *Child Participation and Protection / Mgwirizano Pa Chitetezo Cha Ana* had as one of its objectives, as stated in the Terms of Reference, to give children "a fora [sic] to voice out on issues that affect them by specifically having children's tailored [sic] programs. These child tailored [sic] programs will involve interviewing children on various aspects particularly those affecting them and activities there [sic] are currently engaged [sic] in order to address problems affecting them." The programs were expected to include both interviews with children and children's interviews with other children and adults. Again the contrast to Gogo Breeze's approach to children as

interlocutors was striking. Rather than look for the adults whose responsibility it was to articulate and respond to the grievances of childhood, the
new series took children as capable of not only voicing their own concerns
but also of taking adults to task through interviews.

Although the Terms of Reference stated in its methods section that the
series would deploy "a range of participatory methods to engage children
themselves as well as professionals, traditional leaders and Community
[sic] members themselves," Plan Zambia's method of engaging Breeze
FM was scarcely participatory. It involved signing a contract document in
which the radio station appeared variously as a "contractor" and "consultant." Plan Zambia was to pay Breeze FM a total of ZMK 9,698 (about
US$1,800) in two equal instalments, the latter of which was to become
payable "upon satisfactorily executed, completed and certified works by
Plan Authorised staff [sic]." The Terms of Reference further stated that
"Plan will support the consultant with the relevant information to help
gain more knowledge of issues that will be dealt with throughout the production process of these programs." It stipulated that "pre-recorded programs will be submitted to Plan by the consultant for further editing and
input by Plan Staff [sic] before there [sic] are finally aired on the radio."
Plan Zambia's communications officer had the main responsibility for
overseeing the "works" to be delivered by Breeze FM and told me that she
needed to conduct several meetings to make the broadcasters understand
the issues to be covered during the series. I describe below how a male
presenter was given detailed instructions on how to conduct the launch
program before it went live on air, but Glenda Matoto, who again did the
bulk of the recordings in Chadiza District, saw nothing untoward in Plan
Zambia's policy of screening the programs before their broadcast. When I
had conversations with her about this series, she would draw on the NGO's
participatory rhetoric in saying that the work was done together (pamodzi)
and that, as with the previous series about the girl child, she welcomed
the opportunity to learn (kuphunzira). Yet some of the specific issues on
which Child Participation and Protection / Mgwirizano Pa Chitetezo Cha Ana
was supposed to broadcast raised her doubts in ways that the emphasis
on girls' schooling had not done in the previous series. They included a
campaign against corporal punishment and the expectation that children
should be allowed to participate in decision making over financial matters
in the household.

The increase in children's public presence in Chipata over the past few
years had not escaped Matoto, from children taking on new roles in her
church, including preaching, to billboards condemning corporal punish-

ment (see figure 11). While recognizing the dangers of excess in meting out corporal punishment, Matoto was firmly of the view that it had to remain in adults' disciplinary arsenal. She cited to me the English saying, "Spare the rod and spoil the child." Here she was in agreement not only with many teachers and parents but also with Mtwalo Nzima, her adversary on the *Zam'mabanja* program. For example, a few months before the contract about the new series was signed with Plan Zambia, she had asked Nzima to expound on the merits of beating up misbehaving children. "Don't use empty threats," Nzima bellowed in English after presenting a hypothetical case in which a child was discovered by the mother to have stolen money from her in order to buy sweets.[36] "You had said you could beat," he continued. "Then pick up the whip" (*mwanena kuti mukhoza kumukwapula, to-lani kaliswazi*). This was followed by his imitation of the child's loud cries in the midst of a severe beating. Matoto also expressed private puzzlement over the injunction, by Plan Zambia and other NGOs, to involve children in planning what they called household budgets. She posed me the rhetorical question whether a child knows the value of money. Should he or she be consulted as a member of the household on a par with adults? Behind the NGOs' injunction was the concern that children's access to necessities such as school uniforms and food was undermined by some parents' reck-

FIGURE 11

less spending habits. Whether the concern had any basis in evidence or not, it was another instance of configuring children as equal to adults.

Corporal punishment was one of the themes that the series *Child Participation and Protection / Mgwirizano Pa Chitetezo Cha Ana* was expected to cover, as stipulated in the document titled *Terms of Reference for Child Rights Programs under Tackling Harmful Traditional Practices*. Nzima's self-conscious traditionalism aside, Matoto's endorsement of his view in this instance illustrates the difficulty of regarding corporal punishment simply as a "traditional practice." As was seen above, her aspirations involved leaving the tedium of smallholder farming behind in order to pursue a career in broadcasting along with opportunities for further education. By defining corporal punishment as one of the harmful traditional practices, Plan Zambia turned a deaf ear to what villagers, let alone Zambian professionals, may have had in mind when they endorsed it. Pain might have featured in the disciplinary regimes among Zambians regardless of the extent to which they embodied other signs of tradition.[37] As Caroline Archambault has noted with regard to boarding school students in Kenya's Maasailand, the same people who opposed corporal punishment in terms of children's rights could also mete it out on younger siblings or when they became parents and teachers (2009:299). Opposition to corporal punishment could also be situational in another sense. It served to create alliances with well-resourced campaigns that carried the prospect of contacts, information, and even employment. One example was Matoto's decision not to let her acceptance of using corporal punishment in certain situations to become public on the programs sponsored by Plan Zambia. Yet this situational endorsement of corporal punishment did nothing to alter the distinction on which the new series was erected—the one between tradition and the concept of children's rights as expressed in the UN Convention on the Rights of the Child, such as its prohibition in Article 19 of "all forms of physical or mental violence."

Matoto's predicament was one consequence of Breeze FM's location, through this contract, inside the NGO economy. Her genuine desire to advance some of Plan Zambia's causes and to develop herself in the process could not erase other deeply felt convictions about the proper order in which adults and children were never simply equal. Somewhat different dilemmas characterized those interviewed on Breeze FM who found themselves to varying degrees outside the coveted NGO economy. Both series that Plan Zambia sponsored in 2012–13 had so-called traditional leaders among its local collaborators in order to gain access to the people it wanted to reach. Chief Mpembamoyo was in Plan Zambia's sphere of influence, but he paused on several occasions during his interview with a male presenter on one of the *Because I Am a Girl / Chifukwa Ndine Mtsikana* programs to request further assistance for himself and his attendants (*nduna*).[38] His inclination to use English on a Chinyanja program betrayed his familiarity with the NGO-speak, including the understanding that a central objective was to "sensitize" his subjects about the importance of schooling among girls.[39] In the following extracts, the words that he said in English are italicized. "I am just appealing," he began, "there are *well-wishers*. Plan has tried; Plan *cannot do one hundred percent*. If the government can manage to *sponsor*, I will make a plan. I am prepared to go and *sensitize* people. *If any other organization can come in and help to continue with the program.*"[40] After spending a few moments, at the interviewer's request, reflecting on the importance of schooling among girls, he returned to the need for more resources in his work of sensitization and specified transport as the stumbling block in his efforts. The NGO economy was woven into the chiefly economy in his observation that his subjects would be able to meet other costs during field trips: "*We don't need much, because* when we travel, people cook for us; they cook food for us. *What we want is transport. There is nothing like lunch, no. As long as we inform them in advance,* we come *so and so, they prepare lunch.*"[41] In this confluence of the NGO and chiefly economies,[42] Breeze FM also had a role to play in publicizing the chief's search for partners: "You at Breeze FM know our friends [sponsors], our friends who can help us that this *message*, the importance of schooling among girls, reaches everywhere. *Any way possible* it must happen. We should do that. *I am ready,* the attendants are ready, *but we are lacking sponsorship.*"[43]

Whether the chief's subjects were delighted at the prospect of providing food for those who came to sensitize them about schooling among girls was not broached on the *Because I Am a Girl / Chifukwa Ndine Mtsikana* programs. Their priorities could again be gauged in the other program series running at the same time that also involved field visits by Breeze FM staff. This was the *Chidwi Pa Anthu* series that was discussed earlier as a forum for Gogo Breeze's explorations of similar themes as those on the programs sponsored by Plan Zambia. When the *Child Participation and Protection / Mgwirizano Pa Chitetezo Cha Ana* series was being prepared, he encountered in Chadiza District villagers who had other things in mind than wanting to be sensitized about children's rights.[44] They described their lack of access to clean water, with only two boreholes serving a primary school of one thousand pupils. Plan Zambia's work on this problem rather than on sensitization prompted a man to talk about developments in the neighboring village. "Mine is an appeal to the government that perhaps it could ask NGOs to help us on the issue of water. Plan [Zambia] came to our friends there in Zingalume; it was giving boreholes. In one village it gave two, three boreholes. But we here in Taferansoni are asking that if it is possible, Plan [Zambia] should come here to give us boreholes too as it gave our friends."[45] Gogo Breeze closed this discussion with one of his favorite sayings on such occasions: "When the child asks for a bone, give him/her a bone with flesh, because if you don't do it like that, he/she will point a finger at you tomorrow and say, 'You only gave me such-and-such.'"[46] In this encounter, the NGO economy was in the next village, attractive because of its capacity to reduce daily drudgery. Gogo Breeze rephrased the villagers' request in the idiom of kinship and, as such, evoked a relationship in which future accusations of neglect could be preempted by generosity in the present.

Between Rights and a Riot

Just as the *Child Participation and Protection / Mgwirizano Pa Chitetezo Cha Ana* series was being launched on Breeze FM in early April 2013, rioting erupted in the small town of Katete in Eastern Province. The immediate trigger was a tragic failure of child protection: a grade-twelve secondary-school student had been found dead and mutilated near her school ten days earlier. Rumors spread quickly to assert that parts of her body had been taken to be used for occult purposes.[47] A sense of insecurity grew in tandem with the rumors, exacerbated by a perceived lack of police intervention. The victim's boyfriend was promptly arrested, but popular opinion was that he had committed the crime after receiving an order for body parts from someone far more powerful than himself. Although three more people were eventually arrested by the police, one of whom was a woman, anger and fear in Katete reached a breaking point in the morning hours of April 4. Before the police were able to restore law and order at 11:00 a.m., several stores had been looted, property belonging to store owners destroyed or burned, and shop workers and their management beaten up or intimidated. Reports on the rioting conveyed the retail landscape in the province's towns and trading centers by describing how both Chinese- and South Asian–owned stores came under attack. Yet the primary target of the crowd's fury, and not just of opportunistic looting, was the store owned by a locally prominent Zambian businessman. His reputation in the province had spread along with his business interests, and he had at least one more store in Petauke, another rural trading center. The crowd gathered at his store to make their accusation explicit: he was the one who had ordered the young woman's body parts to advance his business by occult means.

Rumors spread by word of mouth and the apparently neutral reports in the media had a complex relationship during this crisis. It became national news through the ZNBC, which chose to report on the tragedy as a "gang rape," thus playing down the politically volatile rumor of occult machinations among successful entrepreneurs.[48] In Eastern Province, Radio Maria was the first to open the airwaves for listeners' reflections on the incident. Five days before the riot happened, its presenter fielded a number of anxious phone calls, some of which mentioned the incident's occult reverberations while others vented their anger on police inaction. The presenter promised to take the complaints to the Eastern Province Police Commissioner, who soon did dispatch senior police officers from Chipata to Katete, prompted by the provincial minister rather than by this presenter. At Breeze FM, the news about the riot came on a particularly busy day when Michael Daka, the founder-director, had a previously scheduled meeting with the provincial minister to discuss an entirely different matter—the government's potential to start sponsoring a series of programs about its various departments in the province. Daka made his usual point about Breeze FM playing the role of a public-service broadcaster in the absence of the resources it required. The minister seized on this vision for Breeze FM and asked Daka to ensure that the station did what it could to calm tempers down during the present crisis in Katete. Upon his return to the station, I observed Daka summoning the head of the news department to pass on the minister's message. Daka ordered the news to mention that rioting did not benefit anyone and reminded his staff of the unrest that had taken place in Chipata shortly after Breeze FM had been established. Protesters had carried placards crying "Indians Go Home," but Daka attributed Breeze FM's good relations with government officials to his decision never to lend support to such sentiments over the airwaves. Similarly now, he later told me in private, he had achieved a "trade-off" with the minister by agreeing to broadcast the message about maintaining calm while the minister would pursue the idea of a sponsored series on Breeze FM.

Daka could not control everything that went on air. During both Gogo Breeze's late-night shift, as is discussed below, and the morning after the riot when a young male presenter was in charge, the station's regular phone-in times had only one topic. Callers on the morning program were unanimous that the police were to be blamed for violence in Katete. The phone calls and SMS messages began to converge on set phrases, such as congratulations to "the citizens of Katete" (*nzika za Katete*) and, in English, "Well done, people in Katete!" Callers regretting the looting and destruction of property were in the minority. Instead, several mentioned that "things can be replaced but human lives cannot" and proceeded to pour scorn on the police. A recurrent theme was corruption among the police: "the police are trained to receive bribes," "the police only arrest poor people and leave the rich alone," and so on. The presenter did nothing to remind his listeners of the message about maintaining calm that Daka had wanted to put on air the day before. Nor did he offer his own views on the incidents in Katete, preoccupied as he was to simply receive all the calls and messages that came flooding in from all over the province.

The broadcast was markedly different from the launch of the *Child Participation and Protection / Mgwirizano Pa Chitetezo Cha Ana* series that had taken place on Breeze FM the day before, in the afternoon of April 4, the day when the riot had erupted in Katete. This live program, which had as its aim the introduction of children's rights to its listeners, was run by another young male presenter, Matoto's colleague on the Plan Zambia–sponsored programs. He cajoled the listeners into participating in the program no less than eight times during the forty-minute broadcast. Three phone calls were attempted, only one of which did not cut before the caller was able to speak. Alas, it was a wrong number. The only SMS message that was received came after nearly thirty minutes on air: "Good afternoon. We need that project at our district, because some of the children, they don't know some of these rights." The district was Katete.[49]

In the studio were representatives from Plan Zambia, Young Women's Christian Association (YWCA), and the Zambian government. They were well aware of the turmoil in Katete earlier in the day, as they were of the schoolgirl's shocking demise. They were also aware, although it was mentioned less often in news reporting, that the girl had been classified as an orphan and therefore eligible for financial support at school. Her education was being sponsored by FAWEZA, one of the organizations, as mentioned, promoting women's and girls' rights in the province and a sometime sponsor of programs on Breeze FM. None of these details attracted the panelists' comments, whether at their preparatory meeting shortly before the broadcast or when they were on air. Instead, an abstract discussion on the scope and meaning of children's rights ensued, its topic agreed several days before the Katete riot. No one proposed to bring the topic to bear on what was happening in Katete, and the Plan Zambia representative replied to the SMS message by saying that her organization was going to "scale up" its projects to cover parts of Katete and two further districts. The bureaucratic idiom of scaling up in the unspecified future was all she had to offer to the listener in Katete. The rest of the program consisted of the presenter's questions and the panelists' answers regarding the need to recognize children as rights-bearing subjects in their own right and the panelists' reflections on adults' responsibilities to provide them with protection. One example of the distance between life in the province and the panelists' explication of the UN Convention on the Rights of the Child was their discussion on the access to information as stipulated in Article 13. "You want the child to have access to information," one of them stated. "This is information that can be found on the Internet, television, in policies that the government can put in place, like the Ministry of Education." No effort was made to consider the extent to which these sources of information were available to youths in Eastern Province. The presenter addressed the female panelists with the honorific *Madam*. It was consistent with the submissive tone he had adopted at the prebroadcast meeting at which he had merely written down what the panelists told him were the issues and the order in which they should appear on the program. The entire broadcast was conducted in English, except for certain moments in the sole phone call that made it into the program.

PRESENTER: Hello. Good afternoon.

CALLER: Hello.

PRESENTER: Yes, good afternoon. You are through to the program.

[*silence of four seconds*]

CALLER: Who's that? (*Anda?*)

[*silence of three seconds*]

PRESENTER: Eh, you called to participate in the program, right? (*Eh, mwatuma kuti muchite* participate *papologamu, eti?*)

[*silence of three seconds*]

CALLER: Okay.

PRESENTER: Speak out. (*Kambani.*)

[*silence of six seconds*]

PRESENTER: Hello?

CALLER: Hello?

PRESENTER: Yes, speak out. You have called to participate in the program. (*Ee, kambani. Mwatuma kuti muchite* participate *papologamu.*)

[*silence of three seconds*]

CALLER: But it is not this. (*Koma si iyi.*)

[*The line cuts.*]

The contrast to the busy phone lines on Radio Maria's program, broadcast live five days before the riot, was striking. Indeed, both programs on Breeze FM inviting listeners' comments on the Katete incident also had a tremendous listener response, whether on the morning program the day after the riot, as mentioned above, or during Gogo Breeze's late-night shift two days before the riot erupted. Shortly after the murder had taken place on March 23, he had already received a letter from Katete. Because the police had arrested the victim's boyfriend by the time Gogo Breeze came to record the letters program, he refused to align himself with the perspective proposed in the letter.

NAOMI MWIMBA: They say, "We, grandfather, are disappointed with the way soldiers are working here in Soweto in Katete," meaning the police. They say, "They don't work well, because you have heard of the nineteen-year-old schoolgirl. They raped and murdered her"=

GOGO BREEZE: =This story, let me interrupt you.

NAOMI MWIMBA: Mm.

GOGO BREEZE: Because they are saying that the police don't work well.

NAOMI MWIMBA: Ehe.

GOGO BREEZE: The police are working well, because had they not been working well, they would not have arrested that boy. Was it not you reporters, Naomi, who took the story? You told the whole country that the boy was arrested who did violence to the girl studying at Katete Secondary School? When we are talking here, he is in prison [lit., "In a very tight place"].

NAOMI MWIMBA: Mm.

GOGO BREEZE: What about the soldiers, how is it?

NAOMI MWIMBA: They say, "They are arresting ordinary people and giving them to the police."

GOGO BREEZE: That is the work of the police; they investigate. You said in your news that the boy was going out with that girl, is it not what you said?

NAOMI MWIMBA: Yes.

GOGO BREEZE: And also, the head of the police explained how the whole issue was. So, the one who wrote this little letter, if he/she has something to say, he/she should come here to Chipata, to see the officer in charge to explain the whole story.[50]

This exchange was not included in the broadcast version of the letters program, nor was any mention made of the letter from Katete. By the time the letters program went on air, Gogo Breeze had received phone calls from Katete and participated in Chipata in numerous informal conversations about the mounting tension. His faith in the reliability of the police force and news gathering, as expressed in the above exchange, gave way to an appreciation of the anxieties felt on the ground. As he told me, he had understood the incident's potential for sparking accusations about occult machinations, but he had wanted to defuse such suspicions as long as it was possible. Those suspicions—and even accusations—had become so widespread by the time the letters program went on air that his faith in the police would have sounded like he was aloof from popular concerns. Yet behind his change of approach was not simply a populistic desire to speak the language of the people. In the above exchange, the letter writer had addressed him as the grandfather and Gogo Breeze spoke of news journalists as a category separate from himself. Responding to popular concerns as they unfolded was consistent with his status as the radio elder, and here was another instance of his public and private persona merging into one another. What he said on air during the late-evening live program was strikingly similar to what he shared with me during our casual conversations. He was forthright about the ultimately barren wealth that the use of body parts would produce. While fielding phone calls on the live program, he stated, "Money acquired in that way won't stay in the pocket" (*ndalama zija sizikhala m'thumba*). As an example, he described how cars bought with such money would disappear upon the death of their owner, leaving no wealth behind. As for the police, he recognized the extent to which their reputation had been damaged during the crisis. Rather than upholding the virtues of policing as an institution, he issued a criticism by pointing out that many people were afraid of reporting crimes to the police lest they themselves were arrested. "How did you see that?" (*munaona bwanji?*) would be the question they would have to answer from the police cell. The radio elder no longer told his listeners to speak to senior officers in Chipata. Instead, he offered his own services to mediate between his listeners and the police. "If you have seen something suspicious, come and tell us" (*ngati mwaona china chokudabwitsani, bwerani mudzatifotokozere*).

The tide of anger had been rising in Katete for too long to be stemmed by the radio elder's offer of mediation. Yet it has been important to chart the change in his approach in order to discern the alternative he personified between rights and a riot as two responses to the predicament of child protection and participation in the province. Children's rights remained abstract in the NGO-speak, nowhere more poignantly apparent than in the panel discussion that took place while turmoil had engulfed one of the districts in the province. The change in Gogo Breeze's approach was consistent with the way in which he addressed, as has been seen in this chapter, the material and (im)moral conditions of education. Problems with access to clean water, housing for teachers, and road infrastructure featured on his programs, as did the possibility that threats to child welfare could have occult dimensions. Plan Zambia and the radio elder were both didactic in their distinct ways. While the NGO took it as its mission to combat what it called harmful cultural practices in order to promote girls' commitment to schooling, the radio elder shared the high regard for schooling but explored a broader range of factors and actors that undermined it. They went far beyond "tradition" as the catchall for the discontents of education in the province, even as his radio personality was based on customary codes of conduct. An important aspect of that conduct was, as has been seen throughout this book, an intricate ideology of voice. Children's voices were stifled when staged by an NGO but were not necessarily any more audible on the grandfather's programs. Instead, he engaged adults, young and old, in an argument that came closest to ensuring free speech about children's welfare in Eastern Province.

PART FOUR

Coda

SEVEN

Radio Obligations

"What kind of moral or political obligation can ethereal contact compel?" John Durham Peters's (1999:213) question recalls a dilemma from the early history of radio broadcasting. In the 1920s and 1930s, communication in the context of mutual absence was a perplexing proposition in Britain and the United States, where the first steps toward broadcasting were taken. Anxieties about communication breakdown accompanied elated expectations of progress (see Kahn and Whitehead 1992). The search was for "communicative prostheses" that would serve as "compensations for lost presences" (Peters 1999:214). Speaking into the air had to invent its own forms of intimacy and authenticity, a challenge that American commercial radio took on with lasting effects on radio talk. A personal tone and conversational dynamics eventually spread across the world to establish the radio as the most intimate of mass media.

The previous chapters have shown how Gogo Breeze and his colleagues responded to the dilemma of communicative prostheses. The uses of language, for example, have recurred as one key area within which the broadcasters not only sought intimacy but, as was seen in the previous chapter's account of the English-language discussion on children's rights, also allowed their sponsors to assert a measure of distance between their public and themselves. Intimate address was certainly a feature of Gogo Breeze's radio talk, but his grandfatherly prerogative was also to speak in riddles and proverbs and to reject, when the situation warranted it, his interlocutors' attempts to turn intimacy into frivolous informality. Intimacy did not displace hierarchy and moral authority in his radio work, but "the lost presence" in his case did require further effort beyond the judicious use of language. He quite literally fought lost presences by being a frequent sight in urban and rural localities. The encounters he had there, and the grievances he pursued on behalf of specific listeners, were inevitably personalized, but herein lay their significance as communicative prostheses: it was in the obligations he performed for his listeners, whether on air or off, that the intimacy afforded by the radio became flesh, so to speak, a presence that could touch many more people than he was ever able to meet face to face.

By embracing obligations, Gogo Breeze transposed his grandfatherly demeanor from a mere media personality to a presence in his public's lives and made elderhood compelling in spheres where it did not seem to belong, such as labor relations. Obligations, in other words, were what the value of free speech was expected to uphold. Free speech, it will be recalled, would be the ultimate value only if speech did trump all other values. A key question for comparative analysis of free speech as a value is precisely what desires and aspirations it is made to serve and what, on the other hand, would constitute its violation. Chapters 5 and 6, for example, indicated some of the range of desires and aspirations attributed to women and children by various voices on Breeze FM. Not all of them shared the value Gogo Breeze attached to claiming and meeting obligations. Yet his emphasis on obligations was not simply a reversal of the rights talk heard on certain other programs. Rather, Gogo Breeze's radio work recalls the ease with which foundational studies in legal anthropology deployed both rights and obligations as two sides of the same coin, not least because the vernaculars on which they reported made little conceptual distinction between them (see Malinowski 1926; Gluckman 1955). More important than the rights-obligations distinction here is what radio as a medium affords in making them compelling to diverse subjects. Material culture has long been recognized as central to the experience of moral and political obligations, from gift exchange (Mauss 1954 [1924]) to the uses of affective objects in humanitarian work (Malkki 2015:105–31). To that well-established literature this book adds the power of mass-mediated words and voices in generating the kinds of moral sentiments that obligations require if they are to be experienced as compelling (see also Englund 2015b). Radio, to cite Rudolf Arnheim's (1936:14) observation from its early history, is indeed a "sensational" form of expression in its capacity to make senses and sentiments perform the work of communicative prostheses. The question is what makes it sensational in a way that might be different from other media such as movies (see Meyer 2015).

It is the "stranger-sociability" (Warner 2002:56) of mass-mediated publics that has been questioned by the specific combination of radio's technological affordances and Gogo Breeze's insistence on kinship as his preferred register of address. The gist of the preceding chapters has also been to draw attention to the ideologies of voice, including the moral aspects of listening and speaking, when the emphasis on new communication technologies, such as mobile phones, risks diverting scholarship and policy making from such issues to triumphalist accounts of democratization. Closely linked to the sensorial and technological aspects of radio obligations is the economic side of broadcasting. This study has explored the extent to which the ethos of public service can thrive under market conditions. The concluding reflections on this issue address the metanarratives of commodification and modernity in media studies and beyond, while asking whether Gogo Breeze indeed failed to make the market moral. The final section restates multivocal morality as this book's perspective on the value of free speech. It returns to the difference between Gogo Breeze's practice of free speech and *parrhêsia*.

Why Radio Matters

On programs such as *Landirani Alendo* (*Welcome Visitors*) and *Chidwi Pa Anthu* (*Interest in People*), Gogo Breeze upheld a well-established tradition in radio's history to harness it in the service of the "voice of the people." Breeze FM as a whole was erected on the foundation that this sense of service represented. Radio researchers may readily trace precedents to entirely different historical periods and political milieux, such as *Vox Pop*, American network radio's evolving attempt to put "the average people" on air in the 1930s and 1940s (Loviglio 2005:38–69). Its blurring of the line between publics and broadcasters was an early step toward what now characterizes the media field in many parts of the world—the convergence of corporate and consumer uses of media and the rise of citizen journalism (see Jenkins 2006). What *Vox Pop* brought specifically to the use of radio as a medium was to invent the sounds and voices of audience participation, whether as the man in the street, through quiz shows, or on traveling human-interest programs. It also displayed from the outset a tension between liberal and commercial publics in a way that public-service broadcasters in Europe, and indeed for some time in Africa, did not. Although a similar tension at Breeze FM will be discussed below, it is also revealing to consider how much Gogo Breeze's work diverged from *Vox Pop* and other such quests for the voices of the average people.

The first reason to refrain from assuming too linear a development from America's *Vox Pop* to Gogo Breeze's programs is obvious. A twenty-first-century public in provincial Zambia had been introduced to various forms of radio talk, as well as to commercial messages, by ZNBC's varied Chinyanja programming and its broadcast of commercials, well before Gogo Breeze appeared on the airwaves. Even the grandfather appellation, as mentioned in the introduction, had been in use before him (Englund 2015b). A more profound difference is the work Gogo Breeze did to generate his version of the vox populi. While all attempts to capture the ordinary through the airwaves quickly recognized some diversity within "the average people," if only for commercial reasons, Gogo Breeze's ways of addressing his public did not celebrate ordinariness by abstracting a notional man in the street. He refused, as has been seen, those modes of self-identification that came naturally to many of his interlocutors in the streets and villages when they found themselves able to voice their grievances on air. The virtually instinctive urge, molded by the long-standing official emphasis on development, to present themselves as victims to conditions of lack and deprivation found no sympathy with the radio elder (see also Englund 2015a). His mission was to engage people he met in conversations so as to tease out the field of relationships in which they had their grievances. If the government (*boma*) frequently appeared in these conversations as the parent who should provide for its children, it became merely an aspect of the kinship talk within which Gogo Breeze situated many of the grievances he recorded. His public was a poor one, but not without internal differentiation, nor was it untainted by fraud and greed. Kinship terms both blurred the line between the public and the broadcaster in a specifically Zambian way and made it possible to evaluate who had what kinds of obligations to honor. Much as the grandfather appellation summoned a public of grandchildren, every actual encounter had to be described separately, involving, for example, a mother and her son (chapter 3) and different matrilineal segments (chapter 4).

It was this broadcasting of voices that emanated from recognizable persons in relationships rather than from a small number of social types that distinguished Gogo Breeze's radio work from the broad tradition of giving airtime to the vox populi. It also made him a part of his public in a way that neither investigative nor citizen journalism fully does. Although determined to hear all sides in disputes, he did not shy away from expressing his opinions on matters under investigation. The moral authority that enabled him to do so had its sonic as well as its pragmatic dimensions, and much of this book has been devoted to exploring the triad of "the voice, the diction, and the language" that Walter Benjamin (2008 [1931]:391) identified as key to staying tuned to the radio. Public intimacy was a corollary of this triad in Gogo Breeze's radio work, as it is in so much radio broadcasting, but by deploying kinship terms to order the diversity of persons and circumstances he encountered, he also set limits to how intimate affairs could be discussed on air. As was seen in the previous chapter, the popularity of his moral authority involved careful negotiation of those limits, such as when listeners' accounts of their divorces, children born out of wedlock, and HIV status attracted no comment from the radio grandfather if they were looking for a partner to marry. Far from deployed to trap people into fixed roles, the categories of kinship and affinity provided a framework within which key values could be negotiated and the obligations they entailed defined.

Classic ethnographies on Zambia had already showed as much. Kinship and affinity were described in these works as ever-shifting schemes within which hierarchical obligations and historical contingencies were experienced, based on mutually contradictory principles that generated as much animosity as amity (Colson 1958; Gluckman 1965; Turner 1957). Mass-mediated kinship in twenty-first-century Eastern Province not only made the idioms and values associated with kinship newly compelling for people exposed to fresh generational and gendered controversies as well as to evolving migratory processes. In Gogo Breeze's practice, kinship also replicated some of the radio's own affordances. Somewhat comparable to Daniel Fisher's findings on kinship mediated by Australian Aboriginal radio, on Gogo Breeze's programs "kinship itself [came] to typify the kinds of immediacy, intimacy, and connection that radio enable[d]" (2016:49). A key difference was that while in Fisher's study request programs on the radio connected spatially dispersed persons who thought they were kin prior to the radio's mediating efforts, Gogo Breeze's public was summoned to forgo sentiments of mutual strangerhood in order to feel connected as kin. Again the classic ethnographies taught us as much: strangers, from domestic slaves to more recent migrants, could be adopted as members of kin groups (see also Barnes 1954). Yet the technological and sensuous features of radio were crucial to this twenty-first-century version of similar processes. Kinship talk carried, indeed typified, the public intimacy that Benjamin's triad afforded, underpinned by radio's mobile and inexpensive technology. The stranger-sociability of mass-mediated publics came to be modified by radio kinship.

Making Chipata Safe for Capitalism?

It has been a key observation in this book that Gogo Breeze's public intimacy rested not only on radio's sonic and technological affordances but also on the market. As a privately owned radio station, Breeze FM depended on revenue from advertising and sponsored programs. Gogo Breeze himself was a major asset in this regard, an indefatigable member of the station's Marketing Department and a familiar voice in many of the commercials he was able to solicit from local businesses. The introduction presented critical perspectives on the interface between the market and the mass media, but the case of Breeze FM advises caution with what might be an underlying metanarrative of commodification in many of these critical perspectives. The corporate stranglehold on radio broadcasting is apparent enough across the world's ostensibly liberalized mediascapes, from America's urban stations "falling prey to disturbing economically driven homogenization" (Squier 2003:15) to audience participation sponsored by mobile-phone providers in Zambia (Willems 2013). Yet the strategy in this book has been to investigate how the market set the conditions of Breeze FM's work in a double sense. First, much of Gogo Breeze's presence on and off air was informed by his efforts to make the market moral in the lives of his public, whether in his admonition of fraud and greed among petty entrepreneurs or in his criticism of exploitation perpetrated by the province's major economic agents. Second, the station as a whole combined its dependence on the market with an ethos of public-service broadcasting. Both aspects of the market-media interface involved tension and contradiction, but ethnographic insight into these specific sets of relationships and values would be foreclosed if analysis succumbed to the metanarrative of commodification.

The metanarrative has one of its most unremitting examples in the work of Pierre Bourdieu (1998; Bourdieu and Haacke 1995). As discussed in the introduction, he saw a troubling tendency toward the colonization of the media field by the economic field. It would be a pity if the metanarrative was left unexamined just because evidence can be furnished about corporate encroachment. Fieldwork at a radio station in provincial Zambia would be expected to generate further evidence of the corrosive effects of commodification on the value of free speech. Yet precisely because the metanarrative of commodification extends far beyond the study of mass media, such fieldwork must be allowed to unsettle the convictions the metanarrative gives rise to. It is the purity of domains that needs to be questioned. David Graeber readily concedes that what he calls a "human economy" is not necessarily more humane and less brutal than the commodity economy, but he announces "a relatively easy way to identify a human economy" (2009:125). It is one in which the primary concern is "the creation and fashioning of human beings," to be contrasted with the commodity economy as "an autonomous domain of human activity primarily concerned with creating and allocating material possessions, and not primarily about the creation of people and social relations" (Graeber 2012:412). Stephen Gudeman's preferred domains are mutuality and market, "or community and impersonal trade" (2009:18). He does not propose that they map entirely separate socioeconomic systems. On the contrary, "they are dialectically connected," but, ominously, the dialectic "is not without direction" (2009:19). "As the market realm expands," comes the indictment, "it *colonizes* and *debases* the mutual one on which it also relies" (emphases original).

Anthropologists' dismal thoughts on the market arise from, among other influences, particular readings of Karl Polanyi's (1977) work on embedded and disembedded economies, against which the economic historian of early modern Europe can provide a corrective. Reacting to the claims by twenty-first-century "alter-globalists," who seem to hark back toward "a golden age, an age when the economy reflected the values and morality of society from which it was inseparable . . . followed by an amoral economy," Laurence Fontaine (2014:308) demonstrates the plurality of exchange logics and the coexistence of the gift with the market in the period she has investigated. The result is a far less pure distinction between domains than some anthropologists would seem to advocate. Debt and credit arrangements, for example, illustrate how social relations enabled poor people to enter market exchange, with desirable dependence sometimes only a step away from outright exploitation. Fontaine could be writing about workers in Eastern Province when she observes that "debt can be the guarantee of being fed by one's creditors in exchange for one's labour" (2014:300; compare Englund 2015a). The purity of domains in both alter-globalist and certain anthropological thinking exudes certitude that, in Fontaine's view, "likes unanimity, not open debate" (2014:312).

Debate about the morality of market exchange was integral to Gogo Breeze's pursuit of free speech. The domains of kinship obligations and wage labor, for example, were two sides of the same coin in his efforts to make the market moral. Another example is the song quoted in chapter 3, inserted by the radio elder after his evocation of slavery in a contemporary context. The song, like so many of the farmers, traders, and workers whose voices he recorded, asserted the will to prosper through the market but asked for guarantees from moral authority that the market would be just. To recapitulate, there was a parallel between the moral authority in which such demands situated governmental powers and the moral authority with which the radio elder assembled those voices for broadcast. The values of free speech and free market were, in other words, mutually reinforcing, but not in a way that they are seen to be so in mainstream liberal thought. The emphasis on obligations does not replace axiomatic individualism with the equally axiomatic communitarianism promoted by some among Africa's intellectual elites (see Englund 2011:55–58). In the practices described in this book, obligations have been subject to contest as much as to consensus. For them to become morally compelling, the hierarchies they presuppose are vulnerable to the tensions between dependence and exploitation described in attempts to make the market moral.

Even after these reflections, the critical impulse among some activists and social scientists may find reason to be skeptical about the compatibility between market and morality. Far from promoting the communitarian ethos, Gogo Breeze might actually be seen to give vernacular expression to what critics have identified as "neoliberal agency" (see, e.g., Gershon 2011). They might cite as evidence those instances, described in chapter 3 for example, in which he allocated responsibility to beleaguered subjects to find a way out of their predicaments. These instances might be viewed as part of the global trend toward advocating personal responsibility in the service of market fundamentalism. But this interpretation is plausible only if all that has been said above about obligations is put to one side. The very allocation of responsibility rested on the moral authority that the radio elder was able to muster, and at no point did he suggest that the persons he advised would cease to be his grandchildren. A more serious challenge to this perspective on Gogo Breeze's work would be to contend that he whitewashed capitalism. Precisely because the station he worked for depended on raising revenue, critics might point out, his interventions never amounted to a significant threat to capitalist accumulation.

One response to this allegation would be to ask what exactly the critics expect from a radio personality who indeed never questioned the market principle. Beyond the tautological argument that would ensue lies the possibility that the imperative to maintain good business relations compromised the radio elder's resolve to take some entrepreneurs to task. The familiarity he cultivated toward some of Chipata's entrepreneurs of Indian extraction, as described in chapter 1, was unlikely to influence their notoriously parsimonious approach to paying salaries. Yet research for this book did not uncover a single instance of listeners' grievances being overlooked because of the radio elder's familiarity with the targets of their grievances. The specter of compromise can also be qualified by the cases in which he did take on Eastern Province's major economic forces. The mill owners he confronted in chapter 2 controlled a crucial service. The exploitation by the Chinese that he explored in chapter 3 provided a standpoint to make urgent demands on the Zambian government. Rather than contemplating whether he served the interests of capitalism in the abstract, extraneous critics will do well to recognize critical faculties in his efforts to make the market moral.

Multivocal Morality

Alongside the metanarrative of commodification exists another metanarrative that can exert its insidious influence on analysis. It is the metanarrative of modernity in which figures such as Gogo Breeze embody the nostalgic evocation of tradition that seems intrinsic to modernity. While the metanarrative might lead anthropologists to pluralize a singular modernity into multiple modernities (see Englund and Leach 2000), others could dismiss the radio elder as anachronistic. Neither conclusion would do justice to what the previous chapters have described. One reason is that the kind of radio intimacy that Gogo Breeze mediated had been an integral feature of broadcasting in Zambia. The specific radio personalities through whom his predecessors had sought that intimacy have varied, but common to their efforts had been fluency in the languages spoken by their modestly schooled listeners. Whether they therefore came to defend all things traditional over the airwaves is a question that can be explored by considering a submission to the "Administrative Commission of Inquiry into Effectiveness of Zambia Information and Broadcasting Services" in 1967. Alick Nkhata, then Deputy Director General, wrote:

> We firmly believe that a Bemba announcer or Lozi announcer should be able to understand the idiomatic and proverbial aspects of his language, to make broadcasting more interesting. We also believe that he should be able to have some idea of how people live in his tribal area, etc. etc. These qualities are abundant in persons who have had education up to standard six in the rural areas, during the period 1940–1956. We do not see any reason why people of this educational standard with extensive experience either in the teaching or clerical field, should be barred from joining broadcasting as broadcasters. (Heinze 2014, 638)

The metanarrative of modernity raises its head not in this submission but in the recent study in which it has been quoted. Robert Heinze reads it to mean that "Nkhata still adhered to ideas about the path to modernity that had been shaped during colonialism" (2014:638). Crucial to those ideas about modernity, Heinze contends, was to develop "an authentic Zambian style of broadcasting." Yet Nkhata's submission was less about cultural authenticity than the level of educational attainment that present-ers were expected to possess. He argued for a relatively modest level in the new profession, because the ability to communicate with listeners was no less important than the possession of school certificates. At the same time, the "teaching or clerical field" he mentioned hardly delineated an area of tradition. It was the field in which personal advancement beyond the con-fines of rural life had historically been pursued (see Lawrance et al. 2006). As a retired primary-school teacher, Gogo Breeze was one product of the promise that it presented and had precisely the skills and experience that Nkhata was looking for. Michael Daka, the founder of Breeze FM, likewise deemphasized formal qualifications in his search for local talent. To inter-pret these preferences as examples of (neo-)traditionalism would be to ob-scure the pragmatic considerations that came into play when radio broad-casters courted Zambian audiences, whether as public broadcasters in the 1960s or as private ones in the 2000s.

The metanarrative of modernity, in other words, is insidious insofar as it supplies particular assumptions about what sort of radio personality Gogo Breeze was. The radio elder's essential traditionalism would render him rather less appropriate for the study of free speech as a value than what has become evident in the preceding chapters. Reduced to a traditionalist, he could all too easily find his place among the modalities of truth telling by which Michel Foucault (2011) sought to define *parrhêsia*. As frank speech, *parrhêsia* involves particular courage, the will to take "the risk of breaking or ending the relationship to the other person which was precisely what made . . . discourse possible" (Foucault 2011:11). As already argued in the introduction, Gogo Breeze's mass-mediated kinship countenanced no such risk. He addressed grievances and transgressions with a view to remind-ing subjects of their constitutive obligations, and the speech registers in which he did so were multiple, sometimes abrasive, at other times respect-ful or ludic. In Foucault's scheme of truth telling, by contrast, each modal-ity comes with a separate speech register. The prophet and the sage differ from the *parrhêsiast* both in their language ideologies and in the extent to which their knowledge engages the particularities of a situation. While the prophet speaks in riddles, "the *parrhêsiast* leaves nothing to interpretation" (Foucault 2011:16). And while the sage may also "be enigmatic and leave those he addresses ignorant or uncertain about what was actually said," he does dispense advice in the present moment, albeit "in the form of a gen-eral principle of conduct" (Foucault 2011:17). Language ideology and truth telling merge in this neat contrast between the two modalities: "Whereas the sage says what is, but in the form of the very being of things and of the world, the *parrhêsiast* intervenes, says what is, but in terms of the singularity of individuals, situations, and conjunctures" (Foucault 2011:18–19).

If taken as a traditionalist, Gogo Breeze might look like the sage among Foucault's modalities of truth telling. Allusive language was certainly one of his favored registers of speech, as evident in his passion for proverbs and idiomatic expressions, but sharply worded and direct interventions were no less available in his discursive repertoire. Equally important is to recognize that much of what has been described in the previous chapters has involved Gogo Breeze in negotiations over the right sort of conduct in actual situations. Whether he averted the misogynistic impulse in popular culture to attribute blame to women rather than men in adultery (chapter 5) or discovered layers of complexity in a listener's grievances over her father's estate (chapter 4), Gogo Breeze showed a high degree of elasticity in his judgments. Customary codes of conduct were themselves elastic enough to allow the impression that situational considerations were compatible with grandfatherly authority, rather like the repertoire of norms and standards that aided Barotse judges in Max Gluckman's (1955; 1965) classic studies. As such, modalities of truth telling may be possible to distinguish for heuristic purposes, but their ethnographic study throws them into the intricacies of situations.

It is instructive to note where the concept of *parrhêsia*, beyond its origins in ancient Greece, might hold analytical purchase. A recent study claims such a possibility in an argument about contemporary liberal democracy in the Global North (see Boyer 2013). According to this argument, it has reached the sorry state in which "liberalism's promised plurality of competing viewpoints and platforms within 'normal politics' seems more form than substance" (Boyer 2013:283–84). One instance is said to be the way in which debate on public debt liability has been foreclosed by "the gradual homogenization of northern political discourse around the anchor points of neoliberal ideology, for example, that the market is the central institution of society and that individual rights and autonomies are the most positive features of sociality." Among other culprits, "the corporate monopolization of broadcast media production and circulation" has made "the authoritative representations of political and economic issues significantly more homogeneous and experientially repetitive." Against all that stands *parrhêsia* in modes of political communication such as parody and satire (see also Day 2011; Haugerud 2013). Elusive of attempts to fix their position on the political landscape, Northern satirists have been involved not only in generating laughter and hope but also in experiments in direct participatory democracy. As latter-day *parrhêsiasts*, "some satirists are more sincerely committed to truth telling than the political actors that our liberal democratic institutions authorize to act and speak on our behalf" (Boyer 2013:282).

Whatever its merits otherwise, the example helps to clarify the limits of *parrhêsia* as a perspective on the value of free speech. The contrast to the case of Gogo Breeze lies not only in what has already been said about the metanarrative of commodification in understanding mass media and the market. It also obtains between Northern satirists' desire to disrupt the order of things and Gogo Breeze's desire to make people obey their obligations. Both instances entail contentious claims and can precipitate conflicts, but only the satirist, as a defining feature of *parrhêsia*, insists on citizens' capacity for self-government vis-à-vis external authority (see Saxonhouse 2008:30). What a focus on *parrhêsia* may render unthinkable—or deplorable—is the way in which nonelite subjects may themselves adopt rules to facilitate, rather than constrain, political communication (see Brisset-Foucault 2013:244). Throughout this book, the challenge has been to account for the value of free speech when much of the overt concern has been with the customary, the obligatory, and the moral. The challenge, in fact, has been to see beyond the cultural and political homogenization with which this concern could so easily be confused. A renewed interest in the ideologies of voice in understanding the conditions of free speech has been this book's key response to the challenge. *Parrhêsia* may denote a refreshing alternative to scholarship on the First Amendment and French Revolution, but ethnographic work demands more such alternatives, not only a concept derived from ancient Greece. In this book, the alternative notion has been multivocal morality.

Through his liberalism, the radio elder upheld a "plurality of competing viewpoints," but he did so by reserving to himself the moral authority to assemble those viewpoints for broadcast. Drawing inspiration from Mikhail Bakhtin's (1984) perspective on Fyodor Dostoevsky's novels, this book has sought to demonstrate a practice of multivocality that was distinct from the one in which multiple voices were merged into statistical aggregates (chapter 2). It was also a practice that distinguished Gogo Breeze from many of his fellow presenters, who came on air with various commitments to particular viewpoints (chapters 5 and 6). Gogo Breeze did not shy away from expressing his own views either, but their emergence indicated multivocality in a different key. Whether it was the radio granddaughter confronting him in the studio or a casual encounter in the street,

Gogo Breeze formed his views through dialogue. For the dialogue to take place, he had to allow "a genuine polyphony of fully valid voices" (Bakhtin 1984:6). Some of those voices may have been edited out before broadcast, but multivocality was a feature of practically everything he put on air, including when he was alone in the studio. Free speech as multivocal morality was a value that served the higher value of meeting grandfatherly obligations. It ensured that the grandfather became aware of grievances and that he could remind other figures of authority of their obligations. Radio's sonic and technological affordances contributed to making those obligations compelling, dialogically constituted responses to life's injustices.

Confronting Mill Owners

Gogo Breeze's Concluding Words in the Gaga Controversy

Ndinali kunena kuti ngati munali kumvetsera pologomu ya zamakalata, tafika pachigayo china muno muboma la Chipata, nayankhulanso ndi munthu wina amene ali kugwira ntchito ku Petauke ku Nyampinga. Nayenso ali kugaya kumene kuja. Tsono chimene chinali chokondweretsa kwambiri nkhani imene yochokera kuNyampinga ndi ndinakakonde ngati anthu a ku Petauke anakanditume lamya kufotokoza m'mene ziliri. Anandifotokozera kuti ku Petauke kuja kumene kuli chigayo cha wena amene ali ndi chigayo kuno. Anthu a ku Petauke anagwirizana kuti iwo adzitenga gaga wawo; eni yake vigayo aike mtengo umene iwo aufuna osati m'mene akuchitira kuno kuboma la Chipata vigayo vina bevi ayi. Chifukwa nyambo imene ilipo atipatsa mtengo wotsika ngati ufuna kuti usiye gaga. Tsono ngati ufuna kutenga gaga akupatse mtengo wokwera; basi iwe chimtima pyukupyuku and vikhale vigaga. Tsono gaga uja ukakhala, anzathu aja ali kupezere manera. Namwanena kale atukuka, atenga gaga, akagulitsa ku Lusaka kwa aja amene nawonso amapanga chakudya cha nkhuku. Tsopano ena mwanena mawu kunena kuti avigayo afunika kuti azigula gaga kwa mwini wake chimanga ngati afuna, chifukwa iwo ndikamba pano tere, anandiuza ngati munali kumvetsera bwinobwino mupologamu ya makalata kuti munthu wochokera kumudzi ngati afuna gaga pa tin imodzi amamuchaja five sausand. Ine pano panali nthawi ina yake imene ndinalephera kugula vyakudya va nkhuku. Nidye ndinapita makamaka osalephera koma ndinatenga nkhuku zanga zachiboyi nazikomera muchipinda chifukwa zinali kuonoga nyungu panyumba. Ndiye ndinapita kuti ndikaguleko kagaga kotero kuti nkhuku zimenezi ndinazikhomera chipinda zizidya. Anandigulitsa nsaka ten sausand, ndi popeza ukakhala opempha nangonyamula kupatsa ten pin ija. Sindikudziwa ngati ndalama zija zinapita kwa bosi, kanthu kaya, koma ganizo limene anachita anzathu ku Petauke kuvomera mtengo umodzi, alieyense azinyamula gaga wake ndiye nkhani yachipupu ija sidzakhalapo iyayi. Chifukwa tingachite payekhapayekha ndikuti zinthu zidzakhala zovuta, wena adzangopinda mashati kuti "uyu ndi gaga wanga; nanga chimene ukufuna ndi chiyani?" basi ndi nkhonya zayamba, chifukwa cha gaga. Kofunikira anzathu a vigayo kulingana ndi m'mene mwamvetsera; amene amabweretsa chimanga kuvigayo vanu akuti gaga ndi wawo akufuna audzinyamula osati inuyo mudzitenga. Ndiye gogo ali akupemphani popeza anamtuma kuti afufuze nkhani yonse m'mene inachitikira iyi. Inuyo ikani mtengo umodzi woti ngati wabwera kuti mugaye; ndalama yake ndi yakati. Nkhani ya gaga musagwirepo ayi chifukwa ngati mukhuze gaga mwangoputa mlandu. Gaga mwini wake ndi amene ayenera kuti atonge, "oo gaga uyu, ngati mufuna kuti mugule, mundigule mwakati. Or ngati simufuna kundigula ndipita nawo kunyumba." Oweta nkhuku ndi ambiribiri, ndi amene amatenga mankhwala, basi akagula gaga amatenga mankhwala ndi kusakaniza, vakudya va nkhuku vapezeka. Aliyense tsopano safuna kutaya kanthu kamene kangampatse ndalama. Inu a vigayo, gogo ali kukupemphani kuti ikani mtengo umodzi. Gaga musaukhuze chifukwa mawa ndi mkucha mudzangopinda mashati, chinthu chimene sichifunika kuti chitero iyayi. Akankheni gaga monga m'mene a ku Petauke ali kutengera gaga wawo. Nkhaniyi tsopano yapita patali, chifukwa nyumba ya mphepo ya Breeze FM ili patali. Ku Mozambique, ku Malawi, ee titafika ku Malawi tafika ku Mzimba komwe kwa Bangweni ndikuti ku Mzuzu komwe tili konko. Ndiye yafika kutali kumene kuli vigayo vimene vimagaya chimanga chimenechi; natenga gaga mwamvako ndi mawa zidzasinthika. I congratulate people in Petauke amene anangogwirizana chabe kuti gaga ndi wathu; inu wodziwa za kugaya chabe basi. Sikuchitika tero. Nanga ngati chikuchitika ku Petauke ndiye kuti kunoko ku Chipata, nanga kwina kwake kumene ena ali kudandaula kodi sichikhoza kuchitika. Ah, ndi inu anthu ndi kugwirizana zimene zikhoza kuchitika. Koma nkhani ya gaga, tiyeni tipewe inu eni yake vigayo chifukwa idzakuutsirani kaligone mawa ndi mkucha. Kalata yobwerera tere basi ndi yoti mwauza zabwera zina, si apa tere wina akufotokoza za sikinya, ati, "kodi vikoko ndi chiyani vija? Ndi mwini wake ndani?" Namvanso ndafika pena pakenso pachigayo amatenga maleftovers aja, patsani flour; ine, "a-a, imwe bwanji?" Akuti, "timagulitsa." Mudziwa mtengo wake? Ndafufuzaka, twenty five sausand kwacha nsaka ija ya fifty kg. Agula anthu twenty five sausand. Akugulitsa eni yake vigayo uja mpenyadzuwa - ayi ntheradi, anangotenga kumbuli. Ulendo, ee, kuno wasiya twenty, e, wasiya gaga uja wake wasikinya, anzake apezerapo ndalama. A-a, tiyeni tipewe, tipewe. Nkhani ya chiphuphu, ayi napapata, pulizi ee. Nkhani m'mukamwa yatuluka, yatuluka. Kufunikira ndi kupewa. Uja mnyamata tinali kulankhulana dzana ilo, ayi, "ndi profiti yathu." A-a, ndiko kuombera mapiru pamutu pa anthu kapena kudyererana masuku pamutu. Chinthu chimenechi sichofunikira ayi. Mwini wake chimanga ndi mwini wake gaga. Imvani eni yake vigayo achajani mtengo kuti muone ngati angalephere kupereka ndalama imeneyo. Ngati walephera anene yekha, "iyayi kuti popeza ndalephera mutenge gaga," but as far as I know, they will not fail to pay for their gaga kuti atenge apite nawo, chifukwa akapita kunyumba akagulitsa kwa anthu ena amene amaweta nkhuku. Ayi, takambapo, takambapo. Zikomo kwambiri chifukwa chotengako mbali papologamu imeneyi. Mwathandiza gogo kuyankha kalata imene wina anatilembera. Tiye tizitere nthawi zonse tizithandizana ndikuti chalo chiwame.

I was saying that if you were listening to the letters program, we went to a mill here in the district of Chipata. I was talking to someone who is working in Petauke in Nyampinga. He mills there. Now, what is very pleasing is the story from Nyampinga, and I would have been pleased if people in Petauke had phoned me to explain how things are. He explained to me that there in Petauke is a mill owned by someone who owns a mill here. People in Petauke agreed that they should take their husks; the mill owner should put one price that he wants, not like they do here in Chipata in some mills. Because the bait they give us is a low price if you want to leave the husks. Now if you want to take the husks, they should give you a high price; your heart is beating fast. Now, when the husks stay, our friends are finding a ladder. I said already that they develop, they take the husks, they go and sell in Lusaka to those who make chicken feed. Now, some of you said that mill owners are expected to buy the husks from the maize owners if they want them, because while I am talking here, they told me, if you listened well to the letters program that a person coming from a village, if she wants one bucket of husks, they charge her five thousand. There was a time when I myself failed to buy chicken feed. So, I went, not to fail, but I took my African chickens and closed them into a room, because they were destroying pumpkin seeds in the house. So, I went to buy a few husks so that those chickens I had closed into a room would eat. They sold me a bag for ten thousand, and because you are the one who is asking, I just lifted it and gave ten thousand. I don't know if that money went to the boss—who knows?—but the idea that people in Petauke have to accept one price, everyone should take their husks and the issue of bribe will not arise. Because if we do it on our own, things can be problematic, some will just roll up their sleeves that "that's my husks; what do you want?" and so fists will start, because of the husks. It is important for our friends at mills to do how you have heard: those who bring maize to your mills, they say husks are theirs, they want to take them, not you to take them. So, the grandfather is asking you because they sent him to investigate the entire story how it is happening. You, put one price, when they come to mill; its cost is such and such. Don't seize the husks, because if you do so, you just commit a crime. The owner of the husks is the one who should consider, "Oh, the husks, if you want to buy from me, you buy from me like this. Or if you don't want to buy from me, I will go with them home." There are very many keeping chickens; they take medicine, when they buy husks, they take the medicine and mix, chicken feed is ready. Nobody wants to throw away something that might give them money. You, the mill owners, the grandfather is asking you to put one price. Don't touch the husks, because tomorrow or the day after you will just roll up the sleeves, something that is not needed. Do with husks as people in Petauke do with theirs. This story has now gone far, because the radio Breeze FM reaches far. In Mozambique, in Malawi, yes, when we reach Malawi, we reach Mzima there in Bangweni and in Mzuzu we are there. So, it has arrived far away where there are mills that mill that maize, to take the husks; you will hear tomorrow it will change. I congratulate people in Petauke who simply agreed that husks are ours; you only know how to mill. If it is happening in Petauke, so here in Chipata, what about elsewhere where they are complaining that it cannot happen? Ah, if you people agree, it can happen. But the husks issue, let us be careful, you, the mill owners, because it will bring you trouble tomorrow and the day after. The letter that came like that, you said more things, is not here—someone asking about sunflower seeds, saying, "What are the cakes? Who is the owner?" I also heard when I went to one of the mills, they take those leftovers, give us the flour. I am, "A-a, you, what's that?" They say, "We are selling." Do you know the price? I found out, twenty five thousand for a bag of fifty kilograms. People buy with twenty five thousand. Mill owners sell sunflower seeds—no, indeed they take them as ignorant. Off they go, yeah, they left here twenty, eh, they left sunflower husks; their friends find money. A-a, let us be careful, let us be careful. The issue of bribe—I am pleading, please, yeah. The story has left the mouth, has left. What is important is to be careful. That boy I was talking to the other day, says, "It is our profit." A-a, it is stealing wild fruit from people's heads. That thing is not needed. The owner of maize is the owner of husks. Hear you mill owners, charge a price to see if they fail to give that money. If they fail, they should say so themselves, so that "I failed; you take the husks," but as far as I know, they will not fail to pay for their husks to take them with them, because when they go home, they will sell to people who keep chickens. No, we have talked, we have talked. Thank you very much for taking part in this program. You helped the grandfather to answer the letter someone wrote to us. Let's do like that every time to assist each other for the country to be good.

Helping Miriam Nkhoma

Miriam Nkhoma's Letter to Gogo Breeze

Kalata yanu agogo,
Ngati muli bwino agogo zikomo kwambiri. Agogo ine ndine munthu wo-
ponderezedwa. Makolo yanga anamwalira ku Lusaka anali kusewenza mu
OP, koma abanja amene anasankiidwa kukhala administrator siniziwa ngati
ndalama anatenga kapena alibe, chifukwa niwoona kuti nitchaya kamusun-
gunuka.

Agogo chifukwa chamakabirana niichi. Aba amene ali administrator
anandiitana kuno kumudzi kukasaina mapepala ya ndalama ku Lusaka. Pamene tinaziliza anandiuza kubwerera kumudzi ati ndalama zikachoka azan-
diuza. Koma kuli zii, chino chika ndi cha 5 na nyumba kuli zii agogo. Mapepala onse ali na beve, ndithandizeni napapata. Ndizachita bwanji?
Ndine
Miriam Nkhoma

Your letter, grandfather,
If you are well, thank you very much. Grandfather, I am an exploited person.
My parent died in Lusaka while working at the OP, but I don't know if the
family member who was chosen to be the administrator took the money or
not, because I was forced to disappear.

Grandfather, the issue to discuss is this. The family member who is the
administrator called me here in the village to go to Lusaka to sign documents concerning money. When I finished, he/she told me to return to the
village, saying that when the money comes, he/she will tell me. But there is

nothing, now is the fifth year without anything happening, grandfather. All the documents are with him/her, please help me. What should I do?

I am

Miriam Nkhoma

Gogo Breeze's Response to Miriam Nkhoma on the *Makalata* Program

Malinga ndi m'mene amayi akudandaulira ndi nkhani yomvetsa chisoni chachikulu kuti kholo lanu linamwalira. Tsono munasankha m'mwimiliri kuti akuthandizeni kuti mundalama zija zibwere zonse. Koma tsopano monga mwalemba Chinyanja chanu mukuti anakutchayani musungunuke. Mwina akupitani kumphepete, osakuuzani iyayi. Tsono Gogo mulibe muuza iyayi kuti kodi ngati munakhala pansi powafunsa kodi nanga ndalama zija zili poti. Nanga posankha administrator imeneyo, kodi munalipo anthu angati? Chifukwa ngati iye mwaona kuti m'mene akuyendetsera nkhani imeneyo safuna kuti inu abanja mudziwe paja pamene khoti limalamula kuti ngati administrator wasankhidwa ndipo zochita zake ndi zokabisira muyenera kukhalanso pansi monga banja nomchotsapo munthu uja kuti muikepo wina wake. Tsono mukunena kuti munapita ku Lusaka nokasaiyinira mapepala onse ofunikira. Ndingakupempheni mayi, nanga amene akuthandizana nawo? Mukupenyera ndinu amene mukuthandizana naye ndi mdala ngati ndi mzimayi kuti atenge katundu wonse abwere. Tsono pokhala inuyo mthandizi ndi zotani zimene mwachitapo? Ndingakupempheni kuti kulemba nthawi zina, mumalemba pang'ono koma simufotokoza zonse m'mene zikhoza kukhalira. Ndingakupempheni kuti sabata yamawa patsiku la Mande mukabwere kuti mukaonane naye gogo kotero kuti mukabwera tikhala pansi kuti mundifotokozere bwinobwino zonse m'mene ziliri. Nanga administrator uyu ali paubale wotani nainuyo? Kabwereni kuti mufotokoze: mwina ndikhoza kukuthandizani m'njira imeneyo. Koma chodziwika ndi chakuti anthu amene amasankhidwa kukhala maadministrators ndi anthu amene nthawi zina amakhala ndi kampeni kumphasa kufuna kuti adye ndiwo ndi ndalama za amasiye. Tsono kumbukirani kuti katundu wa masiye sibwino kudya mwachisawawa, chifukwa ngati mungodya katundu wa masiye, eh, chidya idyatero, mudzatengapo tsoka. Amayi kabwereni kuti tikaone njira imene tingakhoze kuthandizirana pamenepapa chifukwa nkhani yanu ndi yaikulu ndithu kuti mwina mwake tikapeza mfungulo ndikuti muzingopita kukhoti panthawi yomweyo nokadulira samoni munthu. Basi; kuti khoti likamchotse pautsogoleri wa chuma chimenecho.

Regarding the way the woman is complaining, it is a story that makes one feel very sad that your parent died. Now you chose a representative to help you to get all the money. But now as you wrote your Chinyanja, you are forced to disappear. Maybe he/she making you stay behind, without telling you. Now you haven't told the grandfather whether you sat down to ask them where that money is. What about when choosing the administrator, how many of you were there? For if the one taking care of the issue looks like he/she doesn't want to you, the family members, to know despite the court ruling that the administrator has been chosen and their behavior is to hide things, you need to sit down again as a family to remove that person so that you can put down another one instead. Now you are saying that you went to Lusaka to sign all the required papers. May I ask you, mother, what about the one who is helping as well? You are watching the one who is helping along, whether it is an old man or a woman; he/she might bring all the belongings? Now if you are the helper, what have you done? I would ask you that sometimes when you write, you write a little and don't explain everything about how things might be. I ask you to come next week on Monday to see the grandfather so that when you come we sit down for you to explain well to me how everything is. What sort of kinship does the administrator have with you? Come to explain; maybe I can assist you in that way. But what is known is that the people who are chosen to be administrators sometimes have a hidden agenda to eat the money that belongs to the bereaved. Now remember that it is not good to eat the property of the bereaved by force, because when you just eat the property of the bereaved, eating anyhow, you will pick up misfortune. Mother, come here so that we can see the way we might help each other there, because your story is a big one. Maybe we will find a key for you to go to the court to summon the person. That's it: the court will remove him/her from the leadership over that wealth.

The Conversation between Gogo Breeze and Miriam Nkhoma

[*Miriam Nkhoma's infant cries*]

GOGO BREEZE: Alire uyu; alibe kanthu; osavutika iyayi.

MIRIAM NKHOMA: Oho.

GOGO BREEZE: Monga ndanena kuti kalata yanu yafika ndipo tinayankha. Tsono tilibe kuyankha in full kuti tikukondweretseni pazimene inuyo munafotokoza. Chifukwa chake ndinakamba "aa mubwere kuti mutiuze kuti nkhani yonse imeneyi inali bwanji kuti ifike kuti inuyo mulembe makalata kuti mupemphe thandizo kuchokera kuno kunyumba yamphepo Breeze FM." Poyamba ndingapemphe kwa inu amayi mutiuze dzina lanu, kumene mumachokera. Basi, tiyambapo nkhani m'mene ikhoza kukhalira.

MIRIAM NKHOMA: Ayi, dzina langa ndine Miriam Nkhoma, ndinachokera, pamudzi wathu ndi paKawambe ndili kuchikwati kwa Kangulu. Dandaulo langa; mwadziwa andala anga anamwalira ku Lusaka. Tsopano pamene anamwalira, anandiitana ati "bwerani kuno." So, kupita kuja ndinapeza vonse vapologamu akonza kale. Administrator wasankha, ine kulibe. Nauza kuti "ayi anatha nkhani ya tate wanu, so monse mwamakoti ndinaendamo, tinasayina bwinobwino." Koma chondidabwitsa ndalama lomba sanandipatse. Akuti zinali pochoka, koma mdala ndi five years. Lomba ine maganizo ndikafunseko kuti kapena agogo angathandizeko kuti m'mene zingakhalire. Ndiponso nyumba ya veve mdala anatenga. Sindidziwa ngati anagulitsa kaya anachita chiyani ndiponso na, amdala iwo anakamba kuti "a-a iwe vonsevonse ine ndakonzekeratu." Ngati amwalira ndikamvako. Koma ndidabwa administrator sachitapo chilichonse. China chikukhala chodabwitsa choti ndi m'mene akuchitira vovala vamdala nobweretsa administrator nopereka kwa mayi wawo. Mayi wawo nkolimitsira kumunda, ine osandiuza. So, dandaulo yanga ndi iyo - a, ndidandaule kwa gogo kuti kapena angathandizeko.

GOGO BREEZE: Mm. Nanga posankha administrator, muimiliri ameneyo - inuyo munaliko?

MIRIAM NKHOMA: A-a, kunalibe. Napeza chabe wati anasankhako kwa mdala ku Lusaka.

GOGO BREEZE: Amene anasankha ndani?

MIRIAM NKHOMA: Sindingadziwe bwinobwino; anangouza kuti awa ndi administrator.

GOGO BREEZE: Iwo administratorwo, ali ndi udindo wotani m'banja? Ndi chiyani wawo? Nchimene ndifuna kudziwa.

MIRIAM NKHOMA: Iwowa ndi akulu wawo.

GOGO BREEZE: Atate anu anali wang'ono?

MIRIAM NKHOMA: Ee.

GOGO BREEZE: Ndiye mkulu wawo kutenga udindo?

MIRIAM NKHOMA: Mm.

GOGO BREEZE: Nanga pamene anamwalira atate anu awa, anasiya amano?

MIRIAM NKHOMA: A-a, amayi anamwalira.

GOGO BREEZE: Amayi anamwalira?

MIRIAM NKHOMA: Mm.

GOGO BREEZE: Ndiye mwana wamkulu - aliko?

MIRIAM NKHOMA: Ndi ine amene.

GOGO BREEZE: Mm. Nanga pamene mutaona kuti munasayina - mukafikanso kapena munatuma lamya kapena kwalembera kalata kuti akuuzeni kodi zinthu zikafika poti?

MIRIAM NKHOMA: Ee ndimatuma lamya.

GOGO BREEZE: Amati bwanji?

MIRIAM NKHOMA: Amandiuza "aa, zikadalibe pokonzeka; ndikatuma zikadali pokonzeka. Zikakonzeka ndikuuzani." Ndadabwa lomba mpakana five years. Ndamva pambuyo ndalama zachoka koma ine sizinachoke mpakana lomba.

GOGO BREEZE: Mm. Nanga panthawi yomwe munaganiza kuti mulembe kalata kuno kunyumba yamphepo - munawatumirako lamya kuti ayankhe bwino-bwino m'mene ziliri?

MIRIAM NKHOMA: Ndinawatumirako lamya, koma akulu wa iwo administrator anabwera kuno akuti "osavutika iwe ndi amene amatumatuma malamya, so iwe usavutike. Nati ndifotokozere ndalama ngati zatengedwa adzabwera akufotokozerani amayi anu. Adzatenga iwo amayi wanu nokubweretserani."

GOGO BREEZE: Amayi wanu woti amene akunena?

MIRIAM NKHOMA: Anena akulu a mdala, poti nakhala nawo, so ngati chizolo-werezi ndimati "mayi."

GOGO BREEZE: Oho.

MIRIAM NKHOMA: Ee.

GOGO BREEZE: Nanga amene munazolowerana nawo, amene akuti amayi wanu awo, munawafunsa kodi ndalama bwanji kodi uko?

MIRIAM NKHOMA: Malamya ndimatuma kwa iwo kumene kuja amene ana-sankha administrator.

GOGO BREEZE: Mm.

MIRIAM NKHOMA: Ehe, amene ndikuti mayi ndi amene anasankha administra-tor. Tinene ndi kubele laling'ono, a iwo, atate, amayi wawo ndi waukulu. Iwo aja, amayi wawo ndi wang'ono.

GOGO BREEZE: Oho.

MIRIAM NKHOMA: Ehe. Chifukwa chake anasankha iwo administrator, katundu, vovala, kupereka kwa mayi wawo kukalimitsira kumunda iwo mayi wawo. Ndiitane kuti nivi, koma ndikudabwa kuti iyai, vina vinalimitsidwa ku-munda, ndi m'mene zimakhalira.

GOGO BREEZE: Mm. BaHarri, mwamva nkhaniyi? Kodi ndi m'mene zikhoza kukhalira? Inuyo pokhala mng'ono wanu wamwalira, ndinu wamkulu pabanja; sitidziwa m'mene mumachitira ku Mangalande uko. Kodi mun-gatenge katundu wa mng'ono wanu kugwiritisidwa ntchito, ana pabanja amene anasiyidwa, kodi zingakhale motere?

HARRI ENGLUND: Zikakhala motere ndi iyayi, ndi kulakwa ndithu. Ndiye sizingatheke kwenikweni kwathuko, nanga si malamulo amakhala amphamvu ndithu. Ndiye zonsezi zimakhala ujeni well documented. Amasayinira, ndiye sizingatheke kuti munthu akhoza kuthawa ndi ndalama za anzao pabanja. Sindikudziwa kunoko malamulo amakhala bwanji pankhani imeneyo. Nanga si zikumveka ngati anali kukhoti kale. Nkhani inayambira kukhotiko, koma mpaka pano sizinalongokosoke ayi.

GOGO BREEZE: Kukhoti iyeyo mzimayi sanapiteko.

HARRI ENGLUND: Mm.

GOGO BREEZE: Koma amene ali kukhala ku Lusaka uja ndi amene anapita kukhoti, sitero?

MIRIAM NKHOMA: Eya.

GOGO BREEZE: Atasankha woimilira kuti ndi amene atsatire zonse za uyo womwalira. Ndiye anasayiniranasayinirana, koma amene anasankha uyo, zinthu sakuziyendetsa m'njira yake.

HARRI ENGLUND: Ehe.

GOGO BREEZE: Kotero kuti amayi awo, aunt, titero, because the mother died, aunt, ndi amene anatsimikisira kuti zinthu zakonzeka ndiye "ndibwera nazo ndi ine." Chifukwa chake ndinali kufunsa amayiyo kodi anafotokozapo kalikonse?

MIRIAM NKHOMA: Sanandifotokoze kalikonse.

GOGO BREEZE: Chingakukomereni ndi chiti? Kuti mwafunse amayi wanu amene anakusungani, sitero?

MIRIAM NKHOMA: Mm.

GOGO BREEZE: Kuti kodi ndalama zikalipo potuluka? Ngati mwafunsa akuyankhani, pamenepo pamene tingapeze njira yokuthandizirani.

MIRIAM NKHOMA: Ah, iwo ndi amene ndikukamba ndi mayi poti ndi anti, kumbuyoko ndinakhala nawo pamene anamwalira amayi. Ndi administrator amene.

GOGO BREEZE: Amayi amenewo?

MIRIAM NKHOMA: Ehe. Ndi administrator amene.

GOGO BREEZE: Ali nawo mwamuna wawo?

MIRIAM NKHOMA: A-a, mwamuna alibe. Tsono kumene ndimatumira mafoni, ndikatumira, basi akuti "ayi, sizinachoke." Ndikawatumira sizinachoke. Nthawi zina akadziwa ndi ineyo basi, wakazima foni.

GOGO BREEZE: O-o. [laughs] Zazunza! [laughs] Koma kukamba mpakati ndi mpakati ofesi ya, Office of the President, ndili ndi mbale amene anachita retire posachedwapa ndiyense yakhala less than two years. Some two three months ago ndalama zake zonse anampatsa. Tsono m'mene mukunenera apo mukuti amayi awo ndi amene administrator amene ali mayi wanu amene munakhala nawo, anti wanu titero, ndiye mukatumira lamya, azimitsa. Aa. [*pause of four seconds*] Mwina chotheka pangakhale vuto. Muli nazo mphamvu? Zakuti muyende maofesi?

MIRIAM NKHOMA: Ayi, ndingayende.

GOGO BREEZE: Ine pano, mwana wanga anamwalira. Anasiya mkazi ndi kamwana. Iye wamkazi ndi administrator chifukwa chake ndinakufunsani kodi amano ndi wamoyo. Ndiye anakakhala administrator nothandizidwa ndi mlamu. So ine wanga mwana anamwalira, mkazi wake ndi administrator; mlamu wake angothandiza pobwera pambuyo chabe. Ndi m'mene ziliri. Tsono inuyo pezani njira imene ingakuthandizeni kuti mukafike kuja mukafunse "mm, masiku apitapo ambiri, tiyeni tifikeko, nanenso tsopano ndakula kuti tione m'mene tikhoza kuchitira." Mukati munthu anaononga katundu upeza kuti amakamba ichi chabooka, icho, icho, dziwani kuti apa pali chiyani?

MIRIAM NKHOMA: Sipali bwino.

GOGO BREEZE: Sipali bwino. Timakamba pali Chinyanjanso kuti galu wamkota sakandira?

MIRIAM NKHOMA: Pachabe.

GOGO BREEZE: Pachabe.

[*both laugh*]

GOGO BREEZE: Eh? Mukaona kuti anapondaponda apa ndi apa dziwani kuti ndalama zinabwera anaononga. Tsono zimene munanena kuti nyumba, mukuti anatenga iwo kapena anaigulitsa?

MIRIAM NKHOMA: Iwo akuoneka ngati anatenga nyumba, inali ku Chipata Compound.

GOGO BREEZE: Ehe.

MIRIAM NKHOMA: Iwo anakhala ku . . .

[*pause of three seconds*]

GOGO BREEZE: Anali kukhala kwina?

MIRIAM NKHOMA: Ee.

GOGO BREEZE: Nanga amakhala kuti?

MIRIAM NKHOMA: Amdala ndi amene anakhala ku Chipata Compound.

GOGO BREEZE: Aha.

MIRIAM NKHOMA: Ehe. Veve administrator amakhala kwa Chasanka.

GOGO BREEZE: Nanga ali kuti?

MIRIAM NKHOMA: Ali kwa Chasanka kumene. Tsono nyumba anatenga kumene kuja anati aigulire pafupi.

GOGO BREEZE: Kuthantauza chiyani?

MIRIAM NKHOMA: Kuti aigulitse.

GOGO BREEZE: Ee.

MIRIAM NKHOMA: Ikhale pafupi ndi iwo, ndi m'mene anandifotokozera pamene ndinali ku Lusaka. Akuti "nyumba ija ili kutali, kufunika tiigulitse, tigulire kuno kufupi kuti tidziwona, tiikemo arenti. Basi, ndalama ndikalandira ndikubweretseni."

GOGO BREEZE: Lomba nyumba anagulitsa?

MIRIAM NKHOMA: Sindidziwa pamene apo, anandiuza nyumba koma tinaitenga kuja . . .

[pause of four seconds]

MIRIAM NKHOMA: Lomba tilibe kuona bwinobwino poti tichiteko ndondomeko yeniyeni.

GOGO BREEZE: Ayi, azikamba Chinyanja chenicheni. Anene kuti "nyumba tinagulitsa, koma ndalama zilipo tidakalibe kugula nyumba ina monga tinapangana." Tsono mukapita kuja inuyo mukayamba kufunsa: "Kodi nyumba munagulitsa?" Ngati anagulitsa, nanga ina inagulidwa, akayankhe okha. Osatenga mwandewu koma kutenga ndithu step by step, khwerero after khwerero. Mukafike pamapeto, oh nkhani ili yotero. Lomba popeza mupitirira nkhani ya ndalama ndingapemphe kuti mukhale ndi ndalama zokwana muthumba kupewa zakudya zokupatsani iwo. Chifukwa apa tsopano pali moyo naimfa.

MIRIAM NKHOMA: Ndi zoona ngako.

GOGO BREEZE: Eh?

MIRIAM NKHOMA: Ndi zoona. Nanga ndikafikire kuti agogo?

GOGO BREEZE: Kulibe achibale?

MIRIAM NKHOMA: Ndiwo amene aja aliko komwe.

GOGO BREEZE: Koma musakakhale masiku ambiri. Mwafika lero, usiku, monga Johabe, ngati wanyamuka Johabe five thirty mufika ku Lusaka maeleven hours. Mucheza, mucheza, nthawi ya madzulo, ndiye pamene nkhani imakoma tsopano. Kuti kukhala kunali kwina kwake kukhala kumeneko inuyo mukanakhala komweko nokasayina samoni kuti "achoke paumiliri wa chuma cha atate wanga. Nakula tsopano." Basi. Ndikuti mlanduwa mwathetsa. Ndi katundu wonse umene atate anu anasiya, iwo anabereka ana ndiye kuti udzapite kwa ana awo.

MIRIAM NKHOMA: Kumene using wana awo.

GOGO BREEZE: [laughs]

MIRIAM NKHOMA: Palibe chinanso chimene ndinaganiza. Katundu, ndalama zonse ndi zophunzitsira wana awo.

GOGO BREEZE: Aha.

MIRIAM NKHOMA: Ine ndizivutika.

GOGO BREEZE: Two, zovala. Iwo zovala kutenga zolimitsira, inu wana osadziwa. Ee, "ndi zovala za mdala, inuyo mulibe nazo ntchito iyayi." Koma abanja akhala pansi.

MIRIAM NKHOMA: Mm.

GOGO BREEZE: "Nanga jeketi iyi atenge ndani, nanga izo, atenge ndani?" Ndi m'mene zimakhalira. Tsono iye administrator yekha nutenga zovala zija nokapatsa mayi wawo akalimitsire, ndi mlandu umene anapanga amenewu. Mukhoza kuwafolera kuti afotokoze bwino.

MIRIAM NKHOMA: Ndi chimene ndikudabwa osandiitana kuti wabwera kuno katundu wa atate wako nivi vovala, koma iwo kutenga nupatsa mayi wawo, mayi wawo akuti "oo, nutenga katundu uja, nukupatsako ku Malawi" kumene amalima kumunda kwawo, kwa iwo kwa ndani, mayi wawo.

GOGO BREEZE: Iyayi.

MIRIAM NKHOMA: Osagawireko abanja, atate anali nawo azing'ono awonso, nukupatsako wana wa azing'ono awo, koma kulimitsira kumundako, ndi m'mene zimakhalira?

GOGO BREEZE: Ndiyeno, kupambana kuti mukafunse zonsezi mukapita kuja, kupewa mtera umene umachitika nthawi zina kuti "oo, ndichotse uyu, ativute." Muli konkuno mukhoza kuwadulira samoni kuti akabwera adzafotokoze. Mukayambire pankhani ya zovala.

MIRIAM NKHOMA: Mm.

GOGO BREEZE: Zovala aunti apatsa mawu analimitsira munda, kodi ndi m'mene zimakhalira? Tsono khoti ikaweruza nkhani sandesande, ikapeza kuti sibwino iyayi, monga kumene kwa anzathu, zimene akamba aHarri pano. Amalemberatu kuja, alemberatu, popeza ife pepa iyi, timaiopa kuti tilembepo. Tingosunga chabe m'mutu kuti "a-a katundu ndi wauje wauje." [laughs] Koma anzathu akalemba angosonyeza pepa chabe. Ladzana, eh, dzulo, dzana, pa Satade, Pauline anali pamphepo. Anali kufotokoza nkhani ya will; m'mene ifunikira kutsatiridwa. Tsono izi; mdala alibe polemba, analemba?

MIRIAM NKHOMA: Ee analemba vonse

GOGO BREEZE: E!

MIRIAM NKHOMA: Vonse analemba, mapepa panali nayo, ku OP kuja anatenga mapepa enawo.

GOGO BREEZE: [Turning to Harri Englund] Eeh, it's a big case! [laughs] Nkhani yanu amayi ili ndi umboni. Ili ndi umboni, kuti akabweretse mapepala onse amenewo, muyambire pazovala, zimene munaona ndi maso. Zovala zinabwera ndi anapatsa amao, amao aja analimitsira kumunda, "Ndikufuna kudziwa kodi ndi m'mene zikhalira?" Khoti ikayang'anayang'ana pankhani

imeneyi adzakufunsani, "Chofunika kuti chichitike apo ndi chiyani tsopano?" Kufuna kuti utsogoleri umene ali nawo mayi awa uchoke. Muta-
bwera mwense abanja, abanja akaimilira, "tasankha uyu ndi amene adzatenga udindo."

MIRIAM NKHOMA: Mm.

GOGO BREEZE: Oo, amayi, bweretsani mapepala onse aja. Mukapeza mapepala
aja, ndalama anatenga, ndalama anatenga, nanga ndalamazi zili kuti? Basi,
akagona mukamboliboli.

[all laugh]

GOGO BREEZE: Ine ndizimvako m'mene muchitire, yambani pazovala.

MIRIAM NKHOMA: Mm.

GOGO BREEZE: Bwa?

MIRIAM NKHOMA: Apa zingatheke, koma mukudziwa kuti kuno ndi kumudzi
agogo kuti ndalama muipeze kuti yochokera kuno kufika kuja?

GOGO BREEZE: Ndikuyankhula pazovala.

MIRIAM NKHOMA: Zovala?

GOGO BREEZE: Zovala izi zinabwera kuno kumudzi.

MIRIAM NKHOMA: Ee.

GOGO BREEZE: Umboni muli nawo.

MIRIAM NKHOMA: Ehe.

GOGO BREEZE: Ndiye khoti limene litimfole ndi lakuno.

MIRIAM NKHOMA: Aha.

GOGO BREEZE: Mukafola kuno chisamoni chipita kuja, messenger kuja, akam-
patsa, khoti ee presiding officer, "Kaperekeni samoni pa house number ya-
kutiyakuti." Address yonse ya mayi amene anali kufunda katundu umenewu
mukalembetse pasamoni ya kukhoti. Ndiye ikapita. Mwina akakupempheni,
"Tipatseni chiyani, ndalama kuti tipositire." Basi; kuwapatsa, nkhani yanu
yatha.

MIRIAM NKHOMA: Mm.

GOGO BREEZE: Eeh. Simuona kutalika kwa nkhani yake, chifukwa chake ndikuti, a-a, kabwereni mufotokoze.

MIRIAM NKHOMA: Mm.

GOGO BREEZE: Mm, chifukwa zovala izi zidzaulula nkhani zonse zimene zina-
chitika. Katundu wa masiye musaudalire iyayi, mavuto.

MIRIAM NKHOMA: Ndifunsepo agogo?

GOGO BREEZE: Shani?

MIRIAM NKHOMA: Monga ku OP yakuno moti kukafunse, sizingatheke?

GOGO BREEZE: Mm, pamene anamwalira, anali kuti kugwira ntchito?

MIRIAM NKHOMA: Ndi kumene ku Office of President.

GOGO BREEZE: Ku Lusaka?

MIRIAM NKHOMA: Mm.

GOGO BREEZE: Mapepala muli nawo?

MIRIAM NKHOMA: Mapepa ali nayo komwe ku Lusaka.

GOGO BREEZE: Nanga record ili m'mutu, muidziwa bwinobwino?

MIRIAM NKHOMA: Mm, koma malekodi, ndisaname bodza, koma chabe ndi-nangotenga foni namba yawo kuti ndiziwatumire foni, ya iwo administrator.

GOGO BREEZE: Chikanakhala chapafupi monga ndanena kuti tikanafunsa ku ofesi ya kuno, koma tsopano padzafunika mapepa; kaya ndi pay slip ya mdala anathyoka; kaya ndi kalata; kaya ndi death certificate. Muli nayo, ndi kuti mukanakhala ndi mpata wokuthandizani. Kukafunsa. Koma m'mene ziliri apa, kufunsa kumeneko kudzathandiza ngati mukatenga mayi ame-newo kuti "tiyeni tikafunse kuofesi, kuti ndalama izi zituluke liti," njiranso ina iyi. Ngati mulibe mapepala a amene anamwalira. Muti munali nawo, ndikanene kuti mukalembe, muchite fotokope, muikire mukalata ija yoti ndikhoza kuwafunsa kunoko. Koma kuti palibe ndi kofunika kuti mu-katenge administrator uja naimwe mukapite kuofesi ya OP.

[pause of four seconds]

MIRIAM NKHOMA: Mm.

GOGO BREEZE: Bwa?

MIRIAM NKHOMA: Kaya apa, mm, woimirira mantha.

GOGO BREEZE: Mm.

MIRIAM NKHOMA: Mm. Sindinaonepo, n'zoyamba.

GOGO BREEZE: Oh mama, zichitika! [laughs] Pofuna, pogawana ufa akuti osa-chita manyazi iyayi kapena mantha. Ngati mugawane ufa, mufuna kukhuta nawo kaya!

[all laugh]

GOGO BREEZE: Kuphanga!

MIRIAM NKHOMA: Kuphanga kwake ndi yoipa kaya.

GOGO BREEZE: Ndiye yafika nthawi, yakwana nthawi tsopano kuti nanunso muphangeko. Lomba kuphanga kwanu kudzapangitsa wina kuti akalowe m'ndende, chifukwa sinkhani ya masewera a-a. Bwa?

[pause of three seconds]

MIRIAM NKHOMA: Ah, tione m'mene zikhalire.

GOGO BREEZE: Wati? Moyo ukhale womasuka. Nyumba yamphepo ndi yanu, ngati zakuvutani, bwerani, funsani, tidzayesa kuyankha.

[Miriam Nkhoma's infant cries]

GOGO BREEZE: Let that one cry; no problem; don't worry.

MIRIAM NKHOMA: Oho.

GOGO BREEZE: As I said, your letter arrived and we replied. Now we did not answer you in full to satisfy you on what you described. That is why I said, "You should come to tell us the whole story, how it happened that you wrote the letter to ask for assistance from this house on air, Breeze FM." Firstly, I would like to ask you, mother, to tell us your name, where you are from. That's it, we start the story how it might be.

MIRIAM NKHOMA: No, my name is Miriam Nkhoma. I come from—our village is in Kawambe. I was married in Kangulu. My complaint: you know that my old man died in Lusaka. Now when he died, they [the bereaved] asked me, said, "Come here." So, going there, I found that they had already prepared the whole program. They had chosen the administrator without me. And they said that "no, they finished your dad's case, so I went to all the courts; we signed very well." But what made me wonder was that now they did not give me the money. They said it would come, but now the old man has been dead for five years. Now my thoughts: I should go and ask if the grandfather might help me on how things are. And the old man's house they took. I don't know if they sold it or did what and besides, the old man himself said that "a-a you, everything I have prepared." If he dies, I will hear. But I wonder why the administrator isn't doing anything. The other thing that is strange is what they do with the old man's clothes. The administrator gives them to his/her mother. His/her mother uses them to pay for farm labor, not telling me. So, my complaint—ah, I should complain to the grandfather, perhaps he can help me.

GOGO BREEZE: Mm. What about when choosing the administrator, that representative—were you there?

MIRIAM NKHOMA: A-a, I wasn't. I just discovered that they had chosen at the old man's place in Lusaka.

GOGO BREEZE: Who chose him/her?

MIRIAM NKHOMA: I don't know very well; they just told me that he/she is the administrator.

GOGO BREEZE: This administrator, what sort of responsibility does he/she have in the family? What is his/her role? That's what I want to know.

MIRIAM NKHOMA: He/she is his elder sibling.

GOGO BREEZE: Your dad was the younger one?

MIRIAM NKHOMA: Yes.

GOGO BREEZE: And his elder sibling took the responsibility?

MIRIAM NKHOMA: Mm.

GOGO BREEZE: What about when your dad died, did he leave your mother?

MIRIAM NKHOMA: A-a, mother died.

GOGO BREEZE: Mother died?

MIRIAM NKHOMA: Mm.

GOGO BREEZE: What about a senior child—is there one?

MIRIAM NKHOMA: That's me.

GOGO BREEZE: Mm. What about when you had signed—did you go again or did you phone or did you write a letter so that he/she tells you where things had gotten to?

MIRIAM NKHOMA: Yes, I phoned.

GOGO BREEZE: What did he/she say?

MIRIAM NKHOMA: He/she told me, "Ah, it is not yet ready. I will phone you when it is ready. When it is ready, I will tell you." Now I wonder, for five years. I heard afterward that the money was released, but for me it was not released until now.

GOGO BREEZE: Mm. What about when you thought that you would write a letter here to the house of airwaves—did you phone him/her so that he/she would answer well how things are?

MIRIAM NKHOMA: I did phone him/her, but the administrator's elder sibling came here saying, "Don't you worry, you are the one who phoned, so don't you worry. Let me explain that if the money is taken, your mother will come and tell you. Your mother will take it and bring to you."

GOGO BREEZE: Who is your mother they are talking about?

MIRIAM NKHOMA: They said the old man's elder sibling; namely, I used to live with her, so by habit I call her "mother."

GOGO BREEZE: Oho.

MIRIAM NKHOMA: Yes.

GOGO BREEZE: What about the one you got used to, the one you call your mother, did you ask her about the money there?

MIRIAM NKHOMA: I phoned the one there they chose the administrator.

GOGO BREEZE: Mm.

MIRIAM NKHOMA: Ehe, the one I call mother is the one they chose as the administrator. We should say small breast, his, dad's, mother is the senior one. That one, her mother is the junior one.

GOGO BREEZE: Oho.

MIRIAM NKHOMA: Ehe. That's why they chose her as the administrator, belongings, clothes, giving them to her mother to pay for labor in her mother's field. I am wondering, some things were used to pay for farm labor, that's how it is.

GOGO BREEZE: Harri, did you hear the story? Is that how it can be? While you are alive, your younger sibling dies, you are the senior in your family; we don't know how you do things there in England. Would you be able to take and use your younger sibling's property, while the children in his/her family are left behind, would that be possible?

HARRI ENGLUND: When it is like that, that's to make a mistake really. It couldn't really happen in our place, the laws are very powerful. Everything is well documented. They sign, and it is not possible that a person could run away with family money. I don't know how the law is here regarding this matter. It sounds like they already went to court. The case began in court, but it has not been resolved until now.

GOGO BREEZE: This mother here has not gone to court.

HARRI ENGLUND: Mm.

GOGO BREEZE: But the one who is in Lusaka went to court, isn't that right?

MIRIAM NKHOMA: Yes.

GOGO BREEZE: They chose a representative to follow up on everything to do with the deceased. And they signed and signed, but the one they chose, she is not conducting things the way they should.

HARRI ENGLUND: Ehe.

GOGO BREEZE: That is how her mother, aunt, let's say so, because the mother died, aunt is the one who confirmed that when everything has been prepared, "I will come with them." That's why I was asking this mother if she had explained anything.

MIRIAM NKHOMA: She has not explained anything to me.

GOGO BREEZE: What is it that might satisfy you? That you should ask your mother who looked after you, isn't that so?

MIRIAM NKHOMA: Mm.

GOGO BREEZE: Has the money not been released? If you ask her, she will reply to you, then we will find a way of assisting you.

MIRIAM NKHOMA: Ah, she is the one I am saying is the mother, that is the aunt, previously I lived with her when mother died. She is the administrator.

GOGO BREEZE: That mother?

MIRIAM NKHOMA: Ehe. That's the administrator.

GOGO BREEZE: Does she have a husband?

MIRIAM NKHOMA: A-a, she doesn't have a husband. Now where I phoned, when I phone, she says, "No, it has not been released." When I phone, it has not been released. Sometimes when she knows it is me, that's it, she switches off the phone.

GOGO BREEZE: O-o. [laughs] Things got sour! [laughs] But to talk about facts, inside the Office of the President, I have a relative who retired recently, and it all took less than two years. Some two-three months ago they gave him all the money. Now the way you are saying here, you are saying that the mother who is the administrator who is your mother you lived with, your aunt, let's say so, and when you phone her, she switches off. Ah. [*pause of four seconds*] Maybe there can be a difficulty. Do you have energy? Could you visit offices?

MIRIAM NKHOMA: Well, I can visit.

GOGO BREEZE: Myself here, my child died. He left a wife and a young child. The wife is the administrator, that's why I asked you if your mother is alive. And she was the administrator helped by the brother-in-law. So my child died, his wife is the administrator; her brother-in-law only helps in the background. That's how it is. Now find a way of helping yourself to get there to ask, "Mm, very many days have gone, let's get there, I also have grown up now so that we can see how we do things." A person who has damaged property, you will find he/she will say it had holes, whatever, do you know what that is?

MIRIAM NKHOMA: It is not good.

GOGO BREEZE: It is not good. We say in Chinyanja that an old dog does not dig for what?

MIRIAM NKHOMA: For nothing.

GOGO BREEZE: For nothing.

[*both laugh*]

GOGO BREEZE: Eh? You will go and see that she went here and there, you will know that the money came but she used it. Now what you said about the house, are you saying she took it or sold it?

MIRIAM NKHOMA: It looks like she took the house, it is in Chipata Compound.

GOGO BREEZE: Ehe.

MIRIAM NKHOMA: She lived in . . .

[*pause of three seconds*]

GOGO BREEZE: She lived elsewhere?

MIRIAM NKHOMA: Yes.

GOGO BREEZE: Where does she live?

MIRIAM NKHOMA: The old man lived in Chipata Compound.

GOGO BREEZE: Aha.

MIRIAM NKHOMA: Ehe. The administrator lived in Chasanka.

GOGO BREEZE: Where is she now?

MIRIAM NKHOMA: She is there in Chasanka. Now the house she took there she said she would buy another house close by.

GOGO BREEZE: Meaning what?

MIRIAM NKHOMA: That she would sell it.

GOGO BREEZE: Yes.

MIRIAM NKHOMA: It should be close to her, that's how she explained to me when I was in Lusaka. She said "the house is far away, better we sell it, we should buy here nearby, we'll put in tenants. That's it, when I receive the money, I will bring it to you."

GOGO BREEZE: Now, did she sell the house?

MIRIAM NKHOMA: I don't know how it is there, she told me that the house we took there . . .

[*pause of four seconds*]

MIRIAM NKHOMA: Now we don't see very well what plan we should make.

GOGO BREEZE: No, she should speak proper Chinyanja. She should say that "the house we have sold, but the money is there, we haven't bought another house as we agreed." Now when you go there, you start to ask: "Did you sell the house?" Don't do it in a confrontational way but take step by step, ladder step after ladder step. Toward the end, oh, that's how the story is. Now because you are pursuing the issue of money, I would ask you to have enough money in the pocket to avoid the food they give you. Because here is now both life and death.

MIRIAM NKHOMA: That is very true.

GOGO BREEZE: Eh?

MIRIAM NKHOMA: It's true. Where should I stay, grandfather?

GOGO BREEZE: Are there no relatives?

MIRIAM NKHOMA: She is the only one there.

GOGO BREEZE: But you shouldn't stay for many days. You arrive today at night, such as on Johabe, if you embark on Johabe five thirty, you'll arrive in Lusaka at eleven hours. You chat, you chat, in the evening chatting goes well. Had there been somewhere else to stay there, you would have stayed there to sign the summons so that "she leaves as the representative of my dad's wealth. I have grown up now." That's it. I am saying that you have finished the dispute. And all the belongings your dad left behind, he had children and they should go to his children.

MIRIAM NKHOMA: There she is using her children.

GOGO BREEZE: [*laughs*]

MIRIAM NKHOMA: There is nothing else I have thought of. Belongings, all the money are for educating her own children.

GOGO BREEZE: Aha.

MIRIAM NKHOMA: I have to suffer.

GOGO BREEZE: Two, the clothes. She uses the clothes to pay for farming, without the knowledge of you the children. "Yes, they are the old man's clothes, you have no business with them." But family members should sit down.

MIRIAM NKHOMA: Mm.

GOGO BREEZE: "What about this jacket, who is going to take it, what about these, who is going to take them?" That's how it will be. Now for the administrator to take the clothes on her own and to give her mother to use as a payment for farming, she is making a court case there. You can sue her so that she will explain well.

MIRIAM NKHOMA: That's what I wonder about, not calling me that your dad's belongings have arrived here, here are your clothes, but she takes and gives her mother, her mother says "oo, I take those belongings and give in Malawi," where she cultivates her garden, to whom, to her mother.

GOGO BREEZE: No.

MIRIAM NKHOMA: Without sharing with the family, dad had his younger siblings too, he provided for the children of his younger siblings, but to pay for farming in the garden, is that how it is?

GOGO BREEZE: And so, the best is that you go and ask about all this when you go there, avoiding the medicine that happens sometimes, "Oo, I have to remove this one, she will cause us trouble." While you are here, you can issue summons for her to come and explain. You should start with the issue of clothes.

MIRIAM NKHOMA: Mm.

GOGO BREEZE: Aunt gave the clothes for farming in the garden, is that how it is? Now when the court rules by investigating the case in detail, it will find that this is not good, like where our friends live, what Harri was saying here. They really write down things there, they really write down, while for us paper, we fear writing. We only keep it in our head what belongs to whom. [laughs] But when our friends write, they only have to show paper. The day before yesterday, eh, yesterday, the day before yesterday, on Saturday, Pauline was on air. She was explaining the issue of a will; how it is necessary to pursue it. Now these things; the old man didn't write down, did he?

MIRIAM NKHOMA: Yes, he wrote down everything.

GOGO BREEZE: E!

MIRIAM NKHOMA: Everything he wrote down, the papers were with him, he took the papers to the OP.

GOGO BREEZE: [Turning to Harri Englund] Eeh, it's a big case! [laughs] Your story, mother, has evidence. It has evidence, for her to bring all those papers, you should start with the clothes, what you saw with the eyes. The clothes came and she gave her mother, that mother used them to pay farm labor, "I want to know is this how it should be?" When the court has examined the case, they will ask you, "What is it that has to happen here now?" It is needed that the leadership that the woman has is removed. After you came, all the family members, when family members stand up, "We chose this one who will take the responsibility."

MIRIAM NKHOMA: Mm.

GOGO BREEZE: Oo, mother, bring all those papers. When you find those papers, money that she took, money that she took, where is that money now? That's it, she will sleep in a tight cell.

[*all laugh*]

GOGO BREEZE: I feel how you should do, start with the clothes.

MIRIAM NKHOMA: Mm.

GOGO BREEZE: How's that?

MIRIAM NKHOMA: That's possible, but you know that here is the village, grandfather, where would you find money to go from here to there?

GOGO BREEZE: I am talking about the clothes.

MIRIAM NKHOMA: The clothes?

GOGO BREEZE: Those clothes came here to the village.

MIRIAM NKHOMA: Yes.

GOGO BREEZE: You have the evidence.

MIRIAM NKHOMA: Ehe.

GOGO BREEZE: And the court where to sue is the local one.

MIRIAM NKHOMA: Aha.

GOGO BREEZE: When you file the summons, it goes there, a messenger there, court, yes, the presiding officer, "Go and give the summons to house number such and such." You will go and write on the court summons the whole address for the mother who is hiding the belongings. And so it will go. They might ask you, "Please give us what, money for postage." That's it; to give them, your story has finished.

MIRIAM NKHOMA: Mm.

GOGO BREEZE: Yeah. You won't see that the story is a long one, that's why I am saying, a-h, come and you will explain.

MIRIAM NKHOMA: Mm.

GOGO BREEZE: Mm, because the clothes will reveal how the whole story about things that have happened. One should not count on the belongings of the bereaved, problems.

MIRIAM NKHOMA: I'd like to ask a little, grandfather.

GOGO BREEZE: What is it?

MIRIAM NKHOMA: To go to the OP here, would it not be possible?

GOGO BREEZE: Do you have the documents?

MIRIAM NKHOMA: The documents are with her there in Lusaka.

GOGO BREEZE: What about the record, is it in the head, do you know it well?

MIRIAM NKHOMA: Mm, but the records, you shouldn't lie, but I only took her phone number to call her, that administrator.

GOGO BREEZE: It could have been a short one, as I said, we could have gone to ask at the office here, but now documents are needed; maybe the pay slip the old man had; maybe a letter; maybe the death certificate. If you had it, then you would have had an opportunity to help yourself. To go and ask. But how it is here, asking there will help if you take that mother with you, "Let's go, let's ask at the office when the money will be released," that's another way. If you had the documents, I would tell you to write, to make photocopies, and to enclose them with the letter so that I could have asked them here. But because they are not available, it is needed that you take that administrator and go with her to the office of OP.

[pause of four seconds]

MIRIAM NKHOMA: Mm.

GOGO BREEZE: How's that?

MIRIAM NKHOMA: I don't know there, the representative is scary.

GOGO BREEZE: Mm.

MIRIAM NKHOMA: Mm. I haven't seen such, this is the first time.

GOGO BREEZE: Oh, mama, it will happen! [laughs] When sharing maize flour, do not be embarrassed or fearful. For you to share maize flour, you also want to have a full stomach!

[all laugh]

GOGO BREEZE: Greed!

MIRIAM NKHOMA: That greed is bad.

GOGO BREEZE: And the time has come now for you to be greedy too. Now your greed will make the other one enter the prison, because it is not a light matter. How's that?

[pause of three seconds]

MIRIAM NKHOMA: Ah, we shall see how it will be.

GOGO BREEZE: Right? Feel at ease. The house on air is yours, if you have difficulties, come, ask, we will try to answer.

NOTES

INTRODUCTION

1. MAIKOLO MBEWE: *Ndimafuna ndipeze ma* piecework, *ganyu.*
    RADIO JOURNALIST: *Oh.*
    MAIKOLO MBEWE: *Ndithu, ndithu, malinga ndi mavuto a kwathu ku Malawi.*
    RADIO JOURNALIST: *Mavuto otani, tauzeni?*
    MAIKOLO MBEWE: *Kusowa kwa ndalama.*
    RADIO JOURNALIST: *Zisowa bwa?*
    MAIKOLO MBEWE: *Basi, kusowa si ngati kuno, kwathu kusowa zedi.*
    RADIO JOURNALIST: *Chifukwa?*
    MAIKOLO MBEWE: *Sindidziwa chifukwa chake.*
    RADIO JOURNALIST: *Nanga munakhalapo ndi nthawi yowafunsa akuluakulu kodi chifukwa chiyani ndalama zikusowa tere?*
    MAIKOLO MBEWE: *Mipata imeneyi sipezeka.*
    RADIO JOURNALIST: *Mulibe makhansala?*
    MAIKOLO MBEWE: *Aliko ndithu, koma makhansala amatikutukwana mpakana kutin- yoza. Satipatsa mpata ngati umenewu kuti tikhoza kulankhulana nawo ayi.*
    RADIO JOURNALIST: *Sure?*
    MAIKOLO MBEWE: *Ndithu, ndithu.*
    RADIO JOURNALIST: *Ndiye mukasankha basi, iwo akhala paokha tere?*
    MAIKOLO MBEWE: *Basi.*
    Broadcast on *Landirani Alendo* (*Welcome Visitors*), January 26, 2012.

2. *Gogo wanu wa pamphepo,* Grayson Peter Nyozani Mwale.

3. On the population size and distribution in Eastern Province, see Central Statistical Office (2014a:6–9). The 2010 national census confirmed Zambia's continuing status as one of the most urbanized countries in sub-Saharan Africa, with 40 percent liv- ing in urban areas and 60 percent in rural areas (Central Statistical Office 2012a:5). According to a 2009 survey (OSISA 2010:10), one or more radio sets were owned by 87 percent of Zambian households (94 percent in urban and 84 percent in rural areas). Forty-five percent of households owned a television set (83 in urban and 24 percent in rural areas). Eighty-eight percent of the respondents reported to have listened to the radio every day or within the past seven days.

4. At midnight, the station switched to BBC World Service, "our sister station," as Daka proudly called it.

5. See, for example, Central Statistical Office (2014a:56–57), which included in the "Nyanja group" the closely related Chichewa and Chinsenga but excluded, among others, Chitumbuka. As a lingua franca, Chinyanja's influence has spread far beyond Eastern Province, particularly to Lusaka, where it became the language of the armed forces and continues to appear in popular culture and street slang, sometimes in mixture with Chibemba and English. It is also spoken in vast swaths of Northern Mozambique and in Malawi, where one of its variants, Chichewa, became the subject of standardization and official promotion unseen among Zambian languages.

6. One of the few occasions when Daka went on air was when he was interviewed during the station's tenth-anniversary festivities.

7. Zambia, like other vibrant democracies, does present a lot to discuss for media critics. The limited extent to which the ZNBC has opened up its airwaves to political opposition echoes similar experiences with public broadcasters in the region after democratization. Another contentious issue would be the role of the privately owned newspaper *The Post* in propelling Michael Sata to state presidency in 2011 and its continued partisan reporting until his death in office in 2014. Cases of harassment have come to light, whether by withdrawing broadcasting licenses or by closing down a radio station accused of secessionist sympathies (Simutanyi et al. 2015:6–7). The hotly contested elections of 2016 saw more state-led harassment of some media houses. Whether the Zambian state is more "media-phobic" (Phiri 2010) than others, particularly in its region, is best left to further debate elsewhere.

8. See Nehemas (1998). For a selection of the expanding anthropological literature contributing to this trend, see Cook (2010), Faubion (2011), Laidlaw (2014), and Pandian (2009).

9. On language ideologies, see Schieffelin et al. (1998). Baumann and Briggs (2003: 107) makes the point that oral expression has often been associated with simplified cognitive and social capacities in language ideologies that give primacy to the written word.

10. For key studies on the role of music during decolonization in Africa, see Askew (2002), Chikowero (2015), Moorman (2008), Perullo (2011), and White (2008).

11. For other uses of newspaper cartoons in democratizing Africa, see Nyamnjoh (2005:219–30) and Omanga (2014).

12. The reason would not be a total absence of Mill's influence in Central Africa. One of the pioneering nationalists in Zambia, Harry Mwaanga Nkumbula, is reported to have read Mill (Macola 2010:6). Gogo Breeze's literary influences, as will be discussed in the next chapter, derived from Zambian authors and radio personalities.

13. As chapter 2 makes clear, Mikhail Bakhtin (1984) rather than John Stuart Mill provides intellectual resources to conceptualize multivocality. To dissect a critique that pits the two thinkers against one another would require more space than is available here (see Roberts 2004).

14. Another anxiety, in the context of diminishing state control over the mass media, concerns the threats to press freedom by controversies over blasphemy, as discussed above (see Keane 2009:64).

15. For a distinction between Habermas's early and later work on communicative reason, see Cohen and Arato (1992). For a discussion of the differences between the critiques formulated by Habermas and Bourdieu, see Crossley (2004). Jenkins (2006) offers an influential perspective on the "convergence culture" in which "grassroots" and "corporate" media intersect.

16. Adam Smith's (1976 [1776]) concept of the market was, of course, an attack on collusion and monopoly by unduly corporate private entities.

17. The classic critique of this line of thinking by anthropologists (see Parry and Bloch 1989) has more recently been followed by intriguing work on money in intimate relationships (Cole 2010; Zelizer 2005) and on the imaginative political and economic possibilities presented by new forms of money (Hart 2000).

18. I was afflicted by this laxity in Englund (2006).

19. In a rapidly expanding literature, it remains a moot point whether "neoliberalism" designates anything of political or intellectual import and whether analyst-activists might miss out on emergent possibilities if they failed to see past this notion. For a selection of studies that address these apparently heretic questions in a variety of contexts, see Elyachar (2012), Ferguson (2009), McKay (2012), Muehlebach (2012), and Roy (2012).

20. It gave the founder-director some pleasure, however, to tell the story that when the business was registered, the authorities had queried how he could have an 80 percent share when his bank account had much less money than the Briton's.

21. A once-influential analytical interest in neoliberal subjectivity—the recruitment of subjects to the neoliberal project of self-reliance (see, e.g., Cruikshank 1999; Rose 2007)—would have precluded the inquiry I advocate here into a more complex entanglement between morality, personhood, and the market.

22. Another radio personality in this period was Peter Yumba, who replied to listeners' letters about various issues of personal and public nature. The use of Chibemba on his programs made them considerably less popular in Eastern Province than those featuring Gogo Juli. Some of Yumba's work is available on the website https://scholarblogs.emory.edu/bemba/kabusha-radio-remix/.

23. A literal translation of *Poceza M'madzulo* is "chatting in the evening time."

24. For a further comparison between the radio grandfathers, see Englund (2015b).

25. The decline of Zambia's economy from the 1970s onward has given rise to striking figures and phrases. Between 1974 and 1994, the per capita income in Zambia fell by 50 percent (Ferguson 1999:6). Burdened by external debt and plummeting world prices for copper, Zambia lost the status it had at independence as a "middle-income country." Privatization, as one of the means by which "structural adjustment" was pursued under the instructions of the International Monetary Fund, started in earnest with the change of government in 1991. It was accompanied by "a spectacular looting of the national fiscus, negative growth rates, deindustrialization, deepening debt, and increasing poverty" (Fraser 2010:11). More recently, Zambia has seen its fortunes reversed somewhat, with annual growth rates reaching beyond 7 percent in the early 2010s and the proportion of external debt in the Gross Domestic Product falling from 179 percent in 2002 to 10 percent in 2007 (UNDP 2013:54). What has not changed is some of the language in which these measures are couched, with the United Nations declaring that Zambia has "graduated from a low-income to a lower middle-income country" (UNDP 2013:13). Among Zambian politicians and activists, intense debate rages about how the spoils, including the revenue from fresh investment in the mining sector, are to be distributed (Larmer and Fraser 2007; Lungu 2008).

26. Within the literature on the crisis of reproduction in contemporary Africa, the question of fatherhood is specifically addressed in Colson (2000), Niehaus (2012), and Simpson (2010).

27. The literature on youth in Africa has become too voluminous to be detailed here, but for representative perspectives, see Honwana and De Boeck (2005), Mains (2012), Newell (2012), and Weiss (2009).

28. The Marxist twist to this tale was to argue, with a great deal of disagreement about the terms of the theory, that an alliance had emerged between elders and the labor recruiters of colonial Africa, both keen to keep young, able-bodied men and women under control (see, e.g., Dupré and Rey 1978; Meillassoux 1981). For an African historian's effort to recover aspects of this argument for an analysis of relations of production in rural Malawi, see Mandala (1990).

29. The literature is again extensive, but for new religious forms of authority, see Marshall (2009), and for social networks dependent on various degrees of crime, see Newell (2012).

30. Among such pioneering studies are Cunnison (1959) and van Velsen (1964). They certainly did not anticipate the full range of forms that kinship as "relatedness" would take in anthropological studies decades later, such as sharing food, coresidence, reincarnation, adoption, and so on; nor has their interest in micropolitics and manipulation been central to the so-called new kinship studies, whose overview can be found in Carsten (2000).

31. Writing about a personality on a Nepalese FM radio station, Laura Kunreuther points out how reception can be studied through the process of production: "Kalyan's [the presenter] intertextual production, inspired by multiple popular genres, can itself be seen as a kind of reception and interpretation of the forms that surround him" (2014:213).

32. The sponsor was one of the major retailers in Chipata. It had been established by an Indian whose son was its current manager. The manager, whose name was mentioned in the song advertising the store, was one of those Indian entrepreneurs whom the man who became Gogo Breeze had known for a long time, as discussed in chapter 2.

CHAPTER ONE

1. Interview with Sharath Srinivasan, March 23, 2012.

2. Broadcast on *Chinyanja China*, July 18, 2012.

3. *Nanga inuyo, kodi mukufuna kuti mukaone imvi kumutu kwanu?*

4. *Kuopa zinthu zimene zikhoza kuononga umoyo wanu.*

5. *Kodi munthu amene ngati iye wamera imvi monga m'mene walira agogo wanu tere, kodi mungayerekeze kuti ali kuchita za maula?* Broadcast on *Zotigwera*, March 20, 2012.

6. *Kanthu kaya, chili kwa imwe m'mene mumaganizira, koma zindikirani ichi kuti akuluakulu ndi ofunikira mpakati pathu chifukwa ngati ifeyo tingapezeke ndi mavuto osiyanasiyana akuluakulu ndi amene adziwa kumasulira mavuto amenewo.* (Titled "Diwa lakale silivuta kuliutsa" [Old trap does not fail to entrap], the short story had been about the theft of a chieftainship by a mean person who, after persecuting the elderly along with the blind and the disabled, faced a painful death.)

7. As is discussed later in this chapter, Gogo Breeze did accept the gift of a motorbike in 2013. While it certainly eased the tedium of walking or cycling, particularly as he was advancing in age, he continued to walk within Chipata town as often as possible, partly because the purchase of petrol was a matter of some negotiation with the radio station.

8. Compared to neighboring Malawi, Zambia, on the strength of its copper mines, was

not a major exporter of labor during the high tide of labor migration between the 1940s and 1970s.

9. *Gogo wanu wa pamphepo Grayson Peter Nyozani Mwale.*

10. The term *mtsamunda* derives from the Chinyanja word for colonialism, *utsamunda*, and can therefore be translated as "colonialist." Its negative connotations are reinforced by the literal meaning of "stealing a field," a meaning that appears to be lost on many contemporary Chinyanja speakers.

11. A maternal uncle (*malume*) is a key figure in the lives of his sisters and their children in a broadly matrilineal setting.

12. *Chipembedzo chimene anali kutsatira atate sichinali kufanana ndi chimene chimanenedwa m'Buku Lopatulika.*

13. *Mpingowu ndinasankhira ndekha.*

14. Mwale was old enough to have witnessed the antifederation campaign by nationalists, but his life story made few references to its impact on him.

15. He endorsed, as such, the founder-director's definition of Breeze FM as a secular station.

16. Following the defeat of President Rupiah Banda, himself an Easterner, Michael Sata and his Patriotic Front ascended to power in 2011. Chipata Central, however, was one of the constituencies in Eastern Province, where the balance between the two main parties was by no means clear.

17. Despite his preference for Chinyanja, Gogo Breeze did not articulate his language ideology in terms of a hierarchy between languages and was always keen to adjust to the language that his interlocutors spoke, albeit with some reluctance to use English. Language ideology in this case influenced a particular approach to meaning and its association with the moral authority of elderhood.

18. *Mawu okuluwika ndi mawu amene iwo amabisila Chinyanja inde kwa ana kotero kuti ngati mawu akambidwa ana ang'onoang'ono asamadziwa zimene zikunenedwa ndi akuluakulu ayi pokhapo ngati nkhani imeneyo ikuwafunikira iwo kuti aidziwe.* Broadcast on *Mawu Okuluwika,* February 6, 2012.

19. *Ngati nkhani ndi yooneka ngati ndi yovuta kuti munthu aimvetsetse akuluakulu anali kugwiritsa ntchito mawu okambidwa mwachidule.* Broadcast on *Chinyanja China,* October 7, 2009.

20. *Mawu awa amanenedwa pamilandu mwina ngati pali wina wagwa pamavuto koma asowa chithandizo. . . . Anthu oweruza nkhani amagwiritsa ntchito mawu apafupi kotero kuti mawu aja athe nkhani yonse kwa iwo aja amene amazindikira za Chinyanja china chimene akuluakulu amene iwo anakhalako masiku adzana anali kuwagwiritsa ntchito.* Broadcast on June 2, 2010. I have translated *milandu* as "court cases," customary courts run by village headmen and their coteries of elders. *Nkhani* is translated here as "dispute," but its generic meanings include "story," "news," and "issue."

21. *Samalani! Agogo wanu akukuthandizeni kuti mukonze makhalidwe anu.* Broadcast on *Chinyanja China,* June 2, 2010.

22. *Nthawi imene tili nayo adzukulu anga ndi yabwino kwambiri, chifukwa zakudya zimapezeka ndithu kulingana ndi nthawi m'mene zapezekera. Ndiye pamene mubwera kudzacheza ndi ambuye wanu osaiwala imwe wana kunyamula inde tinkhuni ting'onoting'ono kotero kuti ngati mwafika tizipanga chimoto chakuti tiotchapo zakudya zathu zimene timabwera nazo. . . . Mwachita bwino kubwera nanzanu amene iwo akufuna kuti akamvere nthano zimene agogo wanu amanena. . . . Muchita bwino kuchita motero ndipo ndingakonde kuti muziitana ambiri anzanu amene iwo amangokhalira m'nyumba mwawo.*

Chifukwa ngati adzapitiriza kukhala mwawo motero osamvetsera nthano zimenezi adzakhala wana opulukira. Broadcast on *Zotigwera*, February 21, 2012.

23. *Ngati inuyo mwakhala kale pamipando yanu mwachita bwino. Ngati ena inu mipando mulibe muli ndi kasitoli, inde nakonso kampando kameneko. Ena inu mwina kasitolinso mulibenso, ngati muli ndi chikopa cha mbuzi mukhoza kukhala inde motambalala kuti mumvetsere kupologamu ya tsiku la lero.* Broadcast on *Miyambi Muumoyo Wathu (Proverbs in Our Lives),* June 24, 2012.

24. *Cholinga ndi chofuna kuti inu mukhale anthu odziwa m'mene makolo athu anali kukhalira chifukwa masiku ano ndi chovuta kwambiri kuti anthu kuti awapeze ali pamodzi akusema mipini, akupangira makasu kapena nkhwangwa, ndi owerengeka kwambiri amene amachita zimenezo.* . . . *Tsono leroli mwayi tili nawo wakuti nyumba yanu yamphepo Breeze FM inamangidwa muno muboma la Chipata.* Broadcast on *Chinyanja China,* September 19, 2012.

25. Broadcast on *Makalata*, January 18, 2013.

26. *Akuti ali kupempha chifukwa sakulandira malipiro kwa miyezi itatu tsopano. Tsopano agogo mufikirike kwa mkulu wa kampani imeneyi kuti chomwe afotokoza, akufotokozera anyantchito kuti sali kumvetsera kuti chifukwa chiyani sali kulipiridwa. Mwina inu mungawathandize agogo, adzukulu anu.* Broadcast on *Makalata*, November 4, 2012.

27. Broadcast on *Makalata*, December 23, 2011.

28. *Ndiye alemba tero kuti "Dear Grayson Mwale?"*

29. *Kupanda ulemu. Inu mwalemba kalata uko kumudzi wa Kalunga, dzina lanu mwaikapo kuti ndinu Izeki Jere.* Can you please go back to your school where you did your grade twelve? Ask your English teacher to show you how to address people. *Makalata olemba tere awa, mukuchita ngati mukulembera mnzanu;* we don't write like that. I deserve respect. My granddaughter here deserves respect. And if you write like that it means you don't even qualify to be picked *kukoleji kumene iweyo walemberako. Sitero iyayi, tiyeni tipatsane ulemu ndiye wofunika. Ngati mukulemba kalata ya aplikeshoni timalemba bwinobwino, osalemba m'mene munalembera apa. Mukanalemba monga "Dear Ulutsi," kapena mukanalemba, "The Director," ndi yokuti ndi kalata yopita kwamkulu wapantchito panopa. Koma mungolemba "Dear Grayson Mwale";* that is an insult to me. Can we please learn how to address people? Thank you very much for your letter, but I am not giving you any advice on it or your problem.

30. Even when addressing his listeners and interlocutors as (grand)children, Gogo Breeze would often deploy the second-person-plural *inu.*

31. GOGO BREEZE: *Uli kuti kabudula kuti tione ngati ndi zoona kuti mwaiwalika kabudula mwana?*

    MOTHER: *Uli kung'anda.*

    GOGO BREEZE: *Kung'anda?*

    MOTHER: *Ee.*

    GOGO BREEZE: *Lomba pano pali ng'anda?*

    MOTHER: *A-a, nachoka kukagula malasha*=

    GOGO BREEZE: =*Ayi, wana, wana, muziwaveka. Akauka mwana, mwamveka kabudula, chifukwa ngati mwana aonetsa umaliseche, ndikuti aonetsa umaliseche wa tate, umaliseche wa mayi. Chinthu chimenechi sichoyenerera kuti chidzionekere kubwalo ayi. Tamvana?*

    MOTHER: *Mm.*

    GOGO BREEZE: *Ee, mvekeni mwana kabudula.*

    Equals signs (=) in dialogue indicate overlapping speech.

32. GOGO BREEZE: *Tsono inuyu mukasutha mutenga kalitenda kang'ono koma aja amene ali*

patali sasutha atenga chitenda chachikulu chifukwa cha utsi wanu umene mumachotsa m'mkamwa. Ndiye mukukhoza?

SMOKER: *Aa, sitikukhoza=*

GOGO BREEZE: *=Ngati ndi zoonadi kuti mumakhala ku Katete sinthani. Inu anthu a ku Katete musamasutha fodya chifukwa kusutha fodya kuno ku Chipata tiletsa.*

DRUNKARD: *Mverani ine pano ndikukamba chilungamo=*

GOGO BREEZE: *=Nanga amene mwandiuza kuti ndikumvereni? Ndinu ndani?*

DRUNKARD: *Ine ndine munthu.*

GOGO BREEZE: *Ndi m'mene muyankhiranso?*

DRUNKARD: Yes.

GOGO BREEZE: *Tsopano mwatanthauza chiyani? Musangoyankhe ngati mphemvu chifukwa mphemvu=*

DRUNKARD: *=Kodi munthu=*

GOGO BREEZE: *=imagwera m'thobwa wa eni.*

DRUNKARD: *Anamulenga ndani munthu?*

GOGO BREEZE: *Ayi, pitirizani kusutha. Nanga ndikulalikira pano?*

Broadcast on *Landirani Alendo*, February 16, 2012.

33. On populism as a feature of social science, see Englund (2010), Laclau (2005), and Olivier de Sardan (2005).

34. Broadcast on *Chidwi Pa Anthu* (*Interest in People*), December 17, 2012.

35. *Muziwatuma kuno, "Kaoneni mwana uja, akakumasulireni."*

36. *Tsono mwana azimasula, koma imvi nazonso zidziwe, chifukwa kwa ifeyo sitingakambe monga ngati kukambira ngati* on behalf of *boma. Tikamba kulingana ndi pologamu ya wailesi, koma woyankha mwanayo, ayankha kulingana ndi mwambo. Ife tingotsimikizira kodi ndi zoona zimene akamba mwanayo?*

37. On debates about sovereignty as the power to define rules and their exceptions in the context of humanitarian interventions, see Fassin and Vasquez (2005).

38. On anonymity and local knowledge on a Malawian radio program, see Englund (2011:186–89).

39. *Amene sakufuna ntchito aleke.* Broadcast on *Makalata*, March 16, 2012.

40. *Ukakhala wokuti iweyo uli ndi ndalama, utha kulemba anzako kuti akugwirire. Siku-funika kuwanyoza, chifukwa ntchito ija sikanagwiridwa kuti anthu aja panalibe iyayi. Ndiwo ukamberembere umene tikunena kapena umbava.*

41. *Kampani anaika pa apa, uyu ndi munthu wodziwika kwambiri muno muboma la Chipata. Kalankhuleni naye.*

42. *Nanga inu mafumu, anakupatsani mpando umenewu, kodi ndi wanu? Ngati ndi wanudi mpandowu umene munalandira, gwirani ntchito kulingana ndi m'mene ufumu wanu ufu-nikira kuti inuyo muigwire.* Broadcast on *Zotigwera*, March 20, 2012.

43. "The chief with the scepter" is a literal translation of *mfumu yandodo*, the highest of-fice in the hierarchy of traditional authority.

44. "Paramount Chief" is the title used in English for this rank of traditional authority, but Gogo Breeze deployed Mpezeni's Chingoni title *Inkosi ya Makosi*, "the chief of chiefs."

45. GOGO BREEZE: *Ndipo ndingakupempheni mkulu wanga kuti ngati inuyu ndithu ana-kuchitani tero pitani kwa hedimani, hedimani akutengeni mupite kwa mfumu yandodo. Sindikhulupirira kuti Inkosi ya Makosi Mpezeni angavomere zimene anachita* chair-man *wa cooperative amene analakwitsa, chifukwa Inkosi ya Makosi ifuna anthu wake kuti adzakhala ndi chakudya pamanyumba pawo. Tsono iye uyu munampatsa mpando akubwezerani ndalama m'malo moti apatse kamodzi kathumba, iye watenga mathumba*

awiri, atatu, folo, just because *ndi mtsogoleri mu* cooperative. *No. Ali nawo madoda awo aMpezeni adzakhala nawo pansi akasungulutse—*

GRANDDAUGHTER: *Komanso sali kumva tikulankhula?*

GOGO BREEZE: *Ngati yafika pologamu imeneyo kwa Inkosi ya Makosi ayenera kuti apite mawa uyu munthu uyu kuti akafotokoze nkhani ija, ili tere, tere, tere,* So that *akawaike munsi mwa mtengo wa kachere. Udziwa mtengo wa kachere, m'mene zima-khalira?*

GRANDDAUGHTER: *Mungachite kunena.*

GOGO BREEZE: *Nyerere.*

Broadcast on *Makalata,* February 5, 2012.

46. On another occasion, for example, Gogo Breeze told his public that Paramount Chief Mpezeni would investigate allegations of witchcraft in his territory.

47. *Tinavotera MMD onse awiri khansala ndi MP, koma chodabwitsa chitukuko chomwe chabwera kuno ndi mchere, sopo, mabulangeti ndi masewero a mpira wa miyendo komanso wa manja.* Broadcast on *Makalata,* December 2, 2012.

48. *Anatiuza kuti ngati mwativotera, choyamba misewu, milatho, tidzakonza. Zonse ndatch-ula apa palibe chimodzi chinachitikapo, cholephereka. Funso, agogo, kodi mchere, mpira, mabulangeti ndi chitukuko.*

49. *Tero momwemo ndi chofunikira ife timene tili mtsogolo ngati anthu tinawauza kuti mu-kativotere kenaka tidzakuthandizani zakutizakuti, yesetsani. Ndikudziwa ndi chovuta kuti mupeze mathandizo popeza inuyo mulibe ndalama ayi. Ndalama izi zimaoneka panthawi ya* campaign, *koma tsopano kuti muyang'ane muthumba lanu mukapeza ndithu ayi mu-libe popeza munachotsamo zambiri. Ndiye kuti mubwezeremo zikuvuta, koma yesetsani ku-ona anthu ena amene angakhoze kukuthandizani kuti anthu awa zimene munawalonjeza kuti muyese kukwaniritsa.*

50. *Ndipempha boma la PF, ku Bwanakubwa,* cabinet minister *wa muno mu Chipata, ku-pyolera dziko la Zambia lonse.* Broadcast on *Makalata,* March 16, 2012.

51. *Zikomo kwambiri, madandaulo anu tamva, koma muziyamba kuona kuti "kodi izi ndi zofunikira ndilembere kwa agogo?"*

52. I discuss further the relationship between the market and mass media in chapter 7.

53. This incident was another example of the practice that sometimes made Daka criti-cize Mwale for calling himself Gogo Breeze when he was not actually working for the radio station.

54. Despite the diversification of trade in consumer goods, particularly clothes through *salaula* (second-hand clothing; see Hansen 2000), shopkeepers of Indian origin continued to dominate retail trade in Chipata. They were the descendants of early twentieth-century migrants, who had made Chipata (then Fort Jameson) the other of Zambia's two hubs of Indian settlement (Mufuzi 2011:232). In contrast to the mainly Hindu population of Livingstone's Indians, those in Chipata were predomi-nantly Muslim.

55. For an overview of styles and contents in Benin's radio advertisements, see Grätz (2013).

CHAPTER TWO

1. See http://www.itu.int/net4/itu-d/icteye/.

2. The influence of Chitumbuka on Zambian Chinyanja rendered this plural form as *vigayo* in many of the contributions to the debate.

3. As Gogo Breeze himself had explained on another program, *gaga* can also be used as a synonym for all food: "The word *gaga* means food" (*liwu ili lakuti gaga likutan-*

thauza chakudya). This explanation was a part of the program that takes listeners beyond the ordinary meanings of words. As was his practice with uncommon meanings, Gogo Breeze gave examples of usage: "Do you have *gaga* in your house? If you do not have *gaga*, that is it, you do not have food" (*kodi muli nawo gaga panyumba panu? Ngati mulibe gaga panyumba panu, ndikuti inuyo, ayi ntheradi, mulibe chakudya*). Broadcast on *Mawu Okuluwika*, January 2, 2012.

4. Just under one US dollar. It should be noted that the Zambian kwacha was rebased over the period of my research in 2012–13, and the monetary figures I quote refer to the moment I describe.

5. *Ndi thokoza kwambiri ndimene muna endesela khani ya gaga.* (Here as elsewhere, I have not attempted to change the spelling, orthography, and syntax used in the texts I cite.)

6. *Mdzukulu* is a gender-neutral term like *gogo*, but they can be specified to refer to "female" (*wamkazi*) or "male" (*wamwamuna*). The unmistakably female voice on the *Makalata* program made such specification unnecessary.

7. *Tsono nkhaniyi ndi ya azimai, amene amapita kuchigayo. Sichingakhale kuti munene kuti jenda. Koma siambiri a azibambo amene amapita kuchigayo iyayi. Inuyo ndi amene mumakumana nazo. Patsa mnzako kuti mwina mwake atiunikire kuti mwini wake wa gaga ndi ndani. Kenaka ubwere kwa ifeyo.*

8. Contemporary classics in the scholarship on difference-blind liberalism and democracy include Taylor (1994) and Kymlicka (1995).

9. PAULINE PHIRI: *Ine ndinanyamula chimanga, nanga gaga uja wachokera kuti, mnzanga?*
   JULIANA BANDA: *Kuchimanga changa.*
   PAULINE PHIRI: *Kuchimanga cha ndani?*
   JULIANA BANDA: *Changa.*
   PAULINE PHIRI: *Kupanganso gaga wanga, nanga gaga ndi wa ndani?*

10. *Ndipo popeza malonda wa gaga wachulukadi kubwaloko anthu akutenga gaga kupita nazo kumudzi, nawonso eni yake vigayo akuti iyayi gaga wanga. Inu eni yake chigayo mulibe mphamvu yonena kuti gaga ndi wanu chonde. Ndalama zimene anakupatsani kuti agaire chimene chija anabweretsa. Komanso tili ndi ziweto, gaga uja tikapita kuja tikufuna kuti tipatse ziweto monga tinankhumba, tinambuzi, lomba si gaga wa eni yake chigayo.*

11. *Tsono kuyankhula kwa gogo, iye ntchito yake ndi yofuna kufufuza kuti tione choonadi ndi chiti chimene chimachitika.*

12. *Ndiye ndinatenga njinga yanga imene inayang'ana msewu kuzunguluka kuti ndifufuze pankhaniyi ya gaga ili bwanji. Kodi zoona kuti eni yake vigayo amatenga gaga umenewu? Nanga chifukwa chotengera gaga umenewu ndi chiani? Ndiye ndawapempha eni yake vigayo kuti ayankhulepo, kenaka tione m'mene mapeto ake adzakhala bwanji.*

13. MILL OWNER: *Azipempha.*
    GOGO BREEZE: *Azipempha gaga wake?*
    MILL OWNER: *Ee, azipempha.*
    GOGO BREEZE: *Azipempha kwa inuyo?*
    MILL OWNER: *Ee.*
    GOGO BREEZE: *Ndi wanu gaga?*
    MILL OWNER: *Ee ndi wathu popeza*=
    GOGO BREEZE: =*Ndi wanu bwanji popeza mulibe chimanga iyayi?*
    MILL OWNER: *Obwera kugaya*=
    GOGO BREEZE: =*Kuba sikufunika.*
    MILL OWNER: *Eh?*
    GOGO BREEZE: *Muli kumva?*

MILL OWNER: *Ee, zamveka.*

GOGO BREEZE: *Osabera anthu ayi!*

MILL OWNER: *Okey, okey.*

14. *Alaita akufuna ndalama, wantchito akufuna ndalama, eni yake chigayo akufuna ndalama, ndiye ndinaona kuti ndalama yopereka ichepa koma pali bwino tipeze ndalama mugaga mwina mwake tipeze kang'ono.*

15. *Kodi mukhoza kulanda gaga kwa munthu?*

16. *Ngati simukhoza, chifukwa chiyani upitiriza kumbera munthu wamba?*

17. See Redfield (2010) for different senses in which "neutrality" enters humanitarian causes.

18. Naphiri is the feminine form of the clan name Phiri.

19. GOGO BREEZE: *Maganizo amene anthu atatipatse tsiku lina lobwera patsogolo pamenepo kuti timve ndi zotani, koma ife munomu monga Naphiri wanena kuti gaga ndi wayani?*

    JULIANA BANDA: *Wa mwini chimanga.*

    GOGO BREEZE: *Mwini ndani?*

    JULIANA BANDA: *Wa chimanga.*

    GOGO BREEZE: *Oho, zikomo kwambiri.*

    PAULINE PHIRI: *Chimanga ndi changa ndachokera nacho kunyumba kupita nacho kuchigayo, wina anakandiuza gaga siyani, sindifuna, chimanga sichanga?*

    GOGO BREEZE: *Anafoleledwa?*

    PAULINE PHIRI: *Ah!*

    GOGO BREEZE: *Basi, tero momwemo.*

    PAULINE PHIRI: *Kalata ina.*

20. Broadcast on April 29, 2012.

21. *Tikuyembekezera inuyo kuti mutiuzeko, chifukwa a-a, agogo sangathe kuzindikira bwino-bwino pankhani imeneyo kuti idzakhala motani.*

22. The literal translation of the name would be "the sun of misfortune." In line with the practice on all phone-in programs, Gogo Breeze requested the caller to say his or her name and place before allowing them to continue.

23. The question of so-called serial callers—listeners who frequently call the station regardless of the issue being discussed—cannot be addressed here, but Gogo Breeze confirmed my own impression that the majority of the callers that evening had not called him before. In general, the letters, telephone calls, and SMS messages sent to him tended to be from a wider range of people than on the station's English-language phone-in programs, which seemed to have a more regular cast of callers.

24. As discussed in the next chapter, grandparents and grandchildren have at their disposal relationship categories that can subvert the generational distance between them.

25. Women's lack of participation in radio programs is a much-discussed issue at Breeze FM and other Zambian radio stations. Chapter 5 examines ways in which women's roles became topics of debate on some programs.

26. *Chabwino amama, tulo tabwino amama, zikomo kwambiri. Ndidakalipo ine, kugonanso tsopano iyayi, ndidakalipo ndithu maola angapo anthunthu oti ndipite kunyumba kuka-gona. Inuyo gonani make Mtoliro, zikomo kwambiri chifukwa cha mawu anu.*

27. *Amama ndathokoza kwambiri, tulo tabwino, zikomo kwambiri, alemekezeke Chauta kuti nanunso mayi mwagwapo, chifukwa makamaka chingakhale mupologamu ya zamakalata ndinauza azimai anga, imwe ndi amene zimakukhudzani, mukuti bwanji. Anafotokoza nawonso.*

28. The term *komboni* refers to the history of Zambia's urbanization during which the

growth of urban settlements for Africans began in what were known as mining compounds.

29. *Kumene ndinapita kumene kuja ndinali kutsatira pologamu ya makalata, ee, mdzukulu wanga mayi Phiri pamene wabwera lero wandiuza, "i-i, iwe gogo unakalipa kuno kuNavu-tika." A-a, chifukwa mayankhidwe amene sinakondwere nawo anyamata amene anali kundiyankha ndiye ndinakweza mawu. Popeza kukweza mawu pang'ono basi munthu akuti ndinakalipa koma sinakalipe ayi, nafuna kuti nditenge choonadi.*

30. *Ndikhulupirira kuti eni yake amene ali ndi vigayo ali kumvetsera zimene anthu ali ku-nena. Zikumveka kuti ayi akuti gaga ndi wa mwini wake.*

31. *Ndikhulupirira kuti imwe eni yake ya vigayo muli kumva zimene anthu ali kunena, si gogo amene akunena ayi.*

32. On the thicket of language in Zulu radio drama, see Gunner (2000).

33. The high frequency of Chinsenga usage among some voices on Breeze FM is dis-cussed in chapters 3 and 5, particularly with regard to the language's relatively thin presence in written form and its consequent folksy flavor.

34. The expression *–chiboyi* is a common way in Zambian Chinyanja to refer to anything that is thought to be African or local rather than imported. *Mankhwala achiboyi*, for example, is "traditional" medicine. The expression *–chikuda*, connoting blackness, is more common on the Malawian side of the border, while the origin of *–chiboyi* is in the colonial concept of "boy" as the term for all African males.

35. *Nkhaniyo ndi chimodzimodzi mkulu wanga. Kuti ndiperekenso kwa gulu, nthawi sindilola iyayi.*

36. *Kaligone* uses the diminutive and contains the verb for "sleeping," *kugona*. The allu-sion is to a small thing that is used during someone's sleep.

37. Broadcast on *Makalata*, November 4, 2012.

38. Broadcast on April 25, 2012.

39. *Pomaliza ntchitoyo saoneka olemera kapena kusiyana ndi poyamba paja asanalowe ntchito.*

40. *Munthu mmodzi akamapeza mwai cifukwa ca mphavu za ena.*

41. *Mawu awa ndi olamatu ndi kufunika kugwiritsa ntchito kwambiri.*

42. *Ntchito iliyonse imene muli nayo mumpatsa munthu koma osapatsa malipiro oyenerera, basi ndikuti munthu uja adzachoka panyumba panu pamenepo, pantchito yanu imeneyo, ali osauka kupambana ndi m'mene analiri poyamba.*

43. *Nkhaniyi tsopano yapita patali, chifukwa nyumba ya mphepo ya Breeze FM ili patali. Ku Mozambique, ku Malawi, ee, titafika ku Malawi tafika ku Mzimba komwe kwa Bangweni ndikuti ku Mzuzu komwe tili konko.*

44. *Zikomo kwambiri chifukwa chotengako mbali papologamu imeneyi. Mwathandiza gogo kuyankha kalata imene wina anatilembera. Tiye tizitere nthawi zonse tidzithandizana ndi-kuti chalo chiwame.*

45. Another practice of interactive radio, popular among stations in Lusaka, was to wel-come listeners' requests for songs, but these three stations lacked the capacity to sustain it. They all did play plenty of popular music, both African and Western, although Christian songs tended to predominate on Radio Maria.

46. In its own broadcasts, Feel Free FM did announce that it could be heard in Nyimba and Petauke Districts, a claim that staff members at Breeze FM dismissed as a ploy to attract sponsorship from politicians, NGOs, and advertisers.

47. The practice of paying for airtime applied to virtually all radio stations in Zambia, whether they were public or commercial or community radio (Fraser 2016a:11).

48. Despite being employed by the same university, I was not involved in the design and implementation of the *Africa's Voices* pilot project. I did participate in discuss-

ing certain aspects of interactive radio with the researchers associated with the university's Centre for Governance and Human Rights, and the insights that its director, Sharath Srinivasan, shared with me have been particularly valuable in developing my own understanding.

49. This was the round that witnessed, across the different stations, the highest percentage of messages containing justifications (90 percent).

CHAPTER THREE

1. Broadcast on *Landirani Alendo,* December 1, 2011.

2. GOGO BREEZE: *Imwe anyamata ochepa ndithu, ndevu inangoyamba tsopano apa kumera, koma tsopano mukuthira kachasu m'mutu. Kodi pali phindu lotani pakumwa mowa umenewu?*

   YOUNG MAN: *Aa, makamaka kumowa uyu, nikupaya maganizo wochitika monga vili m'mutu.*

   GOGO BREEZE: *Maganizo wotani?*

   YOUNG MAN: *Monga maganizo woti nayambana ndi munthu=*

   GOGO BREEZE: *=ndiye mufune mukaphe munthu uja? Mukamwa mowa basi maganizo saleka=*

   YOUNG MAN: *=A-a, makamaka aGogo mowa uyu, olo kuti napolomisana ndi mwanamkazi.*

   GOGO BREEZE: *Kuti?*

   YOUNG MAN: *Kuti tikumane pakutipakuti.*

   GOGO BREEZE: *Kukumana pantchito ya?*

   YOUNG MAN: *Yosiya magazino kamba kagawo kameneka ndi, aa, gawo yabwino.*

   GOGO BREEZE: *Tsono iweyo wapita kwamkazi? Mulibe banja?*

   YOUNG MAN: *A-a, nikukamba gawo imeneyi=*

   GOGO BREEZE: *=Ndikuti mwayankhula za mkazi, muli pabanja?*

   YOUNG MAN: *Aa, ndili pabanja=*

   GOGO BREEZE: *=Nanga wasiya bwanji wamkazi?*

   YOUNG MAN: *Aa, ndikukamba kuti=*

   GOGO BREEZE: *=Tafotokozani chinthuchi: mkazi wasiya bwanji?*

3. *Anyamata, anyamata, mukuononga mudzi wa Thondweni ngati mupitiriza kukumwa mowa wotere ndi kusutha fodya. Kuleka! Mudzi uzikhala wolongosoka ndi anyamata amphamvu.*

4. *Nthawi yafika yolima ino, ndikudziwa kuti azimayi ndi amene adzalima kwambiri. Inu, "Ndinkapemphe fodya kwa Jomba kuja," ulendo, zii.*

5. GOGO BREEZE: *Munambereka mwana wanu?*

   MOTHER: *Ngako.*

   GOGO BREEZE: *Kodi munamulangiza tsiku lina kukoma ndi kuipa kwa mowa?*

   MOTHER: *Ngako ee.*

   GOGO BREEZE: *Munamuuza mawu wotani?*

   MOTHER: *Nauza pamowa paliye polifiti, polifiti ya mowa ni kutchayana, ndewu pang'anda ndi azimayi. Koma ngati sukulu yakukangani, kudimba ndi yanu.*

   GOGO BREEZE: *Anamva mawu amenewa?*

   MOTHER: *A-a, akuoneka ngati anaiwala.*

6. GILINI: *Aa, mawu awa ndi ovuta moti inu makolo anga simunandiphunzitse, lomba nalekerera sukulu giledi eleven. Chinandiwawa kwambiri ndi kusowa ndalama, makolo kulibe,* that's why *ndikumwa mowa. Kunena kuti ndilowenso kusukulu, zandisiira.*

GOGO BREEZE: *Tere zimene akukambapo ndi zoona, mukumwa mowa kamba koti ndalama zinakusowani. Munalekeranji kulima kabichi kuti iwe ukapitirize kusukulu?*
GILINI: *Ndili mwana wang'ono,* that's why *nalephera kupeza zonse.*
GOGO BREEZE: *Nanunso mutitidyetsa utsi, sindifuna kudya utsi pano. Zimani fodya wanu, bwanji kodi? Taonani mayi wako awa, mwina mwake unakawagulira duku pamutu. Koma tsopano pagiledi* eleven *unatulukira pawindo, unakhoza?*

7. Broadcast on *Landirani Alendo*, March 29, 2012.

8. *Anthu mwanyamula ndi wa ku Katete, galimoto ikupita ku Katete, mwati mumakhala ku Chipata. Imwe aNg'mbe bodza lotere sifunika, mwamva? Manyamulidwe awa safunika iyayi.* Taxi *imafunika anthu asanu chabe. Oo. Ng'ombe oo, ayi, pitirizani. Ee, mphunzitsi anzanga.*

9. GOGO BREEZE: *Inu musalole=*
TEACHER: *=Ine zimene sindilola, koma chabe ndimangomvera chifundo anyamata amenewa akapanikiza anthu. Motoka ndi zawo izi, amafuna kuti apeze kangachepe.*
GOGO BREEZE: *Tsono kupeza kangachepe, sangakapeze iyayi, chifukwa galimoto ikadzagwa ndiye zonse=*
TEACHER: *=Zonse zionongeka, ndi zoonadi.*

10. A relatively recent dictionary entry for *kangachepe* as "bribe" or "corruption (at low level)" (Paas 2004:150) is consistent with the possibility that money or favors become defined in such a manner. However, the frequent approving use of the idiom, such as in this exchange, suggests that it is not a term for bribes and corruption as *ziphuphu* and *katangale* are, respectively.

11. Broadcast on *Landirani Alendo*, February 16, 2012.

12. The driver's status, established early in the conversation, as someone working for the owner of the bus suggested that either his employer was the one behind this practice or, in another breach of rules, unaware of what the driver was doing.

13. Dialogism, it might be recalled, has been a major way in which commercial radio in particular has sought to avert "one-way flow of communication and anonymous styles of talk" (Peters 1999:214).

14. See, for example, "Mines Are Creating Few Jobs—Scott," *The Post*, April 11, 2014. Commenting on a new report in 2014, Vice President Guy Scott noted that "the direct employment from the mining sector was only 1.7 percent" and that while the country was producing more and more copper, the Copperbelt had "ghost towns."

15. The predicament of abundant labor has given rise to the notion of "surplus people" in a recent critique of economic growth that fails to create more employment opportunities (Ferguson 2013).

16. This was the sponsor whose Zimbabwean representatives were mentioned in chapter 1. The purpose of their sponsorship was to enable Breeze FM to visit rural areas for broadcast material, but unlike some of the NGOs discussed in part 3, it appeared to make few demands on the contents of its sponsored programs.

17. These gatherings may have satisfied the sponsoring NGO's expectation of "focus groups," but the contrast is clear to those uses of focus-group methodology that seek to enhance the success and predictability of particular development projects (see Kratz 2010).

18. A national estimate indicated an increase of about 140 percent in the area used for planting cotton between the 2010–11 and 2011–12 seasons. See pages 16–17 in *Agriculture Today: A Publication of the Ministry of Agriculture and Livestock*, June–December 2012.

19. See "Cotton Crop Goes to Waste in Eastern Province," *Agriculture Today: A Publication of the Ministry of Agriculture and Livestock*, June–December 2012.

20. For the 2012–13 season, many smallholders appeared to have given up cotton, with a reduction of 40 percent in the output projected by the industry. See "Zambia's Cotton Output May Drop by 40%, Says Kaonga," *The Post*, May 1, 2013.

21. *Onani mtengo wa thonje. Takhala olira. Njala iliko.* Broadcast on *Chidwi Pa Anthu*, October 15, 2012.

22. *Pankhani ya kotoni tulira. Chaka chino sitilima ngako milisi, tilime ngako kotoni tipeze ndalama, mwina tikaguleko milisi, koma zonsezi zasefukira, mavuto okha kuno: mankhwala ngongole, mbewu ngongole.*

23. *Timayesako ngakhale kuti tilibe ng'ombe zoti zingatithandize.* Broadcast on *Chidwi Pa Anthu*, October 29, 2012.

24. *Wang'ombe sitimuwerengera chifukwa choti wang'ombe uja alibe mphamvu. Ife amene sitilimira ng'ombe tili ndi mphamvu yopambana wang'ombe. Nthawi imene ng'ombe zamthawa, ndiye kuti sadzalima.*

25. GOGO BREEZE: *Njala bwa?*

    MALE SMALLHOLDER: *Njala iliko monga ulimi wa chino chaka wambiri wapitako straight kuthonje. Pali chiyembekezero kuti thonje imeneyi idzabweretsa chuma chambiri, koma zosautsa zimene tikudandaulira anzathu amene iwo anapita straight kuthonje. Makampani amene amagula thonje anaononga ulimi. Njala iliko chifukwa chakuti ambiri sanalime chimanga analima kotoni kuti tikapeza kandalama aka tidzagula chakudya. Lomba mukotoni muja ndalama yasowa. Adzadya chiyani?*

26. *Muli ndi atsogoleri, akansala, waMP? Ni nchinji chimene wachitapo pankhani ya mandaulo?* Broadcast on *Chidwi Pa Anthu*, October 15, 2012.

27. *Koma kukamba chilungamo, paliye chaka chimo, akansala, waMP, paliye chaka chimo. Mandaulo amva a anthu pamisonkhano ya ahediman. Misonkhano akapanga amaitanitsa mafumu, koma paliye chochitikapo.*

28. *Mwana akalira majikisi kapena masiwiti, mpatseni kuti adye. Osamnamiza bodza kuti mungabweretse jikisi pamene mungabweretse mwala umene mwana sangathe kufuna iyayi.* Broadcast on *Chidwi Pa Anthu*, November 12, 2012.

29. *Sawerengera umoyo wa anthu, amawerengera umoyo wa nyama. . . . Amaiwala chimodzi kuti atabwerera kuno, nokhala kuno, anasungidwa ndi anthu, sanasungidwe ndi nyama. So, chifukwa cha ichi ulimi wathu wakhalanso wobwerera pansi.* Broadcast on *Chidwi Pa Anthu*, October 22, 2012.

30. *Chandigwira mtima ndi ukapolo, m'mene unalipo kale. Kale paja anali kutenga anthu okuda napita naye kumaiko a ku Ulaya kuti akagwire ntchito kumadimba awo a mzimbe. Koma lero mzungu anachoka kwawo nabwera kuno ku Zambia, nabwera kuno ku Afrika, nozapanga kapolo munthu nthaka ili yake. Icho sindidziwa m'mene a boma adzaganizira chifukwa ukapolo umenewu.*

31. He used different renditions of the song on different programs, one sung by an elderly man without accompaniment and the other by a younger man to the tunes and beats emanating from a keyboard. Both versions were broadcast anonymously, without further comment. The version he used on this occasion was sung by the elderly man.

32. *Nilekerenji ine kudandaula pakuti alimi kuno tikungozunzika?*

33. *Kulima timayesa kuchoma padzuwa, nthawi ya msika mwatipondereza / Nikati niyese kulima thonje, uona mtengo wake ni womvetsa chisoni.*

34. *Koma nthawi ya msika, mwatiberanso.*

35. *Chonde aboma tiganizireni. Ife alimi tikungozunzika.*

36. Although I did not specifically investigate the extent to which Chinese nationals interacted with Zambians in Eastern Province, I often heard talk about their poor linguistic skills (whether in English or Chinyanja) and their tendency to keep to themselves. None of the people I got to know well in Chipata had had much personal contact with Chinese nationals.

37. *Yavuta bwanji bizinesi?* Broadcast on *Chidwi Pa Anthu*, November 18, 2012.

38. FEMALE TRADER: Chinese *avuta. Sitigulitsa pano pamastandi chifukwa cha* Chinese.

    GOGO BREEZE: *Wachita bwanji* Chinese?

    FEMALE TRADER: Chinese *anachoka ku Lusaka nogulitsira kuno. Tsopano kugulitsidwa kwake, amagulitsa metodi ya ku Lusaka. Tsone ise munthu tikagulitsa kuno ati* Chinese *achipitsa kuno, so amathamangira* Chinese, *ati* Chinese *agulitsa bwino.*

39. MALE TRADER: *Tikugulitsa bwinobwino. Ee, salaula anali kubwera a ku Malawi; tsopano akubwera a ku Lusaka. Ku Malawi kunavuta. Transport, makastom, amachita kumangitsa anthu. Taoona, a, tiyambe manje kugula mudziko mwathu mwa Zambia. Titukule dziko lathu. Tiyambe kuodala muno mwathu masiku ano. Ndi katundu amene mukuona pamastandipa.*

    GOGO BREEZE: *Aha.*

    MALE TRADER: *Ehe.*

    GOGO BREEZE: Chinese *sakuvutani iyayi?*

    MALE TRADER: Chinese, *ah, agwetsa mtengo. Sativuta kuti atimenya koma kugwetsa mtengo.*

40. *Mwana akalira ndiye kuti akufuna bele kwa mayi wake. Ndiye ngati mayi samlabadira mwana kulira kwake paja pamene mwana adziponya pansi kenaka ayamba kudzipweteka. Tiyeni tione kuti zonse zimene timachita kwa anthu athu zikhala zowakondweretsa nthawi zonse.*

41. *Akugwira m'maso anthu, kukamba chilungamo. Ise alimi sitikondwera chifukwa tikuvutika kuti tipeze vija vinthu kuti tithandizike, koma iwowa akutinyengerera; akutidyera masuku pamutu. Veve akuchita* benefit; *ise koma sitichita* benefit. *So, tipempha ngako kuti atitsegulira misika yolongosoka kuti tigulitse mbewu zathu zimene tikulima* so that *tithandizikeko makamaka pankhani ya ana a masukulu.* Broadcast on *Chidwi Pa Anthu,* October 15, 2012.

42. Incidentally, the woman quoted above used another common idiom on gogo breeze's programs, *kugwira m'maso,* for cheating.

43. NAOMI MWIMBA: *Akuti akafunsako kuli akuluakulu a cooperative, amawanyoza akuti "chokani apa; mukunenanji?"*

    GOGO BREEZE: *"Mukusokosera."*

    NAOMI MWIMBA: *"Mukusokosera." Mwina akulu amene awa a* cooperative *anapatsidwa feteleza koma iwo akufuna kusewenzetsa paokha. Safuna kuti anzawo achite* benefit. *Ndi chomwe akuchiona ndi "tsopano tidzathandizika bwanji?" Aikapo maina a atsogoleri a kabungwe kameneka.*

    Broadcast on *Makalata,* February 24, 2012.

44. *Ncwala* was commonly thought to be a term in the now-extinct Chingoni language. It was the name of the first-fruit ceremony that some in Eastern Province had helped to revive.

45. *Pamande kukakwacha ngati Inkosi Kapatamoyo wabwerako kuchoka kumwambo wa Angoni Ncwala, mukapite kupalasi, mukafotokozere Inkosi kuti awa akuluakulu a m'chigwirizano ichi sanatisunge bwino iyayi. Anatidyera masuku pamutu kotero kuti Inkosi Kapatamoyo akachite nawo anthu amenewa. Tere nikamba pano Inkosi Kapatamoyo ngati iye kulibe kunyumba amayi ali kunyumba, ndipo madoda amene iwo amakhala pamtengo wa*

kachere ali kunyumba, ena a iwo sali kumwambo iyayi, wali kumva. Adzakuyembekeze-
rani kuti paMande. Mukaperekere nkhani imeneyi kuti akaione bwino kuti awa amene
anatenga feteleza. Inuyo wauze kuti mukafunsa akukalipirani.

46. *Ife amene timawalemba ana amasiye, kapena okhalamba, kufuna kuti wena awathandize,*
tiyeni tikhale okhulupirika. Osadyerana masuku pamutu iayayi, watero gogo wanu. Broadcast on *Makalata*, December 16, 2012.

47. Broadcast on *Makalata*, March 8, 2013.

48. *Akuti mwamuna wotere, aGogo. "Mundithandiza bwanji? Chonde ine nasauka; ndichite*
naye bwanji?"

49. GOGO BREEZE: *Mayo! Koma mwamuna mnzanga uyu, mazunzo!*
NAOMI MWIMBA: *Mm.*
GOGO BREEZE: *Tsono, kuipa kwake ndikuti ukwati anamanga chaka chatha.*
NAOMI MWIMBA: *Chaka chatha!*
GOGO BREEZE: *Tsono chaka chatha chimenechi, chimene chili chaka chofunikira kuti*
akaonetse ubwino wake wa umuna.
NAOMI MWIMBA: *Mm.*
GOGO BREEZE: *Ndiye angofuna kudyera masuku pamutu pamkazi, aa, nanga*
zimatero?

50. Marriage guardians (*ankhoswe*) are witnesses, typically sisters or mother's brothers
from both sides of the marriage.

51. *Mudziwanji kuti ndalama zake mwina amataya m'madzi? Tsono agogo akanena ataya*
m'madzi, leka ndikufotokozereni. Madzi ndi azimayi amene amangoyenda mwachi-
sawawa. Afunafuna ndalama usiku; ndi kumene zimapita ndalama zake za mwamuna
wanu uyo. Sinamuone koma ndikukamba m'mene ziliri ngati iye alibe ndalama. "Ndilibe
ndalama, patse iwe." Nanga zake zapita kuti popeza amalandira? Amayi sungani nda-
lama izo zimene munatenga kuboma, zimene atate wanu anazisiya. Zisungeni chifukwa
mwamuna uyo simudzakhala naye nthawi yaitali. Posachedwapa ndikudziwa kuti adza-
kuthawani. Ngati avuta athane nazo ankhoswe. Mukhale pansi, nowafotokozera mavuto
amene mwamuna anu ali nawo. Kotero kuti muone njira imene mukhoza kusungira wana
amenewo.

52. Broadcast on September 19, 2012.

53. *Masiku amenewo panali mwambo waukulu wakuti munthu amene sali mfumu kapena*
wolemera sanaloledwe kudyera pamodzi ndi anthu omveka ndipo otere akapezeka ama-
khala pamlandu waukulu ndithu.

54. *Tinakhazikitsa ufumu wanuwu inu musanabadwe.*

55. *Apa pangotanthauza kuti kawirikawiri mwai wa mfulu umakondanso kufikira mpaka kwa*
anthu wamba koma anthu amene sali mfulu amakhala odzikonda osafuna kuti mwai wao
ukwanirenso ena.

56. This encounter was also a part of Gogo Breeze's life story discussed in chapter 1.

57. *Ndikumbukira tsiku lina kunabwera mtsogoleri wa dziko anandiitana kuti ndikhale mpa-*
kati pawo chifukwa chakuti ndinali kugwira ntchito ina yake. Ndiye tinapita limodzi ku
St Monica kukadya kumene kuja. Ngati ukudya nawo akuluakulu iwo akakhuta nawe un-
gakhute, chingakhale zinthu zotsekemera bwanji - mavuto amenewo. Ndiye kukhala gogo,
wayamba kutenga masikono nayamba kuika muthumba kuti azidya mugalimoto.

CHAPTER FOUR

1. The next two chapters return to these issues by discussing the preponderance of
programs devoted to women's and children's affairs.

2. Axel's argument is about the assumption of an "originary, stable ground"

(2006:374) for communication. He calls "neoliberalism" the historical formation that appears to promote such an assumption.

3. The impetus for the critical study of intimacy, coming from such fields as queer and postcolonial studies, was asserted with particular sophistication by Berlant 1998 and the assembled articles it introduced.

4. In a more material sense, the catchphrase described the concept of soundproofing for listeners who would never enter the studio.

5. This was the series, as mentioned in the previous chapter, that was sponsored by a foreign NGO.

6. *Makosana, mumalemba makalata? Musabise nkhani, chifukwa makalata amene muma-lemba mumafotokoza kuipa kwa aja amene ali ma* executive. (The word Gogo Breeze used for elders, *makosana,* is colloquial, typically used between age mates.)

7. *Ahedimani, fotokozani bwino; mwina ndi inu amene munalandira feteleza ambirimbiri pokhala hedimani. Anakupatsani matumba ambiri kusiyana ndi anthu ena. Fotokozani bwino.*

8. As has been seen, *boma* translates as both "government" and "state."

9. *Tichite bwanji kuti tigawane? Ayi, koma zimatheka feteleza wabwera wochepa. Tichite bwanji? Tiyeni tigawane pang'onopang'ono.*

10. *Ahedimani, musakhale munthu woika kumbuyo mwana amene walakwa.*

11. *Ifenso timavutikira limodzi. Feteleza kulibe.*

12. *Ulimi wabwera pansi chifukwa cha atsogoleri komanso boma. Litiganizire kwambiri ife anthu okhala kuno kumudzi. Umphawi walowa chifukwa cha la feteleza.*

13. GOGO BREEZE: *Tsono tiyeni tipeze umboni pamenepo. Chifukwa ngati munthu, ee, walowa nyumba ya mwini kapena wagwira kamtsikana kamoye, umboni ukhala kuti ka-moyeka kali ndi chiyani, ndi mimba. Si choncho, makosana?*

   CROWD: *Ee.*

   GOGO BREEZE: *Tsopano nkhani imene yatuluka apapa, tiyeni tiyerekeze, munda wanu wa inuyo na munda wanga wa ine amene ndili chairman kapena committee member. Kodi chimanga, popeza chinakula ndipo chinabereka, kuti tipite tsopano tikaone munda wa inu na munda wa chairman, kodi zikafanana?*

   MAN IN THE CROWD: *Zosiyana.*

   GOGO BREEZE: *Zosiyana bwa?*

   MAN IN THE CROWD: *Zosiyana chifukwa choti akuluakulu ndi atsogoleri ali ndi njira ina pakuti chilungamo chimavuta ndi atsogoleri, chimavuta chilungamo.*

   GOGO BREEZE: *Ndipo umboni apapa tili nawo popeza chimanga cha chairman chili bwino pamene chimanga cha ine munthu wamba chimanga chili bwa?*

   CROWD: *Choonongeka.*

14. Maize is more than a means of sustenance in countries like Zambia and Malawi. Maize in its various forms is a common item in ritual exchanges during initiations, weddings, and funerals.

15. The Chinyanja word for justice, *chilungamo,* is derived from the verb *kulungama,* "to stand upright."

16. See, among others, Dodge (1977), Gould (1997:209–30), and Moore and Vaughan (1994:206–31). The issues highlighted in this literature include the colonial and postcolonial policies of enticing Zambians to "return" to agriculture, the boom and bust in hybrid maize cultivation, and its subsidization at the expense of other crops and in areas where input and transport costs rendered it unviable in the long term.

17. *Buku La Alimi,* January–March 2010, pp. 14–15.

18. See appendix B for a transcript and translation of the letter, Gogo Breeze's response on the *Makalata* program, and the subsequent conversation at the station.
19. Broadcast on April 20, 2012.
20. Curiously, Nkhoma did not use the phrase *alongo wawo*, which refers to a sibling of the opposite sex.
21. The name of the compound indicates its origins as a destination for migrants from Eastern Province.
22. Gogo Breeze's expression *akagona mukamboliboli* made us all laugh, because *kamboliboli* evoked the image of a tiny cell where there was not enough room for even turning.
23. For a critique of the stereotype, particularly as it pertains to the uses of literacy, see Gupta (2012:142–44).
24. For further insights into affect and bureaucracy, see Mathur (2016:134–35) and Mazzarella (2009:298).
25. "Psychoanalytical theories of voice," Amanda Weidman has observed, "emphasize its primordiality, its privileged role in creating a sense of self" (2006:10).
26. Matza (2009) elaborates on Russian radio listeners' capacity to question the "neoliberal governmentality" that their psychotherapist-hosts might have been understood to promulgate.
27. Although Gogo Breeze may not be all that different from those healers and diviners whose authoritative statements build on what supplicants tell them, it seems sensible to avoid what Richard Werbner calls "a cynical folktale among would-be streetwise anthropologists—the diviner tells and the client hears what the client expects and wants to hear" (2015:255). Dialogism, here as elsewhere in Gogo Breeze's approach to multivocal morality, is important to keep in focus.

CHAPTER FIVE

1. See, for example, "ZNBC Probes 'Perfecto,'" *The Weekend Post*, April 27, 2012.
2. Such as "Make Wa Junior" (Junior's mom) and "Sikireti Ku Bedi" (Secret in the bed), both revolving around intimate affairs and treacherous women.
3. The slogan formed a part of the HEART (Helping Each Other Act Responsibly Together) Campaign, largely funded by the United States governmental aid agency US-AID. Through television slots, posters, and other print media, it targeted adolescent girls with a view to persuading them to abstain from sex.
4. As a topic in surveys, violence against women was noted to have increased at the national level, with 23 percent of the interviewed women having experienced physical violence in the year prior to the survey in 2001–02 and 33 percent in the year prior to the survey in 2007 (Central Statistical Office 2012b:25). For Eastern Province, the figures were 17 and 20 percent, respectively.
5. Broadcast on December 22, 2011.
6. *Mayi, kuno ku Lusaka, pa hotel ya Mika, nadabwa nazo kuti munakhala kusukulu kwambiri kukonzakonza nkhani ya maphunziro amene tinabwerera kuno, amene. Naimva kuti* gender, responsibility, *chiyani, vizungu amakamba anzathu. Makamaka anthu akufuna kudziwa dzina lanu poyamba.*
7. *Poyamba kumbuyoko panalibe nkhani za azimayi pamene ma* reporters *anali kulemba nkhani zawo pamodzi ndi mapologamu awo?*
8. *Nkhani za akazi* especially *ku Zambia sizinachoke maningi, so tikufuna kuti wamuna ni wamkazi akhale pa* same, same level. Equal, equal.
9. GOGO BREEZE: *Ayi, Chinyanja mukuchita kupatula, chinakakhala Chiwemba=*
    ORGANIZER: =One Zambia, one nation.

10. *Mtima wanena chabe kuti ndifuna kubwerera kumudzi,* not *kubwerera ku Lusaka koma ku Chipata.*

11. *Chovutititsa kwambiri kukhazikika ngati wachokera kunja.*

12. *Adzatengera ntchito yathu.*

13. *Ugwira ntchito ndi mtima wonse, akamba kuti "udzionetsa."*

14. Broadcast on April 9, 2012.

15. *So, pa tsiku la lero tili kuona pali vuto la katisidwe ka ana ochepera zaka ziwiri.* Aunt *Deliwe, mudziwa zambiri pankhani imeneyi, timasulireni.*

16. *Tikanena* malnutrition *tikuti thupi silikulandira izo zakudya zimene liyenera kulandira m'thupi. Makamaka tinene kuti nthawi ya ana ngati ali ndi ana angapo avutika kwambiri chifukwa chakuti vuto lonena lakuti mayi sadziwa kakonzekedwe ka chakudya ndiponso sadziwa kuti tipeze bwanji zakudya zimenezo.*

17. YOUNG MAN: *Lomba* Aunt Deliwe, *kodi ndi chiyani chiletsa mwana kuti sadya mokwana?*

    NGOMA: *Chimene chiletsa mwana kuti sadya mokwana ndi chifukwa cha amayi amenewa sadziwa kudyetsa bwino mwana. Chifukwa chake tifuna kudziwitsa mayi kuti adziwe.*

18. On motherhood as a site of intervention and contestation in colonial and post-colonial Africa, see Hunt (2003); Johnson-Hanks (2006); Mutongi (2007).

19. As mentioned, even those who had settled in Chipata town maintained a strong sense of home in their village of origin. Young mothers would spend some of the time before or after giving birth in the village in order to receive assistance and advice from older female relatives, some of whom could also come to town if the mother was not able to stay in the village. These practices took place under changing conditions, of course, with HIV/AIDS and pregnancies out of wedlock challenging here as elsewhere in contemporary Africa established patterns of intergenerational care. The point here is that such challenges had not reached the stage at which complete ignorance, as Ngoma seemed to suggest, had engulfed the experience of motherhood.

20. YOUNG MAN: *Koma Aunt Deliwe, kuli azimayi ena amazewenza, sangakhale ayamwitse mwana* twenty-four seven. *Amagulako mamiliki kumashopu. Pali vuto bwanji pamenepo?*

    NGOMA: *Vuto lilipo. Amene amazewenza azimayi, kuli zintchito zambiri amapatsa nthawi ya livi kuti akhale ndi mwana, ayamwitse bwino uja mwana. Ndipo* two, *kuonjezera paiyo, munthu amene akufuna kubereka mwana, chachikulu n'chakuti sitifuna kuti aberekebereke, ali kusukulu* girl child *wayamba kale kubereka. N'chifukwa tikufuna munthu achite pulani akakhala ndi mwana akakhala pachikwati mokhazikika bwino, osangobereka mwana chiberekebereke.*

21. On surplus people, see Ferguson (2013) and Li (2010).

22. One test involved preparing a proposal on how one would cover a chief's funeral.

23. *Ngakhale kuti ndi azimayi koma ali kuchita ndithu zitukuko zimene zitha kuphunzitsa azimayi ena amene ali okhalira kuti mwina ali ndi maganizo kuti sangakhoze kalikonse m'miyoyo yawo. Nawonso kuti akamva zimene anzawo akupanga nawonsa mwina angatsatire chitsanzo chimenecho.*

24. Broadcast on November 12, 2012.

25. Broadcast on January 8, 2013.

26. Broadcast on September 18, 2012.

27. Broadcast on August 30, 2011.

28. *Azimayi, azimayi, ndife dziko la Zambia. Azimayi ayenera kukhala olimba, sayenera*

kukhala kumbuyo. Azimayi ndi amene amasunga nyumba, azimayi ndi amene amasunga ana pamodzi ndi amuna. Broadcast on March 12, 2013.

29. Broadcast on April 12, 2012.
30. Broadcast on July 7, 2012.
31. Broadcast on June 28, 2012.
32. Broadcast on March 21, 2013.
33. Broadcast on April 26, 2012.
34. *Ndisanayankhe funso ili chimene ndingakambe ndi chakuti banja lililonse, likakhala banja, chachikulu kwambiri chofunika m'banja ndi ulemu. Mwamuna alemekeze mkazi, mkazi alemekenso mwamuna wake. Chimene chimabweretsa mkangano m'nyumba kapena chimene chimabweretsa ndewu ndi chiyani?*
35. NZIMA: *Mwaziyamba mwekha. Jenda, jenda ndi yakuti* fifty-fifty. *Mwanalume akachite lipoti atatemedwa.*

    MATOTO: *[laughs] Asunga ng'anda ndani?*

    NZIMA: *Nisunge ni wana.*

    MATOTO: *Akuphikirani ndani?*

    NZIMA: *Niphike nekha.*
36. NZIMA: *Nkhani yaikulu ndi yakuti mwanalume ndi mwini wa ng'anda=*

    MATOTO: *=Chabwino.*

    NZIMA: *Mwanalume si wokonsherewa ayi; wokonsherewa ni mwanakazi ni mwanalume.*

    MATOTO: *Mm.*

    NZIMA: *Lomba jenda yanu imene muli nayo ikusokoneza chabe azimayi. Kufuna kulingana ndi mwanalume.*

    MATOTO: *Kodi sitinganene pankhani ya ma* responsibilities, *malamulo a zintchito zimene wina aliyense angachite? Kodi sitikunena za kugawana kwa mphamvu?*

    NZIMA: *A-a, mukufuna kunena kuti newo ni mewo tilingane. Lomba tulingana lini, chifukwa onani ntchito yanu ndi kupyera, kuphika na kusamba. Kupyera m'ng'anda, nili kuntchito.*
37. *Anzima tikanena zantchito monga kutsuka mbale, kuphika zakudya, zakukitcheni, kumbali yakukitcheni azimayi adzakhala olamulira m'mbali yakukitcheni. Koma tikanena malamulo oyendetsera manyumba, mzibambo ndi mutu ndithu wa nyumba.*
38. MATOTO: *Anzima, nafuna kutsiriza; mwandigwira pakamwa.*

    NZIMA: *Tsirizani, chabwino naleka=*

    MATOTO: *=Tikakhala paulamuliro mutu wa nyumba uja ndi mwamuna=*

    NZIMA: *=Mm=*

    MATOTO: *=Wolamulira zonse. Koma tikabwera kuma* responsibilities - *mwachitsanzo Anzima imwe mwachokapo panyumba. Mudzapeza kuti mzimayi uja adzachita* act *ngati* assistant manager, *chifukwa* manager *palibe. Ine pokhala mzimayi ndinene a-a, koma pambali iyi, tichite tere, koma mukabwera tsiku lakutilakuti ndiye mudzabwera amuna anga. Tingakambe ndatenga ulamuliro paja?*

    NZIMA: *Onani, tiyeni tikambe zinthu kulingana ndi m'mene zingamvere, amayi. Nkhani yaikulu tikambe apa ndi yakuti malamulo amene tili nawo kulingana malamulo achikwati. Malamulo achikwati tili nawo, ano masiku, jenda yapaya, chifukwa mwanakazi amangofuna kukhala ndi mphamvu yopambana ndi mphamvu ya mwanalume.*
39. A retired female magistrate was among the potential participants, but she appeared to be in no hurry to give Matoto a definite answer about her availability.
40. It has been observed in the historical literature that the nineteenth-century Ngoni conquest actually involved a conquest of the Ngoni themselves by their wives,

whose languages and matrilineal practices they adopted in present-day Malawi and Zambia (see Langworthy 1975:18).

41. The honor was bestowed on the couple because the father of Nzima's bride was the bishop's domestic servant.

42. *Chimene anafuna n'chakuti ndinene "ee, munthu akhale ndi mitala," koma ine ndinaopa kuti adzayamba kunena "oh, m'Bilizi amavomereza mitala."*

43. *Tikawerenga Buku Lopatulika amanena kuti "mwamuna," mundimvetsa apo?"konda mkazi wako ndiponso mkazi iwe, mvera mwamuna wako," koma Paulo sananene kuti "mwamuna ndi mkazi, mphamvu zanu zilingana; kondanani," kapena ananena m'Chizungu,* "A man must love his wife and the wife must submit to her husband."

44. Both, it can also be added, owed their presence at Breeze FM to its founder-director, who found, at least initially, their expertise and connections useful. As was seen, Ngoma solicited sweet potatoes for his farm, which also benefited from Nzima's advice on agricultural issues over a number of years.

45. The date of the broadcast was April 27, 2012.

46. *Nkhani zakhambamkamwa ndimakonda kuzipewa. Ife kwathu mwina ndi kungomuthandiza mkulu amenewo. Kuti ngati ndi zoona kuti wapangitsa wana ake, wapangitsa mkazi wake, mavuto kamba kakuti waona kamoye, walakwitsa. Kamoye kameneko kadzamthawa, katundu uyu wampatsa mzimayi uyu watsopano sudzakhala wake iyayi. Tili kukhala kukamba nkhani zimenezi kuti zikafika kunoko nkhani zoterezi ndi zochititsa manyazi. Makamaka wopenya uyu wotilembera kalata, ee, wachita bwino, koma tiyeni tithandize onse, azimayi, azibambo. Tiyeni tiyang'ane pamodzi. Tisamwe madzi pazitsime zambiri, chifukwa kumwa madzi pazitsime zambiri, tidzabweretsapo mavuto pathupi lathu kenaka tidzapita kumanda pamene nthawi ikalibe kukwanira iyayi. Imwe abambo amene munachita kumanga restaranti, kumangira* girlfriend, *munalakwa. Nanga wana awo amene munabereka ndi mzimayi amene uyu munatuluka naye mugowelo? Mumsiyire chiyani? Tiyeni tipewe, nkhani zina zake izi, ndapapata, ehe. Aa, imwe, anthu, imwe, aa.*

47. PAULINE PHIRI: *Koma ndi zoona, aGogo. Muumoyo wa munthu chilichonse chimene munthu angachite chili ndi nthawi yake=*

   GOGO BREEZE: *=Taonani tsopano=*

   PAULINE PHIRI: *=Ndipo mdalawa akhoza kuona kuti pakadali pano akuthandizika, koma tsiku limodzi likakwana zonse ndithu zidzaonekera poyera.*

48. GOGO BREEZE: *Ndipemphe amayi awa akhululukire mdalawa. M'mene tauzira tere mwina akagone kunyumba.*

   PAULINE PHIRI: *Wakhululukira kale, chifukwa mzimayi uyu ndi wolimba akadali kunyumba, koma mdalawa n'kofunika asinthe.*

   GOGO BREEZE: *Auze.*

   PAULINE PHIRI: *Tauza kale. Nanga ndipitirire apa?*

   GOGO BREEZE: *Mdala, mutimvetsa manyazi. Taonani agogo walephera kuti alankhule, chifukwa nkhani yanu ndi yomvetsa manyazi, aa!*

49. The 2010 population survey found that among the population age fifteen years and older, 59 percent of males and 60 percent of females in Eastern Province were currently married, with a larger proportion of males (36 percent) than females (20 percent) having never married (Central Statistical Office 2014a:16). In the Zambia section of the World Values Survey in 2007, 81 percent disagreed with the statement that "marriage is an outdated institution," with negligible variation between women and men in their responses, see http://www.worldvaluessurvey.org/wvs.jsp.

50. This desire contrasts with the findings of those studies on contemporary African

situations in which marriage as an institution appears to be contested or even in decline (see, e.g., Cole 2010; Hunter 2010; Johnson-Hanks 2007).

51. Broadcast on *Makalata*, March 22, 2013.

52. *Chodziwika ndi choti monga tanenera pano; zaka ndi zochepera za* twenty-five. *Afunika kuti apitirize maphunziro ake kuti amalize. Akamaliza kukoleji kupita kwina kwake uko kumene ankafune kumanga banja, chikufwa kumwa mankhwala sikuti umoyo wake uwatha iyayi. Anthu amene ali kumwa mankhwala amakhala zaka zopitirira kupambana uja amene sali kumwa iyayi.*

53. *Akuti* status *yake ali pamankhwala, so akulembera amuna aliyense akhalenso pamankhwala ndipo akhalenso pantchito, wakuti angamange naye banja. Waika chipikitchala ndi nambala yake, ndipo ndi mtsikana wooneka bwino.*

54. *Koma tingonena kuti ngati aliko azibambo amene ali ndi zaka zopitirira mzimayi amenewo, nawonso akhoza kubwera kuti aone chipikitchala chimenechi kuti mwina akhoza kumvana kuti amange banja.*

55. *Mzibambo wolemba kalatayi akuti ali ndi zaka* thirty-seven *ndipo akuti akufuna kupeza mkazi wokhulupirika komanso wokongola.*

56. The Chinyanja translation for "virus" had become *kalombo*, the diminutive of "wild beast," conveying therefore a tiny but ferocious threat to health.

57. *Chonde aGogo, ngati angapezeke mayi woti ndimange naye banja ndipo ali ndi wana awiri kapena m'modzi, tingasungane naye m'banja langa.*

58. *AGogo, Mulungu azikudalitseni chifukwa mumamanga mabanja ambiri zedi.*

59. *Ngati muwakonda, kabwereni. Kambewa kamanyazi kanafera kudzenje. Chifukwa mukangonena, "ah, ali mom'muno muboma la Chipata; sindingapite," mwalakwa. Ngati mwabwera mukaonane nawo, mtsikana wanga, ndiye mukaonana nawo adzandiuza, ndikakupatsani malo,* very private place, *eh, mkati kunyumba kwanga, paseli pa chimanga. Mukambiranakambirina, mukatha zonse, mwavomekezana, ndidzakuuzani zoti mukachite. Amyai inu, mulipo ambiri amene muli kuchita nkhani ya maliketi kumakomboni; mulibe mwamuna; wapezeka mwamuna. Iye ali pantchito; akufuna mzimayi amene akuchita nkhani ya maliketi kuti akhoza kumanga naye banja.*

60. *Koma pakukongola iwo adzaone okha. Ngati mzimayi abwera, tiwaitana kuti akaone ngati ndi wokongola. Ndi iwo amene angaone ngati ndi wokongola, chifukwa kuona kwa kukongola kwa ine ndi kwa iwo kudzakhala kosiyana.*

61. Women's involvement in trading, largely through vegetable and fruit vending, increased rapidly after Zambia's independence, if only because of the paucity of other income-generating opportunities available to them (see Bardouille 1981; Hansen 1989; Schuster 1982). The morality of market women's trade and personal comportment is a common theme in the literature on Africa (see, e.g., Clark 2001; MacGaffey 1991; Pietilä 2007).

CHAPTER SIX

1. *Pali zina zake zimene zimachitika kumalo ena ake. Sindikudziwa ngati kwanu ku Lundazi zimachitika makamaka anthu amene amakhala pamaliketi. Mukugulitsa; mupeza kuti kamwana kayenda m'msewu, kayamba kupemphapempha, "Atate anamwalira, amayi anamwalira, anapita ku Malawi," koma amayi wake a mwana ameneyu ndi amene anamtuma kuti apite azikapemphapempha. Kodi kwanu ku Lundazi zoterezi ziliko?* Broadcast on *Chidwi Pa Anthu*, February 11, 2013.

2. *Ndi zoona zimene akulankhula akulu wangawo. Wana amapanga ngati ma* street kids *koma ma* parents *ndi zoona aliko. Ndi vuto limene liliko, koma* problem *imakhala pa*

makolo awo, ndi amene amapangitsa vuto lotere. Amayi alibe chimene angagwire, atate ali kumowa. Ee, vuto liliko; zoona.

3. *Zoona, wana waliko, amakamba kuti ma* street kids *kuno ku Lundazi Market Square. Ndi wana makolo awo* sometimes *kwacha ali kumowa, lomba kuti wana akhale wekha pang'anda ndi njala chiwavuta, chifukwa chake wabwera kuno kumaliketi kuyamba kupemphapempha.*

4. As the literature on Africa has shown, orphaned children rarely face the specter of abandonment but increase the burden of care labor among other relatives than their own parents, such as grandmothers (Geissler and Prince 2010:163; Ingstad 2004:73) and siblings (Wolf 2010).

5. See James (2007) for a succinct account of these attempts in academia and beyond. Boyden (1997) is an example of the anthropological and sociological critiques of the UN Convention.

6. Census figures from Eastern Province do indicate girls' particular difficulties staying in school. In 2000, although the discrepancy between male and female children's attendance was negligible in the seven- to thirteen-years age group, more than two-thirds of females age fourteen to eighteen in rural areas were not attending school, in contrast to nearly 50 percent of boys in this age group attending school in rural areas (Central Statistical Office 2004:51). The trend was compounded in secondary education: "More than 80 percent of the rural females were not attending secondary education compared to less than one third of their urban counterparts" (Central Statistical Office 2004:52). The 2010 census results did not specify rural and urban school attendance according to gender in the same way, but the stark discrepancy between rural (25 percent) and urban (57 percent) secondary-school attendance among the fourteen- to eighteen-year-olds was likely to have a further gendered dimension (see Central Statistical Office 2014b:26).

7. Broadcast on *Because I Am a Girl / Chifukwa Ndine Mtsikana*, October 9, 2012. The other two women in the studio were governmental and NGO representatives.

8. Matoto was a Seventh-day Adventist.

9. *Ine dzina langa ndine Susan Phiri ndine mtsikana. Koma ndithire pondemanga pazimene wakamba mphunzitsi. Makolo angayeseko kuti tisatenge mimba, kutilangiza, koma ise ana sitikumva zokamba makolo. Zikomo.* Broadcast on October 4, 2012.

10. *Ine dzina langa ndine Ester Banda pamudzi wa Jolani Village. Ndithire pondemanga pa zomwe atiphunzitsa alangizi kuti azilowe m'makutu mwathu, komanso ndithire ponde-manga kuti zomwe amatiuza alangizi zimafika m'makutu mwathu koma sitizigwiritsa ntchito. Ise ana tilibe makutu. Alangizi amayesa kulangizako, koma ise ana kuti tizigwiri-tse ntchito, tisowa chabe ulemu. Tilibenso ulemu woti tingamamvetsere makolo. Zikomo.*

11. *Ine dzina langa ndine Justina Mbewe ndine mtsikana. Ndithire ndemanga zomwe akamba alangizi za ukwati, za mimba. Ise ana tilibe makutu, koma makolo amalangiza, kulan-gizadi motsimikiza kuti ana safunika kutenga mimba kapena kupita kuchikwati msanga zaka zikalibe kukwanira. Ukapita kuchikwati zaka zisanafikeko, upezana ndi mavuto am-biribiri; kusunga sungakwanitse. Zikomo.*

12. *Zikomo mkonzi. Ntchito yomwe yakhazikidwa ndi Plan Zambia yakuti Ndine Mtsikana kuidziwa kwake ndikuidziwa kotere. Pomwe inafika tinailandira ndi manja awiri kuti, a-a, wachita bwino watibweretsera ntchito imeneyi yakuti tidziphunzitsa ana athu, chifukwa amapezeka ana ang'ono ali ndi* fourteen years *akupezeka ndi pathupi ndiye timayesetsa kwambiribiri kulangiza wana amenewa kuti, a-a, "simufunika kuchita zimenezi." Tiyeni tithandizane pamodzi ndi anzanga alangizi mpaka kuwaunikira ndithu wana kuti "osa-*

chita kulondola zimenezi malinga ndi maphunziro amene timaphunzira kuti mukakhale umoyo wabwino mtsogolo; tsogolo likhale labwino. Osathamangira mavuto pakuti ise ngakhale makolo anu timakumana ndi mavuto ambirimbiri: vikwati, kumenyewa, kuponderezewa kwambiri ngati osaphunzira. Ngati suphunzira upeza mavuto, sungakwanitse. Kalikonse uchita kupempha kwa azibambo. Ana inu phunzirani kuti mawa tsogolo lanu likakhale labwino. Mukatithandizenso kukhala ngati inenso, mlangizi." Zikomo.

13. *Atsikana amavutika kudziko lino la Zambia. Tsono timawamasulira kuti "inu atsikana mufunika kukhala omvera zimene timakuuzani. Onani akatenga mimba ana awa, mzibambo wopatsa mimba amapitiriza maphunziro awo, koma mzimayi aima; mtsikana uja akubwezera kumbuyo. Mnyamata wopatsa mimba wotenga tsogolo lake apititsa patsogolo."*

14. *Ngakhale munatenga kale mimba monga m'mene ndinachitira ine, musaganize kupita kubanja. Tiyeni tibwerere kusukulu. Zikomo mkonzi.*

15. *Kuleka masukulu ndi choipa ee / Lamulo limakana choipa ee / Kupita kusukulu ndi chabwino ee / Lamulo livomera chabwino ee.* (Rather than evoking specific legislation, *lamulo* referred to law as rules or appropriate codes of conduct.)

16. *Chidwi Pa Anthu,* March 20, 2013.

17. GOGO BREEZE: *Pali vuto lina lake ndalimva chifukwa cha kuyenda kwanga kumeneko. Pali nkhani ndaimva kunena kuti aziphunzitsi, wana amene ali ndi chifuwa chokwera, ayi ndithu, amakhala akazi awo. Kodi kuno kwanu kuno kwa Kagoro nkhani yamtundu umenewu kodi iliko? Ngati iliko n'chiyani chimene mumachitapo?*

    MAN: *Ndi zoonadi nkhani imeneyi yativuta kwambiri. Ena aziphunzitsi awa, mm, akaona azikazi, ah. Tsono makolo ife takambapokambapo, sikhalidwe limeneli, ana saphunzira iyayi. Alekezeni; wana aphunzire. Tinakambapo.*

18. *Alekeze. Timafuna kuti ana a kwa Kagolo aphunzire. Akhalenso ma* teachers. *Akhalenso ma* accountants; *kwabwera banki yatsopano kuno. Tifuna ana awo akaphunzire osati wana aleke iyayi.*

19. *Inu azimayi, ndinamva inu ndi amene mukuti mwana akatha msinkhu, kodi ndi zoona kuti mumamuika m'nyumba nowaululira zonse zija zimene, kanthu kaya, tiuze nkoni, pali bwa?*

20. As has been seen, the idiom *nyumba yomata,* a well-plastered house, was used for this situation and was an inspiration for the idiom *kapinda komata,* the little well-plastered room that Gogo Breeze called the studio at Breeze FM.

21. *Kutsimikiza kuika m'nyumba, timaikadi. Pamene timaika m'nyumba, tsono palibe zimene timapindula, wana ndi opanda matu. Ise kale tinalira pamene mwamuna atatinyenga, kugwira mabele. Tingokwatira kwa makolo, makolo kupita kwa munthu uja, akawalipire. Tsono walero salira.*

22. *Koma ndifunika kunena choona. Awo wana akangochoka kwa makolo awo opanda matu. Ndikakhale naye masiku ochepa singakwanitse kuletsa mwana m'mtima mwake, koma akakhala ochokera kwa makolo ake, achichita. Ngakhale ine mlangizi singachiletse. Koma chinakhazitsidwa ndi mwambo wathu, timatenga mwana, timalangiza. Titalangiza timapereka kwa makolo ake, koma sitimatsiriza mwambo wonse ayi.*

23. *Ise tikafika m'nyumba muja chomwe tiyambira ndi mwana uja, tamtenga mwana, tamuika m'nyumba, choyambirira, tifunika timphunzitse ulemu. Chimakhala choyamba. Na mavalidwe, uja mwana, timphunzitse mavalidwe. Afunika kugwada pansi, koma ngati mwana ni osamvetsa, achoka kwa makolo ake kukhala osamvetsa.*

24. *Amuna anga mulibe chinsinsi / Amuna anga mulibe chinsinsi / Nkhani za m'nyumba tikamba anthu awiri / Nkhani za m'mnyumba tikamba anthu awiri.*

25. Although it was not commented on by Gogo Breeze, the song he broadcast may well have been specifically selected by the women for the occasion to avert attention

from songs of a more obscene character. Studies from Zambia, Malawi, and Mozambique have indicated the weight placed on teachings about sexuality in female initiation ceremonies, including sexual pleasure, reportedly for the benefit of both men and women, through practices such as pelvic movements and elongated labia (see Arnfred 2011; Fiedler 2005; Rasing 2001). This literature is also concerned with comparative perspectives on changes in female initiation among the region's matrilineal peoples in the context of Christianity and NGO-driven attempts to curb the spread of HIV/AIDS (see also Chakanza 1998; Longwe 2006; Mair 1951; Phiri 1998; Rasing 2004; Richards 1956).

26. *Tsono akapezana ndi mwamuna, inuyo makolo achimuna, mukuti, "A-a, ndifunika atipatse kang'ombe - lekeni; nanga wanga mwana." Kodi ndi zoona kuti mumakwatitsa wana ochepa? Chimachitika kwa Kagolo? Ngati chikuchitika, n'chifukwa chiyani?* (Although Chinyanja does not have gendered pronouns, the reference to a girl child is clear in the use of the passive tense for marrying, *kukwatiwa*. The active tense, *kukwatira*, is used for men.)

27. GOGO BREEZE: *Mkulu mnzanga.*

    ELDERLY MAN: *Inde.*

    GOGO BREEZE: *Ndamva kuti mwafuna: "atipatse ng'ombe; ndi wake." Muononga mwana.*

    ELDERLY MAN: *Pankhani yokambidwa apa, sizili tero iyayi. Ise pokhala makolo timayesetsa kuuza ana, "A-a, izi ayi, izi ayi." Mwana ali wochepa; wokwanira zaka eighteen kaya twenty safunika kukwatiwa iyayi. Poyamba aphunzire. Koma kuti pali makolo ena monga wakambira amayi awa, makolo ena amatenga wana uja n'wakwatitsa, koma makolo ena amakhala omvetsa kuti iyayi, wana wang'onong'ono sayenera kutenga banja ayi.*

28. Broadcast on March 5, 2013.

29. GOGO BREEZE: *Anyamata, ndi inu amene mumavutitsa atsikana. Ndaimva nkhani yoti mumauzana kuti "iyayi pitani kwa uja, ee, nalawa." Zili bwanji pamenepo - kodi ndi zoona mumachita kotero?*

    YOUNG MAN: *Zomwe ndifotokozere ndi zakuti atsikana samvera. Atagulira yunifomu makolo veve amapita kusukulu, afuna kuti anyamata aone ndiye ife tikakhumbira paja, tilowa m'mtima mpakana kuti timuone amene uja ali bwanji.*

    GOGO BREEZE: *Zimene mumachita?*

    YOUNG MAN: *Mm.*

    GOGO BREEZE: *Mukukhoza?*

    YOUNG MAN: *Shuwa.*

30. *Mutenga mwana wa eni, gombeza mulibe, mphasa mulibe, mumuononga popititsa kutchile mwana umenewu. Kodi mukukhoza?*

31. GOGO BREEZE: *Mwakamba kavalidwe kwa atsikana. Nanga kavalidwe kwa inu anyamata? Belt wanu mumamanga m'matako m'malo moti mumange m'chiuno. Chimene chikudzetsa zimenezo ndi chiyani, chifukwa ngati mumanga belt wanu m'matako, ndiye kuti mtsikana nayenso akhumbira thako lako. Woipa pamenepo ndi ndani?*

    YOUNG MAN: *Koma tonse ndife oipa. Monga m'mene mwafunsiramo, aGogo, kuipa kwake kuli tere. Akuti, "Uja akuoneka bwino; ali ndi ndalama." Atsikana amafuna kuti onetse zimene zili m'thumba.*

32. *Akhansala, mumaenda m'malo osiyanasiyana, kodi anthu amene mumatsogolera kuno; maukwati a ana ang'onoang'ono, kodi sizichitika? Ngati zimachitika, poti inu pokhala mtsogoleri wa anthu n'chiyani chimene mumachitapo, ngati sichitika, momwemo, tafotokozereni.*

33. *Ee, umo wafotokozera, mwana, kumbuyo uko, zinali kuchitika. Mwana akapatsidwa mimba, makolo anali* forcing *kuti akwatirane cholinga choti apezeke ndi ng'ombe. Koma kulingana ndi kuti kuli mabungwe osiyana pamodzi ndi ise akhansala, kuthandizana, kuphunzitsa wana ubwino wa maphunziro. Tsono ichi chinthu chikukhala chosintha. Ndinene kuti lomba apa ena akufuna kukwatiritsa wana, koma kulingana kogwirizana ndi atsogoleri a mipingo na ife makhansala, tsono icho chinthu chikuoneka kuti kwathu ku Kagolo wana ambiri akupita kusukulu.*

34. Its negative tense, *samvera*, appeared above when the young man claimed that girls "are not disciplined."

35. *Azimayi amene sanapite kusukulu, amene sanaphunzire, alibe ufulu wolankhulira paokha.* Broadcast on May 26, 2011. FAWEZA stands for Forum for African Women Educationalists of Zambia.

36. Broadcast on *Zam'mabanja*, July 7, 2012.

37. See Last (2000) for a case from Northern Nigeria in which physical punishment became associated with schooling while the refusal to beat a child was associated with being backward looking.

38. Broadcast on October 2, 2012.

39. "Sensitization," initially applied in public-health campaigns, became the term of choice for a variety of campaigns and interventions across Africa from the 1990s onward (see Shepler 2005:200).

40. *Ndikungopempha chabe, kuli ma* well-wishers. *Pulani wayesako; Pulani* cannot do one hundred percent. *Ngati boma likhoza kukwanitsa kuchita* sponsor, *ndichita pulani; ndine wokonzeka kupita kukachita* sensitize *anthu.* If any other organization can come in and help to continue with the program.

41. *Ife* we don't need much, because *tikayenda anthu atiphikira; chakudya atiphikira.* What we want is transport. There is nothing like lunch, no. As long as we inform them in advance, *tibwera* so and so, they prepare lunch.

42. Writing about a child-focused NGO in Uganda, China Scherz notes that "Hope Child's demands for goods and collective labor closely mirrored the demands that chiefs, kings, and other patrons made on their clients and followers in Buganda" (2014:56).

43. *Inu a* Breeze FM *mumakhala ndi anzathu, anzathu amene angatithandizire kuti* message *iyi, uthenga uwu, ubwino wa maphunziro a mwana wamkazi, ifike ponseponse.* Any way possible *itheke. Tichite zimenezi, ine* I am ready, *manduna ali* ready, but we are lacking sponsorship.

44. Broadcast on March 11, 2013.

45. *Ine kwanga ndi pempho kwa boma kuti mwina apempheko maNGOs kuti mwina atithandizeko monga pankhani ya madzi. Monga aPulani anabwera kwa anzathu ku Zingalume uko; wakhala kupereka maborehole. Pamudzi umodzi wapereka maborehole awiri, atatu. Koma ifenso kuno ku Taferansoni tikupempha kuti ngati ndi kotheka aPulani abwereko kuno atipatsenso maborehole monga m'mene wapatsira anzathu.*

46. *Mwana akapempha fupa, patseni mnofu kuti adye, chifukwa mukapanda kutero, mawa adzakulozani chala kuti iyayi, ntheradi, "Munandipatsa chakutichakuti."*

47. The alleged use of body parts for occult purposes has recently galvanized media and rumor also elsewhere in Southern Africa (see, e.g., Englund 2006:172–77; Englund 2011:100–101; Gulbrandsen 2012:282–310).

48. "Gang rape" was still mentioned in ZNBC's television news the morning after the riot.

49. See Fraser (2016b) for an account of how the initial lack of participation in phone-

in shows sponsored by the Lusaka City Council on Radio Phoenix improved when figures of authority were brought into the studio.

50. NAOMI MWIMBA: *Akuti "ife, agogo, kuno kwathu ku Soweto ku Katete ndife okhumudwa ndi magwiridwe a ntchito ya asilikali," kapena kuti apolisi. Akuti, "sagwira bwino ntchito, popeza munaimva nkhani ija ya mtsikana mwana wa sukulu wa zaka zakubadwa nineteen. Anamuchita* rape case *nakumuchita* murder"=

GOGO BREEZE: =*Nkhani iyo, ndikugwireko m'kamwa.*

NAOMI MWIMBA: *Mm.*

GOGO BREEZE: *Chifukwa akunena kuti apolisi sakugwira bwino ntchito.*

NAOMI MWIMBA: *Ehe.*

GOGO BREEZE: *Ntchito apolisi akugwira bwino, chifukwa ngati sanagwire bwino, ndikuti mnyamata uyu sanakamugwire iyayi. Sipaja inu atolankhani, aNaomi, mwatenga nkhani? Mwauza dziko lonse kuti mnyamata amene anachita chifwamba kwa mtsikana amene anali kuphunzira ku* Katete Secondary School, *anamgwira. Tikukamba pano tere, ali mkambolimboli.*

NAOMI MWIMBA: *Mm.*

GOGO BREEZE: *Nanga kuneneza asilikali, kodi pali eh?*

NAOMI MWIMBA: *Akuti "anamgwira ndi anthu chabe n'kupereka kwa polisi."*

GOGO BREEZE: *Ndi ntchito yawo ya apolisi; amafufuza. Mwakambamo m'nyuzi zanu, m'nkhani zanu, kunena kuti mnyamata uyu anali kuyenda naye mtsikana uyu, si m'mene mwakambira?*

NAOMI MWIMBA: *Ee.*

GOGO BREEZE: *Tsono iwowo, ndipo mkulu wa polisi nkhani yonse waifotokoza m'mene zinayendera. Tsono awa amene analemba kalata kameneka, ngati ali ndi mawu, abwere kuno ku Chipata, akaonane nawo* officer in charge *kuti akafotokozere nkhani yonse imeneyi.*

REFERENCES

Abreu Lopes, Claudia, and Sharath Srinivasan. 2014. "Africa's Voices: Using Mobile Phones and Radio to Foster Mediated Public Discussion and to Gather Public Opinions in Africa." Centre for Governance and Human Rights Working Paper 9. Cambridge: University of Cambridge.

Archambault, Caroline. 2009. "Pain with Punishment and the Negotiation of Childhood: An Ethnographic Analysis of Children's Rights Processes in Maasailand." *Africa* 79 (2): 282–302.

Archambault, Julie Soleil. 2017. *Mobile Secrets: Youth, Intimacy, and the Politics of Pretense in Mozambique.* Chicago: University of Chicago Press.

Arendt, Hannah. 1970. *On Violence.* London: Allen Lane.

Arnfred, Signe. 2011. *Sexuality and Gender Politics in Mozambique: Rethinking Gender in Africa.* Oxford: James Currey.

Arnheim, Rudolf. 1936. *Radio.* Translated by Margaret Ludwig and Herbert Read. London: Faber and Faber.

Asad, Talal. 2009. "Free Speech, Blasphemy, and Secular Criticism." In *Is Critique Secular? Blasphemy, Injury, and Free Speech,* edited by Talal Asad, Wendy Brown, Judith Butler, and Saba Mahmood, 20–63. Berkeley: University of California Press.

Askew, Kelly M. 2002. *Performing the Nation: Swahili Music and Cultural Politics in Tanzania.* Chicago: University of Chicago Press.

Auslander, Mark. 1993. "'Open the Wombs!': The Symbolic Politics of Modern Ngoni Witchfinding." In *Modernity and Its Malcontents: Ritual and Power in Postcolonial Africa,* edited by Jean Comaroff and John Comaroff, 167–92. Chicago: University of Chicago Press.

Axel, Brian Keith. 2006. "Anthropology and the New Technologies of Communication." *Cultural Anthropology* 21 (3): 354–85.

Bakhtin, Mikhail. 1984. *Problems of Dostoevsky's Poetics.* Translated by Caryl Emerson. Minneapolis: University of Minnesota Press.

Barber, Karin. 1991. *I Could Speak until Tomorrow: Oríkì, Women and the Past in a Yoruba Town.* Edinburgh: Edinburgh University Press for the International African Institute.

———. 2007. *The Anthropology of Texts, Persons and Publics: Oral and Written Culture in Africa and Beyond.* Cambridge: Cambridge University Press.

———. 2012. *Print Culture and the First Yoruba Novel: I. B. Thomas's "Life Story of Me, Ṣẹgilọla" and Other Texts.* Leiden: Brill.

Bardouille, Raj. 1981. "The Sexual Division of Labour in the Urban Informal Sector: Case Studies of Some Townships in Lusaka." *African Social Research* 32:29–54.

Barnes, J. A. 1954. *Politics in a Changing Society: A Political History of the Fort Jameson Ngoni.* Oxford: Oxford University Press.

Barthes, Roland. 1977. *Image—Music—Text.* Translated by Stephen Heath. London: Fontana.

Bauman, Richard, and Charles L. Briggs. 2003. *Voices of Modernity: Language Ideologies and the Politics of Inequality.* Cambridge: Cambridge University Press.

Benjamin, Walter. 2008 [1931]. "Reflections on Radio." In *The Work of Art in the Age of Its Technological Reproducibility, and Other Writings on Media,* edited by Michael W. Jennings, Brigid Doherty, and Thomas Y. Levin, translated by Rodney Livingstone, 391–92. Cambridge, MA: Harvard University Press.

Berlant, Lauren. 1997. *The Queen of America Goes to Washington City.* Durham, NC: Duke University Press.

———. 1998. "Intimacy: A Special Issue." *Critical Inquiry* 24 (2): 281–88.

Bledsoe, Caroline. 2002. *Contingent Lives: Fertility, Time, and Aging in West Africa.* Chicago: University of Chicago Press.

Bloch, Maurice. 1975. "Introduction." In *Political Language and Oratory in Traditional Society,* edited by Maurice Boch. London: Academic Press.

Bolten, Catherine. 2012. "'We Have Been Sensitized': Ex-Combatants, Marginalization, and Youth in Postwar Sierra Leone." *American Anthropologist* 114 (3): 496–508.

Bourdieu, Pierre. 1998. *On Television and Journalism.* Translated by Priscilla Parkhurst Ferguson. Ann Arbor, MI: Pluto.

Bourdieu, Pierre, and Hans Haacke. 1995. *Free Exchange.* Cambridge: Polity.

Boyden, Jo. 1997. "Childhood and the Policy Makers: A Comparative Perspective on the Globalization of Childhood." In *Constructing and Reconstructing Childhood: Contemporary Issues in the Sociological Study of Childhood,* edited by Allison James and Alan Prout, 184–216. Lewes: Falmer Press.

Boyer, Dominic. 2013. "Simply the Best: Parody and Political Sincerity in Iceland." *American Ethnologist* 40 (2): 276–87.

Brisset-Foucault, Florence. 2013. "A Citizenship of Distinction in the Open Radio Debates of Kampala." *Africa* 83 (2): 227–50.

———. 2016. "Serial Callers: Communication Technologies and Political Personhood in Contemporary Uganda." *Ethnos* DOI: 10.1080/00141844.2015.1127984.

Brysk, Alison. 2013. "'Why We Care': Constructing Solidarity." In *Human Rights at the Crossroads,* edited by Mark Goodale, 163–71. Oxford: Oxford University Press.

Carsten, Janet, ed. 2000. *Cultures of Relatedness: New Approaches to the Study of Kinship.* Cambridge: Cambridge University Press.

Cattell, M. G. 1997. "The Discourse of Neglect: Family Support for the Elderly in Samia." In *African Families and the Crisis of Social Change,* edited by Thomas S. Weisner, Candice Bradley, and Philip L. Kilbride, 157–83. Westport, CT: Bergen and Garvey.

Central Statistical Office. 2004. *Zambia 2000 Census of Population and Housing,* vol. 3, *Eastern Province.* Lusaka: Central Statistical Office.

———. 2012a. *Zambia 2010 Census of Population and Housing: Population Summary Report.* Lusaka: Central Statistical Office.

———. 2012b. *Gender Statistics Report 2010.* Lusaka: Central Statistical Office.

———. 2014a. *Zambia 2010 Census of Population and Housing: Eastern Province Analytical Report.* Lusaka: Central Statistical Office.

———. 2014b. *Zambia Demographic and Health Survey: Preliminary Report*. Lusaka: Central Statistical Office.

Chakanza, J. C. 1998. "Unfinished Agenda: Puberty Rites and the Response of the Roman Catholic Church in Southern Malawi, 1901–1994." In *Rites of Passage in Contemporary Africa: Interaction between Christian and African Traditional Religions*, edited by James L. Cox, 168–75. Cardiff: Cardiff Academic Press.

Chaplin, J. H. 1962. "Wiving and Thriving in Northern Rhodesia." *Africa* 32 (2): 111–22.

Chikowero, Mhoze. 2015. *African Music, Power, and Being in Colonial Zimbabwe*. Bloomington: Indiana University Press.

Clark, Gracia. 2001. "Gender and Profiteering: Ghana's Market Women as Devoted Mothers and 'Human Vampire Bats.'" In *"Wicked" Women and the Reconfiguration of Gender in Africa*, edited by Dorothy Hodgson and Cheryl J. McCurdy, 293–311. Portsmouth: Heinemann.

Cohen, Jean L., and Andrew Arato. 1992. *Civil Society and Political Theory*. Cambridge, MA: MIT Press.

Cole, Jennifer. 2010. *Sex and Salvation: Imagining the Future in Madagascar*. Chicago: University of Chicago Press.

Colson, Elizabeth. 1958. *Marriage and the Family among the Plateau Tonga of Northern Rhodesia*. Manchester: Manchester University Press.

———. 2000. "The Father as Witch." *Africa* 70 (3): 333–58.

———. 2010. "The Social History of an Epidemic: HIV/AIDS in Gwembe Valley, Zambia, 1982–2004." In *Morality, Hope and Grief: Anthropologies of AIDS in Africa*, edited by Hansjörg Dilger and Ute Luig, 127–47. New York: Berghahn.

Constable, Marianne. 2005. *Just Silences: The Limits and Possibilities of Modern Law*. Princeton, NJ: Princeton University Press.

Cook, Joanna. 2010. *Meditation in Modern Buddhism: Renunciation and Change in Thai Monastic Life*. Cambridge: Cambridge University Press.

Cooke, Bill, and Uma Kothari, eds. 2001. *Participation: The New Tyranny?* London: Zed Books.

Coplan, David B. 2011. "South African Radio in a Saucepan." In *Radio in Africa: Publics, Cultures, Communities*, edited by Liz Gunner, Dina Ligaga, and Dumisani Moyo, 134–48. Johannesburg: Wits University Press.

Couldry, Nick. 2010. *Why Voice Matters: Culture and Politics after Neoliberalism*. London: Sage.

Crossley, Nick. 2004. "On Systematically Distorted Communication: Bourdieu and the Socio-Analysis of Publics." In *After Habermas: New Perspectives on the Public Sphere*, edited by Nick Crossley and John Michael Roberts, 88–112. Oxford: Blackwell.

Cunnison, Ian. 1959. *The Luapula Peoples of Northern Rhodesia: Custom and History in Tribal Politics*. Manchester: Manchester University Press.

Curran, James. 1991. "Rethinking the Media as a Public Sphere." In *Communication and Citizenship: Journalism and the Public Sphere in the New Media Age*, edited by Peter Dahlgren and Colin Sparks. New York: Routledge.

Day, Amber. 2011. *Satire and Dissent: Interventions in Contemporary Political Debate*. Bloomington: Indiana University Press.

Dean, Jodi. 2009. *Democracy and Other Neoliberal Fantasies: Communicative Capitalism and Left Politics*. Durham, NC: Duke University Press.

———. 2010. *Blog Theory: Feedback and Capture in the Circuits of Drive*. Cambridge: Polity.

Dodge, D. J. 1977. *Agricultural Policy and Performance in Zambia: History, Prospects and Proposals for Change*. Berkeley: University of California Press.

Dupré, Georges, and Pierre Philippe Rey. 1978. "Reflections on the Relevance of a Theory of the History of Exchange." In *Relations of Production: Marxist Approaches to Economic Anthropology*, edited by David Seddon, 171–208. London: Frank Cass.

Elyachar, Julia. 2012. "Before (and After) Neoliberalism: Tacit Knowledge, Secrets of the Trade, and the Public Sector in Egypt." *Cultural Anthropology* 27 (1): 76–96.

Englund, Harri. 2006. *Prisoners of Freedom: Human Rights and the African Poor*. Berkeley: University of California Press.

———. 2010. "The Anthropologist and His Poor." In *Forces of Compassion: Humanitarianism between Ethics and Politics*, edited by Erica Bornstein and Peter Redfield, 71–93. Santa Fe, NM: SAR Press.

———. 2011. *Human Rights and African Airwaves: Mediating Equality on the Chichewa Radio*. Bloomington: Indiana University Press.

———. 2015a. "Forget the Poor: Radio Kinship and Exploited Labor in Zambia." *Current Anthropology* 56 (Supplement 11): S137–S145.

———. 2015b. "Multivocal Morality: Narrative, Sentiment, and Zambia's Radio Grandfathers." *HAU: Journal of Ethnographic Theory* 5 (2): 251–73.

———. 2015c. "Anti Anti-Colonialism: Vernacular Press and Emergent Possibilities in Colonial Zambia." *Comparative Studies in Society and History* 57 (1): 221–47.

Englund, Harri, and James Leach. 2000. "Ethnography and the Meta-Narratives of Modernity." *Current Anthropology* 41 (2): 225–48.

Evans, Alice. 2014. "'Women Can Do What Men Can Do': The Causes and Consequences of Growing Flexibility in Gender Divisions of Labour in Kitwe, Zambia." *Journal of Southern African Studies* 40 (5): 981–98.

Fardon, Richard, and Graham Furniss, eds. 2000. *African Broadcast Cultures: Radio in Transition*. Oxford: James Currey.

Fassin, Didier, and Paula Vasquez. 2005. "Humanitarian Exception as the Rule: The Political Theology of the 1999 *Tragedia* in Venezuela." *American Ethnologist* 32 (3): 389–405.

Faubion, James. 2011. *An Anthropology of Ethics*. Cambridge: Cambridge University Press.

Ferguson, James. 1999. *Expectations of Modernity: Myths and Meanings of Urban Life on the Zambian Copperbelt*. Berkeley: University of California Press.

———. 2009. "The Uses of Neoliberalism." *Antipode* 41 (S1): 166–84.

———. 2013. "Declarations of Dependence: Labour, Personhood and Welfare in Southern Africa." *Journal of the Royal Anthropological Institute* 19 (2): 223–42.

Fiedler, Rachel N. 2005. *Coming of Age: A Christianized Initiation for Women in Southern Malawi*. Blantyre: Christian Literature Association in Malawi (CLAIM) for the Kachere Series.

Finnegan, Ruth. 2007. *The Oral and Beyond: Doing Things with Words in Africa*. Oxford: James Currey.

Fish, Stanley. 1994. *There's No Such Thing as Free Speech, and It's a Good Thing, Too*. Oxford: Oxford University Press.

Fisher, Daniel. 2016. *The Voice and Its Doubles: Media and Music in Northern Australia*. Durham, NC: Duke University Press.

Fontaine, Laurence. 2014. *The Moral Economy: Poverty, Credit, and Trust in Early Modern Europe*. Cambridge: Cambridge University Press.

Fortes, Meyer. 1959. *Oedipus and Job in West African Religion*. Cambridge: Cambridge University Press.

Foucault, Michel. 1986. *The History of Sexuality*, vol. 2, *The Use of Pleasure*. Translated by Robert Hurley. London: Viking.

———. 1988. *The History of Sexuality*, vol. 3, *Care of the Self*. Translated by Robert Hurley. London: Allen Lane.

———. 2001. *Fearless Speech*. Los Angeles, CA: Semiotext(e).

———. 2011. *The Courage of Truth: The Government of Self and Others II*. Edited by Frédéric Gros; translated by Graham Burchell. New York: Palgrave Macmillan.

Fraenkel, Peter. 1959. *Wayaleshi*. London: Weidenfeld and Nicolson.

Fraser, Alastair. 2010. "Introduction: Boom and Bust on the Zambian Copperbelt." In *Zambia, Mining and Neoliberalism: Boom and Bust on the Globalized Copperbelt*, edited by Alastair Fraser and Miles Larmer, 1–30. New York: Palgrave Macmillan.

———. 2016a. "The Political Economy of Sponsored Call-in in Zambia." PIMa Working Paper 5. Cambridge: University of Cambridge, Centre for Governance and Human Rights.

———. 2016b. "Let's Be Responsible Citizens! Contesting the Agenda of a Sponsored Call-In Radio Programme." PIMa Working Paper 6. Cambridge: University of Cambridge, Centre for Governance and Human Rights.

Furniss, Graham. 1996. *Poetry, Prose and Popular Culture in Hausa*. Edinburgh: Edinburgh University Press for the International African Institute.

Gagliardone, Iginio. 2016. "'Can You Hear Me?': Mobile-Radio Interactions and Governance in Africa." *New Media and Society* 18 (9): 2080–95.

Geissler, P. Wenzel, and Ruth J. Prince. 2004. "Shared Lives: Exploring Practices of Amity between Grandmothers and Grandchildren in Western Kenya." *Africa* 74 (1): 95–120.

———. 2010. *The Land Is Dying: Contingency, Creativity, and Conflict in Western Kenya*. New York: Berghahn.

Gershon, Ilana. 2011. "Neoliberal Agency." *Current Anthropology* 52 (4): 537–55.

Geschiere, Peter. 2013. *Witchcraft, Intimacy, and Trust: Africa in Comparison*. Chicago: University of Chicago Press.

Gluckman, Max. 1955. *The Judicial Process among the Barotse of Northern Rhodesia*. Manchester: Manchester University Press.

———. 1961. "Ethnographic Data in British Social Anthropology." *Sociological Review* 9 (1): 5–17.

———, ed. 1964. *Closed Systems and Open Minds: The Limits of Naïvety in Social Anthropology*. Chicago: Aldine.

———. 1965. *The Ideas in Barotse Jurisprudence*. New Haven, CT: Yale University Press.

———. 1968. "The Utility of the Equilibrium Model in the Study of Social Change." *American Anthropologist* 70 (2): 210–37.

Gould, Jeremy. 1997. *Localizing Modernity: Action, Interests and Association in Rural Zambia*. Helsinki: The Finnish Anthropological Society.

Graeber, David. 2009. "Debt, Violence, and Impersonal Markets: Polanyian Meditations." In *Market and Society: The Great Transformation Today*, edited by Chris Hann and Keith Hart, 106–33. Cambridge: Cambridge University Press.

———. 2012. "On Social Currencies and Human Economies: Some Notes on the Violence of Equivalence." *Social Anthropology* 20 (4): 411–28.

Grätz, Tilo. 2013. "Radio Advertising and Entrepreneurial Conjunctions in Benin: Producers, Styles and Technologies." *Journal of African Cultural Studies* 25 (1): 42–56.

Gudeman, Stephen. 2009. "Necessity or Contingency: Mutuality and Market." In *Market and Society: The Great Transformation Today*, edited by Chris Hann and Keith Hart, 17–37. Cambridge: Cambridge University Press.

Gulbrandsen, Ørnulf. 2012. *The State and the Social: State Formation in Botswana and Its Precolonial and Colonial Genealogies*. New York: Berghahn.

Gunner, Liz. 2000. "Wrestling with the Present, Beckoning to the Past: Contemporary Zulu Radio Drama." *Journal of Southern African Studies* 26 (2): 223–37.

———. 2011. "IsiZulu Radio Drama and the Modern Subject: Restless Identities in South Africa in the 1970s." In *Radio in Africa: Publics, Cultures, Communities*, edited by Liz Gunner, Dina Ligaga, and Dumisani Moyo, 163–79. Johannesburg: Wits University Press.

———. 2014. "Soft Masculinities, *Isicathamiya* and Radio." *Journal of Southern African Studies* 40 (2): 343–60.

Gunner, Liz, Dina Ligaga, and Dumisani Moyo, eds. 2011. *Radio in Africa: Publics, Cultures, Communities*. Johannesburg: Wits University Press.

Gupta, Akhil. 2012. *Red Tape: Bureaucracy, Structural Violence, and Poverty in India*. Durham, NC: Duke University Press.

Gwengwe, John W. 1964. *Cinyanja Cina*. Lusaka: Kenneth Kaunda Foundation.

Habermas, Jürgen. 1972. *Knowledge and Human Interests*. Translated by Jeremy J. Shapiro. London: Heinemann.

———. 1989. *The Structural Transformation of the Public Sphere: An Inquiry into a Category of Bourgeois Society*. Translated by Thomas Burger. Cambridge: Polity.

Hansen, Karen Tranberg. 1989. "The Black Market and Women Traders in Lusaka, Zambia." In *Women and the State in Africa*, edited by Jane L. Parpart and K. Staudt, 143–59. Boulder, CO: Lynne Rienner Publisher.

———. 2000. *Salaula: The World of Second-Hand Clothing and Zambia*. Chicago: University of Chicago Press.

Hart, Keith. 2000. *The Memory Bank: Money in an Unequal World*. London: Profile.

Haugerud, Angelique. 2013. *No Billionaire Left Behind: Satirical Activism in America Today*. Stanford: Stanford University Press.

Heinze, Robert. 2014. "'Men Between:' The Role of Zambian Broadcasters in Decolonization." *Journal of Southern African Studies* 40 (3): 623–40.

Herman, Edward S., and Noam Chomsky. 1988. *Manufacturing Consent: The Political Economy of the Mass Media*. New York: Pantheon Books.

Heyman, Steven J. 2008. *Free Speech and Human Dignity*. New Haven, NJ: Yale University Press.

Hill, Jane H. 1995. "The Voices of Don Gabriel: Responsibility and Self in a Modern Mexicano Narrative." In *The Dialogic Emergence of Culture*, edited by Dennis Tedlock and Bruce Mannheim, 97–147. Urbana: University of Illinois Press.

Honwana, Alcinda, and Filip De Boeck, eds. 2005. *Makers and Breakers: Children and Youth in Postcolonial Africa*. Oxford: James Currey.

Hull, Matthew S. 2008. "Ruled by Records: The Expropriation of Land and the Misappropriation of Lists in Islamabad." *American Ethnologist* 35 (4): 501–18.

Hunt, Nancy Rose. 2003. *A Colonial Lexicon of Birth Ritual, Medicalization, and Mobility in the Congo*. Durham, NC: Duke University Press.

Hunter, Mark. 2010. *Love in the Time of AIDS: Inequality, Gender, and Rights in South Africa*. Bloomington: Indiana University Press.

Illouz, Eva. 2003. *Oprah Winfrey and the Glamour of Misery: An Essay on Popular Culture*. New York: Columbia University Press.

Ingstad, Benedicte. 2004. "The Value of Grandchildren: Changing Relations between Generations in Botswana." *Africa* 74 (1): 62–75.

Isichei, Elizabeth. 2002. *Voices of the Poor in Africa*. Rochester, NY: University of Rochester Press.

Jackson, Jennifer. 2013. *Political Oratory and Cartooning: An Ethnography of Democratic Processes in Madagascar*. Oxford: Wiley-Blackwell.

James, Allison. 2007. "Giving Voice to Children's Voices: Practices and Problems, Pitfalls and Potentials." *American Anthropologist* 109 (2): 261–72.

Jeffrey, Robin, and Assa Doron, eds. 2013. *The Great Indian Phone Book: How Cheap Mobile Phones Change Business, Politics and Daily Life*. London: Hurst and Co.

Jenkins, Henry. 2006. *Convergence Culture: Where Old and New Media Collide*. New York: New York University Press.

Johnson, Jessica. 2012. "Living with HIV: 'Stigma' and Hope in Malawi's Era of ARVs." *Africa* 82 (4): 632–53.

Johnson-Hanks, Jennifer. 2002. "On the Limits of Life Stages in Ethnography: Toward a Theory of Vital Conjunctures." *American Anthropologist* 104 (3): 865–80.

———. 2006. *Uncertain Honor: Modern Motherhood in an African Crisis*. Chicago: University of Chicago Press.

———. 2007. "Women on the Market: Marriage, Consumption, and the Internet in Urban Cameroon." *American Ethnologist* 34 (4): 642–58.

Kahn, Douglas, and Gregory Whitehead, eds. 1992. *The Wireless Imagination: Sound, Radio, and the Avant-Garde*. Cambridge, MA: MIT Press.

Kapferer, Bruce. 2006. "Situations, Crisis, and the Anthropology of the Concrete: The Contribution of Max Gluckman." In *The Manchester School: Practice and Ethnographic Praxis in Anthropology*, edited by M. S. Evens and Don Handelman, 118–55. Oxford: Berghahn.

Kaunda, Kenneth. 1966. *Zambia: Independence and Beyond: The Speeches of Kenneth Kaunda*. London: Nelson.

Keane, Webb. 2009. "Freedom and Blasphemy: On Indonesian Press Bans and Danish Cartoons." *Public Culture* 21 (1): 47–76.

———. 2010. "Minds, Surfaces, and Reasons in the Anthropology of Ethics." In *Ordinary Ethics: Anthropology, Language, and Action*, edited by Michael Lambek, 64–83. New York: Fordham University Press.

Kratz, Corinne A. 2010. "In and Out of Focus." *American Ethnologist* 37 (4): 805–26.

Kunreuther, Laura. 2014. *Voicing Subjects: Public Intimacy and Mediation in Kathmandu*. Berkeley: University of California Press.

Kusimba, Sibel, Yang Yang, and Nitesh Chawla. 2016. "Hearthholds of Mobile Money in Western Kenya." *Economic Anthropology* 3 (2): 266–79.

Kymlicka, Will. 1995. *Multicultural Citizenship: A Liberal Theory of Minority Rights*. Oxford: Oxford University Press.

Laclau, Ernesto. 2005. "Populism: What's in a Name?" In *Populism and the Mirror of Democracy*, edited by F. Panizza, 32–49. London: Verso.

Laidlaw, James. 2014. *The Subject of Virtue: An Anthropology of Ethics and Freedom*. Cambridge: Cambridge University Press.

Langworthy, Harry W. 1975. "Central Malawi in the 19th Century." In *From Nyasaland to Malawi: Studies in Colonial History*, edited by R. J. Macdonald, 1–43. Nairobi: East African Publishing House.

Larmer, Miles, and Alastair Fraser. 2007. "Of Cabbages and King Cobra: Populist Politics and Zambia's 2006 Election." *African Affairs* 106 (425): 611–34.

Last, Murray. 2000. "Children and the Experience of Violence: Contrasting Cultures of Punishment in Northern Nigeria." *Africa* 70 (3): 359–93.

Lawrance, Benjamin N., Emily Lynn Osborne, and Richard L. Roberts, eds. 2006. *Inter-*

mediaries, Interpreters, and Clerks: African Employees in the Making of Colonial Africa. Madison: University of Wisconsin Press.

Lekgoathi, Sekibakiba Peter. 2009. "'You Are Listening to Radio Lebowa of the South African Broadcasting Corporation': Vernacular Radio, Bantustan Identity and Listenership, 1960–1994." *Journal of Southern African Studies* 35 (3): 575–94.

———. 2011. "Bantustan Identity, Censorship and Subversion on Northern Sotho Radio under Apartheid, 1960s–80s." In *Radio in Africa: Publics, Cultures, Communities*, edited by Liz Gunner, Dina Ligaga, and Dumisani Moyo, 117–33. Johannesburg: Wits University Press.

Li, Tania Murray. 2010. "To Make Live or to Let Die? Rural Dispossession and the Protection of Surplus Populations." *Antipode* 41 (S1): 63–93.

Lofton, Kathryn. 2011. *Oprah: The Gospel of an Icon.* Berkeley: University of California Press.

Longwe, Molly. 2006. *Growing Up: A Chewa Girls' Initiation.* Blantyre: Christian Literature Association in Malawi (CLAIM) for the Kachere Series.

Loviglio, Jason. 2005. *Radio's Intimate Public: Network Broadcasting and Mass-mediated Democracy.* Minneapolis: University of Minnesota Press.

Lungu, John. 2008. "Copper Mining Agreements in Zambia: Renegotiation or Law Reform?" *Review of African Political Economy* 117:403–15.

MacGaffey, Janet. 1991. *The Real Economy of Zaire: The Contribution of Smuggling and Other Unofficial Activities to National Wealth.* London: James Currey.

MacIntosh, Janet. 2010. "Mobile Phones and Mipoho's Prophecy: The Powers and Dangers of Flying Language." *American Ethnologist* 37 (2): 337–53.

Macola, Giacomo. 2010. *Liberal Nationalism in Central Africa: A Biography of Harry Mwaanga Nkumbula.* New York: Palgrave Macmillan.

Mahmood, Saba. 2009. "Religious Reason and Secular Affect: An Incommensurable Divide?" In *Is Critique Secular? Blasphemy, Injury, and Free Speech*, edited by Talal Asad, Wendy Brown, Judith Butler, and Saba Mahmood, 64–100. Berkeley: University of California Press.

Mains, Daniel. 2012. *Hope Is Cut: Youth, Unemployment, and the Future in Urban Ethiopia.* Philadelphia: Temple University Press.

Mair, Lucy P. 1951. "A Yao Girls' Initiation." *Man* 51:60–63.

Makoni, Sinfree, and Koen Stroeken, eds. 2002. *Ageing in Africa: Sociolinguistic and Anthropological Approaches.* Aldershot: Ashgate.

Malinowski, Bronislaw. 1926. *Crime and Custom in Savage Society.* New York: Harcourt, Brace.

Malkki, Liisa H. 2015. *The Need to Help: The Domestic Arts of International Humanitarianism.* Durham, NC: Duke University Press.

Mandala, Elias C. 1990. *Work and Control in a Peasant Economy: A History of the Lower Tchiri Valley in Malawi, 1859–1960.* Madison: University of Wisconsin Press.

Mano, Winston. 2011. "Why Radio Is Africa's Medium of Choice in the Global Age." In *Radio in Africa: Publics, Cultures, Communities*, edited by Liz Gunner, Dina Ligaga, and Dumisani Moyo, 102–16. Johannesburg: Wits University Press.

Marshall, Ruth. 2009. *Political Spiritualities: The Pentecostal Revolution in Nigeria.* Chicago: University of Chicago Press.

Marwick, M. G. 1965. *Sorcery in Its Social Setting: A Study of the Northern Rhodesian Ceŵa.* Manchester: Manchester University Press.

Mathur, Nayanika. 2016. *Paper Tiger: Law, Bureaucracy and the Developmental State in Himalayan India.* Cambridge: Cambridge University Press.

Matza, Tomas. 2009. "Moscow's Echo: Technologies of the Self, Publics, and Politics on the Russian Talk Show." *Cultural Anthropology* 24 (3): 489–522.

Mauss, Marcel. 1954 [1924]. *The Gift: Forms and Functions of Exchange in Archaic Societies.* Translated by Ian Cunnison. Glencoe, Ill.: Free Press.

Mazzarella, William. 2009. "Affect: What Is It Good For?" In *Enchantments of Modernity: Empire, Nation, Globalization,* edited by Saurabh Dube, 291–309. New York: Routledge.

McKay, Ramah. 2012. "Afterlives: Humanitarian Histories and Critical Subjects in Mozambique." *Cultural Anthropology* 27 (2): 286–309.

Meillassoux, Claude. 1981. *Maidens, Meal and Money: Capitalism and the Domestic Community.* Cambridge: Cambridge University Press.

Meloni, Francesca, Karine Vanthuyne, and Cécile Rousseau. 2015. "Towards a Relational Ethics: Rethinking Ethics, Agency and Dependency in Research with Children and Youth." *Anthropological Theory* 15 (1): 106–23.

Meyer, Birgit. 2015. *Sensational Movies: Video, Vision, and Christianity in Ghana.* Berkeley: University of California Press.

Mill, John Stuart. 1998. "On Liberty." In *John Stuart Mill on Liberty and Other Essays,* edited by John Gray. Oxford: Oxford University Press.

Moore, Henrietta L., and Megan Vaughan. 1994. *Cutting Down Trees: Gender, Nutrition, and Agricultural Change in the Northern Province of Zambia, 1890–1990.* London: James Currey.

Moyn, Samuel. 2010. *The Last Utopia: Human Rights in History.* Cambridge, MA: Harvard University Press.

Moyo, Dumisani. 2011. "Contesting Mainstream Media Power: Mediating the Zimbabwe Crisis through Clandestine Radio." In *Radio in Africa: Publics, Cultures, Communities,* edited by Liz Gunner, Dina Ligaga, and Dumisani Moyo, 49–62. Johannesburg: Wits University Press.

Moyo, Last. 2013. "Critical Reflections on Technological Convergence on Radio and the Emerging Digital Cultures and Practices." *Telematics and Informatics* 30 (3): 211–13.

Muehlebach, Andrea. 2012. *The Moral Neoliberal: Welfare and Citizenship in Italy.* Chicago: University of Chicago Press.

Mufuzi, Friday. 2011. "Indian Political Activism in Colonial Zambia: The Case of Livingstone's Indian Traders." In *Living the End of Empire: Politics and Society in Late Colonial Zambia,* edited by Jan-Bart Gewald, Marja Hinfelaar, and Giacomo Macola, 229–48. Leiden: Brill.

Mutongi, Kenda. 2007. *Worries of the Heart: Widows, Family, and the Community in Kenya.* Chicago: University of Chicago Press.

Mytton, Graham. 1971. *The National Mass Media Audience Survey.* Lusaka: Zambia Broadcasting Service.

Narayan, Deepa, and Patti Petesch, eds. 2002. *Voices of the Poor from Many Lands.* Washington, DC: World Bank.

Navaro-Yashin, Yael. 2007. "Make-Believe Papers, Legal Forms, and the Counterfeit: Affective Interactions between Documents and People in Britain and Cyprus." *Anthropological Theory* 7 (1): 79–96.

Nehemas, Alexander. 1998. *The Art of Living: Socratic Reflections from Plato to Foucault.* Berkeley: University of California Press.

Newell, Sasha. 2012. *The Modernity Bluff: Crime, Consumption, and Citizenship in Côte d'Ivoire.* Chicago: University of Chicago Press.

Newell, Stephanie. 2000. *Ghanaian Popular Fiction: "Thrilling Discoveries in Conjugal Life" and Other Tales.* Athens: Ohio University Press.

Niehaus, Isak. 2012. *Witchcraft and a Life in the New South Africa.* Cambridge: Cambridge University Press for the International African Institute.

Notermans, Catrien. 2004. "Sharing Home, Food, and Bed: Paths of Grandmotherhood in East Cameroon." *Africa* 74 (1): 6–27.

Nyamnjoh, Francis B. 2005. *Africa's Media, Democracy and the Politics of Belonging.* New York: Zed Books.

Olivier de Sardan, Jean-Pierre. 2005. *Anthropology and Development: Understanding Contemporary Social Change.* London: Zed Books.

Omanga, Duncan Mainye. 2014. "'Raid at Abottabad': Editorial Cartoons and the 'Terrorist Almighty' in the Kenyan Press." *Journal of African Cultural Studies* 26 (1): 15–32.

O'Rourke, Kevin C. 2001. *John Stuart Mill and Freedom of Expression: The Genesis of a Theory.* New York: Routledge.

OSISA (Open Society Initiative Southern Africa). 2010. *Zambia: A Survey by the Africa Governance Monitoring and Advocacy Project.* Johannesburg: OSISA.

Paas, Steven. 2004. *Chichewa—Chinyanja—English Dictionary.* Blantyre: CLAIM (Christian Literature Association in Malawi).

Pandian, Anand. 2009. *Crooked Stalks: Cultivating Virtue in South India.* Durham, NC: Duke University Press.

Parry, Jonathan, and Maurice Bloch, eds. 1989. *Money and the Morality of Exchange.* Cambridge: Cambridge University Press.

Perullo, Alex. 2011. *Live from Dar es Salaam: Popular Music and Tanzania's Music Economy.* Bloomington: Indiana University Press.

Peters, John Durham. 1999. *Speaking into the Air: A History of the Idea of Communication.* Chicago: University of Chicago Press.

Phiri, Isaac. 2010. "Zambia: Policies of a Media-phobic State." In *Media Policy in a Changing Southern Africa: Critical Reflections on Media Reforms in the Global Age,* edited by Dumisani Moyo and Wallace Chuma. Pretoria: UNISA Press.

Phiri, Isabel A. 1998. "The Initiation of Chewa Women of Malawi: A Presbyterian Woman's Perspective." In *Rites of Passage in Contemporary Africa: Interaction between Christian and African Traditional Religions,* edited by James L. Cox, 129–46. Cardiff: Cardiff Academic Press.

Pietilä, Tuulikki. 2007. *Gossip, Markets, and Gender: How Dialogue Constructs Moral Value in Post-Socialist Kilimanjaro.* Madison: University of Wisconsin Press.

Polanyi, Karl. 1977. *The Livelihood of Man.* New York: Academic Press.

Porter, Theodore M. 1986. *The Rise of Statistical Thinking, 1820–1900.* Princeton, NJ: Princeton University Press.

Power, Marcus. 2000. "*Acqui Lourenço Marques!* Radio Colonization and Cultural Identity in Colonial Mozambique, 1932–74." *Journal of Historical Geography* 26 (4): 605–28.

Pritchett, James A. 2001. *The Lunda-Ndembu: Style, Change, and Social Transformation in South Central Africa.* Madison: University of Wisconsin Press.

Pype, Katrien. 2012. *The Making of the Pentecostal Melodrama: Religion, Media, and Gender in Kinshasa.* New York: Berghahn.

———. 2016. "'[Not] Talking Like a Motorola': Mobile Phone Practices and Politics of Masking and Unmasking in Postcolonial Kinshasa." *Journal of the Royal Anthropological Institute* 22 (3): 633–52.

———. 2017. "Dancing to the Rhythm of Léopoldville: Nostalgia, Urban Critique and Generational Difference in Kinshasa's TV Music Shows." *Journal of African Cultural Studies* 29 (2): 158–76.

Quennerstedt, Ann. 2009. "Balancing the Rights of the Child and the Rights of Parents in The Convention on the Rights of the Child." *Journal of Human Rights* 8 (2): 162–76.

Radcliffe-Brown, A. R. 1950. "Introduction." In *African Systems of Kinship and Marriage*, edited by A. R. Radcliffe-Brown and Daryll Forde, 1–85. London: KPI.

Rasing, Thera. 2001. *The Bush Burnt, the Stones Remain: Female Initiation Rites in Urban Zambia*. Münster: LIT Verlag.

———. 2004. "The Persistence of Female Initiation Rites: Reflexivity and Resilience of Women in Zambia." In *Situating Globality: African Agency in the Appropriation of Global Culture*, edited by Wim van Binsbergen and Rijk van Dijk, 277–310. Leiden: Brill.

Redfield, Peter. 2010. "The Impossible Problem of Neutrality." In *Forces of Compassion: Humanitarianism between Ethics and Politics*, edited by Erica Bornstein and Peter Redfield, 53–70. Santa Fe, NM: SAR Press.

Richards, Audrey I. 1956. *Chisungu: A Girl's Initiation Ceremony among the Bemba of Zambia*. London: Faber and Faber.

Roberts, John Michael. 2004. "John Stuart Mill, Free Speech and the Public Sphere: A Bakhtinian Critique." In *After Habermas: New Perspectives on the Public Sphere*, edited by Nick Crossley and John Michael Roberts, 67–87. Oxford: Blackwell.

Rose, Nikolas. 2007. *The Politics of Life Itself: Biomedicine, Power, and Subjectivity in the Twenty-First Century*. Princeton, NJ: Princeton University Press.

Roy, Ananya. 2012. "Ethical Subjects: Market Rule in an Age of Poverty." *Public Culture* 24 (1): 105–8.

Sahlins, Marshall. 2011. "What Kinship Is (Part One)." *Journal of the Royal Anthropological Institute* 17 (1): 2–19.

Saxonhouse, Arlene W. 2006. *Free Speech and Democracy in Ancient Athens*. Cambridge: Cambridge University Press.

Scherz, China. 2014. *Having People, Having Heart: Charity, Sustainable Development, and Problems of Dependence in Central Uganda*. Chicago: University of Chicago Press.

Schieffelin, Bambi B., Kathryn A. Woolard, and Paul V. Kroskrity, eds. 1998. *Language Ideologies: Practice and Theory*. Oxford: Oxford University Press.

Schulz, Dorothea. 2012. "Reconsidering Muslim Authority: Female 'Preachers' and the Ambiguities of Radio-Mediated Sermonizing in Mali." In *Radio Fields: Anthropology and Wireless Sound in the 21st Century*, edited by Lucas Bessire and Daniel Fisher, 108–23. New York: New York University.

Schuster, Ilsa M. Glazer. 1982. "Marginal Lives: Conflict and Contradiction in the Position of Female Traders in Lusaka, Zambia." In *Women and Work in Africa*, edited by E. G. Bay, 105–26. Boulder, CO: Westview Press.

Serpell, Robert. 1993. *The Significance of Schooling: Life-journeys in an African Society*. Cambridge: Cambridge University Press.

Shepler, Susan. 2005. "The Rites of the Child: Global Discourses of Youth and Reintegrating Child Soldiers in Sierra Leone." *Journal of Human Rights* 4 (2): 197–211.

Simpson, Anthony. 2003. *"Half-London" in Zambia: Contested Identities in a Catholic Mission School*. Edinburgh: Edinburgh University Press for the International African Institute.

———. 2009. *Boys to Men in the Shadow of AIDS: Masculinities and HIV Risk in Zambia*. New York: Palgrave Macmillan.

Simpson, Anthony, and Virginia Bond. 2014. "Narratives of Nationhood and HIV/AIDS: Reflections on Multidisciplinary Research on the HIV/AIDS Epidemic in Zambia over the Last 30 Years." *Journal of Southern African Studies* 40 (5): 1065–89.

Simutanyi, Neo, Alastair Fraser, and Nalukui Milapo. 2015. "Background Paper: Politics and Interactive Media in Zambia." Politics and Interactive Media in Africa Working Paper Series 3. Cambridge: University of Cambridge.

Smith, Adam. 1976 [1776]. *An Inquiry into the Nature and Causes of the Wealth of Nations.* Chicago: University of Chicago Press.

Smith, David. 2011. "Radio in Zones of Conflict: Abnormal Measures for Abnormal Circumstances." In *Radio in Africa: Publics, Cultures, Communities,* edited by Liz Gunner, Dina Ligaga, and Dumisani Moyo, 256–69. Johannesburg: Wits University Press.

Smyth, Rosaleen. 1984. "A Note on the 'Saucepan Special': The People's Radio of Central Africa." *Historical Journal of Film, Radio and Television* 4 (2): 195–201.

Spitulnik, Debra. 2000. "Documenting Radio Culture as Lived Experience: Reception Studies and the Mobile Machine in Zambia." In *African Broadcast Cultures: Radio in Transition,* edited by Richard Fardon and Graham Furniss, 144–63. Oxford: James Currey.

———. 2002. "Mobile Machines and Fluid Audiences: Rethinking Reception through Zambian Radio Culture." In *Media Worlds: Anthropology on New Terrain,* edited by Faye D. Ginsburg, Lila Abu-Lughod, and Brian Larkin, 337–54. Berkeley: University of California Press.

———. 2010. "Personal News and the Price of Public Service: An Ethnographic Window into the Dynamics of Production and Reception in Zambian State Radio." In *The Anthropology of News and Journalism: Global Perspectives,* edited by S. Elizabeth Bird, 182–98. Bloomington: Indiana University Press.

Spivak, Gayatri Chakravorty. 1988. "Can the Subaltern Speak?" In *Marxism and the Interpretation of Culture,* edited by Cary Nelson and Lawrence Grossberg, 66–111. London: Macmillan.

Squier, Susan M. 2003. "Communities of the Air: Introducing the Radio World." In *Communities of the Air: Radio Century, Radio Culture,* 1–35. Durham, NC: Duke University Press.

Stambach, Amy. 2000. *Lessons from Mount Kilimanjaro: Schooling, Community, and Gender in East Africa.* New York: Routledge.

Sterne, Jonathan. 2005. *The Audible Past: Cultural Origins of Sound Reproduction.* Durham, NC: Duke University Press.

Taylor, Charles. 1994. "The Politics of Recognition." In *Multiculturalism: Examining the Politics of Recognition,* edited by Amy Gutman, 25–73. Princeton, NJ: Princeton University Press.

Tettey, Wisdom J. 2011. "Talk Radio and Politics in Ghana: Exploring Civic and (Un)Civil Discourse in the Public Sphere." In *Radio in Africa: Publics, Cultures, Communities,* edited by Liz Gunner, Dina Ligaga, and Dumisani Moyo, 19–35. Johannesburg: Wits University Press.

Turner, Victor. 1957. *Schism and Continuity in an African Society.* Manchester: Manchester University Press.

UNDP (United Nations Development Programme). 2013. *Millennium Development Goals Progress Report: Zambia.* Lusaka: UNDP.

Vail, Leroy, and Landeg White. 1991. *Power and the Praise Poem: Southern African Voices in History.* Charlottesville: University Press of Virginia.

van der Geest, Sjaak. 1997. "Money and Respect: The Changing Value of Old Age in Rural Ghana." *Africa* 67 (4): 534–59.

———. 2002. "From Wisdom to Witchcraft: Ambivalence towards Old Age in Rural Ghana." *Africa* 72 (3): 437–63.

———. 2004. "Grandparents and Grandchildren in Kwahu, Ghana: The Performance of Respect." *Africa* 74 (1): 47–61.

van Dijck, José. 2009. "Users Like You? Theorizing Agency in User-Generated Content." *Media, Culture and Society* 31 (1): 41–58.

van Velsen, J. 1964. *The Politics of Kinship: A Study in Social Manipulation among the Lakeside Tonga of Nyasaland.* Manchester: Manchester University Press.

———. 1967. "The Extended-Case Method and Situational Analysis." In *The Craft of Social Anthropology*, edited by A. L. Epstein, 129–49. London: Tavistock.

Vaughan, Megan. 2016. "Changing the Subject? Psychological Counselling in Eastern Africa." *Public Culture* 28 (3): 499–517.

Vidali-Spitulnik, Debra. 2012. "'A House of Wires upon Wires': Sensuous and Linguistic Entanglements of Evidence and Epistemologies in the Study of Radio Culture." In *Radio Fields: Anthropology and Wireless Sound in the 21st Century*, edited by Lucas Bessire and Daniel Fisher, 250–67. New York: New York University Press.

Warner, Michael. 2002. "Publics and Counterpublics." *Public Culture* 14 (1): 49–90.

Weidman, Amanda J. 2006. *Singing the Classical, Voicing the Modern: The Postcolonial Politics of Music in South India.* Durham, NC: Duke University Press.

———. 2014. "Anthropology and Voice." *Annual Review of Anthropology* 43:37–51.

Weiss, Brad. 2009. *Street Dreams and Hip Hop Barbershops: Global Fantasy in Urban Tanzania.* Bloomington: Indiana University Press.

Wendland, Ernst. 1979. "Stylistic Form and Communicative Function in the Nyanja Radio Narratives of Julius Chongo." PhD diss., University of Wisconsin–Madison.

———. 2004. *Poceza M'madzulo: Some Chinyanja Radio Plays of Julius Chongo.* Lusaka: UNZA Press.

Werbner, Richard P. 1977. "The Argument in and about Oratory." *African Studies* 36 (2): 141–44.

———. 2004. *Reasonable Radicals and Citizenship in Botswana: The Public Anthropology of Kalanga Elites.* Bloomington: Indiana University Press.

———. 2015. *Divination's Grasp: African Encounters with the Almost Said.* Bloomington: Indiana University Press.

Whyte, Susan R., and Michael A. Whyte. 2004. "Children's Children: Time and Relatedness in Eastern Uganda." *Africa* 74 (1): 76–94.

Willems, Wendy. 2013. "Participation—In What? Radio, Convergence, and the Corporate Logic of Audience Input through New Media in Zambia." *Telematics and Informatics* 30:223–31.

Wolf, Angelika. 2010. "Orphans' Ties: Belonging and Relatedness in Child-Headed Households in Malawi." In *Morality, Hope and Grief: Anthropologies of AIDS in Africa*, edited by Hansjörg Dilger and Ute Luig, 292–311. New York: Berghahn.

Wolfe, Alan. 1989. *Whose Keeper? Social Science and Moral Obligation.* Berkeley: University of California Press.

Yankah, Kwesi. 1995. *Speaking for the Chief: Ọkyeame and the Politics of Akan Royal Oratory.* Bloomington: Indiana University Press.

Zelizer, Viviana A. 2005. *The Purchase of Intimacy.* Princeton, NJ: Princeton University Press.

INDEX

Africa's Voices, 83–85
aid, 17, 89–90
alcohol, 91–92
anonymity, 60, 83
Archambault, Caroline, 184
Arendt, Hannah, 130
Arnheim, Rudolf, 196
Asad, Talal, 12
Auslander, Mark, 24, 26
Australia, 199

Bakhtin, Mikhail, 64–66, 81, 84, 206
Banda, Juliana, 70, 72, 155
Banda, Rupiah, 239n16
Barber, Karin, 65, 66
begging, 165–66
Benjamin, Walter, 198, 199
blasphemy, 12
B1, 135–37, 159, 160, 163, 168
Bourdieu, Pierre, 15, 200, 236n15
Breeze FM: founder-director of (*see* Daka,
    Michael); geographical reach of, 5, 80;
    the market and, 16–21; media technolo-
    gies and, 63–64, 161; religion and, 5;
    revenue of, 6, 59, 143–44, 160, 182
bribes, 40, 47, 57, 58, 60, 77–78, 117, 188,
    247n10
Britain. *See* United Kingdom
bureaucracy, 48–49, 113, 123, 127–30

cartoons, 10, 11–12
censorship, 22, 202–3

Central African Broadcasting Corporation
    (CABS), 21–22
Chadiza, 171, 182, 185
Chewa, 55
Chibemba, 21, 139, 237n22
chiefs, 51, 56, 100, 106, 114–17, 152; Kapa-
    tamoyo, 104; Mpembamoyo, 184–85;
    Mpezeni, 52, 104, 241n44, 242n46;
    Undi, 55
childhood, 165–66, 174, 182
Chiluba, Frederick, 3, 37, 39
Chinese people, 11, 79, 97–99, 101–2, 107,
    186, 203, 249n36
Chingoni, 151, 249n44
Chinsenga, 5, 41, 76, 147, 149
Chinyanja, 3, 5, 41, 59, 72, 76, 82, 139,
    140, 141, 142, 147, 149, 155, 168, 180,
    236n5, 242n2
Chipata, 3, 16, 17, 37, 39, 40, 77, 78, 94–
    95, 96, 113, 117, 128, 135, 140, 143,
    146, 162, 182
Chitumbuka, 5, 140, 141, 242n2
Christianity, 38, 138, 170; Anglican, 152–
    53; Pentecostal, 5, 131; Seventh-Day
    Adventist, 38–39, 48, 91
colonialism, 38, 138, 152, 203, 239n10
Colson, Elizabeth, 23
community radio, 4
Constable, Marianne, 12
cooperatives, 103–4, 115, 117–19
Copperbelt, 4, 21
corporal punishment, 182–84, 260n37